T0311850

Income distribution in less developed countries

Whilst development economics has focused on questions of growth, income distribution – and its implications for growth and for the eradication of poverty – has received less attention. This book, by a leading expert in the field, corrects that imbalance, and gives a comprehensive review of the link between income distribution and the growth of national income. It will be invaluable to students of development economics, and to the staff of national and international agencies concerned with policy making in LDCs.

Most of the existing literature on LDCs is devoted to statistical issues and to policy recommendations based more on their author's ideological preferences than on proper evidence. Dr Sundrum gives a more balanced coverage, discussing the statistical approach, evaluating the quality of the data, simplifying the main concepts of measurement, and concentrating on the basic patterns and trends of income distribution shown by the data. He develops an analytical framework which links theories on the personal distribution of income with substantial discussion of the functional distribution of income. He deals also with policy issues, especially the effects of various policies on both the distribution of income and the growth of the economy, and concludes that there is still considerable scope for growth with equity in less developed countries.

R.M. Sundrum is a leading expert in development economics. A former Director in the World Bank, he is Professorial Fellow in the Economics Department of the Research School of Pacific Studies at the Australian National University, Canberra.

Income distribution in less developed countries

R. M. Sundrum

 Routledge
Taylor & Francis Group

LONDON AND NEW YORK

First published 1990
by Routledge
2 Park Square, Milton Park, Abingdon, Oxon, OX14 4RN

Simultaneously published in the USA and Canada
by Routledge
605 Third Avenue, New York, NY 10017

Routledge is an imprint of the Taylor & Francis Group, an informa business

New in paperback 1992

Typeset by Leaper & Gard Ltd, Bristol

British Library Cataloguing in Publication Data
Sundrum, R.M.
  Income distribution in less developed countries.
  1. Developing countries. Income. Distribution
  I. Title
  339.2′09172′4

ISBN 0–415–07971–3

Library of Congress Cataloging in Publication Data
Sundrum, R.M.
  Income distribution in less developed countries/R.M. Sundrum.
    p.   cm.
  Includes bibliographical references.
  ISBN 0-415-07971-3
  1. Income distribution—Developing countries.   I. Title.
  HC59.72.15886 1990   89–39095
  339.2′09172′4—dc20   CIP

ISBN 13: 978-0-415-07971-6 (pbk)

To
Saras, Ratna, and Raman

Contents

Contents

Tables

Preface

Compared with the attention given to problems of economic growth and development, the distribution of income among individuals and households is much neglected in the training of economists. But it is a subject of great importance. It is the branch of the subject that concerns us most intimately as individuals. It is the source of much of the problems that concern policy-makers. In addition, issues of income distribution are closely intertwined with the process of economic growth and development. This is particularly the case in less developed countries. After decades in which the growth of national income was viewed as the surest way of overcoming the absolute poverty afflicting a large proportion of people in less developed countries, there has been growing doubt whether the growth of national income by itself can solve the problem of poverty without a simultaneous improvement in the distribution of income. There is also some scepticism as to whether the growth of national income can be much accelerated, given the prevailing distribution of income in these countries.

Therefore, since about the mid-1960s, there was a rapid expansion of research work by economists on income distribution. Inevitably, individual researchers have concentrated on particular aspects of the subject. The time is now overdue for a comprehensive review of the literature, not only for the training of students, but also to identify major gaps in the literature which need further research. The main object of this book is to provide such a review.

This is particularly necessary in view of the imbalance in the current literature. A large part of it is concerned with statistical aspects of the subject, such as the invention of an endless stream of new measures of inequality and poverty, and the estimation of econometric equations relating income distribution to other aspects of the economy. Another part has been devoted to recommendations addressed to governments on policies relating to income distribution, not always founded on empirical evidence or on the careful analysis of that evidence. In between, there has been remarkably little work on the analytical framework of the subject, either to explain the patterns uncovered by the statistical research or as the basis for policy recommendations.

The present volume therefore aims to give a more balanced coverage of the subject. Part I discusses the statistical approach. Its principal aim is to evaluate the quality of the data, to simplify the main concepts of measurement which have been presented in the literature in a rather sophisticated form, and to concentrate on identifying the basic patterns and trends of income distribution shown by the data. Then an analytical framework is developed in Part II to provide a bridge between the functional distribution of income, which has been intensively studied in the literature, and the personal distribution of income. The main relationship used to bridge the gap between the two concepts is the distribution of the population according to the factors of production from which they derive their income. The scope of this part of the subject is therefore coterminous with economic theory as a whole, but it is clearly not possible to deal with these theories in much detail within the compass of a single book. Instead, what is attempted is to discuss the main theories from a distributional point of view. However, the discussion is supplemented by more extensive references to the literature than is perhaps customary in such texts. Part III of the book deals with policy issues, especially the effects of various policies on both the distribution of income and the growth of the economy. The book concludes with a discussion of the scope that exists in less developed countries for growth with equity.

It is hoped that the book will be useful to postgraduate and advanced undergraduate students of economics, to academics engaged in research on income distribution in less developed countries, and to the staff of national and international agencies interested in distributional policy in these countries.

The book is the result of a long period of research on the subject, especially during the author's service in the Economics Department, Research School of Pacific Studies, of the Australian National University. The author is grateful to his colleagues for much assistance over nearly two decades. Particular mention, however, must be made of Anne Booth, who not only discussed the issues involved, but also read several drafts of the book.

R. M. Sundrum
Canberra

Chapter one

Introduction

1.1 The growing interest in income distribution

Economics began its scientific career as an enquiry into the wealth of nations. And ever since, the study of the national income, how it differs between countries and how it grows over time, has remained the main concern of economists.

The British classical economists, who laid the scientific foundations of a new approach to the subject, were interested in the national income of countries from the point of view of the welfare of the entire population of these countries; hence, their measure of the economic progress of a country was its per capita income. This was a momentous shift of emphasis from previous writers on political economy, especially those of the Mercantilist school, who were more interested in the power of the state and its rulers.

The classical writers were also interested in how the national income was distributed among different sections of the population, but they distinguished these sections according to their ownership of the various factors of production: land, labour, and capital, that is, the 'functional' distribution of income. As Ricardo (Sraffa edition 1972, vol. 8, pp. 277–8) claimed in a well-known statement: 'Political economy . . . should rather be called an enquiry into the laws which determine the division of the produce of industry among the classes who concur in its formation.'

The main reason underlying this interest in the functional distribution of income was that the classical economists believed that this distribution was closely intertwined with the process of growth itself. Ricardo analysed this interaction with characteristic boldness, working from a few basic assumptions to derive grand theorems about change over long periods of time, so that his work on the subject has come to be known as the 'magnificent dynamics'.

However, in recent times there has been growing interest in the way the national income of countries is distributed among individuals and households in those countries, that is, the 'personal' distribution of income. This growing interest has given rise to a large literature on this topic. The main

1

object of this book is to give a comprehensive review of these studies.

But first we consider the reasons why interest in the personal distribution of income has grown only in recent times. One reason is that in earlier times individuals may have accepted their economic status as a given fact of their lives and thus have been resigned to it. But in our century large groups of people, sometimes indeed entire nations, have become dissatisfied with their present economic status. At the same time they have become increasingly aware that this status can be modified to their advantage, especially by influencing the policies of their governments, and therefore react to their real or imagined grievances by pressing for such actions. These pressures in turn have led to various government interventions with the working of the economic system. The result has been that whereas in the nineteenth century the triumph of classical political economy ushered in a long period of economic growth under free market forces among the Western nations, the time has now come that the governments of these very nations are actively intervening with market forces primarily for distributional reasons. In fact, it is even true to say that the very success of free markets in promoting the overall growth of the national product in these countries has led to the present concern with distributional issues and with various policy interventions to deal with them. Hirsch (1977) has eloquently argued that it is under such a 'distributional compulsion' that the developed market economies (hereafter DMEs) have been moving towards a 'reluctant collectivism'.

There has also been a growing interest in the distribution of income in the less developed countries (hereafter LDCs), though for an entirely different reason. The most striking feature of the LDCs is the large proportion, amounting in some cases to more than half, of the population living in absolute poverty on any reasonable definition. In the early postwar literature on development, such widespread poverty was considered essentially a reflection of the low level of national income relative to population, so that the solution was seen almost entirely in terms of overall economic growth. But since the mid-1960s doubts have begun to set in as to whether economic growth could be accelerated beyond the annual rate of around 5 per cent that many LDCs were experiencing, itself a sharp break from the stagnation of prewar years, and whether, even if these rates could be accelerated, the resulting growth of national income alone could solve the problem of widespread poverty in these countries (Fields 1980: Chap. 7). As an alternative, development economists have begun to look to improvements in the distribution of the national income among persons and households as a more promising way of relieving poverty. In fact, development itself is viewed by some writers primarily in terms of securing a more equal distribution of income, a point of view most forcefully stated by Seers (1969):

The questions to ask about a country's development are therefore: What has been happening to poverty? What has been happening to unemployment? What has been happening to inequality? If all three of these have declined from high levels, then beyond doubt, this has been a period of development for the country concerned.

Thus we see that interest in income distribution has grown in both the developed countries (hereafter DCs) and in the LDCs, though for different reasons. In the DCs, the interest was due to the rapid growth of national income leading to the present state of affluence; by contrast, in the LDCs it was due to the failure to achieve rapid economic growth.

The subject divides naturally into three parts: the quantitative data and their statistical analysis; the economic analysis of the broad patterns of income distribution; and the implications for policies that governments have followed or might follow to improve it. These are described in the following sections, and discussed more fully in later chapters.

1.2 The statistical approach

The first division of the subject is the statistical approach, discussed in Part I of this book. It is primarily concerned with the statistical properties of income distribution, and deals with issues of measurement and the derivation of various quantitative relationships. The central questions addressed are: How is total income distributed among individuals and households? Are there any mathematical patterns which best describe the distribution of incomes? How unequal is this distribution? How can such inequality be measured? What determines the extent of such inequality? In particular, are there any statistical relationships between the degree of inequality and other characteristics of societies taken as a whole? How does income inequality differ between countries? How does it vary over time? What determines differences in income inequality between countries?

An increasing amount of data has now been collected from a number of countries to provide answers to these questions. The nature of these data is discussed in Chapter two. They consist typically of the incomes or consumption expenditures of a sample of individuals or households, presented in statistical frequency distributions, showing the number of individuals or households in various income classes. The data are generally presented for the population as a whole; sometimes the individuals or households are also classified in other ways, but only according to a limited number of demographic or geographic groups such as regions of the country, urban or rural location, age, sex and education of individuals, and size of households. The choice of the data that are collected has been deeply influenced by the statistical approach to the subject. These data often fall short of what are required to answer some of the main questions of interest. Therefore some methods have to be developed to analyse these data to answer these questions at least approximately.

A particularly serious problem is that the concepts, definitions, survey procedures, and statistical reliability of data vary greatly from country to country, so that the data from different countries of different periods are not strictly comparable with one another. Another serious problem is that most of the data refer to the distribution of incomes received by individuals or households during a short period, such as a year or even a few months; hence, they do not throw sufficient light on the economic conditions of people in different economic and social classes, such as would be provided by data on lifetime incomes. While some countries have collected income distribution data for a number of years, few countries have long time series of such data.

The next step in the statistical approach is to summarize these data so that distributions of income in different countries or regions and at different times may be compared with one another. This is usually done by calculating an index of inequality or poverty. A large number of such measures have been proposed in the literature. The methods of their construction and their statistical properties are discussed in Chapter three. The typical procedure followed in constructing measures of inequality is to compare an actual distribution of income with the egalitarian distribution from various points of view. The various measures fall into two major categories, one consisting of measures of dispersion of individual or household incomes without reference to any underlying social welfare function, and the other of measures based on an explicit assumption of such a function. Another aspect of income distribution, distinct from the degree of inequality, is the extent of poverty. The chapter also discusses various measures of poverty which have been proposed. These deal with various aspects of the population living below a specified poverty line. In spite of considerable theoretical differences among these measures of inequality and of poverty, they tend to be highly correlated in practice. The chapter also discusses some aspects of income distribution not covered by measures of inequality or of poverty, and the ways they may be measured.

Although the data from different countries are not strictly comparable, the cross-section data reveal some broad patterns which are discussed in Chapter four. Generally speaking, the distribution of income is more equal in the DCs than in the LDCs, and within the LDCs, it tends to be more equal in Asian countries than in African and Latin American countries. Attempts to explain these variations have relied heavily on the relationship between income inequality and the level of average incomes in different countries. The leading hypothesis in the literature is the so-called Kuznets's law that income inequality rises with per capita income up to a point, and declines thereafter. However, this hypothesis is subject to some serious limitations which are pointed out in the chapter: the statistical relationship between income inequality and income level is not very strong, and even if there is such a relationship, it cannot be taken as indicating a causal connection between the two variables. Therefore a number of other factors are discussed which also influence income inequality in different countries. There is also a discussion of the inter-country variation in the extent of poverty, and the extent to which it is related to variations in income levels and income inequality.

The patterns observed in the cross-section data do not necessarily indicate how the distribution of income changes over time. They can be used for that purpose only on the assumption that all countries follow the same historical path, differing only in the stage they have reached on this path. This is an assumption that cannot be made lightly. It has to be verified against historical time series. The limited data available from a few countries in this form are discussed in Chapter five. They show a considerable diversity of experience about how income inequality changes in the process of economic growth. The data, however, show some interesting regularities concerning inequality of some major components of consumption.

The broad patterns of income distribution are usually much more stable over time than many other economic variables, such as average income levels. But underlying this stability are considerable changes in the fortunes of individuals. The relationship between the fluctuations of individual incomes and the stability of the distribution of income is studied in Chapter six in terms of dynamic probability models of social mobility, which have been discussed more extensively by sociologists than by economists.

The statistical approach has been very useful in organizing the available data on income distribution and exploring some of the relationships between these data and other variables. While this approach is an essential part of the subject, it is not complete by itself. One reason is that by itself, this approach may degenerate into 'measurement without theory'. Another problem is that this approach tends to concentrate excessively on the degree of inequality in a distribution to the neglect of other important aspects. The statistical approach also attempts to derive some broad empirical generalizations in the subject, but even the most robust statistical or historical generalization cannot be relied upon for making projections or devising policies for the future. Whether these generalizations will hold in the future or not depends on what the underlying conditions were which led to the regularities observed in the past, and whether these conditions will also hold in the future. Therefore both the data to be collected and the methods by which they are analysed must be inspired by a theoretical framework.

1.3 The analytical framework

The main objective of Part II of the book, dealing with the analytical framework, is to understand how various economic and social forces operating in the economy influence the distribution of income in that economy. Hence an appropriate point of departure for this part of the study is the concept of a distribution of income which is not affected by such forces. This is clearly not the egalitarian distribution. Instead, a more relevant point of departure is the random distribution of income, determined only by chance. Such a concept is derived in Chapter seven. While the comparison of actual distributions of income with the egalitarian distribution concentrates on the degree of inequality in the actual distributions, the comparison with the random distribution of income suggests that economic and social forces have both equalizing and disequalizing effects on income distribution.

To study these analytical issues empirically, therefore, we require data related to the operation of these economic and social forces. Unfortunately, there is a severe shortage of such information, because most of the data that are routinely collected have been based mainly on the statistical approach.

In developing theories about income distribution, economists have generally followed the model set by the classical economists. In this model, individual incomes are taken to be given by

$$Y_i = L_i w_i + K_i p_i + A_i r_i \qquad (1.1)$$

where Y_i is the income of the ith individual; L_i, K_i, and A_i are the quantities of labour, capital, and land owned by that individual; and w_i, p_i, and r_i are the rates of wages, profit, and rent received by that individual for supplying these resources. Hence any theory of the distribution of the national income of a country among individuals must explain how the productive resources in the economy are distributed among individuals, and what determines the prices individuals receive for supplying these resources to the production process.

The major theories of income distribution in the literature are briefly reviewed in Chapter eight. These theories have concentrated primarily on the prices, and the respective shares in the national income, of the factors of production. The reason these theories have concentrated only on this aspect of income distribution is that they were mainly interested in explaining the growth of national incomes, and only incidentally with income distribution. Therefore they only considered those aspects of income distribution which they considered useful in explaining the growth of national income. The general approach to the subject has been summarized by Samuelson (1964:637) in his influential textbook as follows:

> To understand what determines labour and property's share in national product, and to understand forces acting on the degree of inequality of income distribution, theory studies the problem of how the different

factors of production – land, labour, capital, entrepreneurs and risk-taking – are priced in the market or how supply and demand interact to determine all kinds of wages, rents, interest yields, profits and so forth.

Having narrowed the scope of their concern in this way, most theories then explain these factor prices mainly in terms of competitive market forces, so that all individuals who supply any factor are assumed to get the same price for that factor. An immediate consequence of this assumption is that equation (1.1) can be summed for all individuals in the economy. Then the national income Y of the country can be expressed as

$$Y = Lw + Kp + Ar \qquad (1.2)$$

Neoclassical theory emphasizes the demand side of factor markets; hence it explains the prices of the various factors of production in terms of their marginal productivity. On the other hand, classical economists were more interested in the supply side, and therefore explained factor prices as the result of such long-term forces as population growth and capital accumulation. A number of other theories have also been advanced which combine the classical and neoclassical approaches in various ways.

These theories of factor prices have been applied to study the changing distribution of income among broad social classes, corresponding to the major factors of production. Thus the classical writers were mainly concerned with the disequalizing effect of population growth on a limited area of land through the steady rise in the rent of land relative to the wages of labour, while capital accumulation at a faster rate than population growth has an equalizing effect through the steady decline in the rate of profit. Marxist theory, however, stressed the disequalizing effect of capital accumulation through the exploitation of labour by capitalists. Neoclassical theory has studied the effect of capital accumulation on factor shares mainly in terms of such technical factors as the degree of substitutability between labour and capital, and the bias of technological progress.

One limitation of most of these theories is that their explanation of factor prices is worked out mainly for the case of competitive factor markets. In fact, and especially in the LDCs, there are many other market institutions which have a significant influence on the price of the various factors of production, and on the prices that different individuals receive even for the same factor of production. Another serious limitation of most of these theories is that they have only been concerned with factor prices, whereas according to equation (1.1), the personal distribution of income depends also on the distribution of the factors among individuals and households. This distribution in turn depends on the nature of property institutions prevailing in different countries. Hence a theory of the distribution of income among individuals must take account of the nature and functioning of such institutions.

It is because of the significant influence of institutions on the distribution of income that Mill (1923 edn:199–200) made his sharp distinction between the theory of production on the one hand and the theory of distribution on the other:

> The laws and conditions of the Production of wealth partake of the character of physical truths. . . . It is not so with the Distribution of wealth. That is a matter of human institutions solely. The things once there, mankind, individually or collectively, can do with them as they like. They can place them at the disposal of whomsoever they please, and on whatever terms. . . . The distribution of wealth, therefore, depends on the laws and customs of society. The rules by which it is determined are what the opinions and feelings of the ruling portion of the community make them and are very different in different ages and countries; and might be still more different, if mankind so chose.

The idea is further elaborated as follows:

> Under the rule of individual property, the division of the produce is the result of two determining agencies: Competition and Custom. It is important to ascertain the amount of influence which belongs to each of these causes, and in what manner the operation of one is modified by the other. Political economists generally, and English political economists above others, have been accustomed to lay almost exclusive stress upon the first of these agencies; to exaggerate the effect of competition, and to take into little account the other and conflicting principle. This is partly intelligible, if we consider that only through the principle of competition has political economy any pretension to the character of a science. So far as rents, profits, wages, prices, are determined by competition, laws may be assigned for them. Assume competition to be their exclusive regulator, and principles of broad generality and scientific precision may be laid down, according to which they will be regulated. The political economist justly deems this his proper business: and as an abstract or hypothetical science, political economy cannot be required to do, and indeed cannot do, anything more. But it would be a great misconception of the actual course of human affairs, to suppose that competition exercises this unlimited sway. . . . I speak of cases in which there is nothing to restrain competition; no hindrance to it either in the nature of the case or in artificial obstacles; yet in which the result is not determined by competition, but by custom or usage; competition either not taking place at all, or producing its effect in quite a different manner from that which is ordinarily assumed to be natural to it.

In his comments on this argument, Blaug (1978:188) has suggested that

Mill was referring only to the influence that economic institutions had on the distribution of productive assets among individuals. But it is obvious from the above statement that Mill was also concerned with the influence of different economic institutions on the prices of the factors of production.

In spite of this early recognition of the influence of economic institutions on the distribution of income, it has been neglected in most of the subsequent theoretical work on the subject. Therefore a special attempt is made in the present work to study the factors influencing the distribution of productive assets on the one hand, and to study the determination of factor prices under conditions other than competitive factor markets. This is done separately for the three major factors: incomes from land in Chapter nine, from labour in Chapter ten, and from capital in Chapter eleven. An important conclusion of these chapters is that factor markets are highly fragmented in the LDCs, contrary to the model of competitive markets. Hence the inequality of income distribution as a whole is due not only to the relationship between the prices of different factors of production, but also to differences in the prices that persons get for the same factor of production.

Another aspect of the fragmentation of factor markets is the difference between different sectors of the economy. An important consequence of these differences is that the structure of production both influences and is influenced by the distribution of income. Chapter twelve deals with the relationship between income distribution and the structure of production, including the relative roles of the traditional and modern sectors, and the influence of foreign trade.

Chapter thirteen then brings together the main analytical conclusions of Part II. In particular, it summarizes the factors which explain the empirical evidence, both in the cross-section data and in the historical time trends.

1.4 The policy implications

Part III deals with the main issues of policy relating to the distribution of income. It begins with a discussion of the distributional objectives of policy in Chapter fourteen. The socially desirable distribution of income is a highly controversial subject. Part of the controversy has arisen because although equality is generally accepted as the ideal, there is much less agreement on the question of what constitutes equality. Part of the controversy has also concerned the extent to which the pursuit of equality interferes with the pursuit of other social goals such as rapid growth of national income. However, the definition of the distributional objective of policy is an issue distinct from the extent to which it should be balanced against other objectives. It is argued in Chapter fourteen that the egalitarian distribution of income provides a useful definition of the distributional objective in the long run. Although there are some problems in defining this concept precisely, these problems relate to the ultimate objective, one that cannot be attained in the near future. They are less serious in deciding the choice of policies in the short run. While the egalitarian distribution of income is useful as the long-run objective, the eradication of absolute poverty is an important objective to be attained in the short run. The chapter also discusses whether there is a conflict between the distributional and growth objectives, and if so, how it should be resolved.

Many economists have expressed a rather pessimistic conclusion about conflicts between the equity and growth objectives, but this is because they take a rather narrow view of the instruments of policy. In fact, modern governments have a wide range of instruments at their command which vary considerably in their effects on the two objectives. These instruments may be broadly classified into two groups, one relating to the regulation of various aspects of market forces, discussed in Chapter fifteen, and those involving redistribution of incomes and assets, discussed in Chapter sixteen. Each instrument is discussed in terms of its effects on the two objectives, both in the short run and the long. On the basis of this discussion, it is argued that there is considerable scope for deploying these instruments to promote both objectives at the same time, that is, for achieving equitable growth.

1.5 The special features of LDCs

Because of the growing interest in income distribution, there is now a large literature on the subject. Most of it, however, is either addressed to the distributional problems of DCs or implicitly based on conditions which are characteristic of the DCs. These studies are of little relevance to the LDCs because these countries differ from the DCs in so many respects which crucially affect their income distribution. Therefore, the present study is designed specifically to deal with income distribution in the LDCs.

The most striking difference between DCs and LDCs is, of course, the difference in per capita incomes. But, by itself, this difference in average incomes need not lead to great differences in patterns of income distribution or in the factors influencing this distribution. As far as the effect on the mechanism of income distribution is concerned, a more significant difference is precisely the difference in the institutional aspects of the working of markets, especially factor markets, emphasized by Mill. The standard textbook theory assumes that markets function impersonally, co-ordinating the supplies and demands of anonymous agents. Further, these markets are assumed to be quite efficient in the sense of bringing together all buyers and all sellers of each good or service, so that the same price rules over large parts of the market. Finally, it is assumed that there is a high degree of specialization so that a large variety of productive services are sharply distinguished from one another, and each is traded in a distinct market. The realism of these assumptions is the subject of much controversy even in the developed market economies (DMEs), but they are even more doubtful in LDCs. In these countries, economic transactions between individuals are highly personalized and based on their social status; the functioning of markets is greatly impeded by lack of transport and communications infrastructure, and there is little specialization of economic activities so that individuals perform different roles. The study of income distribution in LDCs must therefore give particular attention to these special features.

Apart from the difference in the working of markets, there is also a difference in economic structure which requires a different approach to the study of income distribution in the LDCs. The main feature of this difference is that agriculture is the dominant sector in the LDCs, employing a large proportion of the labour force and contributing a large share of the national product. Much of the extant literature on income distribution is preoccupied with the relationship between labour and capital, the major factors of production in the industrial sector, which is most important in the DCs. But in considering the problems of agriculture, we have to take into account the relationships among all three of the factors of production distinguished by the classical economists: land, labour, and capital. Further, at the low level of technology and investment which characterize the agricultural sectors of LDCs, we must take full account of the much greater degree of uncertainty affecting production, due both to the vagaries of nature and to the various institutional mechanisms evolved to cope with such uncertainty.

There is yet a third important feature which distinguishes the LDCs from the DCs, namely the fact that the LDCs are currently in the process of development, a process which has largely been completed in the DCs. In this ongoing process of development, the government is likely to play a more significant role. Therefore we must give special attention to the effect of government policies on the distribution of income. Further, during this process the factors affecting income distribution in the LDCs will be subject to more rapid change than in the DCs, with consequent effects on income distribution itself. Therefore we have to take greater account of dynamic interrelations in the case of LDCs.

Part I

The statistical approach

Chapter two

Statistical data on income distribution

2.1 Introduction

The statistical data on income distribution consist of estimates of income that units of the population belonging to various groups receive from different sources over certain periods of time. Such data are usually presented in the form of a frequency distribution, that is, the numbers (frequencies) or proportions (relative frequencies) of units of the population whose incomes fall into a number of income classes. In this form, we use two sets of numbers to summarize the data, namely the incomes of the income classes, and their frequencies.

In this form, the data from different countries cannot be compared easily with each other because the income classes are defined in terms of different currencies. Therefore a more convenient approach that is often used is to arrange the households or individuals in the ascending order of their incomes, and to divide this ranked sequence into a small number of classes, known as fractiles, such as quintiles in the case of five classes and deciles in the case of ten classes. Then the data on income distribution can be summarized by a single set of numbers, the shares of total income received by each quintile or decile. It is in this form that the statistical data will generally be considered in this book.

The data collected in different countries and even in the same country at different times differ in a number of respects, such as the population unit for which incomes are estimated, the groups into which these units are classified, the items of income included and the ways they are estimated, the period over which these incomes are received, and the sources of such incomes. These differences must be noted carefully both in interpreting the data and in making comparisons. Each type of data is suitable for studying a particular aspect of income distribution; therefore we must be careful to ensure that the data we use are suitable for the type of analysis we wish to undertake. Further, comparisons of income distribution between different countries and between different times must be based on the same type of data, or adjusted for any differences that there may be in the data. In this chapter we consider the various types of data that are available and how they can be used for studying different aspects of income distribution.

2.2 Recipient units

There are four types of units for which income data are generally collected: households, economically active persons, income recipients, and individual household members. Each of these units is useful in dealing with particular aspects of the problem, representing different stages in the process by which people earn their income by their productive activity and spend it on their consumption. The unit most frequently used is the household, and the next most common unit is the income recipient.

The household or family is also the most convenient unit for collecting income data. As Kuznets (1976:7) says, the advantages of this unit lie 'in the identification of incomes not clearly assignable to individual persons, in the inclusion within families of both economically active and dependent members of the population, and in being the locus of decisions on income getting and income spending of the individual members'.

But for studying the income of households as a measure of their contribution to productive activity or as a measure of welfare, we must consider individual units within the household. At the point most directly connected with productive activity, the obvious unit is the economically active person. Some countries have collected data on the incomes of such units but such data are not very reliable, especially in LDCs where much of the productive activity is carried on as a family enterprise, and economically active persons working in such enterprises do not always receive incomes separately. This is particularly the case for the category known as unpaid family workers, who constitute a large proportion of the labour force of LDCs. According to the censuses and labour force surveys carried out around 1970, the proportion of unpaid family workers in the labour force was 12.4 per cent for males and 27.9 per cent for females in LDCs, compared with only 2.4 per cent for males and 12.1 per cent for females in the DCs (Sundrum 1983: Table 2.7, p. 25). Even within LDCs, the proportion of unpaid family workers in the labour force varies from sector to sector, being particularly high in the agricultural sector. It is usually difficult to impute reliable values to the contribution of such workers to the family income, and hence their share in this income. Therefore many countries adopt the simpler procedure of collecting income data only for income recipients. In using such data it must be remembered that the income of income recipients includes the contribution of other members of the family or household.

If the average number of economically active persons, or earners, were the same in households at different levels of household income, then the distribution of income among households would be similar to the distribution among earners or among economically active persons. But in fact the number of earners in a household varies quite systematically with household income. The usual pattern of this variation is illustrated by data from a few countries in Table 2.1.

Generally, richer households have a larger number of earners, except for households at the very top of the income scale in some cases. Therefore income distribution in one country or at one time in terms of household units cannot be compared with income distribution in another country or at another time in terms of economically active persons or earners without making some adjustment for such variations in the number of earners with household income.

Similarly, when we are interested in the standard of living of different income groups, the relevant concept is the income or consumption of individual members of the households, 'since it is human beings not households that have stomachs and feel the cold' (Wiles 1978:168). If the average number of members was the same in households at different levels of household income, then the distribution of income among households at different levels of income would be the same as the distribution of income among individuals at different levels of individual income. But in fact household sizes also vary quite systematically with household incomes. The general pattern is illustrated in Table 2.2, showing the variation of household size with household income in selected countries.

The general pattern is that household size increases with household income. Therefore the distribution of income among households at different levels of household income cannot be compared with the distribution of income among individuals without adjustments for differences in household size at different income levels.

In fact, the usual pattern is that household incomes increase with household size, but less than proportionately. Hence the income per household member generally declines with household size. This relationship is illustrated by data from some countries in Table 2.3.

Because of this tendency for larger families to have lower per capita incomes, Dandekar and Rath (1971:13) concluded from their study of India that 'there is therefore little doubt that the size of a household is an important factor pushing it down the ladder'. This pattern was also found by Kuznets (1976:88) in his study of five countries, some developed and some less developed:

[W]hereas larger families or households tended to have larger incomes per family or household – a positive correlation that was found in all five countries (United States, Germany, Israel, Taiwan, and the Philippines) covered in the discussion – the larger units showed *lower per person* income than the smaller units. This *negative* correlation between size of family or household and per *person* (or per consumer) income was quite

Table 2.1 Earners per household by household income

Country/Year	Households ranked by household income						
	Bottom 20%	20%–40%	40%–60%	60%–80%	80%–90%	Top 10%	Average
Malaysia, 1970	1.10	1.33	1.50	1.80	2.12	2.72	1.63
Philippines, 1971							
Urban	1.21	1.30	1.38	1.72	1.89	2.05	1.51
Rural	1.14	1.25	1.32	1.49	1.73	2.01	1.41
National	1.16	1.27	1.36	1.52	1.84	1.97	1.44
Thailand, 1969							
Urban	1.41	1.65	1.88	2.12	2.53	2.85	1.95
Rural	1.20	1.33	1.49	1.60	1.73	1.82	1.48
Sri Lanka, 1973	1.10	1.27	1.32	1.46	1.67	1.72	1.37
Sri Lanka, 1981/82	1.16	1.37	1.52	1.65	1.72	1.60	1.47
USA, 1984	0.83	1.35	1.71	1.98	2.25	2.36	1.64

Sources: Malaysia: Anand (1983), p. 73.
Philippines: Family Income and Expenditures, 1971 (Manila, Bureau of Census and Statistics, Series no. 34), p. 124.
Thailand: Socio-Economic Survey BE 2511–2512 (Bangkok, National Statistical Office), p. 4.
Sri Lanka: Report on Consumer Finances and Socio-Economic Survey, 1981/82 (Colombo, Central bank of Ceylon), pp. 180, 186.
USA: Current Population Report Series P-60 (Washington, DC, Bureau of Census and Statistics), p. 21.

Table 2.2 Household size by household income

Country/Year	Households ranked by household income						
	Bottom 20%	20%–40%	40%–60%	60%–80%	80%–90%	Top 10%	Average
Malaysia, 1970	3.58	4.75	5.38	6.15	6.66	7.31	5.36
Philippines, 1971							
Urban	4.99	5.36	5.67	6.29	6.25	6.49	5.74
Rural	4.80	5.26	5.60	6.06	6.47	6.73	5.66
National	4.84	5.38	5.66	6.05	6.51	6.49	5.69
Thailand, 1969							
Urban	4.29	5.21	6.09	6.51	7.06	7.28	5.85
Rural	5.10	5.30	5.63	6.01	6.20	6.85	5.71
Sri Lanka, 1981/82	3.39	4.55	5.25	5.63	5.89	5.87	4.94
USA, 1984	2.00	2.33	2.67	3.01	3.19	3.28	2.65

Sources: As for Table 2.1.

Table 2.3 Per capita income by household size

| Country/Year/ | Household size | | | | | | | | | | |
Income	1	2	3	4	5	6	7	8	9	10 and over	Average
India 1964–65 (Rs per month)											
Rural	38.3	31.4	28.0	26.3	25.3	24.3	23.7	23.7	25.7		26.7
Indonesia, 1964–65 (000 Rp per month)											
Urban	9.8	10.1	8.9	7.3	7.5	6.6	6.8	6.8	6.9	8.2	7.5
Rural	8.0	7.1	6.1	5.6	5.1	5.1	5.0	5.3	5.7	5.5	5.5
Malaysia, 1970 ($ per month)	137	91	69	58	49	47	41	41	35		43
Philippines, 1971 (000 pesos per month)											
Urban	4.45	2.13	1.57	1.34	1.17	0.91	0.91	0.85	0.72	0.73	1.01
Rural	1.61	0.94	0.70	0.64	0.53	0.48	0.42	0.39	0.39	0.41	0.49
National	2.40	1.26	0.96	0.86	0.72	0.62	0.57	0.51	0.49	0.52	0.65
USA, 1985 (000 $ per month)	16.0	14.8	11.4	9.3	7.3	6.0	—	4.9	—	—	11.0

Sources: India: Vaidyanathan (1974), Table 8, p. 227.
Indonesia: Sundrum (1973), Table 11, p. 93.
Malaysia: Anand (1983), Table 3.2, pp. 69–70.
Philippines: Bureau of Census and Statistics (1973) Family Income and Expenditures 1971 Table 25, pp. 47–8.
USA: Current Population Reports (1985).

striking and was found in all five countries covered. In other words, the rise in income per household (or family) with the increase in its size does not compensate fully for the latter, with the result that income per person (or per consumer, roughly calculated by assigning half-weight to children under 18) declines as size of unit rises.

When household size varies with household income, we cannot compare different countries or countries at different times only on the basis of their household income distributions, although data are best collected initially in this form. Instead, such comparisons should be based on the distribution of persons according to their incomes per capita (or per consumer equivalent), obtained by dividing the income of each household by the number of persons (or consumer equivalents), and attributing this average to each member of the household (see, e.g., Wiles 1978:168–74).

Some countries have published data on the distribution of both household and per capita incomes, from which we can get an idea of the magnitude of the difference between the two kinds of distribution. Some other countries have published data on the distribution of income both by household income class and by household size, from which the distribution by individuals can be derived. For these cases the household and individual distributions can be compared, as shown in Table 2.4.

In most cases, incomes (or consumption expenditures) are distributed more equally among individuals than among households, that is, the lower quintiles of individuals have a higher share of total expenditures than the lower quintiles of households, and the upper deciles of individuals have a smaller share than the upper deciles of households. But in some cases, for example, South Korea, Kenya, and Mexico, the individual distribution is more unequal than the household distribution. The relationship between the two distributions is examined further in Appendix 4.1.

2.3 The measurement of income

The most serious problem in collecting data on income distribution is in estimating the income of households or individuals. To some extent, it is easier to solve in the developed countries, where most transactions are carried out in money terms and most people keep some sort of accounts. Therefore a person's income may be approximated fairly closely by his money income, that is, the amount of money he receives for the goods and services he supplies to others less the amount paid to others for the goods and services used to earn the income. But even in a developed economy, there are serious conceptual and practical problems in allowing for the depreciation of the capital stock used to earn income. Hence even for these countries, Hicks (1966:180) concluded that 'the concept of income [is] one which the positive theoretical economist only employs in his arguments at

Table 2.4 Household and individual distributions of income (percentage share of total income)

Country/Year	Bottom 20%	20%–40%	40%–60%	60%–80%	80%–90%	Top 10%	Total
Bangladesh: 1973–74							
Household	6.8	11.4	16.1	23.5	14.8	27.4	100.0
Individual	8.8	13.6	17.9	21.9	14.4	23.4	100.0
Egypt: 1974							
Household	5.8	10.7	14.7	20.8	14.9	33.2	100.0
Individual	7.6	11.0	14.2	20.1	13.9	33.3	100.0
Fiji: 1977							
Household	3.7	8.8	13.4	20.9	15.5	37.8	100.0
Individual	4.2	9.3	13.3	19.9	15.3	38.0	100.0
India: 1964–65							
Household	6.0	10.0	13.7	19.1	14.1	37.1	100.0
Individual	6.8	10.5	13.8	19.3	14.1	35.5	100.0
Indonesia: 1980							
Household	6.4	10.5	15.5	21.8	15.2	30.6	100.0
Individual	7.7	11.9	16.0	22.2	14.4	27.8	100.0
Iran: 1973–74							
Household	3.8	7.5	12.1	19.2	15.8	41.7	100.0
Individual	5.6	9.0	12.7	19.1	14.9	38.8	100.0
Kenya: 1976							
Household	2.7	6.3	11.5	19.2	14.6	45.8	100.0
Individual	2.5	6.2	11.2	18.8	16.4	45.0	100.0
S. Korea: 1970							
Household	7.4	11.5	15.4	20.9	16.8	28.0	100.0
Individual	6.0	10.5	14.5	21.5	16.5	31.0	100.0
Mexico: 1968							
Household	2.7	6.4	10.2	18.1	15.9	46.7	100.0
Individual	2.6	6.1	10.1	17.3	15.5	48.5	100.0

Philippines: 1971						
Household	3.8	8.1	13.3	21.0	16.9	36.9	100.0
Individual	3.9	8.2	13.1	20.8	16.5	37.5	100.0
Senegal: 1970						
Household	5.5	7.8	10.5	15.3	15.5	45.4	100.0
Individual	5.7	8.1	11.4	16.8	14.9	43.1	100.0
Tanzania: 1968						
Household	5.5	8.0	10.5	15.0	16.0	45.0	100.0
Individual	5.0	8.5	11.5	15.0	15.0	45.0	100.0

Note: Units are ranked by income of unit.

Sources: Lecaillon *et al.* (1984) for India, South Korea, Senegal and Tanzania; van Ginneken and Park (1984) for Bangladesh, Egypt, Fiji, Iran, Kenya and Mexico; Biro Pusat Statistic (1980) *Socio-economic Survey (Susenas)* (1980) for Indonesia; and Bureau of Census and Statistics (1973), *Family Income and Expenditures, 1971* for Philippines.

his peril. For him, income is a very dangerous term.' However, some estimates are needed for practical work and a number of rough adjustments have been evolved to get such estimates.

The problems of measuring income are much more serious in the LDCs. First, owing to the survival of traditional forms of personal relationships, a considerable part of the monies that households receive do not represent income from their productive activities, but rather are receipts for non-economic reasons such as gifts which are, strictly speaking, not income receipts. Second, the economy of LDCs is much less monetized, so that a high proportion of income is received in nonmonetary form, more so for the poorer households. This is particularly so in the case of wages, the whole or part of which may be paid in kind. There is also a large subsistence sector in which the commodities produced by households are mainly for their own consumption, without going through the market. Therefore such nonmonetary receipts and production must be valued at certain imputed prices in order to get a monetary value of income (see Fisk 1975 for some of the problems involved). Third, a large proportion of the labour force is engaged in agriculture, where the flow of income is highly seasonal and very irregular; therefore the income from this sector must be estimated for the season as a whole. Fourth, because of weaker transport and marketing infrastructure, commodity prices vary between different regions to a much greater extent in LDCs than in DCs (see Arndt and Sundrum 1975 for a study of price disparities in Indonesia). Such disparities are particularly large between urban and rural areas. Therefore differences in money incomes do not correspond to differences in real incomes. Finally, it is more difficult to collect data on incomes in LDCs because people in these countries are less accustomed to keeping regular accounts.

The different forms in which incomes are earned in LDCs are particularly important for the study of income distribution in these countries because they vary considerably between different income groups. Some idea of the relative importance of the various forms in which households get their receipts is shown by data from the 1981 socioeconomic survey of households in Thailand, summarized in Table 2.5.

As may be expected, home production for household consumption forms a high proportion (21 per cent) of household receipts in rural areas. However, this form of receipts is quite high (12 per cent) even in urban areas.

Receipts in different forms vary systematically with the levels of household incomes, as shown by data from Indonesia and Sri Lanka in Table 2.6. In the Indonesian case, the proportion of income received in nonmonetary form appears to be quite uniform for all income classes because the survey refers to urban areas of the country at a time when payment of a part of wages in kind was a standard practice for most urban workers. More

Table 2.5 Forms of household receipts: Thailand, 1981 (bahts per month; percentages in parentheses)

Form of receipt	National		Urban		Rural	
Money income	2,388	(70.7)	4,060	(79.8)	1,705	(63.6)
Income in kind	61	(1.8)	152	(3.0)	24	(0.9)
Home production	463	(13.7)	204	(4.0)	569	(21.2)
Others	414	(12.3)	612	(12.0)	333	(12.4)
Total income	3,326	(98.5)	5,028	(98.8)	2,631	(98.2)
Other receipts	52	(1.5)	59	(1.2)	49	(1.8)
Total receipts	3,378	(100.0)	5,087	(100.0)	2,680	(100.0)

Source: National Statistical Office, Bangkok, *Report of the 1981 Socio-economic Survey.*

Table 2.6 Forms of income receipts (households by receipts)

	Bottom 20%	II	III	IV	Top 20%	Total
A. Indonesia, 7 cities: 1968–69						
Form of Receipt	Percentages of total receipt					
Money income	60.5	65.4	67.5	68.2	71.2	68.6
In kind	7.5	9.7	10.8	11.1	10.0	10.1
Home production	5.1	3.9	3.5	4.3	4.8	4.4
Nonincome	26.9	21.0	18.2	16.4	14.0	16.9
Total	100.0	100.0	100.0	100.0	100.0	100.0
B. Sri Lanka, 1981–82						
Region	Percentages of income in kind					
Urban	26.3	14.3	13.4	13.6	15.9	15.5
Rural	31.0	22.8	21.0	20.0	26.0	24.0
Estates	20.0	14.0	12.9	12.2	12.9	12.4
Total	30.0	20.8	18.9	17.7	22.0	21.1

Sources: Indonesia: *Cost of Living Surveys*, Biro Pusat Statistik (1968, 1969).
Sri Lanka: Central Bank of Ceylon (1984), *Report on Consumer Finances.*

commonly in LDCs, the proportion of income received in this form is high at the lower-income levels and declines as income rises, as shown by the Sri Lankan data. Hence income distribution data comprising only monetary forms of income will underestimate the incomes of the poor and over-estimate the degree of inequality, especially in the rural and less monetized sectors of the economy.

Many countries, especially LDCs, collect data on consumption expenditures rather than on incomes, partly because of the difficulty of getting accurate information about incomes, and partly because consumption data may be more relevant for comparing the standard of living of different groups. Then, we must be careful to ensure that the same type of data is used in comparing different periods or different countries because the distribution of consumption will generally be different from the distribution of income. The magnitude of such differences is illustrated in Table 2.7 for a few countries which have collected data on distributions of both income and consumption expenditures.

The differences between incomes and expenditures is quite small in the Indonesian urban survey; they are much larger in the Sri Lankan data. In the Central Bank report on this survey, the differences between income and expenditures were attributed to savings but it is unlikely that savings alone can account for such large differences. It is unlikely that the lower-income groups could afford to spend so much more on consumption than their incomes. It is more likely that incomes have been underestimated relative to consumption expenditures. The differences are even greater in the Philippine data, where average expenditures are reported as being 20 per cent higher than average incomes. This is clearly a case of under-estimating incomes. Therefore for comparison with other countries, the income data have been adjusted to fit with the consumption data (for details, see Rao 1984:115).

In principle, the difference between the two concepts is savings. As the upper-income groups usually save a larger proportion of their incomes, the distribution of consumption will generally be more equal than the distribution of income. However, in practice, even in the case of consumption expenditures, the collection of data in LDCs is a laborious process. Because these expenditures are so irregular, few people can estimate them over any extended period, and it is often necessary for interviewers to check expenditures on a daily or weekly basis, valuing nonmonetary incomes and expenditures at imputed prices. Because of the high costs involved, the data are usually collected from a small sample of households. Such data are also usually collected only for a limited list of consumption items. Therefore many items of consumption bought by the upper-income groups are often omitted. Such data are thus likely to underestimate the consumption of the upper-income groups and therefore to underestimate the degree of inequality.

This problem is particularly serious in the case of durable consumer goods. In this case, the consumption in a given period must in principle be measured in terms of the services derived from such goods in that period, but this raises great problems of valuing such services and making the appropriate allowances for depreciation. This method is therefore used only for some important cases, such as the services derived from owner-

Table 2.7 Income and expenditure: households ranked by monthly household income

	Bottom 20%	20%-40%	40%-60%	60%-80%	80%-90%	Top 10%	Average
A. Indonesia: 7 cities, 1968-69							
Income (000 Rp)	2.53	4.14	5.65	7.96	12.20	21.88	7.46
Expenditure (000 Rp)	2.76	4.52	6.20	8.74	12.06	20.63	7.71
Exp. as % of income	109	109	110	110	99	94	103
B. Philippines, 1971							
Income (pesos)	714	1,510	2,477	3,922	6,303	15,811	3,736
Expenditure (pesos)	1,975	2,718	3,549	4,724	6,885	11,973	4,479
Exp. as % of income	277	180	143	120	109	87	120
C. Sri Lanka, 1981-82							
Income (Rs)	468	784	1,093	1,586	2,390	6,096	1,635
Expenditure (Rs)	658	965	1,309	1,632	2,323	4,007	1,544
Exp. as % of income	141	123	120	103	97	66	94

Sources: Indonesia: Biro Pusat Statistik (1968, 1969) *Cost of Living Surveys.*
Philippines: Bureau of Census and Statistics (1973), *Family Income and Expenditures, 1971.*
Sri Lanka: Central Bank of Ceylon (1984), *Report on Consumer Finances.*

occupied dwellings. In most other cases, the consumption of durable consumer goods is usually valued at the amounts spent in purchasing them. The underlying justification of this procedure is that if 10 per cent of households purchase a durable consumer good in the period under survey, it is implicitly assumed that the average value of consumption of these goods in that period by all households is 10 per cent of their cost price. But even with such adjustments, it is never possible to identify all items of consumption expenditures. Many items, especially those consumed by the upper-income groups, tend to be omitted.

Apart from these conceptual problems, there is also the problem of the statistical reliability of the data on the distribution of incomes or expenditures. This depends on the care with which the data are collected. But even with highly trained staff, it is inevitable that the data reported by individual households will be subject to considerable errors due to genuine mistakes or to misreporting. In the DCs, it may be possible to cross-check the data collected from households against other information, but in LDCs, such other information is itself limited and not very reliable. As far as total expenditure on major items of consumption such as foodstuffs is concerned, it may be possible to compare the results of household surveys with production data, which are usually more reliable. It is usually found in such comparisons that the data collected in household surveys underestimate the consumption estimates derived from production data. If the degree of underestimation is fairly stable over time, the household data could still be used to identify broad trends, but this may not always be true. For example, Srinivasan et al. (1974) and Vaidyanathan (1986) found that the degree of underestimation of consumption expenditures by the National Sample Surveys in India, as compared with the National Accounts data, was quite small and fairly constant before 1965 but increased quite significantly thereafter. In other countries the difference between the two estimates is much greater.

Even if household surveys underestimate consumption expenditures, such errors may not be very serious for the study of income distribution, if all individuals underestimate their incomes or expenditures in the same proportion. However, this is rarely the case. On the one hand, richer individuals tend to underestimate their incomes in order to avoid the envy of others, or for fear of raising their tax liabilities, or provoking policies that might affect them adversely. On the other hand, it has sometimes been found that poorer households tend to exaggerate their consumption expenditures so as not to reveal the extent of their poverty.

2.4 The period of income receipt

Most surveys collect data on incomes and expenditures of persons or households over a relatively short period, such as a year or even a few months. A person's income in such a short period may diverge from the average income of her group or from her own income averaged over a longer period, because it would be affected by a variety of short-term forces. If these forces are due to 'accidental' factors which affect different households in different ways, they may be eliminated by averaging out for large groups of units. But some of these short-term forces may affect large groups in the same way. Kuznets (1975:390) has described them as 'conjunctural' factors. Such factors will not be eliminated by averaging over the group as a whole; they can only be eliminated by averaging incomes over a long period. The distinction corresponds to Friedman's (1957) distinction between 'transient' incomes and 'permanent' incomes. Because consumption expenditures do not vary as much as incomes in the short period, Friedman has suggested that they are more reliable than income receipts as indicative of a household's permanent income.

A more serious problem in using short-period data on incomes is that they catch different individuals at different ages, when they are at different stages of their life-cycle. A person's income generally varies quite systematically with age, being low in youth, rising to a peak in late middle age, and declining with retirement and old age. The extent to which household incomes vary with the age of the head of the household is indicated by the data from some countries shown in Table 2.8.

In all cases, as the age of the head of the household increases, household income rises up to a point and declines thereafter. The decline in the second phase seems to occur at a later stage and more slowly in the LDCs than in the DCs. Because of these differences, Kuznets (1976:89–90) concluded that:

> The combination of this substantial swing in per family income by age of head, with substantial proportions of families at the low income age extremes, introduces a substantial income inequality component into the conventional size distribution of income by income per family or per household in the developed countries . . . Because of the combination of low shares of families or households at the extreme age classes, particularly the old, and the absence of a second, pronounced trough in per family income at the end of the life span, the inequality component introduced by the age-of-head differentials in income per family in the two less-developed countries is appreciably smaller than in the United States and Israel. This suggests that comparisons of size distributions of income among families or households between developed and less developed countries may be significantly biased, if viewed as comparisons of long-term income levels or lifetime incomes: they may exaggerate inequality in the developed countries compared with that in the less developed.

However, when we consider income per person, we must also take

Table 2.8 Variation of income by age of head of household (as percentage of average)

Country/Year	Age of head of household						
	Under 25	25–34	35–44	45–54	55–64	65+	Total
Indonesia (1981)							
Household income	76	95	107	108	102	76	100
Per capita income	119	107	94	96	107	99	100
Philippines (1971)							
Household income	62	83	97	118	121	103	100
Sri Lanka (1981–82)							
Household income	62	114	140	151	——133——		100
Taiwan (1964)							
Household income	71	91	97	110	117	108	100
Israel (1968–69)							
Household income	70	107	115	120	102	53	100
USA (1985)							
Household income	61	96	123	132	110	65	100
Per capital income	70	89	95	116	125	99	100

Sources: Indonesia: Biro Pusat Statistik (1981) *SUSENAS, 1981.*
Philippines: Bureau of Census and Statistics (1973) *Family Income and Expenditures, 1971.*
Sri Lanka: Central Bank of Ceylon, *Report on Consumer Finances and Socio Economic Survey, 1981/82.*
Taiwan, Israel: Kuznets (1975).
USA: Bureau of Census (1985) *Current Population Reports (1985).*

account of another factor, namely the tendency for household sizes to increase with age of head of household up to a point, and decline thereafter. After allowing for this tendency, we find that there is in the United States a tendency for income per person also to increase up to a point and decline thereafter, but the amplitude of this variation is smaller than in the case of household income. The situation in LDCs, as illustrated by the case of Indonesia, is different, with income per person declining with increasing age of head of household up to a point, and increasing thereafter.

A consequence of the systematic variation of income with age is that part of the inequality of income distribution shown by data on annual incomes is due to the differences in the age of the persons involved. Thus even if all individuals had the same stream of incomes at different ages of their life-cycle, the annual data will show considerable inequality (see, e.g., Johnson 1973:207–9). One solution of this problem is to compare individuals on the basis of their lifetime incomes. This is analogous to the study of completed fertility in demographic surveys, but it is much more difficult to undertake such longitudinal surveys of incomes. Even if such surveys could be carried out, there is a further problem, pointed out by Paglin (1975) that in a dynamic society, the lifetime income streams of different generations of people would differ, being higher for the later generations. Thus even if all individuals in each generation had the same lifetime income profiles, the difference in lifetime incomes of different generations would introduce an element of inequality in our data.

An alternative approach is to splice annual data of incomes of people at different ages to construct a lifetime pattern of incomes for different socio-economic groups, showing what their incomes would be on the assumption that current economic conditions will remain constant over their lifetimes. This method is also used in demographic studies to estimate the total fertility of different populations. Lifetime patterns of income constructed in this way for different educational groups are also extensively used in studies of the economic return to education.

A third possible approach is to decompose any measure of inequality of income distribution into two parts, one due to age differences and the other to all other factors. This is discussed in more detail in the next chapter.

2.5 Sources of income

An important influence on the incomes of individuals is the source from which they derive those incomes. Therefore any study of income distribution must consider these sources of income. One way in which the sources of income may be classified is according to whether income is derived from participation in productive activity or from other sources. Different types of income distribution may then be distinguished as follows:

1   primary income distribution, which refers to the way incomes earned from productive activity are distributed
2   secondary income distribution, which refers to the primary distribution of income as modified by direct cash transfers, such as taxes and social security payments
3   tertiary income distribution, which refers to the secondary distribution, as further modified by public sector activities such as the regulation of prices and the provision of public goods and services (Boersma 1978:xviii).

The relationships among these distributions are particularly important in showing the impact of government policies and are considered in later chapters.

In the case of the primary distribution of income, it is useful to subdivide incomes into various categories such as wages, interest, rent, and profits because they can then be explained by the supply and demand for the various factors of production. In DCs, it is relatively easy to separate these categories of income because of the high degree of specialization in these countries. The relative position in DCs is illustrated by the data from the United States (Table 2.9).

It is more difficult to classify incomes into these categories in LDCs because a large proportion of the labour force is self-employed, and their incomes are a mixture of a number of different categories. Some recent estimates for India are shown in Table 2.10.

It is only in the organized sector, accounting for 35 per cent of all incomes, that it has been possible to estimate the various categories of income. This sector is heavily dominated by the public sector, and the position is very close to that observed in the United States for the economy as a whole. In the unorganized sector, typified by the agricultural sector, as much as two-thirds of total income consists of a mixture of various types of income.

Table 2.9 Categories of income: United States, 1976

Category of income	Total income ($ billion)	Percentage distribution
Compensation of employees	1,028	76
Proprietors' income	97	7
Rental income	24	2
Corporate profit	118	9
Net interest	82	6
Total	1,349	100

Source: Dornbusch and Fischer (1978), Table 2.2, p. 31.

Table 2.10 Categories of income: India, 1979–80 (percentage of GDP)

Category of income	Whole economy	Primary sector	Secondary sector	Tertiary sector	Organized sector	Unorganized sector
Compensation of employees	40.1	24.4	48.7	51.1	68.1	25.0
Interest	7.6	5.7	14.7	4.8	13.2	4.5
Rent	4.3	1.9	1.7	8.5	1.6	5.7
Profits and dividends	6.0	3.0	13.9	4.0	17.1	
Mixed incomes	42.0	65.0	21.0	31.6	—	64.8
Total	100.0	100.0	100.0	100.0	100.0	100.0
Amount (Rs. crores)	87,184	33,869	21,238	32,077	30,678	56,506

Source: India: Central Statistical Office (1980) National Accounts Statistics.

But from the point of view of income distribution, what is needed is information on the sources of income at different income levels. One way of collecting such information is the proportion of income that people at different income levels get from different sources. Such data were collected in the 1971 household budget survey of the Philippines and are summarized in Table 2.11. This Table shows the extent to which the lower-income groups derive their income from the agricultural sector, either as farmers or as agricultural labourers. It is interesting to note the high proportion of households at the highest income level which earn their incomes in the form of nonagricultural wages.

Another way in which such data can be collected is by classifying units of the population according to the principal source of their incomes. Most of the data on income distribution collected and published by countries refers to the distribution of income in the population as a whole, or for groups classified according to such criteria as age, sex, region, urban and rural location, education, and so on. These are useful for some purposes, but it is also useful to have such data for groups classified according to social and economic variables which have a more important influence on income distribution, variables such as the ownership of different types of resources, access to market opportunities, the employment in different sectors of the economy, and so on. When the available data on income distribution are based only on a classification of the population into various income classes, writers on the subject have had to study the influence of socioeconomic variables only by searching for relationships between overall income inequality, and the socioeconomic characteristics of societies taken as a whole. In particular, this has led to excessive resort to studies based on international cross-section data, with all their well-known statistical and conceptual problems.

Given the data that are already being collected, it is a relatively simple matter to improve them, simply by classifying income-receiving units by the required socioeconomic variables, in addition to variables such as age, urban and rural location, and educational qualifications, which is already being done by many countries (for further discussion of the need for such data, see Kuznets 1976:93–4). Some examples from a few countries where such data are available are cited in Chapter seven.

Table 2.11 Distribution of income by source: Philippines, 1971

Source of income	Bottom 20%	20%–40%	40%–60%	60%–80%	80%–90%	Top 10%	Average
Percentage of household income from:							
Agricultural wages	11.6	14.3	13.1	10.7	5.5	2.1	10.7
Nonagricultural wages	8.8	17.4	33.7	47.2	57.7	53.5	32.3
Farming	56.3	47.0	31.8	22.0	14.2	10.2	34.4
Other entrepreneurial	16.6	15.9	16.0	16.4	16.5	21.0	16.6
Other	6.7	5.4	5.4	3.7	6.1	13.2	6.0
Total	100.0	100.0	100.0	100.0	100.0	100.0	100.0

Source: Bureau of Census and Statistics (1973) *Family Income and Expenditures 1971.*

Chapter three

Measurement of income inequality and poverty

3.1 Introduction

As described in Chapter two, the statistical data on income distribution is usually presented in the form of a frequency distribution, that is, the proportion of the total population of a country or region falling into various income classes. In order to give sufficient detail, at least ten to twelve income classes must be distinguished. This means that the number of figures used to describe each distribution will be too large to enable comparisons between distributions to be made easily. Therefore there has been great interest in further summarizing the data into one or two statistical constants describing such data, which are used as measures of inequality of income distribution or of the extent of poverty. A number of such measures that have been used in the literature are reviewed in this chapter.

In section 3.2 we consider alternative graphical representations of the statistical data on income distributions. Then in section 3.3 we consider some methods of summarizing such data in the form of measures of inequality of the distribution of incomes from a statistical point of view. In section 3.4 other measures are discussed which approach the subject from an economic point of view. Section 3.5 then discusses some aspects of income distribution other than the degree of inequality, which bring out some important differences between countries, especially between LDCs and DCs. One aspect of income distribution of particular importance in LDCs is the extent of poverty; some statistical measures of this aspect are discussed in section 3.6.

3.2 Graphical representations

The simplest statistical representation of the distribution of income in a country is by means of a frequency distribution, which divides the income range into a number of income classes and shows the relative proportions of individuals or households whose incomes fall into those classes. It is also useful to construct another type of frequency distribution which shows the relative proportions of total income earned by people in these income classes. Graphical representations of these two types of frequency distribution are shown in Figure 3.1, with income level measured on the horizontal axis and relative proportions on the vertical axis. The curve labelled p shows the proportions of individuals or households and the curve labelled q shows the proportions of incomes.

The two curves must intersect at the average income of the population because, at this income, the proportion of units must be equal to the proportion of incomes they receive. Below that average income the relative proportion of earners, shown by the p curve, will be greater than the relative proportion of incomes, shown by the q curve. The area A indicates the extent to which these units receive less than the average income. Correspondingly, above the average income, the q curve will be above the p curve. The area B then indicates the extent to which these units earn more than the average income. It is obvious that the two areas A and B must be equal and will give some indication of the extent to which incomes are unequally distributed.

In fact, if a sufficient number of income classes are distinguished, the q curve can be derived from the p curve and provides little additional information. Therefore we can often describe a distribution only by the p curve. The information provided by the p curve can be presented in various ways. One method of particular interest is illustrated in Figure 3.2, using the data on the distribution of incomes before tax in the United Kingdom in 1967 (cited in Atkinson 1975:11).

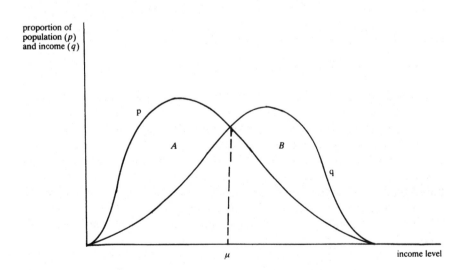

Figure 3.1

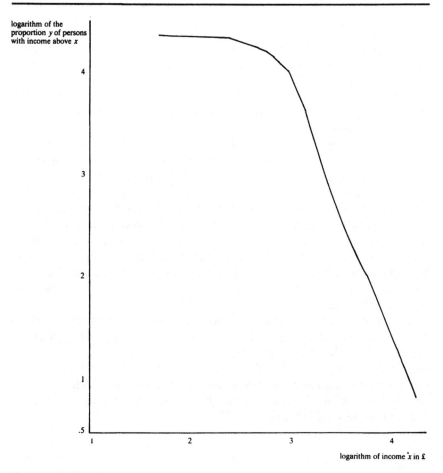

Figure 3.2 Distribution of income in UK, 1967

Source: Atkinson (1975), Table 2.1, p. 11.

In this figure, income is measured on the horizontal axis on a logarithmic scale, while the relative cumulative frequency, that is, the proportion of all units earning more than certain levels of income, is measured along the vertical axis, also on a logarithmic scale. The famous economist, Pareto, drew such curves from data mainly for the upper-income groups from a few countries such as Britain, Prussia, Saxony, and some Italian cities, and found that these curves conformed closely to a downward-sloping straight line on a logarithmic chart. He therefore concluded that all income distributions would conform to the simple law (known as Pareto's Law of Income Distribution)

$$
\begin{aligned}
R(x) &= (x/x_0)^{-\alpha} && \text{for } x > x_0 \\
&= 1 && \text{for } x \le x_0
\end{aligned}
\qquad (3.1)
$$

where $R(x)$ is the proportion of units having incomes above x, x_0 is the minimum income, and α is a parameter. The function $R(x)$ may also be described as a survival distribution function. Further, Pareto found that the income elasticity α of the survival distribution function was approximately 1.5 in all the countries that he studied, and therefore he proclaimed that equation (3.1) provided a universal law with that value of the parameter. It seems that 'Pareto's research on ID [income distribution] was motivated by his polemic against the French and Italian socialists who were pressing for institutional reforms to reduce the inequality in the distribution of income' (Dagum 1982:vol. 4, p. 27). Brown (1976:83) says:

> Pareto's purpose was apparently to reveal an empirical law of such general validity that it would be wise to accept it as a fundamental constraint on economic policy. Neither too much nor too little income inequality should be aimed at, since there is apparently a level of inequality which is a natural feature of human life. Too much inequality will lead to a revolution, while too little will lead to a breakdown of economic life.

However, it has been found that the relationship does not fit more detailed data that have since become available, and is not much used nowadays except in some cases to fit the 'tail' of the distribution of incomes in DMEs. But there are other cases in which Pareto's law fits better, such as the distribution of urban places according to size of population in the DCs.

For most distributions of income actually observed, the p curve of Figure 3.1 is typically skewed, with frequencies falling off from the modal (maximum) value more rapidly to the left (towards lower incomes) than towards the right (towards higher incomes). But if the curve is drawn with the logarithm of incomes on the horizontal axis, the curve loses much of this skewness and tends instead to become a bell-shaped curve, similar to the normal distribution, which has been intensively studied in statistical theory and often used to describe data in the natural sciences. Therefore the log-normal distribution (i.e., the case in which the logarithm of a variate follows the normal distribution) is often used to fit data on incomes, especially in the middle range of the distribution.

A problem in using the above graphical representations to compare different distributions is that, because the horizontal axis measures the actual incomes received by various groups, they differ from one another not only because of differences in distribution but also because of differences in average incomes. Therefore an alternative graphical representation is often used to compare different distributions. This method is illustrated in Figure 3.3.

To construct this diagram the population is first arranged in an ascending order of incomes. Then the cumulative proportion P of units earning less than a given level of income is measured on the horizontal axis, and the

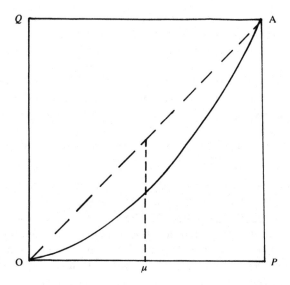

Figure 3.3

corresponding cumulative proportion Q of total income earned by these units is measured on the vertical axis. The values of P and Q for various levels of income are then plotted in a series of points and joined by a curve, known as the 'Lorenz curve' of the distribution. It will start at the origin, corresponding to the lowest income, where both P and Q are zero, and go to the point corresponding to the maximum income, where both P and Q are unity. In between, the proportion of units will be less than the proportion of income, and so the Lorenz curve will be a convex curve lying below the diagonal line. The diagonal line itself can be interpreted as the Lorenz curve of a distribution in which income is equally distributed among all units of the population.

To interpret the diagram, take a point on the horizontal axis, showing the cumulative proportion of persons earning less than a given level of income. At that point the vertical distance between the diagonal and the Lorenz curve will be the difference between the cumulative proportion of persons and the cumulative proportion of incomes, and will therefore be equal to the difference in the areas under the p and q curves of Figure 3.1, to the left of the specified income level. It follows therefore that the vertical distance between the diagonal and the Lorenz curve will be a maximum at the mean level of income.

Hence we can say that, the further the Lorenz curve of a distribution is from the diagonal, the more unequal the distribution. If the Lorenz curve of a distribution lies entirely above that of another, we can unambiguously say that the first distribution is more equal than the second, because the first distribution can be derived from the second by a series of income transfers from the rich to the poor. The interpretation becomes more difficult when the Lorenz curves of two distributions intersect each other, as sometimes happens.

3.3 Statistical measures of inequality

The aspect of income distribution with which economists have been most concerned is the inequality of incomes, that is, the extent to which incomes differ from each other in any actual situation. A number of indices of inequality have therefore been proposed to measure this aspect of income distributions. A particularly convenient method of constructing such indices of inequality is to measure the extent to which an actual distribution of income deviates from the case in which all incomes are equal, that is, the egalitarian distribution of income. It is easy to see that many such measures can be devised, and have indeed been proposed in the literature. We shall not attempt to describe all of them (for a comprehensive review, see Kakwani 1980: Chap. 5; and Nygard and Sandstrom 1981). Instead we shall consider only a sample of the most frequently used measures just to give a flavour of the discussion.

One method of measuring income equality is to use the parameters of any mathematical function which happens to fit the observed data satisfactorily. For example, if the actual distribution of incomes can be described by the Pareto function (equation 3.1), then the parameter a of that function has been suggested as a possible measure of inequality (for some problems in using this parameter as a measure of inequality, see Samuelson 1965; and Muellbauer 1976:94). If the observed data conform closely to the log-normal distribution described in section 3.1, then the standard deviation of such a distribution can be used as a measure of inequality.

The measures of inequality most often used in practice are derived directly from the data, rather than from mathematical functions fitted to such data. To explain the construction of such indices, we note that the data can be presented in a number of alternative ways, as shown in Table 3.1.

Given such data, various measures of inequality can be derived by comparing each of these representations of the data with what they would be in the case when all incomes were equally distributed. This amounts to saying that one distribution is more unequal than another if it is further removed from an equal distribution. For this purpose, one convenient approach is to use the various measures of dispersion commonly used in statistical methods of summarizing data. Various measures of inequality derived in this way are described below.

Table 3.1 Alternative presentations of income distribution data

Income class	Average income	Proportion of units	Cumulative proportion of units	Proportion of total income	Cumulative proportion of total income
1	x_1	p_1	P_1	q_1	Q_1
2	x_2	p_2	P_2	q_2	Q_2
3	x_3	p_3	P_3	q_3	Q_3
k	x_k	p_k	$P_k = 1$	q_k	$Q_k = 1$
All classes	μ	1	—	1	—

3.3.1 The range and decile ratio

The simplest statistical measure of dispersion is the range, the difference between the largest and smallest of the observed values. For convenience of comparison of different groups, this measure may be normalized by dividing by the respective mean values. The main advantage of this measure is that it can be computed very easily just by observing the two extreme values, but because it does not make any use of the information provided by the other observations, it was dismissed by Sen (1973a:31) as a 'non-starter'. However, this measure has been defended by Wiles (1974) on the argument that there is usually little difference in the relative incomes of people in the intermediate levels, and therefore what is needed is a measure of the extent to which the top incomes differ from the bottom incomes; hence 'one of the most despised (and simple!) of all measures of inequality, the "range" or (the highest income to the lowest) the mean, is one of the best. Alone among all the indices commonly discussed, it points us in the right direction.'

One problem with the range is that the extreme values on which it is based are subject to large sampling fluctuations and are therefore unsuitable for identifying the stable features of any distribution. Therefore in applying this measure, Wiles uses the ratio between the incomes of the top and the bottom 10 per cent of the population. Although this measure ignores much of the information collected, it still describes an aspect that is often of much interest to the general public, namely how big the difference is in the standard of living between the richest and the poorest members in a society. It is more sensitive than most other measures in the sense of being much more variable between societies and over time.

3.3.2 Relative mean deviation

Most other measures of inequality are constructed by considering how far a given distribution differs from a completely egalitarian distribution. The simplest of these measures is obtained by taking the average of all the differences between the class incomes x and the mean income of the population, divided by the mean income, that is,

$$K = \Sigma \, p_i \left| \frac{x_i - \mu}{\mu} \right| \tag{3.2}$$

These differences will be negative for low incomes and positive for high incomes. It is a property of the arithmetic mean that the sum of these negative deviations would be exactly equal to the sum of the positive deviations, so that the algebraic sum of all deviations would be zero. Therefore for a measure of inequality we take the average of the absolute differences, divided by the mean income, for comparing different distributions. This is well known in statistical theory as the relative mean deviation. It was introduced by Von Bortkiewicz in 1898 and widely used in studying income distributions by Kuznets; it may be described as the K measure. It corresponds to the area A (or B) in Figure 3.1, and has the simple economic interpretation of being equal to the proportion of total income that must be transferred from the rich to the poor in order to make all incomes equal.

3.3.3 Coefficient of variation

Another way of averaging the differences between the x values and the arithmetic mean is to take their quadratic mean, that is, the square root of the mean of the squared differences:

$$S = [\Sigma \, p_i(x_i - \mu)^2]^{1/2} \tag{3.3}$$

This quantity is well known in statistical theory as the standard deviation. It has a simple geometric interpretation in the case of a population divided into k income classes with equal numbers of units. Then the average incomes in these classes for any actual distribution of income (as shown in the first column of Table 3.1) can be represented by a point, say X, in k-dimensional space. The corresponding equal distribution of income is then represented by another point, say P, all of whose co-ordinates are equal to the average income μ. Then the standard deviation is $1/k$ times the Euclidean distance between X and P. For comparing distributions with different means, this measure may be normalized to have a range from zero to unity by dividing it by its maximum possible value. Because we are dealing with non-negative values, this maximum has the value $\mu \, (k - 1)^{1/2}$, attained when the top class gets all the income. In practice, the index is most often used in the form S/μ and is known as the coefficient of variation. In this form it has been extensively used as a measure of the variation of incomes among different regions within a county, following Williamson (1965).

The above definition of S is based on the deviations of the observed incomes from their mean, representing the case of the equal distribution. But it is also a measure of how unequal the observed values are from each other for it can be shown that S^2 is, in fact, half the expected value of the squared difference between the incomes of any pair of units x and y chosen at random (Kendall and Stuart 1963: vol. 1, p. 47).

3.3.4 Hirschman index

The standard deviation is based on the distance between a given distribution and the egalitarian distribution in x-space. Similarly, we can construct a measure of inequality based on the distance in q-space, that is, the distance of the point representing the quantities q (the observed proportions of income in the various classes) from the point representing the quantities p (which are the proportions of income to be expected when all units have the same income). In the case in which classes are defined to have the same number of units each, this measure is given by

$$H = \left(\sum q^2 - \frac{1}{k} \right)^{1/2} \tag{3.4}$$

This measure can also be converted to an index varying from zero to unity by dividing it by its maximum possible value of $\{(k-1)/k\}^{1/2}$ attained when the top class gets all the income. The quantity $\sum q^2$ was introduced by Hirschman (1945) to measure the concentration among commodities in the exports of countries.

This measure can be given a simple diagrammatic illustration when the population is arranged in ascending order of their incomes and divided into three groups of equal size. Then any distribution of total income among the three groups can be represented by a point P in an equilateral triangle, as shown in Figure 3.4. In this diagram, the shares of the three income classes are given by the perpendicular distances of the point P from the three sides of the triangle. Thus A represents the share of the bottom group, B that of the middle group, and C that of the top group. The centre E of the triangle represents the case of an equal distribution, while the point O that of the most unequal distribution, in which the top class gets all the income. In

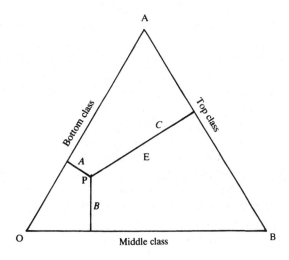

Figure 3.4

such a representation the Hirschman index, as defined above, will be the ratio of the distance PE to the distance OE. It then follows that the Hirschman index of inequality will be constant for all points on any circle with centre at E.

3.3.5 Gini index

Then we have another measure of inequality based on the differences between the quantities Q (the cumulative proportions of income received by the various classes) and the values they would have under an egalitarian distribution, that is, the quantities P. If the income classes are arranged in ascending order, each of these differences will be positive, given by the vertical distance between the Lorenz curve and the diagonal line. The sum of all these differences corresponds to the area between the Lorenz curve and the diagonal. Twice this area is known as the Gini index, and is one of the most commonly used measures of inequality of income distributions.

Apart from its geometric counterpart in the Lorenz diagram, it has an interesting statistical interpretation in terms of the quantity known as the mean difference. Just as the arithmetic mean of the incomes of a group of individuals is the expected value of the income of an individual chosen at random from the group, the mean difference is the expected value of the difference between the incomes of a pair of individuals chosen at random. It is calculated by taking the average of the difference between all possible pairs of observations. The Gini index of a distribution is its relative mean difference divided by twice the mean income:

$$G = \frac{1}{2\mu} \Sigma \left| x_i - x_j \right| \tag{3.5}$$

(Kendall and Stuart 1963: vol. 1, pp. 46–7; a simpler derivation is given in Appendix 3.1). Hence if the Gini index of a distribution is 0.4, we can say that the expected difference between any pair of observations chosen from the distribution at random is 0.8 times the mean income.

This interpretation gives us a simple way of adjusting the Gini index when the base from which incomes are measured is changed. For example, it may be argued that we are really interested in the inequality of incomes measured from a subsistence level of income, say m. This change will not alter the value of the mean difference, but the mean value of the incomes measured from this change will now become $\mu - m$. Therefore the Gini index G_m of incomes measured from this base will be higher than that of incomes measured from zero, according to

$$G_m = \frac{\mu}{\mu - m} G \tag{3.6}$$

There is also an interesting economic interpretation for the Gini index. Just as the relative mean deviation, described above as the K measure, is the proportion of total income that must be transferred from the rich to the poor in order to make all incomes equal, the Gini index is also the proportion of such transfers, with the difference that each transfer is weighted by the number of units across which it is made (see Appendix 3.1 for proof, and some simple ways of calculating the index).

Like the Hirschman index defined above, the Gini index can also be indicated in a diagram such as Figure 3.4 for the special case of a population divided into three equal classes. Then, while the Hirschman index is represented by the distance of the point P from the point E, the Gini index for this case is simply the horizontal distance between the two points. This means that the Gini index will be constant for all points lying on any vertical line drawn to the left of E.

It is sometimes useful to be able to decompose a measure of inequality of income distribution into various components. For example, the income of a person may be derived from different sources. Then we might wish to break up the overall inequality into components corresponding to each source of income. The population may also be divided into different groups. Then we might be interested in breaking up the overall inequality into components corresponding to the different groups of the population. In the case of the standard deviation or variance, formulae for such decompositions are easily derived from the usual methods of the analysis of variance. We consider some results that have been established for the decomposition of the Gini index.

First, we introduce a new concept. Let x_i be the income of the ith person, and let y_i be another variable related to income, such as income from a particular source or expenditure on a particular commodity. Let $P(x)$ be the proportion of persons with incomes less than x, and let $Q(y)$ be the cumulative share of y for all persons with incomes less than x. The curve showing $Q(x)$ as a function of $P(x)$ is the Lorenz curve illustrated in Figure 3.3. For any other variable y, the curve showing $Q(y)$ as a function of $P(x)$ is known as the concentration curve of y with respect to x. This curve starts at $(0,0)$ and ends at $(1,1)$ like Lorenz curves, but would differ at other points. In particular, it need not always lie entirely below the diagonal. By analogy with the Gini index of x, which is twice the area between the Lorenz curve and the diagonal, the concentration index of y with respect to x is defined as twice the area between the concentration curve of y and the diagonal line. The concentration index of y with respect to x is related to the Gini index of y by the formula

$$C_y = \frac{\rho(y, r_x)}{\rho(y, r_y)} G_y \qquad (3.7)$$

where $\rho(y, r_y)$ is the correlation between the y values and their ranks, and $\rho(y, r_x)$ is the correlation between the y values and the ranks of the corresponding x values. It follows that, if y is a monotonically increasing function of x, the concentration index of y will be equal to its Gini index, and it will be equal to its Gini index but opposite in sign if y is a monotonically decreasing function of x. In other cases, the absolute value of C_y will be less than G_y (for proofs, see Kakwani 1980:174).

Then we have a simple result expressing the Gini index of income in terms of the concentration indices of incomes from different sources:

$$G = \Sigma \, b_i C_i \qquad (3.8)$$

where b_i is the proportion of income that the population gets from the ith source, and C_i is the concentration index of incomes from that source (Kakwani 1980:178).

3.3.6 Decomposable measures

Next we consider the case in which a population is divided into a number of groups. Then we have a certain amount of inequality within each of these groups and a certain amount of inequality between these groups. The most convenient way of measuring the inequality between groups is by calculating the inequality for the population as a whole on the assumption that there is no variation of incomes within groups, that is, that all persons within a group have the same income, equal to the group mean. Then it would be convenient if the overall measure of inequality could be decomposed exactly into the between and within components, also measured in the same way. It turns out that all measures of inequality which have this property must be based on the quantity

$$\frac{1}{a^2 - a} \left[\frac{1}{n} \Sigma \left(\frac{y_i}{\mu} \right)^a - 1 \right] \qquad a \neq 0, 1$$

$$\Sigma \frac{y_i}{\mu} \log \left(\frac{y_i}{\mu} \right) \qquad a = 1 \qquad (3.9)$$

$$- \Sigma \log \left(\frac{y_i}{\mu} \right) \qquad a = 0$$

(Bourguignon 1979; Cowell 1980; Shorrocks 1980). The basic element of this formula is the quantity $(y_i/\mu) - 1$, which is the normalized difference between the income of the ith person and the mean income of the whole population, that is, a quantity that measures the difference between the actual and the egalitarian distribution. In order to see how this index can be decomposed into its between and within components, note that we can write

$$\left(\frac{y_i}{\mu}\right)^a - 1 = \left(\frac{\mu_i}{\mu}\right)^a \left[\left(\frac{y_{ij}}{\mu_i}\right)^a - 1\right] + \left[\left(\frac{\mu_i}{\mu}\right)^a - 1\right] \quad (3.10)$$

where y_{ij} is the income of the jth person in the ith group, and μ_i is the mean income of the ith group. Summing over i and j, we then get

$$I = \Sigma \, p_i \left(\frac{\mu_i}{\mu}\right)^a I_i + I_B = \Sigma \, p_i^{1-a} q_i^a \, I_i + I_B \quad (3.11)$$

using $q_i = p_i \mu_i / \mu$.

It is easy to see that the coefficient of variation belongs to this family of inequality measures for the case $a = 2$. A measure belonging to this class for $a = 1$ was proposed by Theil (1967) on the basis of statistical information theory, and may be described as the T measure:

$$T = \Sigma \, q_i (\log y_i - \log \mu) \quad (3.12)$$

This can be viewed as another way of comparing a given distribution with the corresponding egalitarian distribution, devised by taking the difference between the logarithms of the observed incomes y and their mean value μ, instead of the difference between their numerical values as in 3.2. The T measure weights these logarithms by the respective shares of total income received by each individual or group. It is then easy to derive the decomposition formula:

$$T = T_B + \Sigma \, q_i T_i \quad (3.13)$$

where T_i is the inequality measure within the ith class, calculated in the same way as T is for the whole population, and T_B is the inequality measure between groups, also calculated in the same way as T, but assuming that all incomes within a group are uniform and equal to the group mean.

Yet another measure suggested by Bourguignon (1979), which may be described as the L measure, is the special case of this class of measures for $a = 0$. This is defined in terms of differences in the logarithms of observed incomes and the corresponding mean income, but weighting them by the proportion of persons in each income class:

$$L = \Sigma \, p_i (\log \mu - \log y_i) \quad (3.14)$$

This measure can also be viewed as

$$L = \log \mu - \log g \qquad (3.15)$$

where g is the weighted geometric mean of observed incomes. Like the T measure, it can also be decomposed exactly into a between and a within component:

$$L = L_B + \Sigma p_i L_i \qquad (3.16)$$

The only difference is that, to get the within component, the inequality measures of the various groups are weighted by their shares of population, while for the T measure the weights are the shares of total income received by the various classes.

We may also consider to what extent the Gini index can also be decomposed in terms of the Gini indices of population subgroups (see Bhattacharya and Mahalanobis 1967; Rao 1969; Mangahas 1975; and Pyatt 1976). We first consider the case in which the population is divided into two groups, say the poor and the rich, such that there is no overlap of incomes between the two groups. Let p_1 be the proportion of the poor in the population, and hence $p_2 = 1 - p_1$ the proportion of the rich. Also, let μ_i and G_i be the mean incomes and the Gini indices of the two groups, with μ and G the mean income and Gini index of the population as a whole. Then the decomposition of the Gini index is shown in Table 3.2, using its interpretation in terms of the mean difference. From this, we easily get

$$G = p_1^2 \frac{\mu_1}{\mu} G_1 + p_2^2 \frac{\mu_2}{\mu} G_2 + p_1 p_2 \left| \frac{\mu_2 - \mu_1}{\mu} \right| \qquad (3.17)$$

This result may be illustrated as in Figure 3.5.

To extend this result to the case of k non-overlapping groups, let p_i be the population share, q_i the income share, μ_i the mean income, and G_i the Gini index of the ith group. Then in calculating the mean difference, a proportion p_i^2 of all possible pairwise comparisons will be between units

Table 3.2 Decomposition of Gini index: Two disjoint classes

Ways of choosing two observations	Probability	Mean difference
(i) Both from the poor	p_1^2	$2\mu_1 G_1$
(ii) Both from the rich	p_2^2	$2\mu_2 G_2$
(iii) One from each group	$2p_1 p_2$	$\mu_2 - \mu_1$
Total	1	$2\mu G$

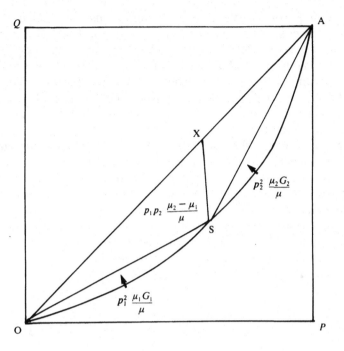

Figure 3.5

within the ith group, and a proportion $2p_ip_j$ will be between units chosen from the ith and the jth groups. Then we get

$$G = \sum_i p_i^2 \frac{\mu_i}{\mu} G_i + \sum_i \sum_j p_i p_j \left| \frac{\mu_i - \mu_j}{\mu} \right|$$

$$= \sum_i p_i q_i G_i + \sum_i \sum_j p_i p_j \left| \frac{\mu_i - \mu_j}{\mu} \right|$$

(3.18)

The first term of the righthand side is the weighted average of the group Gini indices. This term is the 'within-group' component of the overall Gini index, and may be written G_W. The second term expresses the mean difference of observations taken from different groups in terms of their mean values; it must be noted that this is valid only for the case of non-overlapping groups, because then all these differences will be of the same sign. This term is the 'between-group' component of the overall Gini, and may be written G_B. In fact, it is the Gini index for the whole population calculated on the assumption that all units in any group have the same income, equal to the group mean, that is, assuming no variation within groups.

The decomposition in the case of several groups is illustrated in Figure 3.6. The curved line OABC is the Lorenz curve for the whole population, while the segmented line OABC is the Lorenz curve drawn on the assumption that incomes of all units within a group are the same and equal to the group mean. If the dotted rectangle is expanded to a unit square, the line AB will be its diagonal, the curve AB will be the Lorenz curve for that group, and the area between the line and the curve will correspond to the Gini index of the group.

Figures 3.5 and 3.6 show that the Gini index calculated from grouped data will be smaller than that calculated from data on individual incomes. The difference arises because, as seen from equation (3.18), the grouped method neglects the within-group inequality. In order to get a more accurate estimate of the Gini index from grouped data, Kakwani (1980: Chap. 7) proposed fitting a beta-function to the Lorenz curve based on grouped data. However, this method does not make much difference if data are available for 10 or more income groups.

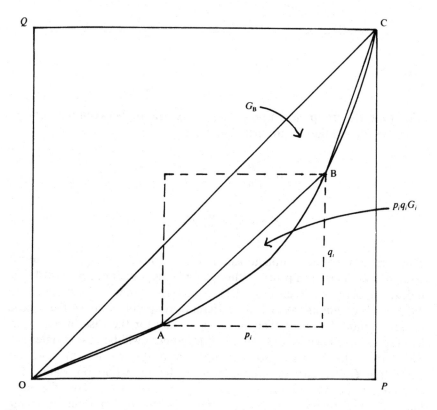

Figure 3.6

A simpler alternative is to consider the case in which the population is divided into just two non-overlapping groups, as illustrated in Figure 3.5. Then the Gini index is just double the area of the triangle OSA. This measure of the Gini index assumes that there is no inequality within each of the two groups, and will therefore underestimate the true value. The degree of such underestimation will be a minimum when the population is divided into two groups at the mean income, for then, as noted in Figure 3.1, the vertical distance of the Lorenz curve from the diagonal will be a maximum, and equal in fact to the *K* measure discussed in section 3.3.2. This measure was calculated for the 50 countries considered by Kakwani (1980:388–9). As expected, the estimate of this form of the Gini index was less than the estimate from the data grouped into deciles. But the degree of underestimation was remarkably uniform, varying only from 26 to 31 per cent, with an average of 29 per cent for all countries. We get the same average degree of underestimation for all DCs, all Asian LDCs, and all African LDCs in the sample, and the average was 27 per cent for the Latin American countries in the sample. Therefore a simple adjustment can be made to adjust for the degree of underestimation involved even when the data are divided into just two groups at the mean income level.

Equation (3.18) gives a very simple decomposition of the Gini in the case of non-overlapping groups. The main reason is that, in this case, the segmented line OABC will touch the curve OABC at a number of points. Then it follows that the income share of the bottom group coincides with that of the poorest *p* proportion of the population and so on. But we do not get such a neat decomposition when there is some overlap of incomes between different groups. Then the position will be as shown in Figure 3.7. Now the segmented line OABD will not touch the Lorenz curve OCD of the whole population because the income share of the lowest group will not coincide with that of the poorest *p* of the population, but will be higher. The overall Gini will then consist of another term, corresponding to the area between the curves OABD and OCD, which may be written G_C. This point is overlooked by some authors who take G_B alone as their measure of the between-group component of inequalities (see, e.g., Paglin 1975 for the case of age groups).

These are only some of the measures of inequality most commonly used in the literature. Many more can be, and have been, constructed. For example, there are any number of mathematical transformations of the Lorenz curve, and each can be made to yield a measure of inequality by comparison with the case of the egalitarian distribution. Rather than pursue these any further, we consider a different class of inequality measures in the next section.

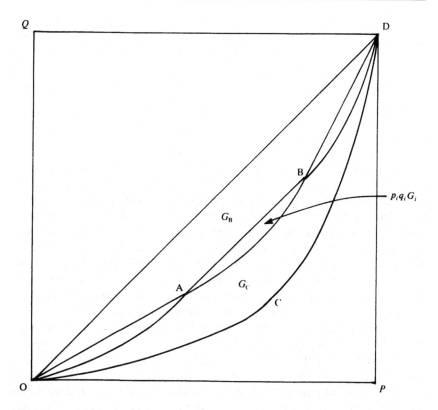

Figure 3.7

3.4 Welfare measures of inequality

3.4.1 The welfare approach

This alternative class of inequality measures is based on the social welfare consequences of income distribution. In particular, they are based on a welfare function which attains its maximum value when a given total income is divided equally among all members of the society. Thus, like the statistical measures discussed earlier, these welfare measures of inequality are also based on a comparison of actual distributions with the egalitarian distribution.

The major difficulty with this approach is that, by concentrating on the total utility of all members of society, it neglects inequalities in the utilities of individuals. Another difficulty is the specification of a utility function which is widely acceptable. In a sense, the statistical measures of inequality discussed earlier can also be interpreted in terms of an implicit welfare function, but such welfare functions may not be widely acceptable. Thus it has been shown that the way the Gini index ranks different distributions does not correspond to any welfare function with properties usually assumed to be desirable in this context (see, e.g., Atkinson 1970); instead, it is based on a welfare function in which individual incomes are weighted by their rank orders, a procedure which is not intuitively very persuasive. Some examples of inequality measures derived from the welfare approach are discussed below.

3.4.2 The Dalton index

The first measure of inequality based on this approach was proposed by Dalton (1920; see also Meade 1976:118–21 for a lucid exposition). He assumed that the utility of an individual was a concave function $u(x)$ of his income x, that is, the marginal utility was a diminishing function of income, and that this function was the same for all individuals. He also assumed that social welfare of a society of n individuals was the simple sum of their individual utilities. Then he argued that because of the concave utility function, a transfer of income from a rich to a poor person will increase total welfare because the gain to the transferee will be greater than the loss to the transferor. From this it follows that the total welfare of society will be maximized when all incomes are uniform and will then be equal to $nu(\mu)$. He therefore proposed as his measure of inequality

$$D = 1 - \frac{\Sigma\, u(x_i)}{nu(\mu)} \qquad (3.19)$$

which shows the proportionate loss of total welfare due to the inequality in the actual distribution of income.

Apart from the fact that the measure takes account only of total welfare but not the distribution of utilities, one weakness of this measure is that its value depends crucially on the specific form of the assumed utility function; indeed, it is not invariant even under simple positive linear transformations of the utility function (Kakwani 1980:92). Therefore an alternative measure to overcome this difficulty was proposed by Atkinson (1970).

3.4.3 Atkinson's measure

The Atkinson measure is defined as follows:

$$A = \Sigma\, p_i(x_i - \mu_e) \qquad (3.20)$$

While the relative mean deviation, described in section 3.3.2, was based on the differences between the x values and the arithmetic mean, the Atkinson measure takes the deviations not from the arithmetic mean but from a quantity μ_e, described as the 'equally distributed equivalent income'. This quantity is interpreted as the income which, if received by every member of the population, would give the same total welfare as the distribution of incomes actually observed. If all members received the arithmetic mean income, total welfare would be greater than that derived from the actual unequal distribution because the population is getting the same total income, but this income is now distributed more equally and therefore yields higher total welfare. Therefore the equally distributed equivalent income which gives society the same total welfare will be less than the mean income. Then the welfare advantage of the equal distribution is reflected by the extent to which the equally distributed equivalent income is less than the mean income. The Atkinson measure is based on this difference, normalized by expressing it as a ratio to mean income.

The approach is therefore similar to that of the Dalton measure, except that the Dalton measure is defined on the utility space while the Atkinson measure is defined on the income space. Thus just as the Dalton measure indicates the proportionate loss of total utility due to the unequal distribution of income, the Atkinson measure indicates the proportionate loss of national income. But in order to avoid the difficulty of the Dalton measure that it depends on the nature of the utility function, a specific form of the utility function is chosen which leaves the Atkinson measure invariant under positive linear transformations. It is easy to see that for this condition to be satisfied, the elasticity of the first derivative of the utility function must be constant, that is, that utility functions must be of the type

$$
\begin{aligned}
u(x) &= A + B\,\frac{x^{1-\varepsilon}}{1-\varepsilon} \quad \text{for} \quad \varepsilon \neq 1 \\
&= \log_\varepsilon x \qquad\qquad \text{for} \quad \varepsilon = 1
\end{aligned}
\tag{3.21}
$$

for which the elasticity of the first derivative is constant. If we assume such a form for the utility function, the Atkinson measure becomes

$$
A = 1 - \frac{g_{i-\varepsilon}}{\mu}
\tag{3.20a}
$$

where the quantities $g_{1-\varepsilon}$ are known as means of order $1 - \varepsilon$ and equal to the ordinary geometric mean when ε is zero. It is a well-known result in the mathematical theory of inequalities that these means are increasing functions of $1 - \varepsilon$ for unequal values of x, and are constant for equal values of x (Kendall and Stuart 1963: vol. 1, pp. 37–8). Therefore the Atkinson index based on differences between means of different orders has some merit as a measure of inequality from a mathematical point of view. But the value of the index and the way it ranks distributions still depend on the chosen value of the parameter ε.

More important than taking the deviations of x from a different central value representing equality is the fact that, although some of these deviations are positive and others negative, the proposed index is based on their algebraic sum, unlike the absolute sum used in the relative mean deviation. This is because like the Dalton measure, the Atkinson measure is only interested in the effect of unequal incomes on total welfare, rather than on the inequality of individual welfares.

3.4.4 Welfare comparison of income level and income inequality

The welfare measures discussed above were only concerned with comparing societies differing in their income distribution. But the welfare of societies depends not only on their income distributions but also on their mean incomes. It would generally be agreed that a society is to be preferred to another if it has a higher mean income and also a more equal distribution. A more serious problem arises if the society with a higher mean income has a more unequal distribution than another.

An attempt has been made to solve this problem by extending the welfare approach to compare societies on the basis of both their mean incomes and their income distributions. This comparison is based on the concept of the 'generalized Lorenz curve', which is the ordinary Lorenz curve with its vertical heights at all points multiplied by the mean income (Shorrocks 1983). Thus if $L(p)$ is the ordinary Lorenz curve showing the cumulative income share q as a function of the cumulative population share p, and if μ is the mean income, then the generalized Lorenz curve $GL(p)$ is given by

$$GL(p) = \mu L(p) \tag{3.22}$$

It is then proposed that a society should be preferred to another if its generalized Lorenz curve is everywhere higher than that of the other society.

The test is based on two assumptions. One is the usual assumption that a society is to be preferred to another, other things being equal, if it has a more equal distribution; in particular, that a transfer of income from one individual to a poorer individual which does not change their ranking will increase social welfare. The other assumption is that an increase in the income of any one individual without any change in other incomes will increase social welfare; in particular, that a society is to be preferred to another if the income of each fractile group is equal to or higher in the first society than in the second. The application of the test on these assumptions is illustrated in Table 3.3 by a simple example.

There are two possibilities. Suppose $b_i > a_i$ for all i, so that society B is

Table 3.3 Hypothetical distributions of income by quintile groups

Quintile group	Distribution A		Distribution B		Distribution C	
	Average income	Cumulative income	Average income	Cumulative income	Average income	Cumulative income
1	a_1	A_1	b_1	B_1	$c_1 = a_1$	$C_1 = A_1$
2	a_2	A_2	b_2	B_2	$c_2 = a_2 + a_3 - b_3$	$C_2 = A_3 - B_3$
3	a_3	A_3	b_3	B_3	$c_3 = b_3$	$C_3 = A_3$
4	a_4	A_4	b_4	B_4	$c_4 = a_4$	$C_4 = A_4$
5	a_5	A_5	b_5	B_5	$c_5 = a_5$	$C_5 = A_5$

Source: Compiled by the author.

preferred on the second assumption. Then $B_i > A_i$ for all i so that the same conclusion also follows from the generalized Lorenz curve test. But sometimes we may have $B_i > A_i$ for all i but b_i not greater than a_i for all i. For example, we may have $b_3 < a_3$. Then consider the distribution C derived from A by transferring $a_3 - b_3$ from the third quintile to the second, so that society C is to be preferred to A. But society B is to be preferred to C because $b_i > c_i$ for all i. Therefore even in this case society B is to be preferred to A as indicated by the generalized Lorenz curve test.

But sometimes even generalized Lorenz curves may intersect. This will happen if the distribution with the higher mean is also very unequal. Then, just as the ordinary Lorenz curves are ranked by a measure of inequality such as the Gini index G, the generalized Lorenz curves may aso be ranked by an index such as

$$\mu(1 - G) \tag{3.23}$$

suggested by Sen (1974), where μ is the mean income. If one distribution has a higher mean income and lower inequality then another, this measure will rank the two distributions in the same way as the generalized Lorenz curves. But it will also rank distributions according to both mean income and inequality in the case where the generalized Lorenz curves intersect. Similarly, Kakwani (1980:77) has suggested an alternative measure:

$$\frac{\mu}{1 + G} \tag{3.24}$$

All these welfare measures, however, suffer from a basic limitation, namely the assumption that the welfare of individuals depends only on their own incomes and that social welfare depends on the welfares of the individual members of the society determined by their individual incomes. But an important aspect of the inequality of income distribution is the fact that individual welfare depends not only on one's own income but also on how that income compares with the incomes of others. This is not only because of feelings of envy, but also because persons with large incomes exercise considerable power over the economy as a whole, and hence over the welfare of its less fortunate members. Thus even the small difference between Gini indices of 0.4 and 0.5 represents a great difference between the two economies. But the Sen index (3.23) suggests that two societies with these degrees of inequality should be considered equivalent from a welfare point of view, if the more unequal society has an average income 20 per cent greater than the less unequal society. Many observers would consider this difference in mean incomes to be too small to compensate for such a big difference in the degree of inequality.

3.4.5 A comparison

It is rather embarrassing to have so many measures of inequality, and there has been much discussion of the differences between these measures. But much of this discussion is only of theoretical interest. For the distributions usually found in practice, there is a remarkably close agreement among all measures. For example, using a sample of theoretical distributions, Champernowne (1974) found that the Gini index had a rank correlation of 0.996 with the Theil index, and 0.993 and 0.901 with the Atkinson index with $\varepsilon = 2$ and 3 respectively. Similarly, we find high correlations of the Gini index with a number of other inequality measures for the distributions that have been actually observed, as shown in Table 3.4.

3.5. Other aspects of inequality

There are a number of aspects of income distribution, and the above measures of inequality deal with only one. Therefore we consider some measures dealing with some other aspects of inequality.

Consider the case in which a population is divided into two classes of people, the rich and the poor. We can distinguish two aspects of inequality, namely the proportion π of the population in the poor class, and the ratio R of income in the rich class to that in the poor class. From (3.9), we see that the Gini index of the whole population is related to π and R as follows:

$$G = \frac{\pi^2 G_p + (1 - \pi)^2 RG_r + (R - 1)\pi(1 - \pi)}{\pi + R(1 - \pi)} \qquad (3.9b)$$

The relationship between the three parameters G, π, and R, for given values of G_p and G_r may be illustrated as in Figure 3.8. Figure 3.8a shows how a given overall inequality, as measured by G, may result from various combinations of π and R. Figure 3.8b shows that, for a fixed π, G will increase steadily with R, but Figure 3.8c shows that, for a fixed R, the value of G increases with π up to a point and declines thereafter.

Another aspect of inequality relates to the inequalities in different parts of the distribution, such as whether there is more inequality in the upper part of the range or the lower part. The simplest way of describing this aspect of a distribution is to consider the case in which a population is divided into three equal classes, arranged in ascending order of incomes, with their respective shares of total income equal to a, b, and c. Then the difference $b - a$ is a simple measure of the inequality at lower incomes, and the difference $c - b$ the corresponding measure for higher incomes. We can then measure the pattern of inequalities in the distribution by the ratio

Table 3.4 Correlation of inequality measures with Gini index

Distributions (number)	Hirschman index with 3 classes	K measure	Information measure	Atkinson measure $\varepsilon = 1.5$
(A) LDCs (33)	0.9877	0.9944	0.9867	0.9218
Asia (11)	0.9781	0.9915	0.9781	0.9691
Africa (10)	0.9838	0.9936	0.9840	0.8882
Latin America (12)	0.9935	0.9963	0.9887	0.8528
DCs (17)	0.9989	0.9981	0.9893	0.9406
LDCs and DCs (50)	0.9924	0.9965	0.9893	0.8951
(B) Households				
LDCs (27	0.9986	—	—	—
DCs (16)	0.8887	—	—	—
Total (43)	0.9992	—	—	—
(C) LDCs (53)	0.9948	—	0.9616	—
Household (22)	0.9966	—	0.9680	—
Economically active popn. (18)	0.9918	—	0.9665	—
Individuals (13)	0.9947	—	0.9720	—

Sources: (A) Fifty distributions selected by Kakwani (1980: Table 17-1, pp. 386–7) from Jain (1975).
(B) World Bank (1984) World Development Report, 1984 (Washington, DC), Table 28, pp 272–3.
(C) Lecaillon et al. (1984), Table 4, pp 26–7.

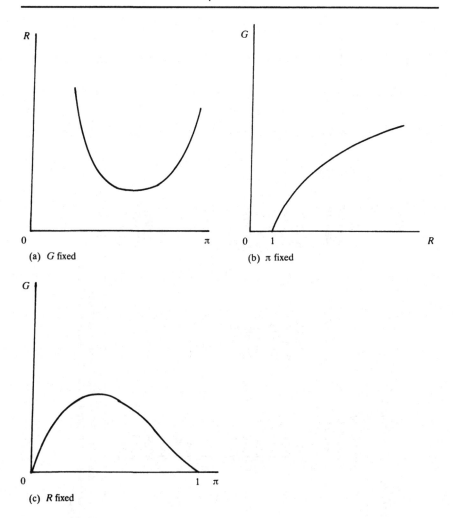

Figure 3.8

$$w = \frac{c - b}{b - a} \tag{3.25}$$

In terms of the diagram in Figure 3.4, where P represents a given distribution and E the corresponding egalitarian distribution, the quantity w is indicated by the slope of the line joining P to E. Therefore this measure represents a different aspect of income distribution from overall inequality, which is represented by the distance PE for the Hirschman index and the horizontal distance between P and E for the Gini index.

A more sophisticated measure of this aspect of income distributions has been suggested by Kakwani (1980: Chap. 17). Starting from the Lorenz curve of Figure 3.3, he makes a transformation of co-ordinates such that the diagonal becomes the horizontal axis; then the Lorenz curve may have different shapes, as illustrated in Figure 3.9.

In this diagram, the curve in Figure 3.9a is skewed towards the point (0,0) and may be said to be negatively skewed, while the curve in Figure 3.9b is skewed towards the point (1,1) and may be said to be positively skewed. To measure the extent of skewness, Kakwani uses the ratio of the parameters α and β of the beta-distribution fitted to the Lorenz curve after transforming it as described above. This measure of the skewness of the Lorenz curve is closely related to the measure w defined above. The

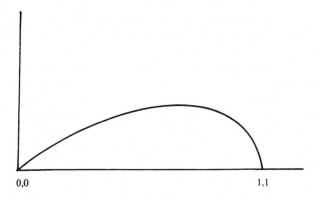

0,0   1,1

(a) Negatively skewed Lorenz curve

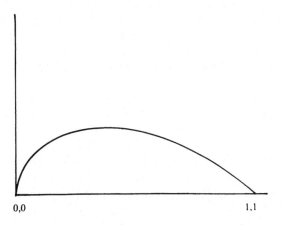

0,0   1,1

(b) Positively skewed Lorenz curve

Figure 3.9

average values of the two measures for various groups of countries are shown in Table 4.2; it is found that the two measures are quite highly correlated (0.70 for the sample of 50 countries studied by Kakwani 1980: Table 17.2, pp. 388–9, being 0.45 for LDCs and 0.69 for DMEs). On the other hand, there is little correlation between the skewness of the Lorenz curve and the Gini index (0.13 for LDCs and 0.35 for DMEs).

3.6 Measurement of poverty

One aspect of income distribution that is of particular interest is the extent of poverty, that is, the extent to which some people in society have a standard of living below some specified poverty line. There are two approaches to defining the poverty line. According to one approach, the poverty line is a relative concept, fixed in relation to the average income of the community as a whole. This is the approach generally followed in the DCs. On such a definition, the poverty line varies between countries and over time with the average level of income, and is an aspect of the pattern of income distribution. In contrast, the poverty line in LDCs is usually based on an absolute concept of a minimum standard of living below which a person cannot satisfy his or her basic needs of food, clothing and shelter. When the poverty line is defined in this way, the extent of poverty in a country depends both on the average income and the pattern of distribution of the country. Following this approach, the poverty line is sometimes defined in terms of nutrition, for example, as the income that is just sufficient to buy the amount of calories and proteins required to sustain life at a given standard of efficiency. It was hoped that such a poverty line could be specified only on the basis of physiological considerations, but it has proved difficult to do so, and the question has generated much controversy.

Once a poverty line is fixed, the simplest measure of the extent of poverty is P_0, the proportion of the population below the poverty line. In the DCs, because of the relative concept of the poverty line, the proportion of poor people varies only around 10 to 15 per cent of the population at the bottom of the income scale, who are somehow left out of the normal functioning of the economic system, such as the aged, the handicapped, and the unemployed. But because of the absolute concept used in LDCs, the proportion of poor people varies much more depending on the average incomes of countries. Using a poverty line estimate of an annual income of US$80 per person, converted to local currencies at purchasing power parities, Ahluwalia et al. (1979) estimated that the population living in poverty in 1975 was about 38 per cent of the population of a large sample of LDCs. Using a nutritional standard, the UN (1979) estimated that a quarter of the population of LDCs were living below 1.2 times the basic metabolic rate.

The above measure only counts the number of poor people but does not take any account of the extent to which their incomes are below the poverty line. Therefore another measure of the extent of poverty is the 'poverty gap', defined as

$$P_1 = P_0 \left(\frac{k - \mu_p}{\mu} \right) \tag{3.26}$$

where k is the poverty line income, μ_p is the average income of the poor, and μ is that of the whole population. This measure shows the extent to which the incomes of the poor fall short of the poverty line k as a proportion of total income. This is the proportion of total income that must be transferred from the non-poor to the poor in order to raise all the poor to the poverty line level of income.

But even this measure does not quite capture the extent of poverty. For example, it implies that the suffering of the poor is proportional to the extent to which their incomes fall below the poverty line, but most people would consider that the suffering associated with a deficit of 10 rupees below the poverty line was much greater than just twice that associated with a deficit of 5 rupees. Therefore it is desirable that the extent of poverty should be taken as being more than proportional to the deficits of income below the poverty line. A particularly simple definition could be based on a quadratic function of the deficit, such as

$$P_2 = \int_0^k \left(\frac{k - y}{\mu} \right)^2 f(y) \mathrm{d}y \tag{3.27}$$

It can then be seen that all three definitions are special cases of the general definition proposed by Foster *et al.* (1984):

$$P_\alpha = \int_0^k \left(\frac{k - y}{\mu} \right)^\alpha f(y) \mathrm{d}y \tag{3.28}$$

This definition yields the three previous definitions for the values $\alpha = 0, 1, 2$.

Another measure of poverty which has come into fairly wide use is that proposed by Sen (1976):

$$\frac{P_0}{\mu} [k - \mu_p(1 - G_p)] \tag{3.29}$$

where the measure is normalized by dividing by μ rather than by k as in Sen's original version. In addition to allowing for the proportion of people living below the poverty line and the extent to which their incomes fall short of the poverty line, this measure also takes account of the inequality of the incomes of the poor. Sen's measure of poverty was derived from certain axioms based on welfare considerations. But a more relevant approach to the measurement of poverty may be to consider the effect of transferring incomes from the non-poor to the poor so as to eradicate poverty completely on the inequality of income distribution measured, for example by the Gini index.

Writing equation (3.17) for the case in which the two groups are the poor and the non-poor respectively, we have for the Gini index prior to the transfer

$$G = \frac{\pi^2 \mu_p G_p}{\mu} + \frac{(1-\pi)^2 \mu_r G_r}{\mu} + \pi(1-\pi) \left(\frac{\mu_r - \mu_p}{\mu}\right) \qquad (3.17 \text{ bis})$$

Assuming that the transfers are carried out in such a way that none of the persons initially above the poverty line is pushed below the poverty line, the Gini index after the transfers will be

$$G' = (1-\pi)^2 \frac{\mu_r' G_r'}{\mu} + \pi(1-\pi) \left(\frac{\mu_r' - k}{\mu}\right) \qquad (3.30)$$

where primes on variables indicate their values after the transfer. The first term in (3.17) involving G_p drops out because all poor persons now have the same income. Further, because the average income in the society as a whole will not be affected by the transfers, we also have

$$\pi\mu_p + (1-\pi)\mu_r = \pi k + (1-\pi)\mu_r' \qquad (3.31)$$

Therefore

$$(1-\pi)(\mu_r - \mu_r') = \pi(k - \mu_p) \qquad (3.32)$$

and

$$\pi[(\mu_r - \mu_p) - (\mu_r' - k)] = \mu_r - \mu_r' \qquad (3.33)$$

Subtracting (3.30) from (3.17), and using (3.32) and (3.33), we get

$$G - G' = \frac{\pi}{\mu}[k - \mu_p(1 - \pi G_p)] + \frac{(1-\pi)^2}{\mu}[\mu_r G_r - \mu_r' G_r'] \qquad (3.34)$$

Suppose also that the eradication of poverty is financed by transferring a uniform amount from each member of the non-poor population. This method of taxation will not affect the mean difference of incomes among the non-poor; hence

$$\mu_r G_r = \mu'_r G'_r \qquad (3.35)$$

Therefore the second term on the righthand side of (3.34) will vanish. Then the reduction in the overall Gini index due to the eradication of poverty by this method of transfers will be given by the first term on the righthand side of (3.34). This term is the same as the Sen measure of poverty except for the coefficient of G_p but it has a more direct intuitive interpretation.

Appendix 3.1 Interpretations of the Gini index

1. A simple way of calculating the Gini index from grouped data is as follows. In the Lorenz diagram shown in Figure 3A.1, $AB = p_i$, $AD = Q_{i-1}$, and $BC = Q_i$.

The area of the trapezium ABCD is $\frac{1}{2} p_i(Q_i + Q_{i-1})$, and the total area under the Lorenz curve is

$$\frac{1}{2}\Sigma p_i(Q_i + Q_{i-1})$$

Therefore the Gini index, which is twice the area between the diagonal line and the Lorenz curve, is

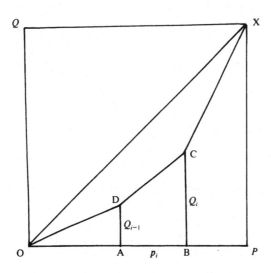

Figure 3A.1

$$G = 1 - \Sigma p_i(Q_i + Q_{i-1})$$

2. An alternative method of calculating the index is as follows. In the Lorenz diagram shown in Figure 3A.2,

$$
\begin{aligned}
OA &= P_{i-1}, & OB &= P_i, \\
AC &= Q_{i-1}, & BD &= Q_i, \\
CF &= P_{i-1} - Q_{i-1}, \\
DE &= P_i - Q_i
\end{aligned}
$$

The area of the trapezium CDEF is

$$
\begin{aligned}
&\tfrac{1}{2}(P_i - P_{i-1})[(P_{i-1} - Q_{i-1}) + (P_i - Q_i)] \\
&= \tfrac{1}{2}(P_{i-1}Q_i - P_iQ_{i-1})
\end{aligned}
$$

The Gini index, which is twice the sum of these areas, is therefore

$$G = \Sigma(P_{i-1}Q_i - P_iQ_{i-1})$$

3. The relationship of the Gini index to the mean difference may be derived as follows. Let x_i be the income in the ith income class; P_i the proportion of persons in that class, with $P_i = \Sigma^i p_j$; and q_i the proportion of income in that class, that is, $q_i = p_ix_i/\mu$ and $Q = \Sigma p_ix_i/\mu$. Then,

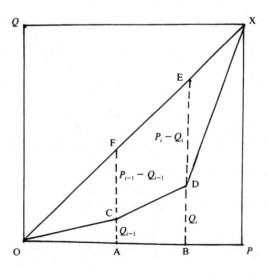

Figure 3A.2

$$\text{mean difference} = \Sigma\Sigma\, p_i p_j \,|\, x_i - x_j\,|$$

$$= 2 \sum_i^k \sum_j^i p_i p_j (x_i - x_j)$$

$$= 2 \Sigma\, [p_i x_i \Sigma\, p_j - p_i \sum_j^i p_j x_j]$$

$$= 2\,\mu\Sigma(q_i P_i - p_i Q_i)$$
$$= 2\,\mu\Sigma\,(P_i Q_i - P_i Q_{i-1} - P_i Q_i + P_{i-1} Q_i)$$
$$= 2\,\mu\Sigma\,(P_{i-1} Q_i - P_i Q_{i-1})$$
$$= 2\,\mu\,G$$

Hence

$$G = \frac{1}{2\mu} \sum_i \sum_j p_i p_j \,|\, x_i - x_j\,|$$

4. The interpretation of the Gini index in terms of weighted transfers from rich to poor to get an equal distribution follows from its definition in terms of the relative mean difference. In the ungrouped case of n persons,

$$G = \frac{\Sigma\,|\,x_i - x_j\,|}{2n(n-1)\mu}$$

Consider a transfer of amount t from the ith to the $(i - s)$th person arranged in ascending order of income. This transfer reduces the difference between their incomes by $2t$; this amount is transferred across s persons and each difference occurs twice. Each such transfer reduces the numerator by $4st$. Therefore considering all the transfers required to make the distribution an egalitarian one, we get

$$G = \frac{2\,\Sigma ts}{n(n-1)\mu}$$

Example: Consider an initial distribution of five persons with incomes 1, 4, 6, 7, and 12. The Gini index of this distribution is $^5\!/_{12}$. We can derive it in terms of weighted transfers as follows:

Step 1:   Transfer 1 from the fourth to the second person, that is, a weighted transfer of $1 \times 2 = 2$. The distribution is now 1, 5, 6, 6, 12.

Step 2:   Transfer 1 from the fifth person to the second person, that is, a weighted transfer of $1 \times 3 = 3$. The distribution is now 1, 6, 6, 6, 11.

Step 3: Transfer 5 from the fifth person to the first person, that is, a weighted transfer of $5 \times 4 = 20$. The distribution is now 6, 6, 6, 6, 6.

The total weighted transfers being 25, we have

$$G = \frac{2 \times 25}{5 \times 4 \times 6} = \frac{5}{12}$$

In the case of grouped data, the transfer of 1 unit of income from a person in the *i*th income class to a person in the *j*th income class, where $j < i$, must be weighted by $n + 1$ where n is the number of persons in the intervening classes. Thus the relationship between the Gini index and the K measure is analogous to the relationship between the Spearman and Kendall rank correlation coefficients.

For a general proof of this interpretation, the Gini index can be expressed as

$$G = \frac{2}{\mu} \int_8^{\infty} x[F(x) - \tfrac{1}{2}]f(x)dx$$

where $f(x)$ is the frequency and $F(x)$ the cumulative frequency, at income x. Then, it has been shown that the effect of transferring a small amount from a person with income $(x - h)$ to a person with income x is given by

$$\frac{dG}{dx} = \frac{2}{\mu}[F(x) - F(x - h)]$$

(see Kakwani 1980:73). The term in the square brackets refers to the proportion of all persons with incomes between x and $x - h$. Therefore the effect of the transfer on the Gini index depends on the number of persons across whom the transfer is made. This result is sometimes interpreted as meaning that the Gini index gives more weight to transfers near the mode of the distribution than at the tails. By comparison, the coefficient of variation is equally sensitive to transfers at all levels of income (Kakwani 1980:72–3, 87).

Chapter four

Cross-sectional patterns of income distribution

4.1 Introduction

In Chapter two, we considered the statistical data required for the study of income distribution and the types of data that have been collected in many countries on the subject. In most cases the available data fall far short of what we require, but in spite of these shortcomings they give us a rough picture of certain patterns of income distribution prevailing in different countries at different times. Of these patterns, those relating to historical changes in income distribution are discussed in the next chapter. Here we consider the patterns shown by the latest available data from a cross-section of countries. Some of the typical differences between countries are summarized in section 4.2. One of the major factors used in the literature to explain these differences is the level of per capita income. The evidence for this relationship is discussed in section 4.3. This evidence shows that although there is some relationship between income levels and the distribution of income, the relationship is rather weak. Therefore we must also consider other factors which are associated with differences in income distribution between countries. Unfortunately, sufficient data are not available from many countries to study the role of many of these factors. A few factors for which cross-section data from different countries are available are examined in section 4.4. Apart from this, we also analyse the effect of some of these factors by considering how they affect the distribution of income within countries. Finally, in section 4.5 we consider the factors influencing the extent of poverty in LDCs.

4.2 International differences

There are four major compilations of international data on income distribution. The first major source is Jain's (1975) compilation for the World Bank. This data set brings together 405 distributions from 81 countries for various dates. Choosing the more recent and comprehensive cases from these data, we get 75 distributions. These are described below as World Bank-I.

This compilation brings together the data as they were published in the national sources. Because of the wide variation between them in concept, definition, method of collection, and reliability, they are not entirely suitable for making detailed comparisons and have been subject to considerable criticism. Therefore in recent years the World Bank has selected some of the more reliable data from national sources, made certain adjustments, and published the results in the series of *World Development Reports*. Taking the distributions published in 1985, and substituting more recent data published in 1987 wherever available, we get 51 cases of household income distributions. These are described below as World Bank-II. Although some effort was made to adjust them for errors and for comparability, the World Bank has cautioned that they are still subject to considerable error.

In view of the shortcomings of much of the data available at the time, the International Labour Office (ILO) decided to make a further selection of new, comparable, and relatively reliable estimates. One such set is the compilation of data for 53 distributions by Lecaillon *et al.* (1984), which is referred to below as ILO-I. Then van Ginneken and Park (1984) generated a set of 23 household distributions and 13 individual distributions which they considered more suitable for international comparisons. These are referred to as ILO-II.

We first consider the differences between developed market economies and less developed countries in three major regions. The data from the above sources are summarized in Table 4.1 in the form of the income shares of the four bottom quintiles and the two top deciles of the population, averaged for different groups of countries. The general pattern shown by these data is that the distribution of income is generally more equal in the DMEs than in the LDCs. The simplest measure of inequality for comparing these distributions is the ratio of incomes in the top decile to those in the bottom quintile, a slight modification of the measure recommended by Wiles. For the household distributions in the World Bank-I compilation, this ratio was 9.6 for DMEs and 17.1 for LDCs (23.6 in Africa, 21.9 in Latin America, and 10.2 in Asia). Similar values are found in the data from the other sources. This is also the case for the World Bank-II estimates, which are given only for households. The distribution among income recipients is also more equal in the DMEs than in the LDCs, but in this case, the difference is smaller.

Within the LDCs there is a tendency for the distributions in Africa and the Middle East to be very unequal, and those in Asia to be much less unequal, both in the case of households and of income recipients. One reason for the lower inequality in Asian countries is that the share of the bottom groups is quite high, sometimes higher than in even the DMEs. Kuznets (1955:22) and Myrdal (1968:566) have suggested that this is because the standard of living in these countries is already so close to the subsistence level that it cannot be depressed any further.

The ILO-I estimates are given only for LDCs. They are shown separately for households, income recipients, and individuals. There seems to be a tendency for the distributions among income recipients to be more unequal than those among households, and the distributions among individuals to be less unequal. The ILO-II estimates are given both for DMEs and LDCs, and for households and individuals. They also show that distributions are more equal in the developed than in the less developed countries. These data also indicate that the individual distributions tend to be more equal than the household distributions but, as mentioned above, this is considered in more detail below.

Next we summarize the data in terms of various measures of inequality in Table 4.2. The values of the Gini index confirm the conclusions derived from Table 4.1 that LDCs generally have higher inequality than DMEs, and within LDCs, the Asian countries generally have less inequality than other LDCs. In fact, in the case of the distribution among individuals, inequality is lower in Asia than in the DMEs.

Table 4.2 also shows that LDCs and DMEs differed greatly in respect of the skewness of the Lorenz curve. Kakwani (1980: Chap. 17) found that with only one exception, his sample of 33 LDCs had negatively skewed Lorenz curves; and with only two exceptions, his sample of 17 DMEs had positively skewed Lorenz curves. This difference is shown even more clearly in terms of the w measure of the pattern of inequalities.

Table 4.2 gives the measures of inequality separately for household and individual distributions of income. There does not seem to be any systematic relationship between the household and individual distributions. The average Gini index of individual distributions is greater than that of household distributions in some regions and smaller in others. This may be partly due to the fact that the averages refer to different groups of countries in each case. Therefore we consider the relationship between the two distributions in the countries for which data are available for both distributions, as shown in Table 2.4. The Gini index of these distributions is shown in Table 4.3.

In most cases the inequality of individual distributions is less than that of household distributions, but there are quite a few cases – Kenya, South Korea, and Mexico, and also in the case of families in the United States – where the individual distribution is more unequal than the household distribution; there are other cases in which the Gini index is very close for the two distributions. Observing such cases van Ginneken and Park (1984:99) pointed out that 'we do not know of any work which has demonstrated under what conditions the Gini index of household income inequality is higher than that of household income per head'.

Lecaillon *et al.* (1984:34) found that 'in most cases the Gini coefficients are the same, or approximately the same, for the distribution by households

73

Table 4.1 International differences in income distribution

Country group (number of countries)	Percentage share of total income in:						
	Bottom quintile	Second quintile	Third quintile	Fourth quintile	Ninth decile	Top decile	Total
I. World Bank-I							
(a) Households							
DMEs (13)	6.0	10.9	15.7	22.7	16.0	28.7	100.0
LDCs (35)	4.5	8.3	12.7	20.2	15.9	38.4	100.0
Africa and							
Middle East (10)	3.6	7.2	11.6	19.4	15.7	42.5	100.0
Latin America (12)	3.7	7.5	12.0	20.0	16.4	40.5	100.0
Asia (13)	6.3	10.2	14.5	21.3	15.5	32.2	100.0
(b) Income recipients							
DMEs (16)	5.4	10.7	15.4	22.3	16.0	30.2	100.0
LDCs (21)	5.6	9.2	13.1	19.5	14.6	38.0	100.0
Africa and							
Middle East (12)	4.5	7.3	11.2	17.8	14.3	44.9	100.0
Latin America (6)	4.0	8.3	12.9	20.1	15.6	39.1	100.0
Africa (3)	8.3	11.8	15.3	20.6	13.9	30.1	100.0
II. World Bank-II							
(a) Households							
DMEs (21)	6.5	12.2	17.3	23.6	15.6	24.8	100.0
LDCs (30)	4.6	8.5	13.1	20.2	15.7	37.9	100.0
III. ILO-I LDCs							
(a) Households (22)	4.5	7.9	12.0	18.8	15.6	41.2	100.0
(b) Econ. active pop. (18)	4.1	7.0	10.7	18.2	14.8	45.2	100.0
(c) Individuals (13)	5.6	8.7	12.1	19.0	13.9	40.7	100.0

IV. ILO-II

(a) Households							
DMEs (8)	6.7	12.1	16.9	23.5	15.5	25.3	100.0
LDCs (1)	4.4	8.6	12.9	19.9	15.4	38.8	100.0
(b) Individuals							
DMEs (7)	8.7	13.0	17.0	22.2	14.9	24.2	100.0
LDCs (6)	5.2	9.2	13.2	19.5	15.1	37.8	100.0

Source: Compiled by the author.

Table 4.2 Measures of inequality: An international comparison

Inequality measures	Asia	Africa	Latin America	LDCs	DMEs
A. Households					
Gini index	0.410	0.539	0.522	0.490	0.382
Skewness of					
Lorenz curve	1.076	1.144	1.129	1.108	0.945
w measure	2.84	4.05	4.35	3.61	2.24
B. Individuals and income recipients					
Gini index	0.357	0.545	0.502	0.468	0.401
Skewness of					
Lorenz curve	1.400	1.311	1.069	1.232	0.899
w measure	4.10	4.34	4.25	4.26	2.02
C. Correlation of Gini index with skewness	0.36	−0.03	−0.12	0.13	0.35

Sources: Gini index: Jain (1975); skewness of Lorenz curve: Kakwani (1980).

and for the distribution by individuals, and that the former may be taken, therefore, as referring to the latter'. But most other writers have assumed that individual distributions are more equal than household distributions and have usually explained this observation by the tendency for household sizes to increase with household incomes. This explanation is so widely accepted that when Lecaillon *et al.* (1984:30) found in an analogous case that the Gini index of the distribution of income among earners (i.e. the economically active population) was greater than that of households in LDCs, they concluded that this must be due to a tendency for the number of earners per household to fall with rises in the average income of the household, and even advanced an explanation along the lines of the backward sloping supply curve of labour. But as we have seen in the cases for which data are available, the number of earners per household also generally tends to increase with household income (Table 2.1). Further, even in the case of those countries included in Table 4.3 for which the individual distribution is more unequal than the household distribution, household size generally increases with household income.

This is because the relationship between the two distributions depends not only on how household size varies between income classes, but also on the variation of household size within income classes in the case of grouped data. Such size variation within income classes tends to increase the value of the Gini index, and therefore has an effect opposite to that of the usual size variation between income classes. The relationship between the two

Table 4.3 Gini index of household and individual distribution

| Country (Year) | Gini index of income distribution of: | |
	Households	Individuals
LDCs		
Bangladesh (1973–74)[a]	0.351	0.279
Egypt (1974)[a]	0.401	0.376
Fiji (1977)[a]	0.472	0.464
India (1975–76)[b]	0.420	0.380
Indonesia (1980)[c]	0.391	0.344
Iran (1973–74)[a]	0.507	0.453
Kenya (1976)[a]	0.548	0.554
South Korea (1970)[b]	0.351	0.395
Malayasia (1970)[d]	0.513	0.498
Mexico (1968)[a]	0.563	0.574
Philippines (1971)[e]	0.478	0.478
Senegal (1970)[b]	0.513	0.490
Tanzania (1968)[b]	0.509	0.508
DCs		
Denmark (1976)[a]	0.310	0.268
France (1975)[a]	0.388	0.350
West Germany (1974)[a]	0.365	0.319
Ireland (1973)[a]	0.319	0.294
Spain (1973–74)[a]	0.371	0.337
Sweden (1979)[a]	0.312	0.225
UK (1979)[a]	0.313	0.272
USA		
Families (1957)	0.356	0.395
(1975)	0.376	0.397
Households (1967)	0.408	0.407
(1985)	0.412	0.413

Sources: [a]van Ginneken and Park (1984); [b]Lecaillon *et al.* (1984); [c]Biro Pusat Statistik (1980) *SUSENAS 1980*; [d]Anand 1983; [e]Bureau of Census and Statistics (1973) *Family Income and Expenditures (1971)*. [f]Bureau of Census (various isues) *Current Population Report, Series 60*.

distributions depends on the net effect of the two factors, which may be positive or negative depending on particular cases. These effects are discussed in more detail in Appendix 4.1.

4.3 Relationship between income inequality and mean income

Next we consider the factors influencing the variation of income inequality between countries. The dominant hypothesis in the literature is that income inequality is related to the level of per capita income. More specifically, the hypothesis, as recently stated by Lecaillon *et al.* (1984:4), is that 'income inequality at first increases during the process of development, and then diminishes once a certain level has been reached'. According to this hypothesis, the relationship between income inequality and per capita income may be described by a curve in the shape of an inverted U, with an upward phase in which income inequality increases with increases in per capita income, and a downward phase in which income inequality declines with increases in per capita income. This generalization is often referred to as Kuznet's law.

If this generalization is valid, then it has a very important implication for policy relating to income distribution in the LDCs. Thus if during a given period income inequality in these countries shows a tendency to increase, then according to this law it would have to be treated as an inevitable consequence of an increase of per capita incomes in the early stages of growth. It could then be argued that it is only in the later stages of their growth that there would be a 'trickle down' of the effects of growth and a reduction of income inequalities to the level that now obtains in the DCs. This implication that efforts to reduce income inequality will only be successful in the later stages of growth is so serious that we must consider the basis of this law more carefully.

It is frequently implied in the literature that this relationship is a generalization from the historical experience of the developed countries. For example, Ahluwalia (1974:17n) says: 'This relationship can be traced to Kuznets's (1955) study of historical data for the developed countries in which he observed that whereas the degree of inequality had declined steadily during this century, this was not true of the early stages of their growth when inequality *probably* increased' (italics added). Similarly, Oshima (1970:7) says, 'Professor Simon Kuznets, a pioneer in this field, *speculated* in his American Economic Association presidential address in 1954, that inequality tends to widen in the earlier phases of growth and then to narrow in the later phases of growth. Since then most of his studies and those of others on the topic have fully confirmed this finding' (italics added).

In fact, however, the hypothesis was advanced by Kuznets in a very tentative way. His historical research provided support only for the downward phase of the relationship. Further, the historical data show that the reduction of inequality occurred rather late in the process of development and then it was not simply a relationship between inequality and income level, but the result of many other factors. As far as the upward phase of the relationship characterizing the earlier phase of growth is concerned, Kuznets based his very tentative remarks mainly on certain theoretical speculations, and on a comparison of developed and less developed countries. Even then, he recognized the role of many factors influencing income distribution in addition to the level of per capita income. As he summarized his argument on a later occasion (Kuznets 1966:216–7):

[T]he size distribution of income and the developed countries is subject to a variety of factors, some making for narrowed inequality, others for wider. The actual trends are a net balance of these forces, and to account for them one should be able to measure the changing effects of pushes upward and of pulls downward. This we cannot do without data that are not now available. It seems plausible to assume that in the process of growth, the earlier periods are characterised by a balance of counteracting forces that may have widened the inequality in the size distribution of total income for a while because of the rapid growth of the non-A sector and wider inequality within it. It is even more plausible to argue that the recent narrowing in income inequality observed in the developed countries was due to a combination of the narrowing inter-sectoral inequalities in product per worker, the decline in the share of property incomes in total incomes of households, and the institutional changes that reflect decisions concerning social security and full employ-ment. But these are conjectures that, while consistent with the existing data, have so far only an imprecise empirical base.

Although Kuznets's law is often stated as describing a historical process, subsequent writers have mostly examined it on the basis of contemporary international data from a cross-section of countries at different income levels. In his 1963 paper, Kuznets used such a cross-section including 11 LDCs and 7 DCs. Since then data have become available from a larger number of countries. A number of authors have used these data to show that the cross-section pattern among countries is consistent with Kuznets's law. For example, some authors have classified countries according to their per capita incomes, and found that income inequality increases with per capita income up to a point and then declines at higher income levels (Table 4.4).

Table 4.4 Income inequality and per capita income (number of countries in brackets)

GDP per capita (US$)	Average values of Gini index:		
	Paukert	Ahluwalia Jain	Lecaillon et al.
LDCs			
Below 150	0.424 (14)	0.449 (10)	0.437 (9)
150–330	0.506 (14)	0.551 (14)	0.521 (12)
330–700	0.492 (11)	0.523 (11)	0.545 (10)
700 and over	0.430 (14)	0.462 (6)	0.487 (8)
DCs	0.388 (13)	0.363 (13)	0.381 (8)

Sources: Paukert (1973); Ahluwalia (1976); Lecaillon *et al.* (1984), Table 9, p. 41.

What the table shows is that the developed countries, which are the richest, have a lower inequality than the LDCs; among the LDCs, the poorest countries have lower inequality than the others. There also seems to be lower inequality for the richest LDCs, but the number of countries in this group is quite small.

These results only show the cross-sectional pattern of income inequality but they have been used as evidence of temporal changes according to Kuznets's law. For example, Lydall (1977:3) says:

> Although Paukert's data were of very variable quality, and even in some cases of definition, his results suggest that the *current pattern of differences* between countries is consistent with Kuznets' original hypothesis about *changes* in distribution during the process of economic growth.

However, such cross-sectional analysis is not entirely suitable for deriving intertemporal patterns of change; for that, we must consider data on historical changes such as those discussed in the next chapter.

A number of authors have also applied regression analysis to the cross-section data to derive a relationship between income distribution and the level of per capita income. We consider some examples. Selecting 118 household distributions from 71 countries from Jain's (1975) compilation, referred to above as the World Bank-I source, Lydall (1977:4a) regressed the Gini index G on per capita income X (in US dollars at 1971 prices) to get

$$G = 0.784 - 0.050 \log X - \frac{12.18}{X} + \text{dummy variables}$$
$$R^2 = 0.38; \ X^* = \$243 \tag{4.1}$$

According to this equation, G increases with income up to \$243 and declines thereafter. Lydall therefore concluded that the equation is consistent with Kuznets's hypothesis.

Other studies used the income share of various fractile groups as the dependent variable of the regression equations. For example, Lydall also obtained the following results:

$$S_1 = 3.070 + 0.312 \log X + \frac{154.85}{X} + \text{dummy variables}$$
$$R^2 = 0.31; \ X^* = \$497 \tag{4.2}$$

$$S_2 = 0.420 + 1.438 \log X + \frac{358.31}{X} + \text{dummy variables}$$
$$R^2 = 0.33; \ X^* = \$249 \tag{4.3}$$

$$S_6 = 53.926 + 4.596 \log X - \frac{919.47}{X} + \text{dummy variables}$$

$$R^2 = 0.36; \; X^* = \$200 \tag{4.4}$$

where S_1 is the income share of the bottom 20 per cent, S_2 that of the next 20 per cent, and S_6 that of the top 5 per cent. These results also show that income inequality increases with per capita income up to a point, shown as X^*, and declines thereafter, again consistently with Kuznets's hypothesis.

Another set of regressions was obtained by Chenery and Syrquin (1975:49) as follows:

$$B_{40} = 0.466 - 0.119 \log Y + 0.010 (\log Y)^2$$
$$\quad (2.98) \quad (2.26) \qquad (2.40)$$

$$R^2 = 0.12; \; Y^* = \$384 \tag{4.5}$$

$$T_{20} = -0.228 + 0.292 \log Y - 0.027 (\log Y)^2$$
$$\quad (0.75) \quad (2.84) \qquad (3.19)$$

$$R^2 = 0.29; \; Y^* = \$223 \tag{4.6}$$

where B_{40} is the share of the bottom 40 per cent, T_{20} the share of the top 20 per cent, and the figures below the regression coefficients are t ratios. These equations are also consistent with Kuznets's hypothesis, with the turning points occurring at the values of Y^* shown alongside.

However, such regressions are not entirely satisfactory in establishing the influence of income levels on income inequality. This is partly because in many cases these regressions have only a low degree of explanation. Further, when they have a higher degree of explanation, they are based on data on both developed and less developed countries. It is true that, as we have seen, income inequality is lower in DCs compared with LDCs. However, this cannot be ascribed only to the fact that incomes are higher in DCs than in LDCs because the two groups of countries also differ in many other respects. Therefore cross-sectional analysis using data from both groups suffers from the effect of double clustering (see Sundrum 1983:32, 131), and may attribute to per capita income the effects of other variables. One way of checking this argument is to compare such regressions with results based on data only from LDCs. Some examples computed by Ahluwalia (1976:311) are shown below:

DCs and LDCs:
$$B_{40} = 70.57 - 44.38 \log Y + 8.31 (\log Y)^2 + 11.95 D$$
$$\quad (5.38) \quad (4.61) \qquad (4.82) \qquad (5.54)$$

$$R^2 = 0.59; \; Y^* = \$468 \tag{4.7}$$

$$T_{20} = -57.58 + 89.95 \log Y - 17.56(\log Y)^2 - 20.15 D$$
$$\phantom{T_{20} =} (2.11) \quad (4.48) \qquad (4.88) \qquad\qquad (6.83)$$
$$R^2 = 0.58; \ Y^* = \$364 \tag{4.8}$$

LDCs only:
$$B_{40} = 106.80 - 74.69 \log Y + 14.53(\log Y)^2$$
$$\phantom{B_{40} =} (3.83) \quad (3.25) \qquad (3.10)$$
$$R^2 = 0.24; \ Y^* = \$371 \tag{4.9}$$

$$T_{20} = -99.74 + 123.80 \log Y - 24.18(\log Y)^2$$
$$\phantom{T_{20} =} (1.50) \quad (2.35) \qquad (2.26)$$
$$R^2 = 0.12; \ Y^* = \$363 \tag{4.10}$$

where D is a dummy variable for socialist countries. From these results, Ahluwalia (1976:309) concluded that 'the cross country regressions provide a substantial measure of support for the hypothesis that there is a U-shaped pattern in the secular behaviour of inequality. . . . Taking the results from the full sample to begin with, there is clear evidence of a non-monotonic relationship between inequality and the level of development.' But the regressions for LDCs only have a much smaller degree of explanation than those for DCs and LDCs combined. This suggests that the relatively high R^2 values of equations (4.7) and (4.8) are mainly due to the inclusion of the DCs. By contrast, equations (4.9) and (4.10) based on data from LDCs only show a much weaker relationship between income levels and income inequality. Subject to this weakness, the equations continue to show the Kuznets's pattern of variation, with turning points at the values of Y^* shown with these equations.

However, the data from which these equations were derived are rather old, and of doubtful comparability. Further, the income variable used is based on converting estimates in national currencies to US dollars at official exchange rates. Therefore it might be useful to repeat the analysis with more recent and more reliable data, such as those described above as World Bank-II estimates, which are available for 30 LDCs. In doing so, we use estimates of the income variable in terms of international purchasing power parities which have become available (Summers and Heston 1984). On this basis we find:

$$B_{40} = 125.553 - 30.204 \log Y + 2.003(\log Y)^2$$
$$\phantom{B_{40} =} (2.09) \quad (1.76) \qquad (1.66)$$
$$R^2 = 0.23; \ Y^* = \$1881 \tag{4.11}$$

$$T_{20} = -36.27 + 25.168 \log Y - 1.749(\text{Log } Y)^2$$
$$\phantom{T_{20} = }(0.29) \quad (0.70) \qquad\quad (0.69)$$
$$R^2 = 0.02; \; Y^* = \$1333 \tag{4.12}$$

$$G = -1.074 + 0.419 \log Y - 0.028(\log Y)^2$$
$$(0.88) \quad (1.21) \qquad\quad (1.16)$$
$$R^2 = 0.09; \; Y^* = \$1776 \tag{4.13}$$

Now we find that the R^2 values are much lower and that the regression coefficients are very different and much less significant. Further, we find that the turning points are much higher; the equations therefore show that income inequality generally rises with per capita income for most of the range of incomes actually observed in LDCs, and that the nonmonotonic relationship in the regression equations is mainly due to a few countries with high per capita incomes and low inequality, such as South Korea and Hong Kong.

While the cross-section regressions show a tendency for income inequality to increase with per capita income up to a point, some authors have also argued that there is an actual increase in the extent of poverty in the early stages of growth. For example, Chenery et al. (1974:xiii) say, 'It is now clear that more than a decade of rapid growth in underdeveloped countries has been of little or no benefit to perhaps a third of their population'. And Adelman and Morris (1973:189, 192) claimed that 'development is accompanied by an absolute as well as a relative decline in the average income of the very poor', and that 'hundreds of millions of desperately poor people throughout the world have been hurt rather than helped by economic development'. But as Little (1976:102) pointed out,

> The rapid growth refers to the Third World, but the fact that as much as a third of the people may have benefited very little is presumably because South Asia has grown very slowly. It is not because a third of the people in rapidly growing countries have benefited very little or not at all.

To investigate the behaviour of different groups further, we calculate the elasticities of various percentile income shares with respect to per capita income. The results are shown in Table 4.5 for the sample of 30 LDCs and 21 DMEs in the World Bank-II compilation. This shows that the incomes of all groups, including the bottom quintile, rise with growing incomes. But the share of the bottom quintile increases less than proportionately with per capita income, while the shares of the upper income groups, especially the ninth decile, increase faster, leading to increasing inequality at higher income levels. By contrast, in the DMEs it is the top decile which is least elastic with respect to per capita income, and this is the main reason why

Table 4.5 Elasticity of income shares with respect to per capita income

Income share	LDCs	DCs
Bottom quintile Q_1	0.74	1.01
Second quintile Q_2	0.93	1.09
Third quintile Q_3	0.99	1.10
Fourth quintile Q_4	1.07	1.04
Ninth decile D_9	1.08	0.98
Tenth decile D_{10}	0.98	0.86

Source: Compiled by the author.

income inequality declines with rising incomes in those countries.

An alternative version of Kuznets's hypothesis was tested by Kakwani (1980: Chap. 17). According to this interpretation, the skewness of the Lorenz curve declines with increasing per capita income, leading to a steady rise in the share of the middle income groups. To test this version, Kakwani considered the relationship between per capita income and a measure of skewness in a sample of 50 DCs and LDCs. The correlation between these variables is negative (−0.57). However, this high negative correlation is mainly due to the difference between DCs and LDCs. As we have noted, the skewness of the Lorenz curve is positive in almost all LDCs and negative in almost all DCs. But the relationship is much weaker within each of these groups, the correlation coefficient being only −0.19 within LDCs and −0.24 within DCs. Therefore we have to conclude that it is not so much the level of per capita income which influences income distribution, but rather other aspects of the level of development.

However, all such relationships are based on the cross-section pattern. Economists, even those who use such cross-section analysis, are aware of its many pitfalls. Thus Ahluwalia *et al.* (1979:466–8) say:

> It is important to emphasize that the average cross-country relationship should not be interpreted as an iron law. Individual countries that are able to establish the preconditions for a more egalitarian distribution of income and to stimulate growth in such a policy environment, as illustrated by Yugoslavia, Taiwan and Korea, may well be able to avoid or moderate the phase of increasing inequality. But there are a number of reasons why such a pattern is likely to emerge with a continuation of past policies, especially in the nonsocialist countries characterised by sharp inequalities in the initial distribution of productive wealth (including land). . . . The use of the Kuznets curve in projections also implies that the distribution of income will improve in countries with a

per capita income above 800 ICP dollars without specifying the effort required to redirect government policies. Needless to say, we cannot assume that this improvement will take place automatically.

An alternative analysis was carried out by Papanek (1978:265) also using regression methods and using the Gini index as the dependent variable, but dividing the sample into four groups according to level and type of economic development. He summarizes his conclusions as follows:

1   There is no convincing support from cross-country analysis for the hypothesis that an n-shaped or inverted U-shaped relationship exists between per capita income and income distribution.
2   Instead, there are probably four groups of countries with differences in average per capita income and inequality, which may permit in cross-country analysis an inverted U form to be imposed on the data.
3   Within these four groups – the developed, Eastern European, raw material exporters and other LDCs – no clear relationship is observed between per capita income and income distribution.
4   There is some tendency for inequality to increase as countries move from an essentially agricultural, subsistence economic structure with incomes around $150–200. But there is no very good evidence that inequality continues to increase thereafter in less developed countries.
5   For the LDC, inequality is correlated with dependence on raw material exports.

These results suggest that future levels of inequality cannot be projected only on the basis of the patterns observed in the cross-section data. As Papanek (1978) put it:

That Rhodesia's income was quite unequal when per capita income reached $200 does not really suggest that the income of, say, Pakistan or India, will become much less equally distributed when their per capita income increases from $100 to $200.

So far we have been considering the relationship between income inequality and level of income at roughly the same point of time. But inequality may also be related to income in other ways. For example, changes in income inequality during a given period of time may be related to growth of income during that period. As pointed out above, this relationship cannot be inferred from the cross-section patterns observed at a point of time. A better approach would be to use time series data and examine whether different rates of growth of income have any effect on the changes in income inequality. Some results of this approach are discussed in the next chapter. Then there is a third possible relationship, namely one between the growth of income over a period of time and the degree of inequality at a point of time during that period. For example, we might use such data to see whether the level of inequality depends on the rate of growth, in particular whether faster-growing countries tend to have higher inequality, as is sometimes argued.

To examine this possibility, LDCs and DCs for which data are available were classified according to their rates of growth and levels of inequality in Tables 4.6 and 4.7. There is clearly no relationship between the two variables. Ahluwalia (1976:338) analysed similar data by regression methods using the rate of growth as an additional explanatory variable and reported that:

> The results obtained from this exercise reject the hypothesis that a faster rate of growth leads to greater inequality. . . . While there may be a secular time path for inequality which developing countries must traverse, and which contains a phase of increasing inequality, there is at least no evidence that countries which traverse this path at a fast pace are worse off *at the same level of development* than countries which traverse it at a slow pace.

The exercise was repeated using the income distribution data for LDCs from the World Bank-II set and the rates of growth for the period 1973–83 as given in the *World Development Report* of 1985. Again it was found that there was only a weak relationship between the Gini coefficients and the rates of growth; according to this analysis, the correlation between the variables is in fact negative (−0.21), that is, countries that grew faster tended to have lower inequality than the slow growing countries.

In view of these results we have to conclude that the degree of income inequality prevailing in countries is not primarily influenced by their per capita incomes or their rates of economic growth. Instead, it is influenced by more deep-seated factors, which change slowly in the normal course of events unless they are altered by violent disturbances such as wars or revolutions. Therefore the distribution of income remains fairly stable over long periods of time. It just happens that, as a result of such deep-seated factors, the distribution of income is more equal in the Asian type of countries with their lower average incomes compared with the Latin American type of countries with their higher incomes. Similarly, income inequality is lower in the DMEs which have higher incomes than in the LDCs with their lower incomes. Putting all these countries together then reveals an inverted U-shaped relationship between income inequality and income level, which has been widely taken as evidence for Kuznets's law. But this cross-section pattern does not give us any insight into how the growth of income alone is likely to influence the distribution of income in any particular country over time.

Table 4.6 Rates of growth and income inequality: LDCs, 1970–81

Income inequality	Rates of growth		
	Low	*Medium*	*High*
Low:	Bangladesh (4.1; 0.37)		Egypt (8.1; 0.47)
	El Salvador (3.1; 0.40)		Hong Kong (10.0; 0.39)
	India (3.7; 0.40)		S. Korea (9.0; 0.37)
	Sri Lanka (4.3; 0.41)		Thailand (7.2; 0.42)
Medium:	Argentina (1.9; 0.43)	Costa Rica (5.2; 0.48)	Indonesia (7.8; 0.42)
	Venezuela (4.5; 0.49)	Philippines (6.2; 0.45)	Malaysia (7.8; 0.49)
		Trinidad and Tobago (5.5; 0.43)	
		Turkey (5.4; 0.49)	
High:	Peru (3.1; 0.56)	Ivory Coast (6.2; 0.55)	Brazil (8.4; 0.60)
	Zambia (0.4; 0.53)	Kenya (5.8; 0.55)	Mexico (6.5; 0.52)
		Mauritius (6.2; 0.52)	
		Panama (4.5; 0.56)	

Note: Figures in parentheses are rates of growth 1970–81 and Gini coefficients for latest available year respectively.
Sources: World Bank (1984) *World Tables*; World Bank (1987) *World Development Report, 1987*.

Table 4.7 Rates of growth and income inequality: LDCs, 1970–81

Income inequality	Rates of growth		
	Low	*Medium*	*High*
Low	Netherlands (2.7; 0.27)	Belgium (3.0; 0.27)	Ireland (4.0; 0.31)
	W. Germany (2.6; 0.30)	Finland (3.1; 0.31)	Japan (4.5; 0.28)
	Switzerland (0.7; 0.30)		
Medium	Denmark (2.1; 0.33)	Spain (3.4; 0.32)	Israel (4.0; 0.33)
	Sweden (1.8; 0.32)		Norway (4.5; 0.31)
	UK (1.7; 0.32)		
High	New Zealand (3.0; 0.38)	Australia (3.3; 0.40)	Canada (3.8; 0.34)
		France (3.3; 0.35)	Portugal (4.4; 0.41)
		Italy (2.9; 0.36)	
		USA (2.9; 0.34)	

Note: Figures in parentheses are rates of growth 1970–81 and Gini coefficients for latest available year respectively.
Sources: World Bank (1984) *World Tables*; World Bank (1987) *World Development Report, 1987.*

4.4 Influence of other factors

In the last section, we discussed attempts to explain the differences in inequality between countries in terms of their per capita incomes. In this section we consider how far these differences were associated with other factors. In order to consider such relationships, Chenery and Syrquin (1975:61) extended their regression equations, shown in (4.5) and (4.6) above, by the addition of other variables such as school enrolment (E), primary export shares (X), and the share of primary production in GDP (P) and obtained the following results:

$$B_{40} = \text{income effect} + 0.068\,E - 0.126\,X + 0.157\,P$$
$$\qquad\qquad\quad (1.56) \qquad (2.98) \qquad (1.69)$$

$$R^2 = 0.24 \qquad\qquad\qquad (4.5\text{a})$$

$$T_{20} = \text{income effect} - 0.223\,E + 0.286\,X - 0.329\,P$$
$$\qquad\qquad\quad (3.08) \qquad (2.99) \qquad (2.14)$$
$$R^2 = 0.52 \qquad\qquad\qquad (4.6\text{a})$$

On the basis of these results they concluded that while the level of income does not explain a large part of the intercountry variation, the addition of the above variables led to a 'notable improvement in the regression results'.

A more extensive regression analysis was carried out by Ahluwalia (1976) using data from both DCs and LDCs. His results are shown in Table 4.8 for B_{40} (the income share of the bottom 40 per cent) and in Table 4.9 for T_{20} (the income share of the top 20 per cent). These results may be compared with equations (4.7) and (4.8) respectively based only on the income variable. As far as the income variable is concerned, the equations of Tables 4.8 and 4.9 also show a nonmonotonic relationship. However, here the turning points are much higher, so that the downward phase of inequality is now mainly confined to the DCs. Hence Ahluwalia (1976:338) concluded that 'the operation of these processes appears to explain some of the improvement in income distribution observed in the later stages of development, but they do not serve to explain the marked deterioration observed in the earlier stages'. But because these regressions are based on data from both DCs and LDCs, what they really show is that inequality is lower in the DCs than in the LDCs, a difference that may be explained by a number of variables which differ markedly between the developed and the less developed countries, other than per capita income.

The addition of the new variables, however, has not raised the R^2 values significantly. This is partly because the new variables are highly correlated with the old and therefore do not add to the degree of explanation. In order to assess the role of the new variables by themselves. Ahluwalia also calculated some regressions with these variables while omitting the income

Table 4.8 Regression of B_{40} on income and other variables

Explanatory variable	(1)	(2)	(3)	(4)	(5)	(6)
Constant	100.90	103.3	74.50	85.66	66.01	76.32
	(3.5)	(3.8)	(4.01)	(6.59)	(2.80)	(5.58)
(log Y)	−59.65	−63.09	−43.85	−51.44	−38.60	−47.35
	(3.0)	(3.6)	(3.54)	(5.29)	(2.30)	(4.60)
(log $Y)^2$	9.62	10.54	7.01	8.41	6.78	8.00
	(2.7)	(3.6)	(3.3)	(4.91)	(2.39)	(4.24)
E_1	0.06	0.07	—	—	—	—
	(1.7)	(2.1)				
E_2	0.04	—	0.03	—	—	0.04
	(1.0)		(1.0)			(1.29)
L	—	—	0.05	0.06	—	0.05
			(2.13)	(2.61)		(2.21)
A	−0.19	−0.18	0.03	—	−0.16	—
	(1.7)	(1.7)	(0.48)		(1.0)	
A^2	—	—	—	—	0.003	—
					(1.17)	
U	—	—	0.06	0.06	0.03	—
			(1.73)	(1.85)	(0.27)	
GP	−1.44	−1.62	−1.16	−1.16	—	—
	(1.7)	(2.3)	(2.47)	(2.48)		
GY	0.52	0.63	—	—	—	—
	(1.9)	(2.6)				
DD	−0.04	—	—	—	—	—
	(0.0)					
DS	10.08	10.13	8.70	9.18	12.09	10.57
	(3.9)	(4.4)	(5.40)	(5.98)	(8.49)	(7.55)
R^2	0.56	0.57	0.68	0.68	0.61	0.65
TP ($)	1,260	984	1,343	1,144	702	911

Notes:
E_1	— primary enrollment rate	GP	— growth rate of population
E_2	— secondary enrollment rate	GY	— growth rate of GNP
L	— literacy rate	DD	— dummy for developed countries
A	— agricultural share of GDP	DS	— dummy for socialist countries
U	— urban ratio	TP	— turning point

Sources: (1) and (2): Ahluwalia (1974: 28); (3) and (4): Ahluwalia (1976: 316); (5): Ahluwalia (1976: 319); (6): Ahluwalia (1976: 324).

variable. These results are summarized in Table 4.10. Then we see that these equations have nearly as high R^2 values as the equations (4.7) and (4.8) based only on the income variable. This shows that the international differences in inequality can be explained nearly as well by these structural variables as by the income variable used to test Kuznets's law. Further, comparing the equations of Table 4.10 among themselves, it seems that the coefficients of the agricultural variable are just as significant as those of the urban ratio or the educational variables.

Table 4.9 Regression of T_{20} on income and other variables

Explanatory variable	(1)	(2)	(3)	(4)	(5)	(6)
Constant	−57.35	−10.2	−8.71	−1.59	36.06	−57.34
	(0.9)	(0.2)	(0.26)	(0.05)	(0.73)	(2.11)
$(\log Y)$	81.51	52.4	49.62	43.58	80.42	85.15
	(1.8)	(1.7)	(2.24)	(1.97)	(2.29)	(4.16)
$(\log Y)^2$	−13.07	−9.29	−7.98	−7.16	−15.64	−14.42
	(1.6)	(1.6)	(2.10)	(1.87)	(2.64)	(3.84)
E_1	−0.11	—	—	—	—	—
	(1.4)					
E_2	−0.15	−22.6	−0.15	−0.16	—	−0.17
	(1.7)	(3.2)	(2.63)	(2.86)		(2.70)
L	—	—	−0.09	−0.11	—	−0.09
			(2.29)	(2.60)		(1.81)
A	0.25	—	−0.26	−0.23	−0.28	—
	(0.9)		(2.15)	(1.87)	(1.17)	
A^2	—	—	—	—	0.002	—
					(0.66)	
U	—	—	—	—	0.07	—
					(0.20)	
U^2	—	—	−0.09	—	−0.005	—
			(1.58)		(0.92)	
GP	1.29	—	3.61	3.48	—	—
	(0.7)		(4.28)	(4.09)		
GY	−0.77	—	—	—	—	—
	(1.22)					
DD	−3.53	—	—	—	—	—
	(0.6)					
DS	−18.33	−16.7	−9.44	−9.29	−19.66	−16.46
	(3.1)	(3.6)	(3.27)	(3.17)	(6.59)	(5.92)
R^2	0.50	0.50	0.75	0.75	0.59	0.67
TP ($)	1312	661	1291	1108	327	896

Notes:
E_1 — primary enrollment rate
E_2 — secondary enrollment rate
L — literacy rate
A — agricultural share of GDP
U — urban ratio
GP — growth rate of population
GY — growth rate of GNP
DD — dummy for developed countries
DS — dummy for socialist countries
TP — turning point

Sources: (1) and (2): Ahluwalia (1974: 28); (3) and (4): Ahluwalia (1976: 316); (5): Ahluwalia (1976: 319); (6): Ahluwalia (1976: 324).

The main weakness of the above results is that they are based on cross-section analysis. The problem is that countries differ in many respects, and such cross-section analysis by itself cannot identify which of these factors really have a causal influence on income distribution. A better approach is therefore to study how individual factors affect incomes within the same country. One way of doing this is to see how incomes differ between groups

Table 4.10 Regression of B_{40} and T_{20} on factors other than income

Explanatory variable	Dependent variable					
	B_{40} (1)	B_{40} (2)	B_{40} (3)	T_{20} (4)	T_{20} (5)	T_{20} (6)
Constant	18.56 (14.25)	16.06 (10.71)	11.70 (10.99)	39.54 (13.73)	52.08 (15.25)	58.76 (28.60)
A	−0.48 (4.64)	—	—	1.16 (5.01)	—	—
A^2	0.008 (4.61)	—	—	−0.02 (4.63)	—	—
U	—	−0.023 (3.04)	—	—	0.28 (1.62)	—
U^2	—	0.003 (3.69)	—	—	−0.005 (2.53)	—
L	—	—	−0.008 (3.69)	—	—	0.02 (0.49)
E_2	—	—	0.066 (2.53)	—	—	−0.22 (4.32)
DS	11.66 (8.11)	11.07 (7.50)	9.69 (6.05)	−20.11 (6.33)	−18.14 (5.39)	−14.85 (4.92)
R^2	0.56	0.54	0.51	0.49	0.43	0.56

Sources: (1), (2), (4), and (5): Ahluwalia (1976: 319); (3) and (6): Ahluwalia (1976: 324).

within countries which differ with respect to these factors. We have already noted some of these factors in Chapter two. For example, incomes of households tend to increase with the age of the head of household up to a point, and then decline thereafter. We also found that the incomes of households increase with their size, but less than proportionately, so that incomes of individuals decline with household size. These two factors are often related, as household size varies in the course of the life-cycle of the head of the household. We now consider a number of other factors which lead to income differences within countries.

4.4.1 Urban–rural income differentials

A typical feature of income distribution is the fact that average urban incomes are higher than average rural incomes. Some estimates of this differential observed in a few countries are given in Table 4.11. These estimates refer to the income differential between urban and rural areas in nominal terms, but from the point of view of income distribution, we are more interested in the differential in real terms. The differential in real terms will be different from that in nominal terms because the prices of many basic commodities are generally higher in urban than in rural areas.

However, it is unlikely that the price difference is as high as some of the income differences shown in the table. Therefore it is typically the case that urban incomes are higher than rural incomes in real terms as well. The cross-section pattern shows a tendency for the urban–rural differential to increase with per capita income, being quite small in the poorest Asian countries and much larger in the richer LDCs, especially in Latin America. The urban–rural differential is a significant component of overall income inequality; therefore the tendency for this differential to be greater in the richer LDCs is an important reason for the tendency for income inequality in LDCs to increase with per capita income.

4.4.2 Income differential between agricultural and nonagricultural sectors

The main reason that incomes are higher in urban than in rural areas is the fact that nonagricultural incomes are generally higher than agricultural incomes, and agriculture is mainly concentrated in rural areas and non-agricultural work in urban areas. For some countries we also have estimates of incomes in these sectors; these are summarized in Table 4.12. Again we see a tendency for the income disparity between the two sectors to increase with per capita income, together with a tendency for the agricultural share of the labour force to decline.

The corresponding position in DCs is shown in Table 4.13. It is interesting to see that the dualism between agricultural and nonagricultural incomes exists even in the DCs and, with some notable exceptions, there is a tendency for the disparity to decline with rising per capita incomes. However, in these countries the agricultural share of the labour force is

Table 4.11 Urban–rural income differential sectors in LDCs

Country/Year	Urban as percentage of rural
Bangladesh (income): 1977–78	148
(expenditure): 1977–78	130
India (income): 1967–68	135
(expenditure): 1977–78	140
Malaysia (income): 1970	216
Philippines (income): 1971	208
(expenditure): 1971	196
Sri Lanka (income): 1981–82*	164
Brazil (income): 1970	281
Colombia (income): 1970	232
Costa Rica (income): 1971	208
Honduras (income): 1967–68	539

Note: *Rural including estate sector.
Source: Jain (1975).

Table 4.12 Income differential between agricultural and nonagricultural sectors in LDCs

Country/Year	Per capita income ($) 1970	Agricultural share of labour force (%)	Agricultural income as percentage of nonagricultural income
Madasgascar: 1970	647	81	14
Zambia: 1972	722	67	18
Philippines: 1976	781	53	43
Senegal: 1970	852	74	19
Ivory Coast: 1970	1,028	66	25
Swaziland: 1974	1,044	82	11
South Korea: 1970	1,112	52	40
Malaysia: 1967	1,242	50	54
Colombia: 1972	1,355	31	42
Turkey: 1970	1,408	49	48
Iran: 1972	1,749	47	49
Mexico: 1968	2,005	47	41

Sources: Per capita income in US$ at international purchasing power parities: Summers and Heston (1984).
Agricultural share of the labour force and agricultural incomes as percentage of nonagricultural incomes: Lecaillon et al. (1984: 69).

Table 4.13 Income differential between agricultural and nonagricultural sectors in DCs

Country	Per capita income ($) 1965	Agricultural share of labour force (%) 1965	Agricultural income as percentage of nonagricultural income 1965–67
Italy	2,823	24	49
Austria	3,322	19	39
UK	3,814	3	106
Netherlands	3,825	9	91
Belgium	3,834	6	110
Norway	3,893	15	91
France	3,929	18	47
West Germany	4,422	10	45
Denmark	4,704	14	57
Canada	4,939	11	69
Sweden	5,210	11	54
USA	6,100	5	60

Sources: Per capita income in US$ at international prices: Summers and Heston (1984).
Agricultural share of labour force: World Bank, *World Development Report*, 1985.
Agricultural income as percentage of nonagricultural income: UN *Economic Survey of Europe, 1969*, cited in Cornwall (1977: 51).

much smaller. Therefore the income disparity between the two sectors has a much smaller influence on overall inequality.

Associated with the difference in incomes there is also some difference in income inequality. More data are available on these differences for urban and rural areas than for the two sectors. Therefore we illustrate these differences by data on the Gini index for urban and rural areas in Table 4.14. From this sample, we see that urban income distributions are, with few exceptions, more unequal than rural distributions. This suggests that nonagricultural incomes are also generally more unequally distributed than agricultural incomes.

In the course of economic development, there is a steady shift of the labour force from the agricultural to the nonagricultural sector. This means a shift of individuals from the sector with the lower incomes and lower inequality to the sector with the higher incomes and higher inequality. Kuznets (1955) and a number of later writers have suggested that this process is the main explanation for the variation of overall income inequality with per capital incomes in accordance with Kuznets's hypothesis. This argument is discussed further in Chapter twelve.

4.4.3 Income differentials by education

One of the most important factors influencing individual incomes is the level of education. Therefore it may be expected that the distribution of income in a country would be related to its educational position. Such a relationship was shown to some extent by the regression equations of income distribution on educational variables, shown in Tables 4.8, 4.9, and 4.10, based on cross-section data. But a weakness of such cross-section

Table 4.14 Gini index of urban and rural income distributions

Country/Year	Urban	Rural
Bangladesh (1966–67): Household incomes	0.399	0.334
(1978–80): Expenditure	0.342	0.328
Brazil (1970): Economically active population	0.556	0.476
Columbia (1970)	0.552	0.476
Costa Rica (1971)	0.418	0.367
Honduras (1967–68)	0.501	0.486
India (1967–68): Income	0.465	0.477
(1977–78): Expenditure	0.345	0.336
Malaysia (1970): Income	0.504	0.464
Philippines (1971): Income	0.453	0.458
Sri Lanka (1981–82): Income	0.542	0.498

Sources: Jain (1975); for Sri Lanka, Central Bank of Ceylon (1984) *Report on Consumer Finances and Socio-Economic Survey 1987/82.*

analysis is that the difference in income distribution between countries may be due to a wide variety of factors other than the differences in the educational conditions. An alternative approach which avoids this difficulty is to consider how educational differences affect income distribution within countries.

The first point to consider is the distribution of the adult population according to educational attainments. The data for a few Asian LDCs are shown in Table 4.15, together with data from the United States for comparison. In this table the average level of education is shown by the mean years of schooling. LDCs generally have a lower average level of education than DCs. Among the LDCs, Indonesia is an example of a country with a low average level of education, while the Philippines and Sri Lanka are examples of countries with a high level of education. Within each country, the level of education is higher in urban than in rural areas. This is one reason for the difference in average incomes between urban and rural areas, and between the agricultural and nonagricultural sectors. The Indonesian data also show that the mean years of schooling is higher for the younger age groups than for the older. This is generally the case for most LDCs because the educational system has been expanded rapidly in recent years in these countries.

The next feature of the educational situation is the inequality of the educational distribution of the population. A convenient measure of this inequality is the Gini index, denoted by $G(E)$, of the distribution of years of schooling. The general pattern is for educational inequality to decline with increases in the mean years of schooling. Thus $G(E)$ is greater for LDCs than for DCs; among LDCs, countries with a higher average level of education have a more equal distribution of education. Further, within LDCs, $G(E)$ is lower in urban areas that have a higher level of education than rural areas. A particularly interesting case of the relationship between $G(E)$ and the mean years of schooling is shown by the Indonesian data which show these values for different age groups. They show that $G(E)$ is generally higher for the older age groups which have a lower average level of education. Thus with the increase in the average level of education over time, there has been a steady decline in the inequality of the distribution of education.

Next we must consider the relationship between the distribution of education and the distribution of income. For this purpose, Table 4.16 shows the incomes of individuals (or households in the case of Indonesia and the Philippines), expressed as a percentage of the average level of income, according to level of education.

The most important feature is the universal tendency for the incomes of individuals to rise with their educational qualifications. Indeed, Blaug (1974:27) has described this association as 'one of the most striking findings of modern social science'.

Table 4.15 Distribution of the adult population by educational attainment

Country/Year	Percentage of the adult population with educational qualification							Mean years of schooling	G(E)
	None	Below primary	Primary	Below secondary	Secondary	Tertiary	Total		
Indonesia, 1981	32.5	27.2	25.1	6.8	6.8	1.6	100.0	3.98	0.51
Urban	16.7	20.6	28.3	14.1	15.9	4.4	100.0	6.15	0.39
Rural	40.2	30.4	23.5	3.2	2.4	0.3	100.0	2.94	0.54
By age:									
Below 25	8.9	31.1	34.9	11.4	13.1	0.6	100.0	5.72	0.33
25–34	11.8	28.0	34.9	10.3	12.7	2.3	100.0	5.71	0.36
35–44	22.5	29.9	28.2	8.5	8.4	2.5	100.0	4.73	0.44
45–54	40.9	28.8	20.6	4.3	4.0	1.4	100.0	3.17	0.57
55–64	52.4	23.8	17.9	3.6	1.8	0.5	100.0	2.40	0.64
65 and over	68.5	16.3	11.5	2.7	0.8	0.2	100.0	1.55	0.76
Philippines, 1971	12.1	37.8	19.4	9.8	8.8	12.1	100.0	6.22	0.39
Urban	4.5	19.5	17.9	13.2	16.7	28.2	100.0	9.00	0.29
Rural	15.4	45.7	20.1	8.3	5.4	5.2	100.0	5.02	0.40
Sri Lanka, 1981–82	14.9	—	37.3	30.3	16.2	1.3	100.0	6.98	0.27
USA, 1985	—	7.2	6.2	12.2	36.1	38.3	100.0	12.30	0.15
White	—	6.4	6.3	11.5	36.3	39.4	100.0	12.50	0.15
Black	—	12.7	5.6	19.2	36.1	26.4	100.0	11.20	0.17

Sources: Indonesia: Biro Pusat Statistik (1987) *SUSENAS 1981.*
Philippines: Bureau of Census and Statistics (1973) *Family Income and Expenditures, 1971.*
Sri Lanka: Central Bank of Ceylon (1984) *Report on Consumer Finance and Socio-Economic Survey 1981/82.*
USA: Bureau of Census (1985) *Current Population Report, Series 60.*

Table 4.16 Income differentials by education

Country/Year	Income of educational category as percentage of average:							
	None	Below primary	Primary	Below secondary	Secondary	Tertiary	Total	G(Y/E)
Indonesia, 1981	62	79	100	171	222	405	100	0.25
Urban	50	65	84	124	157	272	100	0.26
Rural	79	97	111	177	223	449	100	0.13
By age:								
Below 25	62	74	91	132	178	221	100	0.19
25–34	67	64	80	131	197	338	100	0.25
35–44	52	71	94	157	220	355	100	0.29
45–54	61	84	114	219	289	461	100	0.25
55–64	65	99	131	255	319	832	100	0.25
65 and over	74	118	146	363	248	585	100	0.20
Philippines, 1971	61	71	90	101	141	217	100	0.24
Urban	66	67	82	77	99	152	100	0.19
Rural	73	84	99	116	165	229	100	0.16
Sri Lanka, 1981–82	52	—	82	109	161	190	100	0.19
USA, 1985	—	51	65	68	90	135	100	0.18
White	—	50	63	69	89	133	100	0.18
Black	—	67	76	77	98	141	100	0.15

Sources: As for Table 4.15.

However, the rate at which incomes increase with educational level varies between countries. Incomes rise with educational level more slowly in the DCs like the United States than in the LDCs, because the average level of education is higher in the DCs than in the LDCs. There is a greater scarcity of highly educated workers in countries where the average level of education is low; therefore people with higher educational qualifications command a higher income differential in countries with a limited overall supply of educated people. For the same reason, income differentials by educational level are greater in LDCs with a lower stock of education than in LDCs with a larger stock.

A convenient way of summarizing the influence of education on income inequality is by calculating the Gini index, denoted by $G(Y/E)$, of the inequality of incomes between educational classes, that is, the Gini index calculated by taking the average incomes of different educational classes and assuming that all members within an educational class earn the average income of that class. The table shows that $G(Y/E)$ declines as the average educational level rises. This shows even more clearly the tendency for income inequality of countries and groups within countries to decline with increasing level of education.

Thus we see that the progress of education affects income distribution in two ways; first, by making the distribution of education itself become more equal, and second, by reducing the income differentials associated with education, and hence making the distribution of income become more equal.

There are many other factors which also affect the distribution of income among individuals and households such as the source of income – wages, rent, interest, or profit – and employment status, occupation, and sector of employment, but unfortunately there are not enough data for the sort of statistical analysis that we have done for the case of education. Therefore the economic analysis of these other factors is discussed in Part II.

4.5 Variations in the extent of poverty

An aspect of income distribution that is of special concern in LDCs is the extent of absolute poverty. International variations in the extent of such poverty are discussed in this section. For this purpose, it is desirable to have a uniform standard for the absolute poverty line. For the present analysis, we might take this to be a per capita income of US$150 at 1970 prices. On this basis Kakwani (1980:392–5) derived from the World Bank-I data estimates of the proportion of people below the poverty line in 30 LDCs around the year 1970. These estimates vary from 1.2 per cent in Hong Kong to 58.2 per cent in Malawi, with an average percentage of 35 in Asia, 25 in Africa, and 13 in Latin America.

An alternative set of estimates was made by Ahluwalia *et al.* (1979) for a sample of 36 LDCs accounting for 80 per cent of the population of developing countries, excluding China. They used a poverty line of $200 in ICP dollars, that is, US dollars adjusted for purchasing power parities. According to these estimates, the extent of poverty ranges from 5 per cent in Argentina, Mexico, and Yugoslavia to 60 per cent or over in Bangladesh, Burma, and Ethiopia. The extent of poverty is much influenced by the per capita income of the countries concerned, with an average of 13 per cent for high-income countries (per capita income greater than ICP $750 in 1975), 31 per cent in middle-income countries (per capita income between ICP $350 and 750), and 51 per cent in low-income countries (per capita income below ICP $350). For the sample of 36 countries, the total population in poverty was estimated at 644 million, being 38 per cent of their total populations. Of this, 510 million poor people were in the low-income LDCs.

The two main influences on the extent of poverty in a country are its per capita income and the inequality of its income distribution. Using Kakwani's data, we find the following relationship of the extent of poverty (POV) on per capita income Y in ICP dollars and G, the Gini index of inequality in the distribution of income:

$$POV = 24.54 - 0.117\,Y + 0.00005\,Y^2 + 88.44\,G$$
$$\quad\; (3.08) \quad (8.92) \quad\;\; (6.18) \qquad\;\; (6.27)$$

$$R^2 = 0.89 \tag{4.14}$$

This result shows that both the level of income and the degree of income inequality have significant effects on the extent of poverty.

From this equation we can estimate the relationship between the level of the country's average income and the degree of inequality required to keep the extent of poverty constant. Table 4.17 illustrates this trade-off, starting from a base position in which the average income is $300 and G is equal to 0.3, at which point the extent of poverty according to the above regression is 20.48 per cent.

These results may be compared with the trade-off between income level and income inequality corresponding to some of the tests proposed in the literature based on measures of social welfare. Consider two societies consisting of five members each, with respective incomes as shown in Table 4.18. Society B will be judged to be welfare superior by the generalized Lorenz curve test discussed in section 3.4.4. Note, however, that if we take the poverty line to be 10, the extent of poverty in society B is greater than in society A.

Consider next the welfare test using the Sen index (3.23) based on both the level of income and the degree of inequality. The income levels for different values of the Gini index corresponding to constant values of this

Table 4.17 Trade-offs between per capita income and income inequality

Income inequality G (1)	Income Y needed to keep poverty at base level (2)	Income Y needed to keep welfare index at base level (3)	Poverty at income levels (3) (4)
0.35	352	323	22.9
0.40	408	350	25.1
0.45	469	382	26.9
0.50	535	420	28.4

Notes: Base income ICP $300; G − 0.30; POV − 20.48%.
Source: Estimated by author.

Table 4.18 Welfare comparisons of two distributions

	Society A		Society B	
Individual	Individual income	Cumulative income	Individual income	Cumulative income
1	5	5	7	7
2	7	12	8	15
3	11	23	9	24
4	14	37	15	39
5	23	50	31	70

Source: Compiled by author.

index are shown in column (3) of Table 4.17. Then we see that the increases of income needed to maintain poverty at the same level as the degree of inequality rises are almost double those needed to keep this particular measure of welfare constant. Column (4) of the table shows the variations in the extent of poverty associated with the combinations of income level and income inequality that keep this measure of social welfare constant at the base level. In so far as the eradication of poverty is a major problem in LDCs, a weakness of such welfare criteria is that they may judge a society to have a higher social welfare than another even if it has a greater extent of poverty.

Appendix 4.1 Distribution of income among household and among individuals

As discussed in the text, the relationship between the household and the individual distributions of income depends on two factors, namely the variation of household size between income classes, and the variation of household sizes within income classes. The first factor would generally tend to make the individual distribution more equal than the household distribution. This can be seen most simply in the case of ungrouped data, using the coefficient of variation as our measure of inequality. Writing Y as household income, m as household size, and $y = Y/m$ as individual income, we have the standard result

$$\sigma^2(y) = \frac{\mu_y^2}{\mu_m^2} \left(\frac{\sigma_Y^2}{\mu_Y^2} + \frac{\sigma_m^2}{\mu_m^2} - 2\rho \frac{\sigma_Y \sigma_m}{\mu_Y \mu_m} \right) \qquad (4A.1)$$

where the μ are means, the σ are standard deviations, and ρ is the correlation coefficient between household size and household income (see, e.g., Kendall and Stuart 1963: vol. 1, p. 232). The expectation of a ratio is not the same as the ratio of expectations, but if we assume that these two quantities are approximately equal and take $E(Y)/E(m)$ as equal to $E(Y/m)$, we get

$$CV^2(y) = CV^2(Y) + CV^2(m) - 2\rho\, CV(Y)CV(m) \qquad (4A.2)$$

where CV stands for the coefficient of variation. Hence we have

$$CV^2(y) < CV^2(Y) \quad \text{if} \quad \rho > \frac{CV(m)}{2CV(Y)} \qquad (4A.3)$$

Generally, $CV(m)$ will be quite small relative to $CV(Y)$. Therefore we have the approximate result that $CV(y)$ will be less than $CV(Y)$ if ρ is positive, that is, if household size tends to increase with household income, and conversely.

This result follows even more directly if we take logarithms of incomes and household size and use the standard deviation of these logarithms as our measure of inequality. These results, however, are strictly applicable to the case of ungrouped data. The proof of the result is a bit more complex in terms of the Gini index for the case of grouped data and is therefore briefly indicated. In order to isolate the two factors involved, we shall assume that all households in any income class are of the same size, though this size varies between income classes. Then, applying the usual formulae, we have for the Gini index of the household distribution

$$G_H = 1 - \Sigma \frac{h_i}{H}(Q_i + Q_{i-1}) \qquad (4A.4)$$

where h_i is the number of households in the ith income class arranged in ascending order of income, H is the total number of households, Q_i is the cumulative share of income up to and including the ith class, and Q_0 is taken as 0.

Next we consider the individual distribution. First, we assume that household sizes do not increase faster than household incomes as we go from one income class to the next, so that the ranking of individuals will be the same as the ranking of the households to which they belong. Then we have the convenient result that the Qs for the classes of individual incomes are the same as those for the classes of household incomes. Hence the Gini index of the individual distribution is given by

$$G_1 = 1 - \Sigma \frac{h_i m_i}{H \tilde{m}} (Q_i + Q_{i-1}) \qquad (4A.5)$$

where m_i is the household size in the ith income class and $\tilde{m}$ is the average household size for the whole population given by

$$\tilde{m} = \frac{\Sigma h_i m_i}{H} \qquad (4A.6)$$

Subtracting (4A.5) from (4A.4), we have

$$G_H - G_1 = \frac{1}{H^2 \tilde{m}} \{ (\Sigma h_i)[\Sigma h_i(Q_i + Q_{i-1})] - (\Sigma h_i m_i)[\Sigma h_i(Q_i + Q_{i-1})] \}$$

$$= \frac{1}{H^2 \tilde{m}} \Sigma_{j>i} h_i h_j (m_j - m_i)[(Q_j - Q_i) + (Q_{j-1} - Q_{i-1})] \quad (4A.7)$$

From the fact that Q_i is an increasing function of i, it then follows that $G_H > G_1$ whenever $m_j > m_i$ for $j > i$, and conversely.

This completes the proof that, in the case in which there is no variation of household size within income classes, the Gini index of the household distribution will be greater than that of the individual distribution, when household size increases with household income, and conversely. To get some idea of the orders of magnitude involved, we consider the case of ten income classes in which household incomes increase in geometric progression, that is, $Y_{i+1} = Y_i(1 + r)$, and consider two cases: (A) the case in which household size increases with household income, according to $m = 2.8 + 0.2i(i = 1, 2, \ldots, 10)$, and (B) the case in which household size decreases with household income, according to $m_i = 5.2 - 0.2i$. The results are shown in Table 4A.1.

Next we consider the effect of the variability of household sizes within income classes. In order to isolate this effect from the first factor considered above, we assume that the size distribution, and hence the average household size, is the same for all household income classes. The fact that

Table 4A.1 Gini index of household and individual distribution (with household size constant within each H-decile)

r	Gini index of households	Gini index of individuals with household size	
		increasing (A)	Decreasing (B)
0.1	0.1549	0.0715	0.2343
0.2	0.2852	0.2048	0.3618
0.3	0.3897	0.3131	0.4626
0.4	0.4717	0.3991	0.5406
0.5	0.5353	0.4667	0.6006
0.6	0.5850	0.5205	0.6469
0.7	0.6242	0.5625	0.6830
0.8	0.6556	0.5968	0.7116
0.9	0.6810	0.6248	0.7346
1.0	0.7020	0.6480	0.7533
1.1	0.7194	0.6674	0.7688
1.2	0.7341	0.6839	0.7818
1.5	0.7660	0.7210	0.8105
2.0	0.8000	0.7590	0.8391
3.0	0.8333	0.7977	0.8672
4.0	0.8500	0.8173	0.8811

household size varies within a household income class means that although all households in that class have the same income, or at least incomes within a narrow range, the individuals in those households will have very different incomes depending on the sizes of the household to which they belong. Therefore for any one income class, it follows that individual incomes vary to a greater extent than household incomes. The problem is to verify that this result is also true when we consider all income classes together.

To analyse the problem, we make some simplifying assumptions. We consider the case of households divided into ten equal classes, referred to as H-deciles, such that all households in a decile have the same income. We assume also that the household income increases in geometric progression at the rate r from one H-decile to the next. We also assume that the maximum household size is 5. Then the individual incomes for households of different sizes in the various H-deciles will be as shown in Table 4A.2.

First consider the case in which $r > 4$. It follows immediately that all individual incomes in any H-decile will be higher than the individual incomes in all lower H-deciles. Hence the ranking of individuals according to their individual incomes will be identical with their ranking according to the incomes of the households to which they belong. Further, the number of individuals will be the same for all H-deciles. Hence if the individuals are also grouped into ten equal classes, to be known as P-deciles, these

105

Table 4A.2 Individual incomes by H-deciles

H-decile	Household size				
	1	2	3	4	5
1	Y	$Y/2$	$Y/3$	$Y/4$	$Y/5$
2	$Y(1 + r)$	$\dfrac{Y(1 + r)}{2}$	$\dfrac{Y(1 + r)}{3}$	$\dfrac{Y(1 + r)}{4}$	$\dfrac{Y(1 + r)}{5}$
3	$Y(1 + r)^2$	$\dfrac{Y(1 + r)^2}{2}$	$\dfrac{Y(1 + r)^2}{3}$	$\dfrac{Y(1 + r)^2}{4}$	$\dfrac{Y(1 + r)^2}{5}$
...					

P-deciles will coincide with the H-deciles and there will be no difference between the household and individual distributions. But $r > 4$ represents a very unequal distribution of income; for instance, with $r = 4$, the Gini index of the household distribution will be 0.85, much higher than any observed in practice.

Therefore we have to consider some lower values of r. Then we have the interesting result that, for the range $\sqrt{5} < 1 + r < 5$, the overlap of the P-deciles over the H-deciles follows a particularly simple pattern shown in Table 4A.3, where $a + b + c = k$, the number of households in each H-decile, taken as ten in this example.

With the simplifying assumptions made above, the household and individual Gini indices can be easily calculated by summing up the geometric series. Then we get the result that

$$G_I > G_H \text{ if } a > c(1 + r) \tag{4A.8}$$

Table 4A.3 Distribution of households into H-deciles and P-deciles

H-decile	P-decile						Total
	I	II	III		IX	X	
I	$10 - a$	a	0	...	0	0	10
II	c	b	a	...	0	0	10
III	0	c	b	...	0	0	10
IV	0	0	c	...	0	0	10
...	...	...	...		...	...	...
IX	0	0	0	...	b	a	10
X	0	0	0	...	c	$10 - c$	10

It is easy to see that this is the condition which makes the total income of the bottom P-decile less than that of the bottom H-decile, and the total income of the top P-decile greater than the total income of the top H-decile, two indications that the individual distribution is more unequal than the household distribution.

To see whether the condition (4A.8) is satisfied, we need the values of a, b, and c. These values depend on r and the common size distribution assumed for all H-deciles. The values of a and c are shown in Table 4A.4 in terms of $n_i (i = 1, 2, \ldots, 5)$ where n_i is the number of households of size i in each H-decile. It can easily be verified that the condition (4A.8) is satisfied in all these cases.

This proves that $G_I > G_H$ for values of $1 + r$ down to $\sqrt{5}$, but even these represent a very unequal distribution of income. For instance, when $1 + r = \sqrt{5}$, G is still as high as 0.74. Therefore we have to consider still lower values of r. But from now on, the case of a general size distribution becomes too complex to handle. Therefore we consider only a special distribution with $n_1 = n_5 = 1$, $n_2 = n_4 = 2$, and $n_3 = 4$. The values of G_H and G_I for various values of r are shown in Table 4A.5.

Hence we can conclude that the variability of household sizes within income classes, by itself, tends to make $G_I > G_H$. This effect therefore operates in the opposite direction to the effect of household sizes increasing with household income by itself.

These results may be illustrated by an application to the 1971 Philippines data on income distribution, shown in terms of deciles in Table 4A.6. We see that the Gini indices of the household and individual distributions are virtually the same. To explain this result, we consider the two factors distinguished above. The hypothetical distribution (A) shows what the individual distribution would have been if household size varied between classes but not within classes; its effect is to reduce G_I below G_H. The hypothetical distribution (B) shows what the individual distribution would have been if all H-deciles had the same size distribution of households, that is, the same as the national distribution actually observed. Its effect has been to raise G_I above G_H. The two factors have had opposite effects which offset each other almost exactly. The small residual that remains may be attributed to differences in the size distribution between H-deciles which has not been allowed for.

In passing, we may note an alternative approach used by Paglin (1975). He was mainly concerned with the fact that as a norm for the measurement of income inequality, household incomes should be allowed to vary with the life-cycle of the head of household. He therefore took the observed pattern of the variation of household income with age of the head of household as the norm, and measured the divergence of the actual household distribution of income from this norm by the within component of the Gini index, given by $G_B = G - G_W$ where G_B is the component of the Gini

Table 4A.4 Values of a and c

r		Condition on n_i	a	c
$3 < r < 4$	(i)	$n_1 \leqslant 5n_5$	n_1	$\dfrac{n_1}{5}$
	(ii)	$n_1 \geqslant 5n_5$	$5n_5$	n_5
$2 < r < 3$	(i)	$n_1 \leqslant 5n_5$	n_1	$\dfrac{n_1}{5}$
	(ii)	$5n_5 \leqslant n_1 \leqslant 5n_5 + 4n_4$	n_1	$\dfrac{n_1 - n_5}{4}$
	(iii)	$n_1 \geqslant 5n_5 + 4n_4$	$4n_4 + 5n_5$	$n_4 + n_5$
$1.5 < r < 2$	(i)	$n_1 \leqslant 5n_5$	n_1	$\dfrac{n_1}{5}$
	(ii)	$5n_5 \leqslant n_1 \leqslant 5n_5 + 4n_4$	n_1	$\dfrac{n_1 - n_5}{4}$
	(iii)	$5n_5 + 4n_4 \leqslant n_1 \leqslant 5n_5 + 4n_4 + 3n_3$	n_1	$\dfrac{n_1 - 2n_5 - n_4}{3}$
	(iv)	$n_1 \geqslant 5n_5 + 4n_4 + 3n_3$	$3n_3 + 4n_4 + 5n_5$	$n_3 + n_4 + n_5$
$\sqrt{5} \leqslant 1 + r \leqslant 2.5$	(i)	$n_1 + 2n_2 \leqslant 5n_5$	$n_1 + n_2$	$\dfrac{n_1 + 2n_2}{5}$
	(ii)	$5n_5 \leqslant n_1 + 2n_2 \leqslant 5n_5 + 2n_2$	$\dfrac{n_1 + 5n_5}{5}$	n_5
	(iii)	$5n_5 + 2n_2 \leqslant n_1 + 2n_2 \leqslant 5n_5 + 4n_4 + 2n_2$	n_1	$\dfrac{n_1 - n_5}{4}$
	(iv)	$5n_5 + 4n_4 \leqslant n_1 \leqslant 5n_5 + 4n_4 + 3n_3$	n_1	$\dfrac{n_1 - n_4 - 2n_5}{3}$
	(v)	$5n_5 + 4n_4 + 3n_3 \leqslant n_1$	$3n_3 + 4n_4 + 5n_5$	$n_3 + n_4 + n_5$

Table 4A.5 Gini index of household and individual distributions: The special case

r	G_H	G_I
0.2	0.2852	0.3451
0.3	0.3897	0.4337
0.4	0.4717	0.5019
0.5	0.5353	0.5598
0.6	0.5850	0.6052
0.7	0.6242	0.6430
0.8	0.6556	0.6894
0.9	0.6810	0.7127
1.0	0.7020	0.7169
1.1	0.7194	0.7328
1.2	0.7341	0.7457
1.5	0.7660	0.7707
2.0	0.8000	0.8026
3.0	0.8333	0.8343
4.0	0.8500	0.8500

Table 4A.6 Income share by deciles: Philippines, 1971

Deciles	Household (1)	Average household size (2)	Individual distributions Hypothetical A (3)	Hypothetical B (4)	Actual (5)
1	1.44	4.67	1.86	1.27	1.35
2	2.38	5.02	3.05	1.82	2.55
3	3.42	5.22	4.14	2.74	3.57
4	4.66	5.54	5.18	4.54	4.66
5	5.85	5.50	6.54	5.31	5.86
6	7.42	5.80	8.04	6.98	7.26
7	9.23	5.91	9.30	8.38	9.15
8	11.79	6.18	11.60	11.81	11.65
9	16.88	6.51	16.06	16.34	16.47
10	36.93	6.47	34.25	40.81	37.48
Gini index	0.4780	——	0.4338	0.5160	0.4779

index for income inequality between age classes. As noted earlier, G_B is not entirely satisfactory as a measure of the between component in this case of overlapping groups. But using this measure he argued that there has been a significant decline in income inequality in the United States, contrary to the popular opinion that income inequality has remained fairly stable, based on the overall Gini index.

Paglin's main justification for taking the observed variation of household incomes with age as the norm was that it corresponded to variations in household size in the course of the life-cycle of the household head. But if this is the main justification, a better measure of inequality is provided by the Gini index of the individual distribution. However, when we use this index, it can be seen from Table 4.3 that there has been little change is inequality in the United States in the postwar period.

Chapter five

Historical changes in income distribution

5.1 Historical trends in DCs

In the last chapter, we considered international differences in income distribution. We also considered ways in which such cross-section data have been used to identify factors which may have influenced income distribution. However, such cross-section analysis is subject to some serious weaknesses and is not very reliable, especially for projecting future trends in income distribution. Such analysis is useful only when it can be assumed that all countries are traversing the same dynamic path, and that individual countries are at different points on this path. If this assumption is valid, then international cross-section data can be used to identify the nature of this path and to estimate its parameters. But the underlying assumption that all countries are following the same path is a very doubtful one. The actual path followed by countries may be influenced by a wide variety of other factors based on their historical evolution and their economic institutions. Therefore we must also consider historical evidence about changes in income distribution of individual countries over time. Further, as the distribution of income changes only slowly over time, we must consider trends over fairly long-term periods.

Such data are extremely limited. Some estimates have been made for a few developed countries. Although our main concern in this book is with income distribution in LDCs, it is worth considering whether the historical experience of the DCs can throw any light on the forces influencing income distribution more generally. The estimates for DCs are very rough results, based on fragmentary data. As Kuznets (1963:12) remarked, 'It may not be an exaggeration to say that we deal here not with data on the distribution of income by size but with estimates or judgments by courageous and ingenious scholars relating to size distribution of income in the country of their concern.' He has brought together a number of such estimates, which are summarized in Table 5.1. Over the long periods spanned by these estimates, there was, as Kuznets (1966:207) pointed out, 'a perceptible narrowing in inequality in the size distribution of income if judged

Table 5.1 Historical changes in income distribution in DCs

Countries	Year	Income shares of		
		Top 5%	Top 20%	Bottom 60%
UK	1880	48	58	——
	1913	43	59	——
	1929	33	51	——
	1938	30	51	——
	1949	24	48	——
	1957	18	42	——
Prussia	1854	21	——	——
	1875	26	48	34
	1896	27	45	——
	1913	31	50	32
	1928	26	49	31
Saxony	1880	34	56	27
	1896	36	57	27
	1913	33	54	28
	1928	28	50	31
W. Germany	1913	31	50	32
	1928	21	45	34
	1936	28	53	27
	1950	24	48	29
	1955	18	43	34
	1959	18	43	34
Netherlands	1938	19	49	31
	1949	17	46	34
	1954	13	39	40
Denmark	1870	37	——	——
	1908	30	55	31
	1925	26	53	25
	1939	25	51	27
	1949	19	45	32
	1955	18	44	32
Sweden	1930	30	59	19
	1935	28	58	19
	1945	24	52	23
	1948	20	45	32
	1954	17	43	34
USA	1917–19	24		
	1919–28	25	54	26
	1929	30	54	26
	1935–36	27	52	27
	1941	24	49	29
	1944–47	21	46	32
	1950–54	21	45	33
	1955–59	20	45	32

Source: Kuznuts (1966:208–11).

by the declines in the shares of the upper ordinal groups; less marked if judged by the rise in the shares of the lower ordinal groups'. He also pointed out that 'the scanty empirical evidence suggests that the narrowing of income inequality in the developed countries is relatively recent and probably did not characterise the earlier stages of their growth' (Kuznets 1963:5).

To Kuznets (1955:262), the 'long-term constancy, let alone reduction, of inequality in the secular income structure is a puzzle'. This is because he was impressed with the strength of long-term forces operating in market economies which tended to widen inequalities. Based on this impression, he concluded that a widening of inequalities must have characterized the earlier phases of economic growth in the developed countries. This was the origin of the Kuznets's hypothesis of a phase of increasing inequality followed by a phase of declining inequality in the course of income growth. He was aware that 'no adequate empirical evidence is available for checking this conjecture of a long secular swing in income inequality; nor can the phases be dated precisely' (Kuznets 1963:18). But he went on to say, 'To make it more specific, I would place the early phase in which income inequality might have been widening, from about 1780 to 1850 in England; from about 1840 to 1890, and particularly from 1870 on in the United States; and from the 1840s to the 1890s in Germany' (Kuznets 1963:18). This conclusion is quite plausible, for although there are no quantitative historical data on the distribution of income, there is much other indirect and qualitative evidence to suggest the widening of inequality in this period, when there was a transition from the pre-industrial to the industrial civilization in these countries. This is the sort of evidence on which Marx, for example, based his thesis of the increasing misery of the masses in the process of capitalist development.

However, these changes in inequality were not simply the consequence of the growth of per capita income, and this relationship cannot be used to explain or project the distribution of income in other countries, as many later writers on the Kuznets's hypothesis have tended to do. Instead, the historical trends of income distribution in the DCs were affected by significant institutional changes. The widening inequality of the earlier phase was much influenced by the initial position derived from the feudal past of these countries. Similarly, there were important institutional changes which led to the declining inequality in the later phases. For example, Ahluwalia et al. (1979:468–9) argued that 'the low inequality observed in the developed countries today is as much the result of institutional evolution resulting from particular historical and political factors as of their level of development. . . . The most important of these developments was the strengthening of organized labor and its subsequent political role in developing a welfare state'. Bacha (1977) has gone further to argue that the observed reduction in inequality in the developed countries over the first half of this century arose from social and political changes following World War I that are not likely to be replicated in countries approaching industrial maturity today. In particular, statistical generalizations derived from the historical experience of the DCs cannot be applied to the current or future experience of LDCs without checking whether the conditions underlying that generalization would also apply in future.

5.2 Recent changes in DCs

More data are available on changes in income distribution in the DCs in recent periods, especially in the period since World War II. These data are summarized in Table 5.2. The data have been compiled from different sources. Therefore care must be taken in comparing these results because they may be based on different concepts and definitions, and may not be

Table 5.2 Recent changes in income inequality in DCs

Country	Persons		Households	
	Year	Gini index	Year	Gini index
Australia	—	—	1966–67[a]	0.30
			1975–76[a]	0.40
Canada	1965[b]	0.37	1965[c]	0.39
	1971[b]	0.40	1971[c]	0.43
	1975[b]	0.37	1975[c]	0.42
	1979[b]	0.37	1979[c]	0.41
	1982[b]	0.37	1982[c]	0.40
	1983[b]	0.37	1983[c]	0.41
Denmark	1953[d]	0.39	1976[a]	0.29
	1963[d]	0.38	1981[a]	0.33
	1953[e]	0.40		
	1963[e]	0.39		
	1966[e]	0.37		
Finland	1952[d]	0.40	1977[a]	0.29
	1962[d]	0.46	1981[a]	0.31
	1952[e]	0.41		
	1962[e]	0.47		
France	1956[d]	0.47	1956[e]	0.48
	1962[d]	0.50	1962[e]	0.52
			1970[a]	0.41
			1975[a]	0.35
West Germany	1955[d]	0.48	1968[e]	0.39
	1960[d]	0.46	1969[e]	0.33
	1964[d]	0.45	1970[e]	0.39
	1955[e]	0.52	1973[a]	0.38
	1960[e]	0.51	1974[a]	0.36
	1964[e]	0.48	1978[a]	0.30

Italy	—	—	1969[a]	0.39
			1977[a]	0.36
Japan	—	—	1962[e]	0.39
			1965[e]	0.38
			1968[e]	0.39
			1969[a]	0.31
			1979[a]	0.28
Netherlands	1952[d]	0.43	1967[a]	0.35
	1962[d]	0.43	1975[a]	0.27
	1952[e]	0.45	1977[a]	0.28
	1962[e]	0.44	1981[a]	0.27
	1967[e]	0.45		
New Zealand	1967–68[e]	0.39	1966[e]	0.31
	1968–69[e]	0.39	1981–82[a]	0.38
	1969–70[e]	0.41		
	1970–71[e]	0.37		
	1971–72[e]	0.36		
Norway	1957[d]	0.38	1970[a]	0.30
	1963[d]	0.35	1982[a]	0.31
	1957[e]	0.39		
	1963[e]	0.36		
Spain	—	—	1964–65[d]	0.39
			1974[a]	0.35
			1980–81[a]	0.32
Sweden	1954[d]	0.36	1972[a]	0.30
	1964[d]	0.40	1979[a]	0.30
	1954[e]	0.37	1981[a]	0.32
	1964[e]	0.41		
	1967[e]	0.39		
UK	1954[d]	0.39	1960[e]	0.35
	1964[d]	0.39	1968[e]	0.34
	1954[e]	0.41	1973[a]	0.31
	1964[e]	0.40	1979[a]	0.32
	1967[e]	0.36		
USA	1957[f]	0.39	1947–51[h]	0.37 (0.30)
	1975[f]	0.40	1952–56[h]	0.37 (0.28)
	1967[g]	0.41	1957–61[h]	0.36 (0.27)
	1985[g]	0.41	1962–66[h]	0.36 (0.23)
			1967–72[h]	0.35 (0.24)
			1967–72[i]	0.37
			1973–78[i]	0.37
			1979–84[i]	0.38

Sources: (a) World Bank, *World Development Reports*, various issues.
(b, c) M. Wolfson (1986), 'Stasis Amid Change – Income Inequality in Canada, 1965–83', *Review Income and Wealth* 32 (4):337–76.
(d) UN, *Incomes in Post-war Europe* (1967), Chap. 6, p. 15.
(e) S. Jain, *Size Distribution of Income* (World Bank, 1975).
(f, g, i) US, *Current Population Reports, Series 60* (various issues); (f) refers to persons in families; (g) refers to persons in households; (i) refers to income at 1984 constant dollars.
(h) M. Paglin (1975), 'The Measurement and Trend of Inequality', *American Economic Review* 65 (4):598–609; figures in parentheses refer to Paglin's Gini indices adjusted for changes in age distribution.

strictly comparable. In particular, as pointed out in the last chapter, there is no systematic relationship between measures of inequality derived from the distribution of income among individual persons, and among families or households. Therefore these two types of measures have been reported separately.

At least until the early 1970s, this was a period in which the DCs enjoyed a long period of rapid economic growth. The average per capita income (in terms of ICP dollars as estimated in Summers and Heston 1984) of the countries included in the table increased two and a half times between 1950 and 1980. But in spite of this rapid increase in per capita income, there does not seem to be any definite trend one way or the other in the inequality of income distribution of these countries during this period. A few countries showed a decline in inequality, a few others showed an increase, but there was no significant change in most of the countries. This is yet another indication that there is no systematic relationship between the level of income and the inequality of income distribution.

The changes in income inequality during this period have been studied in more detail in two developed countries. In the case of Canada, Wolfson (1986:337, 369) concluded:

> The conventional wisdom in Canada is that income inequality has not changed at all since the Second World War. When data are used to support this contention, it is frequently observed that the share of income going to the bottom 20 per cent of the population (the bottom quintile) is about 4 per cent while the amount received by the top quintile is about 40 per cent, and neither figure has changed significantly over time. This apparent stability in the distribution of income is surprising in view of the major economic and social changes that have occurred. . . . Given the overall stability in income inequality, it might be (simplistically) concluded that the equalizing tendencies of macroeconomic factors, high interest rates and stagnant growth, have just offset the disequalizing social factors of 'baby boomers' leaving home, lower fertility, higher divorce and separation rates, and higher female labour force participation.

In the case of the United States, Paglin (1975:603–4) was also concerned with 'the widely accepted conclusion that there has been no significant reduction of inequality from 1947 to 1972 despite the massive spending on education and training programs, the more generous cash and merit good transfers, and the legislative and judicial actions directed at bringing minorities and underprivileged groups into the mainstream of the economy'. Table 5.2 shows that the inequality of household incomes has also remained stable from 1967 to 1984. However, Paglin went on to argue that 'a very substantial part of the traditional area of inequality (one-third to one-half) is simply a function of the diversity in the ages and size of families, and the lifetime income pattern typical of a technically advanced society'. He therefore calculated a new index of inequality, described as the Paglin–Gini index, simply by subtracting the concentration ratio of family incomes with respect to age of head of household. He then concluded that 'in contrast to the traditional view, inequality has declined 23 per cent in the 25-year period, 1947–72' (Paglin 1975:605).

However, as a number of comments on the Paglin paper published in the *American Economic Review* of 1977 pointed out, the allowance he made for the age factor in deriving his adjusted measure of income inequality was not correct because of the overlap of incomes between age classes. In subtracting the inequality of incomes at different ages to estimate what he thought was a better index of income inequality, Paglin's main argument was that household sizes varied sytematically with age of head of household. But if this is the main reason for his adjustment, a much simpler way to allow for such changes in household size is to calculate the index of inequality for individuals rather than for families or households. When this is done for a few years at long intervals, again we find from Table 5.2 that there has been no significant change in inequality in the United States.

Thus the recent experience of DCs shows that income inequality is not really a function of per capita income. Instead, it changes only slowly over time, under the influence of various institutional factors which may act in one direction or the other.

5.3 Recent changes in LDCs

Statistical data on historical trends in inequality are even more limited in the LDCs, to the point of being non-existent. Currently a considerable amount of historical research is going on in attempts to date the emergence of mass poverty in these countries, but no reliable conclusions have emerged so far. Therefore we can only study changes in income distribution in the LDCs for a more recent period, especially since World War II, when a considerable amount of data began to be collected. But even for this period, data about changes in income distribution covering fairly long periods of time are available only for a few countries. Some of the available data are summarized in Table 5.3.

In the last chapter, we argued that it is risky to draw any strong conclusions comparing income distributions in different countries because of significant differences in concepts, definitions, and methods of collecting data in these countries. It might be thought that such dangers will be minimized when comparing data on income distribution collected in the same country in different years. However, this is not always the case. For example, discussing the three surveys carried out in Malaysia, Anand (1983:42) argued that

Table 5.3 Recent changes in income inequality: LDCs

Country	Year	Units	Gini index
(A) Rising inequality			
Argentina	1953	H	0.413[a]
	1961	H	0.435[a]
	1970	H	0.435[f]
Bangladesh	1963–64	H	0.33[a]
	1973–74	H	0.379[b]
	1976–77	H	0.383[f]
	1978–79	H	0.334[b]
	1981–82	H	0.369[f]
Brazil	1960	IR	0.590[c]
	1970	IR	0.647[c]
Colombia	1962	IR	0.525[c]
	1964	IR	0.597[c]
	1970	IR	0.562[c]
Mexico	1963	H	0.527[d]
	1968	H	0.522[d]
	1975	H	0.557[d]
	1977	H	0.496[d]
Philippines	1956	H	0.48[e]
	1961	H	0.50[e]
	1965	H	0.51[e]
	1971	H	0.49[e]
	1985	H	0.45[f]
Thailand	1962–63	H	0.414[g]
	1968–69	H	0.429[g]
	1975–76	H	0.439[h]
	1981	H	0.446[h]
(B) Mixed trends			
India	1953–57	H	0.343[c]
	1960	H	0.473[c]
	1964–65	H	0.421[c]
	1967–68	H	0.478[c]
	1975–76	H	0.402[f]
Indonesia	1970	P(exp)	0.327[j]
	1976	P(exp)	0.368[j]
	1980	P(exp)	0.344[j]
	1981	P(exp)	0.332[j]
	1984	P(exp)	0.333[j]
Malaysia	1957–58	H	0.371[k]
	1967–68	H	0.562[k]
	1970	H	0.513[k]
South Korea	1966	H	0.342[c]
	1968	H	0.305[c]
	1969	H	0.298[c]
	1970	H	0.372[c]
	1971	H	0.360[c]
	1976	H	0.371[f]
	1980	H	0.389[n]
	1982	H	0.357[n]

Sri Lanka	1953	H(IR)	0.457 (0.489)[m]
	1963	H(IR)	0.443 (0.489)[m]
	1969–70	H	0.340[f]
	1973	H(IR)	0.343 (0.400)[m]
	1978–79	H(IR)	0.419 (0.482)[m]
	1981–82	H(IR)	0.437 (0.500)

(C) Declining inequality

Costa Rica	1961	H	0.521[a,c]
	1971	H	0.445[a,c]
Pakistan	1963–64	H	0.387[c]
	1966–67	H	0.355[c]
	1968–69	H	0.336[c]
	1969–70	H	0.336[c]
	1970–71	H	0.330[c]
Peru	1961	EAP	0.612[c]
	1970–71	EAP	0.594[c]
	1972	H	0.561[f]
Taiwan	1953	H	0.56[n]
	1959–60	H	0.44[n]
	1964	H	0.360[p]
	1966	H	0.358[p]
	1968	H	0.362[p]
	1970	H	0.321[p]
	1972	H	0.318[p]
	1974	H	0.319[p]
	1976	H	0.307[p]
	1978	H	0.306[p]
	1980	H	0.303[p]
	1982	H	0.308[p]
	1984	H	0.312[p]
	1985	H	0.317[p]

Notes: H — household; IR — income recipients; EAP — economically active population; P(exp) refers to distributions of per capita consumption expenditures of persons.

Sources: a. G.S. Fields (1980), *Poverty, Inequality and Development* (Cambridge, CUP), pp. 88–93.
   b. Bangladesh Bureau of Statistics (1984), *Bangladesh Statistical Yearbook.*
   c. S. Jain (1975), *Size Distribution of Income* (World Bank).
   d. J. Bergsman (1980), *Income Distribution and Poverty in Mexico* (World Bank Staff Working Paper no. 395), p. 15.
   e. A. Berry (1978), 'Income and Consumption Trends in the Philippines, 1959–70', *Review Income and Wealth* 24 (3):313–31.
   f. *World Development Report,* various issues (World Bank).
   g. P. Chanthaworn, 'The Decomposition Analysis of the Sources of Income Inequality in Thailand, 1962/3 and 1968/9', cited in Medhi Krongkaew (1987), *The Current State of Poverty and Income Distribution in Thailand* (paper presented at Thai Conference at Australian National University, 1987).
   h. S. Jitsuchon (1987), 'Sources and Trends of Income Inequality: Thailand, 1975/6 and 1981), cited in Medhi Krongkaew (1987).
   j. Biro Pusat Statistik (various issues), *Socio-Economic Surveys of Indonesia* (SUSENAS).
   k. S. Anand (1983), *Inequality and Poverty in Malaysia* (Oxford, OUP).
   m. Central Bank of Ceylon (1984), *Report on Consumer Finances and Socio-Economic Survey, 1981/2.*
   n. W. Kuo (1975), 'Income Distribution by Size in Taiwan', in *Income Distribution, Employment and Economic Developments in Southeast Asia* (Tokyo, JERC and CAMS).
   p. Republic of China (1987), *Taiwan Statistical Yearbook.*

these differences are not indicative of actual changes in inequality over time, and might be wholly due to differences in income concept and coverage. More fundamentally, I show that the three surveys are not comparable with each other, and that *no* conclusion can be drawn from them about change in inequality.

The problem may not be so serious in other cases in which the same system of data collection has been used regularly.

Subject to this caution, we find that of the 16 countries covered by Table 5.3, inequality rose in seven countries, fell in four, and the trend was mixed in the remainder. The sample is too small to support any elaborate statistical analysis. Classifying the countries in the sample according to these trends in inequality and their rates of growth of GDP in the decade 1970–81, we get the picture shown in Table 5.4. This suggests that there is no perceptible relationship between trends in income inequality and rates of growth of GDP. In particular, we see that among the countries with a high rate of growth, there are some in which income inequality has risen and some in which it has fallen significantly.

The countries can also be cross-classified by the average level and trends in income inequality. The result of such cross-classification is shown in Table 5.5. Again we see a rather mixed picture. All trends of income inequality, rising and falling, are found in countries with low or medium levels of inequality. All the countries in the sample with high inequality, however, have experienced further increases of inequality.

Of special interest are the newly industrializing countries (NICs) of Asia which have experienced high rates of growth of GDP as well as falling degrees of inequality. One factor which explains both the rapid growth and the falling inequality trend is the rapid expansion of their education. The

Table 5.4 Classification of LDCs by trends in income inequality and rates of GDP growth

	Trends in income inequality		
Rate of growth of GDP	Rising	Mixed	Falling
Low	Bangladesh	India Sri Lanka	
Medium	Argentina Philippines	Malaysia Indonesia	Costa Rica Pakistan
High	Brazil Columbia Mexico Thailand	S. Korea	Peru Taiwan

Sources: World Bank (1984) *World Tables*; World Bank (1987) *World Development Report, 1987.*

Table 5.5 Classification of LDCs by levels and trends in income inequality

Level of income inequality	Trends in income inequality		
	Rising	Mixed	Falling
Low	Bangladesh Thailand	India S. Korea Sri Lanka	Pakistan Peru Taiwan
Medium	Argentina Philippines	Indonesia Malaysia	Costa Rica
High	Brazil Columbia Mexico		

Sources: World Bank (1984) *World Tables*; World Bank (1987) *World Development Report, 1987.*

changes in the postwar period for these countries are summarized in Table 5.6. The table shows the steady rise in the mean years of schooling of the labour force. It also shows the decline in the inequality of educational attainments shown by the index $G(E)$. This decline in educational inequality associated with the rising average level of education has been an important factor in the decline of income inequality in these countries.

5.4 Changes in inequality of components of consumption

The data considered in the last section referred mostly to the distribution of incomes. The LDCs have more often collected data for a number of years on the distribution of consumption and some of its major components. These data are considered in the present section. As discussed in Chapter two, the data on the distribution of consumption are generally more reliable than those on the distribution of incomes. Where incomes differ from consumption expenditures, the difference lies mainly in the amount of savings. In most LDCs the bulk of these savings are made by the top income groups. Therefore for most of the population, consumption expenditures are a good proxy for incomes.

As the upper-income groups generally save a larger proportion of their incomes, the inequality of incomes will be greater than that of consumption expenditures. The magnitude of these differences is shown in Table 5.7 for some countries where data are available both on the distribution of incomes by income classes and the distribution of consumption expenditures by expenditure classes.

The difference between the Gini index of incomes and of consumption expenditures is very small in Bangladesh. This is partly because of the low rate of savings in that country, but it may also be because incomes were

121

Table 5.6 Distribution of labour force by educational qualification

Country/Year	Percentage of labour force with educational qualification							Mean years of schooling	G(E)
	None	Below primary	Primary	Below secondary	Secondary	Tertiary	Total		
Hong Kong									
1961	20.2	6.4	46.3	13.6	9.4	4.3	100.0	5.96	0.36
1971	16.2	5.5	46.1	12.2	15.2	4.9	100.0	6.58	0.33
1976	13.9	—	45.4	15.8	19.1	5.8	100.0	7.31	0.30
1980	10.4	—	38.1	16.9	24.5	9.4	100.0	8.21	0.27
S. Korea									
1960	44.7	—	39.5	7.3	6.2	2.4	100.0	4.13	0.31
1970	23.8	—	43.6	26.4		6.1	100.0	6.31	0.37
1980	16.0	—	35.5	20.1	21.8	6.7	100.0	7.55	0.31
Singapore									
1966	54.1	—	29.2	13.3		3.4	100.0	3.59	0.62
1972	20.6	—	36.9	36.2	4.4	2.0	100.0	6.29	0.62
1977	13.8	—	35.2	40.5	7.7	2.7	100.0	7.09	0.26
1980[a]	22.5	—	50.0	16.2	7.7	3.6	100.0	5.92	0.35
Taiwan									
1965	26.0	—	54.3	9.0	7.5	3.1	100.0	5.44	0.37
1970	26.0	—	52.7	12.1	10.5	3.9	100.0	6.10	0.34
1975	15.9	—	47.9	15.4	14.7	6.1	100.0	6.94	0.31
1980	9.0	—	39.6	19.8	20.8	10.9	100.0	8.87	0.26

Note: [a]The 1980 data for Singapore are from the Population Census, and give higher proportion of workers in the lower educational categories than the data for earlier years taken from the Household Surveys.

Source: Fields (1985), Table 8.9, pp. 350–1.

Table 5.7 Gini index of distribution of income (*Y*) and of consumption expenditures (*E*)

Country (Year)	Gini index of Y	Gini index of E	Concentration index of E
Bangladesh (1978–79)			
National	0.359	0.343	0.331
Urban	0.365	0.364	0.350
Rural	0.354	0.335	0.325
Philippines (1971)			
National	0.490	0.404	0.324
Urban	0.453	0.378	0.315
Rural	0.458	0.356	0.254
Sri Lanka (1981–82)	0.451	0.371	0.316

Sources: Bangladesh: Bangladesh Bureau of Statistics (1984) *Bangladesh Statistical Yearbook*.
Philippines: Bureau of Census and Statistics (1973) *Family Income and Expenditure, 1971*.
Sri Lanka: Central Bank of Ceylon (1984) *Report on Consumer Finances and Socio-Economic Survey, 1981–82*.

reported by households on the basis of their consumption expenditures. The differences are much greater in the Philippines and Sri Lanka. In the case of the Philippines, this may be partly due to a considerable underestimation of incomes compared with consumption expenditures, as noted in section 2.3.

The Gini index of the inequality of consumption expenditures can be calculated when the data on the distribution of these expenditures are given for groups of the population classified according to their consumption expenditures. However, in some cases the data on consumption expenditures are only available for groups classified according to their incomes. In these cases the inequality is measured by the concentration ratio of consumption expenditures with respect to income classes. The values of this index are shown in the last column of Table 5.7. The difference between these concentration ratios and the corresponding Gini indices is quite small in Bangladesh, but much greater in Sri Lanka and the Philippines.

In many cases data are available on expenditures of different components of consumption. Then we can calculate measures of inequality of these components, such as the concentration ratios of expenditures on these components with respect to total consumption expeditures. Some illustrative values of these concentration ratios are shown in Table 5.8.

The inequality of expenditures on any commodity is related to the income elasticity of demand for that commodity. For example, if the income elasticity of demand for a commodity is low, the expenditure on

Table 5.8 Inequalities of components of consumption

	Concentration ratio with respect to income of expenditures on:					
Country/Year	Total	Food	Basic food	Other food	Non-food	Clothing
Bangladesh (1978–79)						
National	0.331	0.321	——	——	0.362	0.364
Urban	0.350	0.313	——	——	0.422	0.389
Rural	0.325	0.321	——	——	0.337	0.353
Philippines (1971)						
National	0.324	0.239	0.120	0.153	0.422	0.370
Urban	0.315	0.226	0.116	0.273	0.393	0.343
Rural	0.254	0.201	0.120	0.258	0.330	0.320
Sri Lanka (1981–82)	0.316	0.207	0.156	0.233	0.465	0.417

Sources: As for Table 5.7.

that commodity by different income groups will differ to a smaller extent than their incomes or total expenditures. The relationship is quite simple in the case of the linear expenditure demand system; in this case Kakwani (1980:187) has shown that

$$\eta_i = \frac{G_i}{G} \qquad (5.1)$$

where G is the Gini index of total expenditure, G_i that of the expenditure on the ith commodity, and η_i is the expenditure elasticity of that commodity at the mean expenditure level.

The measures of inequality of various components of consumption can therefore be used to study how income elasticities of demand for various commodities vary with income level. As pointed out by Cornwall (1977:101) and Pasinetti (1981:71–5), the income elasticities of commodities generally decline with rising incomes. Each commodity goes through different stages. Its consumption starts at a certain income level, when it behaves like a 'luxury' with a high income-elasticity; then it becomes a 'necessity' with a low income-elasticity, and finally reaches a 'satiation' point when income elasticity is zero. Different commodities pass through these stages at different income levels and can therefore be arranged in a hierarchical pattern according to these income levels. Basic foods are the lowest in this hierarchy, meaning that they go through these stages and reach a satiation level at a lower level of income than other commodities. Then we have other foods, and after that manufactures and various types of services in that sequence. Among the non-food items, clothing tends to have a lower position in the hierarchy than other commodities.

Some indication of these patterns is given by fairly long time series of concentration ratios of expenditure on various commodity groups, which are available from some countries. The longest time series is that produced by the National Sample Surveys of India. The concentration ratios from these data are summarized in Table 5.9. There has been a slight decline in the overall inequality of consumption expenditures in both urban and rural areas, but the most striking feature of Table 5.9 is the sharp decline in the inequality of basic foods consumption, especially in urban areas. This is partly due to the increased availability of basic foods in the country, which enabled the lower-income groups to approach the consumption level of the upper-income groups. It is also partly due to a steady rise in the expenditure on food as a proportion of total expenditure, as shown in Table 5.10.

Another striking feature of the data summarized in Table 5.9 is the steady rise in the inequality of expenditures on clothing in India, both in rural and in urban areas. This is probably related to the slow growth in the availability of clothing during this period. In fact, it has been estimated that the per capita availability of clothing has remained stable and even declined to some extent during the postwar period (Sundrum 1987:156).

The position in India may be compared with that in Indonesia, another country at a similar stage of development. The data on concentration ratios of various categories of consumption expenditures are summarized in Table 5.11. Again we find that while there has been a slight decline in the

Table 5.9 Changes in inequalities of consumption by major categories: India (average of annual estimates)

| Period | Concentration ratios with respect to total expenditures of: | | | | | |
	Total consumption	Food	Basic food	Other food	Non-food	Clothing
(A) Urban areas						
1951–54	0.376	0.278	0.115	0.397	0.494	0.399
1954–58	0.377	0.278	0.113	0.389	0.514	0.542
1958–64	0.354	0.263	0.097	0.368	0.494	0.551
1964–68	0.339	0.235	0.082	0.374	0.471	0.579
1968–78	0.331	0.253	0.181	0.355	0.367	0.556[a]
(B) Rural areas						
1951–54	0.338	0.277	0.199	0.397	0.453	0.337
1954–58	0.338	0.252	0.184	0.385	0.488	0.532
1958–64	0.315	0.243	0.165	0.357	0.481	0.540
1964–68	0.293	0.234	0.179	0.345	0.432	0.570
1968–78	0.299	0.235	0.146	0.351	0.460	0.572[a]

Note: [a]Average of 1968–74.
Source: Sundrum (1987:146, 150, 155).

Table 5.10 Percentage of consumption expenditure spent on food: India
(average of annual proportions)

Period	Expenditure on food		Expenditure on foodgrain	
	Urban	Rural	Urban	Rural
1951–55	54.9	65.4	22.6	39.2
1955–61	59.9	68.6	24.0	41.1
1961–67	57.2	69.0	23.7	43.4
1967–74	66.1	74.8	25.3	43.7

Source: Sundrum (1987:151–2).

Table 5.11 Changes in inequalities of consumption by major categories:
Indonesia

Year	Concentration ratios of per capita expenditures in:					
	Total	Food	Cereals	Other foods	Non-food	Clothing
(A) Urban areas						
1969	0.333	0.306	0.136	0.399	0.400	0.364
1970	0.329	0.301	0.151	0.389	0.400	0.378
1976	0.346	0.278	0.293	0.363	0.464	0.353
1980	0.355	0.274	0.080	0.349	0.476	0.357
1981	0.335	0.222	0.071	0.278	0.462	0.363
1984	0.324	0.244	0.067	0.298	0.418	0.287
(B) Rural areas						
1969	0.330	0.316	0.203	0.415	0.383	0.368
1970	0.345	0.336	0.225	0.430	0.382	0.398
1976	0.310	0.280	0.172	0.377	0.413	0.389
1980	0.309	0.278	0.155	0.362	0.398	0.350
1981	0.290	0.223	0.113	0.294	0.419	0.368
1984	0.283	0.252	0.130	0.323	0.349	0.283

Source: Biro Pusat Statistik (various issues) SUSENAS.

inequality of total consumption, there have been much larger changes in
the inequality of particular types of consumption. Thus we see that the
inequality in the food consumption has been lower than that of non-food
consumption and has also declined over time, while that of non-food
consumption has tended to rise. The decline of inequality has been particularly marked in the case of basic foods such as cereals. In one respect,
however, the Indonesian experience has been different from that of India,
namely in that the inequality of clothing expenditures has also declined in

Indonesia, whereas it had increased in India. This may be attributed to the fact that there was a substantial increase in clothing availability in Indonesia during the period covered by Table 5.11, whereas it had remained almost constant in India in the postwar period.

Chapter six

Dynamics of income distribution

6.1 A model of socioeconomic mobility

So far we have been considering the distribution of income at a point of time, and how it is influenced by various other aspects of the economy. This has been the main thrust of most statistical analyses of the subject. One problem with this approach is that while the pattern of income distribution as a whole changes very slowly over time, the factors usually assumed to influence it, such as per capita income, change more rapidly. By contrast, the incomes of individual units of the population change more rapidly, even when the distribution of income as a whole remains fairly stable. These changes in individual incomes are explained in the literature by a different set of arguments, based, for example, on the factors of production owned by these individuals and the prices they receive for them. Therefore we need a theory to explain how a stable or slowly changing pattern of income distribution as a whole may be derived from the more rapidly changing fortunes of individual members of society. Some aspects of such a more general theory are discussed in Part II of this book on the analytical framework. But in this chapter we discuss a contribution to such a theory based on some statistical models that have been developed in the study of socioeconomic mobility.

The idea underlying these models is that the income, or other socioeconomic characteristics, of individuals at one point of time is one of the most powerful factors influencing their incomes in the next, and hence later points of time. This influence then leads to some important dynamic relationships governing the distribution of income over time. Such relationships are considered in this chapter. For the empirical study of such relationships we need data not only on the distribution of income at different dates, but also data on how the incomes of particular individuals and households have varied over time. Unfortunately, such longitudinal observations of individual incomes are extremely scarce in LDCs. Therefore much of the present chapter will be devoted to a theoretical discussion of the dynamic relationships of income distribution.

Such theoretical models have been extensively studied in the context of social mobility. The study of such mobility is of interest for various reasons; Atkinson (1981) has classified them under three headings. First, greater mobility may be desired for its own sake. Second, greater mobility may be desirable as instrumental in leading to greater economic efficiency; for example, the more freely individuals can move from one occupation or industry to another, the more successful society will be in adjusting its production to changing conditions of technology or market opportunities. Thus one reason that the DCs have enjoyed higher rates of economic growth on a sustained basis may be due to their greater social mobility; these economies are said to be more flexible (Cornwall 1977:20–2). In contrast, most LDCs tend to have less mobility because the economic relations between individuals depend so much on their personal characteristics, such as their social status, which in turn depend greatly on the accident of birth, and therefore does not change in the course of their lives. Therefore LDCs are slower in adjusting to changing external conditions. But we shall be more concerned with the third consideration, in which greater mobility is desired as instrumental in improving the conditions of income distribution. It is for this purpose that we consider how the methods evolved for the study of social mobility can be used for studying the dynamics of income distribution in this chapter.

We start with a simple way of describing social mobility, that is, the extent to which individuals move in and out of a certain number, k, of classes. Let $n_t(r,s)$ be the number of units in the class r at time t who move into class s at time $t+1$. Also let

$$N_t(r) = \sum_{s}^{k} n_t(r,s) \tag{6.1}$$

be the total number of units in the class r at time t. Then the ratio

$$p_t(r,s) = \frac{n_t(r,s)}{N_t(r)} \tag{6.2}$$

can be interpreted as the probability of a unit moving from class r to class s during the tth time interval. Obviously,

$$\sum_{s}^{k} p_t(r,s) = 1 \tag{6.3}$$

Now arrange the quantities $p(r,s)$ in a square matrix P_t with $p_t(r,s)$ as the element in the rth row and sth column. Then the matrix P_t is a very convenient way of describing the mobility between classes in a given period. It can be used to show how the distribution of individuals among these classes changes from time to time. If N_t is the row vector of elements $N_t(r)$, then we have the simple relation

$$N_{t+1} = N_t P_t \tag{6.4}$$

between the distribution at two consecutive points of time, derived directly from the definition of the quantities $p(r,s)$.

When the classes into which we group individuals are defined according to some basic characteristics, and society is going through a fairly stable phase regarding these characteristics, the probabilities of transition between these classes will also be fairly constant over time. The first step in building up a statistical model is to assume that these ratios are constant over time; then they are known as transitional probabilities. This is an important step of the argument, for it involves the idea that the probabilities of people moving from one class into another at time t depend only on their class at time $t-1$ and not on other factors, such as their class in periods before $t-1$. On this assumption, the matrix P_t can be written without a time suffix. When this assumption is satisfied, the process is known as a Markov chain, whose movement is governed by the matrix P and the initial situation.

Sometimes it may be desired to summarize the matrix P by a single measure of mobility so that we can describe one society as being more mobile than another. The basic idea in the measurement of mobility is that the larger the diagonal elements, the greater the tendency for individuals to remain in the same class. Therefore a society may be said to be more mobile, the smaller the elements in the diagonal line, and the larger the elements off the diagonal. But we may also incorporate other considerations. For example, we may give more weight to a move across many classes than to one across fewer classes. A number of such measures have been suggested in the literature (see, e.g. Bartholomew 1982).

But from some points of view, our interest may not be in movement as such. We may be more interested in how far a person's ability to improve her lot, that is, to move to a 'higher' class, depends on the class of her origin. This aspect of mobility is sometimes described as 'generation dependence' to distinguish it from mere movement. Thus one of the goals of society has long been defined in terms of equality of opportunity. This is measured, for example, by the extent to which the probability of reaching some of the highest classes in society, shown by the terms in the columns at or near the right side of the matrix P, is the same for all initial classes. The ideal would then be the case where all the terms in each column are equal. A society with such a matrix of transitional probabilities has been described as the 'perfectly mobile' society (Prais 1955).

Using the matrix P of transitional probabilities to describe the movement of people between classes over time, equation (6.4) shows how the distribution of the population in various classes at one time may be derived from the distribution in the previous period. Applying this result repeatedly, the distribution at any time may be derived from the initial distribution at time $t = 0$.

The method is illustrated by considering some numerical examples. For example, suppose the transition matrix has the following form:

$$P = \begin{bmatrix} 0.60 & 0.30 & 0.10 \\ 0.20 & 0.70 & 0.10 \\ 0.05 & 0.15 & 0.80 \end{bmatrix}$$

This represents the case in which 60 per cent of the people in the first group remain in the same group in the next period, while 30 per cent move to the second group and 10 per cent to the third group; and so on. Given such probabilities of movement from group to group, we can calculate the expected number of persons in the various groups starting from any given initial distribution. Two examples of such change are worked out in Table 6.1. This table shows the interesting result that although we start with two different initial situations, the distributions steadily converge to the same pattern in the long run. This is an example of an important result of matrix theory that, if the matrix P remains constant and obeys certain conditions, then the influence of the initial distribution becomes less and less, and the influence of the matrix P becomes more and more dominant, so that in the limit the vector N describing the distribution of the population depends

Table 6.1 Changing distribution of the population over time

Time	Case A			Case B		
	1	2	3	1	2	3
0	50	35	15	30	50	20
1	38	42	20	29	47	24
2	32	44	24	28	45	27
3	29	44	27	27	44	29
4	28	43	29	27	43	30
5	27	43	30	26	43	31
6	26	43	31	26	42	32
7	26	42	32	26	42	32
8	26	42	32	26	42	32
9	26	42	32	25	42	33
10	25	42	33	25	42	33
∞	25	42	33	25	42	33

only on the matrix P. (In the language of matrix theory, N is said to be the eigenvector corresponding to the largest eigenvalue of the matrix P; for the matrices considered above, it can be shown that this largest eigenvalue will be unity.) This limiting vector, showing the distribution into the various classes, is usually referred to as the equilibrium distribution corresponding to the transition matrix P, but it is an equlibrium only in a macroscopic sense, that is, in the sense of a stable distribution of income as a whole, rather than the probabilities for any particular individual to be in the various income classes (Feller 1968:395).

The condition required for the existence of such an equilibrium distribution is that the matrix P should be irreducible, that is, it cannot be partitioned into smaller matrices along the diagonal such that all elements outside these smaller matrices are zero. For example, a matrix of transition probabilities will be irreducible in this sense if there is some finite probability that a person can move from any class to any other. When the matrix is reducible, it means that there are some classes from which a person cannot move to certain other classes directly or indirectly. Whether the matrix P is reducible or not is therefore an important question, depending on the basic economic and social institutions of a country. If these institutions are such that some people, say in the lower class, have little chance of improving their position, then the matrix P will be reducible; this means that these people will be locked into the small set of classes in which they find themselves initially.

When the matrix is irreducible, the Markov chain process is said to be ergodic. Then there will be an equilibrium distribution associated with it. The derivation of the equilibrium distribution requires a great deal of computation when the number of classes is large, but it can be derived very easily in the case of three classes. Then, writing p_{ij} for the transition probability from the ith to the jth class, and a, b, and c for the proportions in the three classes in the equilibrium distribution, we have

$$\frac{a}{c} = \frac{P_{21}P_{32} + P_{31}(1 - P_{22})}{(1 - P_{11})(1 - P_{22}) - P_{12}P_{21}} \tag{6.5}$$

$$\frac{b}{c} = \frac{P_{12}P_{31} + P_{32}(1 - P_{11})}{(1 - P_{11})(1 - P_{22}) - P_{12}P_{21}} \tag{6.6}$$

The above model is extremely versatile and can be applied to many different cases. For example, it is a standard model used in demography to study changes in the age distribution of a population. In that subject it is used to derive the stable age distribution of a population, which is subject to the same conditions of fertility and mortality over long periods of time. In fact, on the basis of this theory the elements of the transition matrix indicating the conditions of fertility and mortality are sometimes derived from the age distribution of populations, which have been observed to be fairly stable over time. But here we are interested in the application to the distribution of income. Some results about the distribution of income and its changes over time are discussed in the following sections, dealing with mobility between income classes in section 6.2 and between socioeconomic classes in section 6.3.

6.2 Mobility between income classes

We first consider the case in which the population is divided into groups classified according to their incomes. The matrix P now indicates the rates at which people in different income classes move to other classes in a given period. For this application, we make the simplifying assumption that the total number of units receiving income is constant over time, that is, that each unit goes on receiving incomes until he retires or dies, when he is followed by a single heir. This means that the matrix P will have the property that all elements in any row will add up to unity. Corresponding to any such matrix P will be an equilibrium distribution of income. Such an equlibrium distribution N must satisfy the equation

$$N = NP \qquad (6.7)$$

As stated above, the equilibrium distribution can be derived from the transition matrix, that is, as the eigenvector corresponding to the largest eigenvalue of the matrix, which will be unity. But this is usually a complex task in the general case. Therefore we consider some simple cases in which the equilibrium distribution can be derived by solving the equation (6.7) directly.

Case (i)

For our first example we consider a model advanced by Champernowne (1953) in which income classes are defined in such a way that the class sizes increase in geometric progression. It is then assumed that a person in a certain income class may remain in the same class in the next period, move one step upward, or move down at most to s classes, and that the probabilities of all these moves are independent of the initial class. Then the matrix of transitional probabilities consist of p_0 along the principal diagonal, p_1 along the diagonal line just above the principal diagonal, and p_{-i} for the ith diagonal line below the principal diagonal, as shown in Figure 6.1 (for the case $s = 2$).

These probabilities are subject to a further restriction

$$\begin{bmatrix} p_0 & p_1 & 0 & 0 & 0 \\ p_{-1} & p_0 & p_1 & 0 & 0 \\ p_{-2} & p_{-1} & p_0 & p_1 & 0 \\ 0 & p_{-2} & p_{-1} & p_0 & p_1 \\ 0 & 0 & p_{-2} & p_{-1} & p_0 \end{bmatrix}$$

Figure 6.1

$$\sum_{u=-s}^{1} u p_u < 0 \tag{6.8}$$

This condition implies that, while some individuals may move upward, the average movement of all individuals in each class is downward; this condition is necessary to avoid an explosive rise of incomes in the long period. To find the equilibrium distribution, we try the solution

$$N(r) = cb^r \tag{6.9}$$

For this solution, b must satisfy the equation

$$\sum_{-s}^{1} p_u b^{1-u} - b = 0 \tag{6.10}$$

One root of this equation is clearly $b = 1$, for which the equilibrium distribution has the trivial solution of the same frequency for all classes. The equation will have another real positive root $0 < b < 1$. The equilibrium distribution corresponding to this root then becomes the Pareto distribution discussed in section 3.2.

Case (ii)

For the second example, we consider the case in which the movement of individuals is restricted to not more than one step up or down, but the probabilities of the permitted movements differ from class to class. This is the case considered by Johnson (1973:211; see also Feller 1968:396, 402). This model can therefore be described by three probabilities for each class, say the rth, as follows: $p_{r,\,r}$ the probability of remaining in the same class, $p_{r,\,r+1}$ the probability of moving one step up, and $p_{r,\,r-1}$ the probability of moving one step down. Then it can be shown quite easily that in the equilibrium distribution

$$\frac{n_{r+1}}{n_r} = \frac{p_{r,\,r+1}}{p_{r+1,\,r}} \quad (r = 1,2, \ldots, k-1) \tag{6.11}$$

The difference from the previous case is that now the ratios of frequencies in successive classes do not have to be the same for all classes. Case (ii) is therefore a more general form of case (i) and includes the latter as a special case. Equation (6.11) states that the ratio of the equilibrium numbers in two adjacent classes equals the ratio of the probabilities of movement between them in the two directions.

Case (iii)

In the previous case, the movement from any class was described by the transition probabilities out of that class into the two neighbouring classes. Champernowne (1973) has generalized this model further by considering the proportionate changes from any class as random variables with a normal distribution with means and variances varying from class to class. In case (ii), the ratio of the frequencies in consecutive classes in the equilibrium distribution, that is, the slope of the frequency curve in logarithmic scale, was given by the transition probabilities around those classes. Champernowne has shown that in his more general model, this slope b of the frequency curve in logarithmic scale is given approximately by

$$b = 2I_1/I_2 \qquad (6.12)$$

where I_1 is the mean and I_2 is the variance of the normal distribution of income changes in each class. These means and variances can be derived from data showing changes of income distribution in any given time interval. If these means and variances can be assumed to be constant over time, then the above equation shows the slope of the frequency curve for each class. As these means and variances may differ from class to class, we get an equilibrium distribution for which the slope b also varies in different parts of the income scale, as in case (ii).

6.3 Mobility between socioeconomic classes

A basic assumption of the model used in the last section is that the change in the income of an individual is entirely due to her movement from one income class to another. In practice, however, it is more likely that the change in an individual's income is due to two different factors: her movement from one socioeconomic class to another, and the change in the incomes of people in each of these classes. It is important to distinguish between these factors because they typically operate at different speeds. Thus movements between socioeconomic classes usually operate rather slowly, while incomes in some socioeconomic classes may change much more rapidly. We therefore summarize an approach suggested by Robinson and Dervis (1977) which makes this distinction.

For such an analysis, the authors distinguish socioeconomic classes such as large and small capitalists; large and small landowners; professionals; white-collar workers; organized, unorganized, and unemployed workers in urban areas; and small farmers and landless workers in rural areas. In order to use such a classification, data must be collected for the movement between these classes over a fairly long period. Such data are not available for any large sample, but the authors suggest that the matrix of the transitional probabilities will be strongly diagonal in structure, as there is little likelihood of substantial movements between classes widely differing from each other, even over periods as long as a decade. In fact the authors suggest, on the basis of their experience of conditions in Turkey, that as many as 63 of the 100 possible entries in the matrix are likely to be so small that they may be taken as zero. The most significant movements are likely to be those associated with rural–urban migration, upward mobility in the urban labour market, the upgrading of labour qualifications in the educational system, and the accumulation of capital. Movement between such social and economic classes has been intensively studied by sociologists (for a survey of some basic contributions, see Coxon and Jones 1975).

But while movement between these classes is generally slow, the average incomes of these classes may increase greatly, either as a result of the general progress of the economy or as the result of specific policies of the government. Therefore we may consider two types of policies, one which affects mobility between these classes, that is, which influences the transition probabilities, and the other which affects the incomes of individual classes.

To illustrate the method of analysis that may be applied, the authors consider two situations, one involving low mobility, and the other high mobility. They also consider two cases of income growth, one tending to equalize incomes between classes and the other to make these incomes increasingly unequal. For the case of three classes only, arranged in order of decreasing average incomes, they consider the following numerical examples:

Low mobility:

$$M_A = \begin{bmatrix} 1.00 & 0.0 & 0.0 \\ 0.10 & 0.85 & 0.05 \\ 0.0 & 0.10 & 0.90 \end{bmatrix}$$

High mobility:

$$M_B = \begin{bmatrix} 1.00 & 0.0 & 0.0 \\ 0.18 & 0.80 & 0.02 \\ 0.05 & 0.20 & 0.75 \end{bmatrix}$$

Unequalizing growth:

$$r_A = \begin{bmatrix} 5.0 \\ 3.5 \\ 2.5 \end{bmatrix}$$

Equalizing growth:

$$r_B = \begin{bmatrix} 4.0 \\ 4.5 \\ 5.6 \end{bmatrix}$$

The outcomes of the four possible policy combinations are then found to be as shown in Table 6.2. It is found that the effects of higher mobility on income inequality are generally smaller than the effects of income policies. This result, however, depends on the numerical values assumed in this hypothetical example, but it gives a feel for the sort of results that may be expected and the magnitude of the problems involved in policies to influence the distribution of income.

In a sense, this was the method used by Ricardo in his pioneering study of income distribution (see Chapter eight for a detailed discussion); however, his model was mainly based on the changing incomes of different socioeconomic classes rather than on movement between these classes. More recently, some writers have developed the concept of a social accounting matrix. In this concept, the population is divided into various socioeconomic classes. This distribution is then used to study how the average incomes of these classes change over time, and affects both

Table 6.2 Effects of mobility and income growth

Variables	Group	Base percentage	Strategies $M_A r_A$	$M_A r_B$	$M_B r_A$	$M_B r_B$
Percentage share in population	1	15	18.50	18.50	23.75	23.75
	2	35	34.75	34.75	38.00	38.00
	3	50	46.75	46.75	38.25	38.25
Mean income	1	1000	1628	1480	1628	1480
	2	300	423	466	423	466
	3	90	115	147	115	147
Gini index		0.473	0.515	0.461	0.492	0.443

Source: Robinson and Dervis (1977).

economic growth and the distribution of income. However, most applications of this method do not take much account of the mobility of individuals between various classes. Therefore the model is more useful to study the effect of relatively short-term influences than the long-term effects of inter-class mobility.

6.4 Dynamic measures of inequality

Most of the measures of inequality, such as those reviewed in Chapter 3, are concerned with the distribution of incomes prevailing at a point of time, that is, with a static 'snapshot' picture of income distribution. The distribution of income at a point of time may be compared with the position of individuals at various heights on the income ladder. The measures of inequality derived from such a distribution or its Lorenz curve may be interpreted as measuring the steepness of the income ladder. But behind such a static picture there are some important dynamic movements. One is the movement of the ladder itself, such as the motion of an escalator, representing a rise in all incomes such as might occur during a period of economic growth. Another important dynamic feature is the movement of people up and down the income ladder, discussed in the preceding two sections, depending on the extent of social mobility. This dynamic aspect is very important from a policy point of view because a highly unequal distribution of income at a point of time, that is, a steep income ladder, may be tolerated to a greater extent and may even be preferred if it is combined with a high degree of social mobility which offers individuals at the bottom of the ladder a better chance of moving up the ladder. Thus, for example, static inequality is usually taken to be greater in the United States than in Great Britain, but it is claimed that this is compensated by greater social mobility in the United States.

Given these dynamic movements in income distribution, we cannot confine our measures of inequality only to the static aspect. Therefore Adelman and Whittle (1979) have considered the problem of defining a dynamic measure of inequality. They first make projections of the time stream of the incomes of individuals for certain periods in the future, based both on the factors affecting individual incomes, such as age, and on the factors affecting the mobility of individuals between income classes. After considering various measures of inequality defined on these time paths of incomes, they propose a measure of inequality calculated from the discounted values of the future streams of incomes of individuals as the preferred method of taking account of both the static and the dynamic aspects of income distribution. This is an important advance over the static measures of inequality commonly used in the literature.

The analytical framework

Chapter seven

Introduction to part II

7.1 From the statistical approach to the analytical framework

In Part I we reviewed the statistical approach to the study of income distribution in both its descriptive and analytical roles. As a descriptive method, this approach has made a useful contribution by summarizing a large body of information and by bringing out certain interesting patterns in the distribution of income in different countries and its variation over time. However, it has been less successful in explaining these patterns. The statistical approach to explaining these patterns has followed three main lines: (i) treating the variations of individual incomes primarily as random phenomena subject to probabilistic laws; (ii) the explanation in terms of purely statistical regularities observed in historical experience or international cross-section data; or (iii) the explanation in terms of the statistical relationships between aspects of income distribution and such macroeconomic variables as the per capita income of countries.

As pointed out in previous chapters, the statistical approach by itself is inadequate in various ways. It is largely based on cross-section data from a number of countries. The statistical data brought together in Chapter four showed some significant differences in income distribution among these countries. Broadly speaking, we found that income was more equally distributed in DCs than in LDCs, and within LDCs, income was more equally distributed in many Asian countries than in most countries of Africa and Latin America. Apart from these broad differences between groups of countries, there were also some differences within these groups of countries.

At the same time, per capita income was higher in DCs than in LDCs, and within LDCs it was higher in the Latin American countries and many of the African countries for which data are available than in the Asian countries. The combination of the observed differences in income inequality and in per capita income has been widely used as evidence of a systematic relationship of income inequality with per capita income, with income inequality being low in countries at a low level of per capita income, higher in countries at an intermediate level of income, and again low in countries at a high level of income. This inverted-U relationship represents the cross-section version of Kuznets's law. However, we found in Chapter four that the statistical relationship between income inequality and the level of per capita income was not a strong one. The cases in which regressions on per capita income explained a large part of the variations in measures of income inequality were based on data from both DCs and LDCs. But if we consider only data from LDCs, the degree of explanation is much smaller. Therefore most of the correlation must be attributed to the 'double clustering effect' based on the large differences between DCs and LDCs. In both cases there is some evidence of a non-monotonic relationship, positive at low levels of income and negative at higher levels, but the estimates of the turning point are much larger in the case of regressions based on LDC data than in regressions based on data from both DCs and LDCs.

The relationship between income level and income inequality observed in these cross-section studies is also often assumed to hold for changes in income distribution in the process of economic growth. But this conclusion is valid if it can be assumed that all countries are following the same dynamic path, differing only in the stage they have reached on this path. This is not an assumption that can be made lightly, and represents one of the main weaknesses of cross-sectional analysis. In fact, as shown in Chapter five, such limited time series data as are available show that historical trends of income inequality in the process of economic growth do not always show the same pattern of change that is suggested by the cross-section data. The only relationship that is well supported by historical data is the decline in income inequality in the DCs, and this decline occurred only since the early decades of this century, fairly late in the economic development of these countries.

Even if the statistical relationships between income inequality and levels of income were stronger, it cannot be inferred that differences in income inequality are due to differences in levels of income. This is because countries with different degrees of income inequality differ not only in their average incomes but also in many other respects. Thus, apart from their higher income levels, DCs differ from LDCs in many other aspects of their economic systems, such as the working of their factor markets and the development of their economic and political institutions, which have significant effects on their income distributions. Similarly, Latin American LDCs differ from their Asian counterparts not only in their per capita incomes but also in other aspects of their economies such as the distribution of productive resources among individuals and households, the working of their factor markets, and the nature of their economic and political institutions. Therefore to explain the cross-sectional differences of income distribution among countries, we must consider a number of factors apart from differences in income levels.

Finally, even if it is found that there is a strong association of the kind postulated in Kuznets's law, we cannot rely solely on such statistical generalizations for the purpose of economic analysis. Such statistical relationships must be explained in terms of more fundamental economic and social forces. Then we may find, for example, that the observed association between income distribution and income levels arises because both are influenced by other economic and social factors. Or we may find that such an association arises only under certain conditions which were fulfilled in the past in some countries, but may not be fulfilled in other countries at other times.

Therefore the statistical approach discussed in Part I must be supplemented by a more analytical approach based on the working of various economic and social forces. This is the task of Part II of this book. We begin by considering a suitable point of departure for this purpose.

7.2 The random distribution of income

One of the main concerns of the statistical approach is the measurement of income inequality. For this purpose, as shown in Chapter three, the most convenient point of departure is the egalitarian distribution in which all members of society get the same income. It is by comparing actually observed distributions of income with such an egalitarian distribution that various measures of inequality have been proposed in the literature. But in an analytical study we are more interested in how the distribution of income is influenced by the sort of economic and social forces that operate in the real world. An appropriate point of departure for such a study is therefore a distribution which is not affected by such forces. The egalitarian distribution is certainly not one to be expected in the absence of such forces. There is no more reason that incomes should be equal in the absence of such forces than that heights or weights or IQs should be equal. A certain amount of inequality is inherent in the 'infinite variety' of human affairs. Therefore a more suitable point of departure for our analytical study is a distribution of income governed entirely by chance, that is, a random distribution of income.

One way of interpreting the concept of a random distribution of income is to treat the incomes of individuals as independent random variables, in the statistical sense of a variable which takes different values with probabilities given by some mathematical function or other. However, there are two difficulties with this approach. One is that when individual incomes are treated as independent random variables in this sense, the total income is also a random variable. But individual incomes are not entirely independent of each other, if only because the total productive resources of a country are limited at any time. Hence the model does not fit the case, typically considered in theories of income distribution, in which total income is given, and the problem is only to see how such a total income is distributed among members of a society. The other difficulty is that on this approach, the way income is distributed depends crucially on the probability function assumed for the distribution of individual incomes. Thus it is well known that, if individual incomes are distributed according to a uniform distribution, the Gini index of income distribution will be 1/3; in the case of the exponential distribution, it will be 1/2; and in the case of the log-normal of Pareto distributions, the Gini index will depend on the parameters of these functional forms. This raises the question of which probability function is most appropriate to describe the distribution of the income variable.

Probability theorists have shown that the exponential distribution of individual incomes has a special claim to be considered in this context because it embodies the notion of complete randomness (Feller 1968:73). Specifically it has been shown that if individual incomes were each distributed according to an exponential function, subject to the condition that they add up to a given total, then the corresponding shares are distributed as if they were the lengths of the intervals into which a rod of unit length is divided by a random set of points, that is, the random partition of a given line (Feller 1966:75). This model has been used to explain the surprising degree of accuracy with which waiting times or the duration of telephone conversations follow the exponential law (Feller 1968:458-9).

In view of the importance of this result, and the difficulty of following the proofs given in probability texts, an alternative derivation may be given as follows using methods more commonly employed in the economic study of income distribution. The simplest way to proceed is to start with the case in which a given total income is divided between two persons at random. This is analogous to the problem of breaking a rod of unit length into two parts at random. To solve this problem, we assume that all points at which the rod is broken into two parts are equally probable. It is then easy to see that, if the length of the smaller part is x, the x can vary from 0 to 1/2, and all values in this range are equally probable. Therefore the expected value of the smaller part will be 1/4, and that of the larger part 3/4. Hence the expected value of the Gini index will be 1/4. Alternatively, we can use the fact that the difference between the two parts takes all possible values from 0 to 1 with equal probabilities. As the Gini index of these two parts is related to the difference between them, it also follows that all possible values of the Gini index will have the same probability, that is, the Gini index will have a rectangular distribution. But in this case of a division into two parts, the maximum value of the Gini index will be only 1/2. Therefore the expected value of the Gini index will be 1/4.

This example might suggest that the Gini index has a rectangular probability distribution also in cases in which income is randomly distributed to more than two persons. But this is not the case, as can be seen quite simply in the case of a random division into three parts. This case is illustrated diagrammatically in Figure 7.1. As in the case of Figure 3.4, each point in the equilateral triangle represents a particular distribution of income, the distance of the point from AB representing the smallest share, that from AC the middle share, and that from BC the largest share. All possible points will therefore be restricted to lie within the triangle AED, where E corresponds to the case of the egalitarian distribution and D is the midpoint of AB. Then the random division of a given total into three parts means that all points in the triangle AED are equally probable. Given this wide range of possible outcomes, we consider only the average of these outcomes, which corresponds to the centroid of the triangle AED. At this point the expected values of the three parts will be 2/18, 5/18, and 11/18, giving an expected value of the Gini index of 1/3. Alternatively, we may note that the probability distribution of the Gini index for this case is a triangular distribution, with values ranging from a minimum of 0 to a maximum of 2/3, as shown in Figure 7.2. From this distribution, again, we get an expected value of the Gini index of 1/3.

For the random division of a given total into more than three parts, we consider only the average result of all possible outcomes. The mathematical derivation is greatly simplified by considering the first difference of income shares, that is, $u_i = x_i - x_{i-1}$, where x_i is the ith income share when these shares are arranged in ascending order, and x_0 is taken as 0. Note that in the case of three parts, the first differences follow the simple pattern 1/9, 1/6, and 1/3. In fact, it can be shown that this pattern is generally true, and that the expected values of the first differences are given by

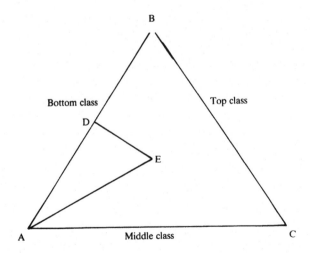

Figure 7.1

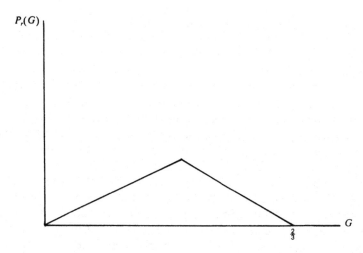

Figure 7.2

$$E(u_i) = \frac{1}{k(k+1-i)} \tag{7.1}$$

From this we can easily derive the expected values of the shares x_i, and also the corresponding expected value of the Gini index. The values for a few cases are shown in Table 7.1. The expected values of the Gini index are then given by the formula

$$E(G) = \frac{k-1}{2k} \tag{7.2}$$

This result can also be derived by an alternative argument. As in the case of division into three parts, the distribution of the Gini index corresponding to the random division into more than three parts is also symmetric. When there are k members in the population, the Gini index ranges from a minimum of 0 to a maximum of $(k-1)/k$ in the case in which one individual gets all the income. Hence the expected value of the Gini index is as given in (7.2).

Finally, we consider the case of a division of total income to a large number of units in the population. To analyse this case, we take the limit of (7.1) as k tends to infinity to get

$$\frac{d^2 Q}{dP^2} = \frac{1}{1-P} \tag{7.3}$$

where P is the cumulative proportion of income-receiving units and Q is the cumulative share of their incomes. Integrating this differential equation, we get

Table 7.1 Expected values of income shares and Gini index in the random distribution of income into k parts

Expected values	$k = 2$	$k = 3$	$k = 4$	$k = 5$	$k = 6$
$E(x_1)$	1/4	2/18	3/48	12/300	30/1080
$E(x_2)$	3/4	5/18	7/48	27/300	66/1080
		11/18	13/48	47/300	111/1080
			25/48	77/300	171/1080
				137/300	261/1080
					441/1080
$E(G)$	1/4	1/3	3/8	2/5	5/12

$$Q = P + (1 - P) \log(1 - p) \tag{7.4}$$

This is the equation of the Lorenz curve of the case in which individual incomes are independently distributed according to the exponential distribution (Kakwani 1980:37–8), with a Gini index of 1/2. This limiting value of the Gini index is also given by taking the limit of (7.2) as k tends to infinity. Hence we have an alternative derivation of the probability theorem stated at the beginning of this section, that the random distribution of income corresponds to the case in which individual incomes are distributed according to an exponential law, subject to a fixed total.

It was noted in Chapter three that Pareto claimed to have discovered a universal law of income distribution according to which the distribution of income in all places and all times was given by the function (3.1). It is a remarkable coincidence that when this function was fitted to distributions from many countries, the parameter α was found to be approximately 1.5. The coincidence is that for this value of the parameter, the Gini index of the Pareto distribution is 0.5 (Kakwani 1980:34), the same as the random distribution of income. But the similarity between the two distributions stops there, for the two distributions are in fact quite different, as shown in Table 7.2. It will be noticed that, although the two distributions have the same Gini index of 0.5, the income shares of the lower deciles of the Pareto distribution are higher than those of the random distribution, while the shares of the upper deciles are also higher.

7.3 Equalizing and disequalizing forces

When the egalitarian distribution is taken as the standard for comparison, we naturally find that observed distributions are more unequal than the egalitarian. Such comparisons therefore tend to focus attention on the disequalizing effect of economic and social forces. But, as argued above, the egalitarian distribution is not a particularly suitable standard for

Table 7.2 The Pareto and random distributions of income

Decile	Decile income shares (%) of	
	Pareto distribution $\alpha = 1.5$	Random distribution
1	3.45	0.52
2	3.72	1.63
3	4.04	2.88
4	4.45	4.32
5	5.00	5.99
6	5.69	8.01
7	6.73	10.53
8	8.46	13.93
9	12.06	19.16
10	46.40	33.03
Total	100.00	100.00

comparison in analytical studies. Instead, a more relevant standard for comparison is that with the random distribution. Some observed distributions of income are compared with this standard in Table 7.3. Then we find that, although the inequality of income distribution of LCDs in some regions of the world is very close to that of the random distribution, income distributions of LDCs in other regions, especially in Asia, and of DCs, are much less unequal. From this, we may conclude that while some of the economic and social forces which operate in the real world may have a disequalizing effect on the distribution of income, there are others which have an equalizing effect. For example, the fact that, even in countries with a very unequal distribution of income, the share of the bottom quintile is higher than that in the random distribution suggests the presence of some equalizing forces at this end of the income scale. A similar equalizing tendency is also seen in the case of the DCs, in which the share of the upper deciles is lower than that of a random distribution.

In the analytical approach the distribution of income is explained by two types of forces, one related to the distribution of productive assets among individuals and households, and the other to the prices these individuals and households receive for their productive assets. It is obvious that any tendency for increasing concentration of the distribution of assets will have a disequalizing effect on the distribution of income. As noted in section 5.1, Kuznets was so impressed with the power of this disequalizing effect that he was puzzled by the decline of inequality in the DCs since the beginning of this century. But the distribution of assets does not always tend to become unequal. In some cases it may actually become more equal over time, and then have an equalizing effect on the distribution of income.

Table 7.3 Comparison of actual with random distribution of income

Income group	Household income shares (percentage) in:					
	Random distribution	Africa	Latin America	Asia	LDCs	DCs
Bottom 20%	2.15	3.6	3.7	6.3	4.5	6.0
20–40%	7.20	7.2	7.5	10.2	8.3	10.9
40–60%	14.00	11.6	12.0	14.5	12.7	15.7
60–80%	24.46	19.4	20.0	21.3	20.2	22.7
80–90%	19.16	15.7	16.4	15.5	15.9	16.0
Top 10%	33.03	42.5	40.5	32.2	38.4	28.7
Gini index	0.500	0.539	0.522	0.410	0.490	0.382

Source: Derived from Table 4.1.

Similarly, the differences in the levels of income that individuals receive from different factors of production may have both an equalizing and a disequalizing effect on the distribution of income. Inequality due to these differences is a case of vertical inequality. In the early stages of development, certain factors of production, such as land and capital, may be in such scarce supply that they earn high rates of remuneration and thereby have a disequalizing effect. But in the later stages of development, the accumulation of capital will reduce the rate of profit on such assets and thus have an equalizing effect.

A certain part of income inequality is also due to different prices that individuals receive for even the same factor of production. Inequality due to these differences may be considered a case of horizontal inequality. Under perfect competition, these prices will be equal for all suppliers of the same factor of production. Because of this effect, competition is one of the most powerful equalizing forces in the economy. But competition may not be perfect; the weakness of competition will then have a disequalizing effect. Therefore an important source of differences in income inequality between countries is the force of competition. Competition is generally stronger in the DCs, and is part of the explanation of the lower inequality of income distribution in those countries. By contrast, the weaker force of competition in the LDCs is part of the explanation of the higher inequality in those countries.

Some of the major theories of income distribution in the literature have been mainly concerned with the way in which competitive market forces determine the levels and variation of the prices of different factors. These are reviewed in Chapter eight. But this is only one way in which economic and social forces influence the distribution of income. We must also consider other ways in which these forces affect the distribution of income, such as the imperfect working of factor markets and the distribution of assets. These effects are considered in Chapters nine to eleven dealing with the three factors of production: land, labour, and capital. Then in Chapter twelve we consider effects operating through the product markets, especially through the structure of production. But before going to those chapters, we consider some empirical information about the relative incomes of individuals and households deriving their incomes from different factors of production.

7.4 Income distribution from an analytical point of view

7.4.1 Income ratios and population shares

Most theoretical studies of income distribution have only been concerned with the ratio of incomes received from different factors of production. However, these income ratios are only one element contributing to income inequality. Income inequality depends also on the proportions of the population earning their income principally from these factors of production. To examine this relationship, consider a simple example in which a proportion λ of the population earns income only from their labour, at an average wage level W, while the rest of the population earns their income at the average level R representing, say, profits. Writing $\rho = R/W$, the average income y in the population is given by

$$y = \lambda + (1 - \lambda)\rho \qquad (7.5)$$

From equation (3.17) we also find that the Gini index of income inequality in this two-class society is given by

$$G = \frac{\lambda G_1 + (1 - \lambda) \rho G_2 + \lambda(1 - \lambda)(\rho - 1)}{\lambda + (1 - \lambda)\rho} \qquad (7.6)$$

where G_1 and G_2 are the Gini indices for the two classes. This formula shows that the Gini index depends on both λ and ρ. The relationship between the three variables is illustrated in Figure 7.3. Each curve of this figure shows the combinations of λ and ρ for which G is constant. These G curves are convex from below. The figure shows that, for any fixed value of λ, G will be higher, the higher the value of ρ.

But the relationship between G and λ is more complex. For a fixed value of ρ, G starts at a low level for low values of λ, then increases as λ increases up to a point, shown by the minimum point of the G curves, and then declines with further increases in λ. The minimum points of the G curves can be derived simply by calculating the value of λ at which the

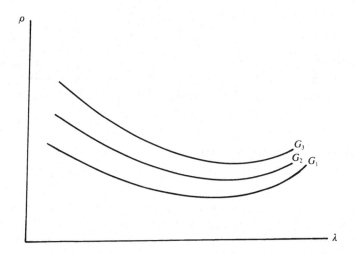

Figure 7.3

value of ρ is a minimum for any given value of G. These values of λ are given by

$$\lambda_m = \frac{[(G - G_1)(G - G_2)(1 + G_2 - G_1)]^{1/2} - (G - G_2)}{G_2 - G_1} \quad (7.7)$$

At these values of ρ, the minimum value of ρ is given by

$$\rho_m = \frac{G - G_1}{G - G_2} \left(\frac{\lambda}{1 - \lambda} \right)^2 \quad (7.8)$$

In the special case in which $G_1 = G_2 = k$, we have

$$\lambda_m = \frac{1 + G - k}{2} \quad (7.7a)$$

$$\rho_m = \left(\frac{1 + G - k}{1 - G + k} \right)^2 \quad (7.8a)$$

Both y and G thus depend on the two parameters ρ and λ. Therefore we cannot expect to get a relationship between G and y independently of these parameters. At the best, we can eliminate one of these parameters from (7.5) and (7.6) and express G as a function of y and the other parameter. For example, eliminating ρ from these equations and taking the simple case in which $G_1 = G_2 = 0$, we get

$$G = \lambda \left(1 - \frac{1}{y} \right) \tag{7.9}$$

This shows that, if λ is constant, then G will increase with y. But λ need not be constant, and may decline as y rises; if λ declines sufficiently rapidly, then an increase in y may be associated with a decline in G, as has been observed in the DCs since the beginning of this century.

7.4.2 Income shares and population shares

Much of the theoretical literature on income distribution has been concerned with the shares of total income received by each factor of production. This is only one aspect of the personal distribution of income. For a fuller analysis, we must also consider the proportion of the population earning incomes from each of these factors of production, as in the case of the income ratios. In order to see how these population shares and the income shares corresponding to different factors of production together determine income inequality, consider the case of only two factors of production, labour and capital. Then the decomposition formula (3.17) for the case of non-overlapping groups can be written in terms of the population shares λ_1 and λ_2 and the income shares π_1 and π_2 as follows:

$$G = \lambda_1 \pi_1 G_1 + \lambda_2 \pi_2 G_2 + \lambda_1 \pi_2 - \lambda_2 \pi_1 \tag{7.10}$$

where G_1 and G_2 refer to the Gini indices of the two groups.

The case in which $G_1 = G_2 = 0$ has a simple geometric interpretation. In this case, the Lorenz curve will be as shown in Figure 7.4. This figure illustrates the case of two groups, with incomes being uniform within each group. Then OSA is the Lorenz curve of the distribution, and the Gini index will be twice the area of the triangle OSA. But because the horizontal distance between O and A is equal to unity, the Gini index will be equal to the vertical distance RS. It is easy to see that this distance is just the difference between the population share and the income share of either group, that is,

$$G = \lambda_1 - \pi_1 = \pi_2 - \lambda_2 \tag{7.11}$$

The corresponding formula for the case of three groups is

$$G = (\lambda_1 + \lambda_2)(\lambda_1 - \pi_1) + (\lambda_2 + \lambda_3)(\pi_3 - \lambda_3) \tag{7.12}$$

These equations illustrate how income inequality depends not only on income shares but also on the population shares of groups classified according to their ownership of various factors of production.

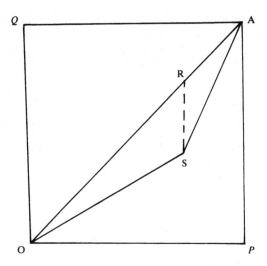

Figure 7.4

7.4.3 The data

In the statistical approach the data on income distribution are usually considered in the form of proportions of the population in various income classes, or the proportions of total income accruing to various deciles of the population. But in economic analysis, it is more important to consider the income shares and the population shares of groups classified according to their ownership of various factors of production. Unfortunately, not many countries have provided such data. Such estimates have been made in a few countries in the course of compiling the social accounting matrix. For example, some estimates made in the 1977–78 social accounting matrix for India are summarized in Table 7.4.

The poorest households are those of landless agricultural labourers and small farmers, whose incomes are mainly derived from their labour. Next are the marginal workers in urban areas, who also derive their income mainly from their labour. Similar incomes are also earned on the average by medium farmers who derive their income partly from their labour and partly from their land. Higher incomes are earned by regular workers in urban areas, probably because of their greater skills and educational qualifications. The high income of large farmers is mainly derived from their land ownership. The richest category are the people who earn their income from capital.

Estimates for a slightly more detailed classification have been made for South Korea in 1968, and are summarized in Table 7.5. Again we see a pattern similar to that in India, namely that capitalists earn the highest incomes, farm operators' incomes vary with their farm sizes, and

Table 7.4 Per capita income by socioeconomic category: India, 1977–78

Social class	Percentage of population	Average per capita income (Rs)
Rural		
Landless agricultural workers	8.4	622
Small farmers	23.7	502
Medium farmers	25.3	829
Large farmers	11.0	2,024
Urban		
Regular workers	17.9	2,008
Management workers	11.2	811
Capitalists	2.5	3,148
Total	100.0	1,133

Source: de Janvry and Subbarao (1986:49).

Table 7.5 Per capita income by socioeconomic category: South Korea, 1968

Socioeconomic category	Percentage of labour force	Per capita income (000 won)
Employees		
Engineers	0.5	435
Technicians	1.3	225
Skilled workers	8.5	108
Apprentices	2.5	53
Unskilled workers	9.8	109
White-collar workers	7.2	259
Government workers	7.2	161
Own Account Workers		
Manufacturing	2.3	157
Services	9.4	198
Capitalists	1.3	729
Agricultural workers		
Labourers	5.5	49
Farm size 1	12.8	65
Farm size 2	13.9	85
Farm size 3	13.7	112
Farm size 4	4.0	131
Total	100.0	132

Source: Adelman and Robinson (1978:73).

employees' incomes vary with their skills.

In interpreting these tables, it must be noted that, however carefully various socioeconomic groups are defined, it will generally be the case that each group will derive incomes from more than one factor of production. This is particularly the case in LDCs. Therefore it is desirable to have some estimates of incomes derived from different sources for each category of households. An example is given in Table 7.6, which summarizes estimates made in the course of compiling a social accounting matrix for Indonesia in 1975.

While agricultural workers earn most of their income from their labour, other categories of employees earn a considerable part of their income from other factors of production as well. Similarly, farm operators earn their income not only from their land but also from the profits of operating the land, and to some extent also in the form of wages. It is particularly noteworthy that the high incomes of professional employees and the more skilled urban workers are due not only to higher wages and salaries for their labour, but also to high returns derived from capital.

Such estimates have also been made for Thailand for 1981, and are shown in Table 7.7 for the whole kingdom. An interesting feature of these estimates is that farmers who rent in the land they operate earn nearly as much income as those owning land, but they earn more in the form of wages for their labour. We also note that the more skilled employees earn a considerable part of their high incomes from other sources such as capital. The Thai data are also available separately for urban and rural areas, and are summarized in Tables 7.8 and 7.9.

The general pattern of the distribution of income among socioeconomic categories is the same in both urban and rural areas, but in each case, average incomes are higher in urban areas than in rural areas.

Table 7.6 Individual incomes by socioeconomic category and type of income: Indonesia, 1975

Socioeconomic category	Average annual income (000 Rpl) by type:					
	Percentage of workers	Total	Wages and salaries	Profits	Land	Other capital
Farm operators						
< 0.5 ha	22.3	122.0	18.6	57.8	28.8	16.8
0.5–1 ha	11.9	165.4	12.4	64.7	72.0	16.3
1 ha and over	13.3	251.9	9.6	66.7	160.1	15.5
Employees						
Agricultural	9.8	86.8	74.7	4.3	7.8	—
Production	1.1	161.9	45.6	37.1	—	79.2
Clerical	1.2	149.7	26.9	49.6	—	73.2
Professional	0.3	528.9	248.8	21.5	—	258.6
Nonagricultural workers						
Rural: Unskilled	17.9	169.8	64.6	45.3	9.9	50.0
Skilled	5.9	233.3	112.9	53.0	8.1	59.3
Urban: Unskilled	10.7	340.6	110.2	57.8	1.1	171.5
Skilled	5.7	637.5	271.5	56.8	1.6	307.6
Total	100.0	210.6	61.1	51.6	39.5	58.4

Sources: Central Bureau of Statistics, Jakarta (1982) *Social Accounting Matrix, Indonesia 1975.*

Table 7.7 Household incomes by socioeconomic category of households and source of incomes: Thailand, 1981

Socioeconomic category	Percentage of household	Average annual household incomes (Bahts) by type:				
		Total	Wages and salaries	Profits from farm	Non-farm profits	Other sources
Farm operators						
Owning land	43.0	2,586	140	1,968	76	402
Renting land	9.1	2,772	235	1,994	97	446
Own account workers						
Entrepreneurs, trade, and industry	12.5	5,403	404	462	3,787	750
Professional, technical, and administrative	0.1	5,804	228	111	3,982	1,483
Employees						
Professional, technical, and administrative	4.8	6,778	5,253	192	222	1,111
Farm workers	6.5	1,776	1,021	378	37	340
Skilled	1.7	2,124	1,386	265	75	398
Clerical	7.6	4,688	3,503	169	240	776
Production	7.9	3,496	2,571	244	121	560
Inactive	6.8	3,385	264	257	122	2,742
Total	100.0	3,384	962	1,172	570	680

Source: National Statistical Office, Bangkok (1985) *Report of the 1981 Socio-Economic Survey, Thailand.*

Table 7.8 Household incomes by socioeconomic category of households and source of incomes: Thailand, urban areas, 1981

Socioeconomic category	*Average annual household incomes (Bahts) by type:*					
	Percentage of household	*Total*	*Wages and salaries*	*Profits from farm*	*Non-farm profits*	*Other sources*
Farm operators						
Owning land	2.4	4,300	185	3,094	114	907
Renting land	4.0	4,644	302	3,436	168	738
Own account workers						
Entrepreneurs, trade, and industry	27.8	7,700	617	314	5,785	984
Professional, technical, and administrative	0.3	7,203	254	112	5,073	1,764
Employees						
Professional, technical, and administrative	10.3	8,715	6,903	67	287	1,458
Farm workers	2.6	2,517	1,706	198	38	575
General workers	2.3	2,929	2,252	103	128	446
Clerical	24.8	5,348	4,136	53	288	871
Production	16.7	4,270	3,338	89	168	675
Inactive	9.0	4,575	482	100	147	675
Total	100.0	5,916	2,624	351	1,763	1,178

Source: National Statistical Office, Bangkok (1985) *Report of the 1981 Socio-Economic Survey, Thailand.*

Table 7.9 Household incomes by socioeconomic category of households and source of incomes: Thailand, rural areas, 1981

Socioeconomic category	Percentage of household	Average annual household incomes (Bahts) by type:				
		Total	Wages and salaries	Profits from farm	Non-farm profits	Other sources
Farm operators						
Owning land	53.0	2,567	139	1,955	76	397
Leasing land	10.4	2,592	228	1,856	90	418
Own account workers						
Entrepreneurs, trade, and industry	8.8	3,630	241	577	2,245	567
Professional, technical, and administrative	0.02	1,606	149	—	709	748
Employees						
Professional, technical, and administrative	3.4	5,340	4,029	285	173	853
Farm workers	7.4	1,711	961	394	36	320
General workers	1.6	1,837	1,077	331	56	373
Clerical	3.4	3,490	2,356	380	153	601
Production	5.7	2,935	2,013	357	87	478
Inactive	6.3	2,968	187	312	113	2,356
Total	100.0	2,759	552	1,375	275	557

Source: National Statistical Office, Bangkok (1985) Report of the 1981 Socio-Economic Survey, Thailand.

Chapter eight

Theories of income distribution

8.1 The neoclassical theory

The economic literature does not contain much that can be described as a theory of income distribution, in the sense of a theory explaining the distribution of income among individuals and households. Instead, the standard works of each major school of thought usually have a section described as a theory of distribution, explaining how factor prices are determined and how they in turn determine the shares of total output accruing to each of these factors of production. Often these questions are addressed because of the role of factor prices and factor shares in the study of economic growth. The prices and income shares of factors of production are not sufficient by themselves to explain the personal distribution of income; however, as discussed in Chapter seven, they are a necessary ingredient of a complete theory of income distribution. Therefore the analyses of factor prices and factor shares, as considered in the major theories of economics, are briefly reviewed in this chapter.

We begin with the neoclassical theory. It is so well known that only a brief summary will be given here. This theory is based on the assumption of maximizing behaviour on the part of producers and consumers, and has been worked out most fully for the case in which there is perfect competition and where markets work efficiently so that they speedily attain their equilibrium positions. In the short period, the stocks of the various factors of production are assumed to be given and to be fully utilized.

Under these assumptions the competitive market forces ensure that factor prices are equal in all sectors of the economy, and the profit-maximizing behaviour of entrepreneurs leads to each factor being employed up to the point at which its marginal product equals its price. Hence resources are optimally allocated to different uses so as to maximize the total output of all goods, valued at the prevailing market prices. This leads to a definite relationship between total output and the stocks of the various factors of production, represented by an aggregate production function. Therefore the prices of the factors of production are determined by their respective marginal productivity in each industry, and hence for the economy as a whole, at the given levels of their supply.

For the theory to apply consistently to all factors of production, payment to each factor at its marginal productivity must exhaust the total product. Initially, this 'adding-up' problem was solved by assuming that production is subject to constant returns to scale, and relying on the Euler's theorem property of linear homogeneous production functions. In modern textbooks it is more common for this problem to be solved by assuming that firms are free to enter or leave an industry; then firms at the margin will be operating at their minimum average cost, at which the payment to factors according to marginal productivity will exhaust the total product. However, the assumption of linear homogeneous production functions continues to be used in much theoretical work.

The great attraction of the theory is that it explains factor prices in a country entirely in terms of its factor endowment, and the state of technology as represented by the aggregate production function. Thus the low wages of labour in LDCs, compared with DCs, is explained by the abundance of labour relative to other factors of production and the low productivity of labour at the prevailing technology. Similarly, the high rates of profit and rent in LDCs reflect the high marginal productivity of capital and land due to their relative scarcity.

This analysis is then used to derive some dynamic theorems about the behaviour of factor prices and factor shares as the stocks of factors grow over time. For example, an increase in the stock of capital relative to labour will raise the average and marginal products of labour, and lower those of capital. At the same time, there will also be an increase in output per worker. Then whether the share of labour increases or falls in the process of capital accumulation depends on the changes in marginal products. These changes in turn depend on the ease with which capital can be substituted for labour as measured, for example, by the elasticity of substitution. This concept is defined as the proportionate change in the ratio of factor quantities divided by the proportionate change in the ratio of their marginal products. From this definition, it follows that the share of capital in total product would rise, remain constant, or decline in the course of capital accumulation according to whether the elasticity of substitution was greater, equal to, or less than unity.

The marginal productivity theory of factor prices has also been used to study the effect of technological progress on the shares of various factors. For example, Hicks (1932; 121–3) classified inventions as labour-saving, capital-saving, or neutral according to whether they raised, lowered, or kept constant the ratio of the marginal product of capital to that of labour. On this definition, other things being equal, labour-saving inventions would lower the ratio of wages to profits. But because of a special interest in the effect of technological progress on the shares accruing to the two factors, later definitions have been based on the effect of inventions on these shares. Thus, for example, an invention is classified as neutral if it keeps the factor shares constant, as labour-saving if it reduces the share of labour, and as capital-saving if it reduces the share of capital. But whether factor shares are constant or not depends not only on the type of inventions but also on what happens to the relative stocks of the two factors. Three special cases have been distinguished: technological progress is said to be Harrod-neutral if it keeps factor shares constant along a path on which the output–capital ratio is constant; to be Hicks-neutral if it keeps factor shares constant along a path on which the capital–labour ratio is constant, and to be Solow-neutral if it keeps factor shares constant along a path on which the output–labour ratio is constant.

According to this theory, the effect of capital accumulation on factor shares in total output depends on the elasticity of substitution and the bias of technological progress. However, there are few reliable estimates of these parameters which can be used to explain the observed changes in factor shares. In fact, it has often been the case that broad trends in factor shares have been used to derive some ideas about the elasticity of substitution and the bias of inventions.

Thus it has been taken as a stylized fact of the historical experience of DCs that factor shares have been fairly stable over long periods. Therefore attempts have been made to identify the conditions on the elasticity of substitution between capital and labour and the nature of technological progress that will lead to this result. For example, the alleged stability of factor shares may be due to the elasticity of substitution between capital and labour being one. But this is too much of a coincidence. Therefore Hicks (1932) offered the explanation that the elasticity of substitution was really less than one, but that this was offset by predominantly labour-saving technological progress in these countries.

More recently, neoclassical writers have developed a theory of growth specifically to explain such stylized facts of the growth experience of the DCs. For example, assuming that a constant proportion of income is saved and invested to increase the stock of capital, Solow (1956) and Swan (1956) showed that the endogenous rate of capital accumulation will steadily converge to any given exogenous rate of population growth. This property of the model is known as dynamic stability. The theory has been extended to two sectors; the dynamic stability of the model depends on there being sufficient substitutability between capital and labour, or alternatively on such a casual property of technology as the condition that consumer goods must be more capital-intensive than capital goods. In such models, however, per capita income and the shares of the two factors remain constant over time. Then the observed growth of per capita income is attributed entirely to technological progress of various types.

There have also been studies that explain technological progress as an endogenous process. Thus Hicks (1932; Chap. 6) argued that while some innovations were autonomous, others were induced by changes in relative factor prices. He used this theory to explain the predominance of labour-saving inventions in the DCs as the result of rising wages. This theory was criticized by Salter (1960) but continues to be followed by other writers. For example, Hayami and Ruttan (1985) have used this type of argument to explain the variations of agricultural techniques in different DCs as the response to variations in relative factor prices. If valid, the theory has important implications for long-term trends in income distribution, for it shows that changes in technology would offset the effects of changes in relative factor supplies, and thereby tend to reduce variations in relative factor prices.

8.2 The classical theory

While the neoclassical theory is a very general one, it has been worked out most fully for the case of two factors of production, labour and capital. The classical theory, which dealt mainly with the agricultural sector, dealt with three factors of production: land, labour, and capital. The stock of land is assumed to be fixed over time. Hence the classical economists gave special emphasis to the role of diminishing returns to an increasing application of labour and capital on a fixed stock of land. While neoclassical theory generally assumed that the stock labour was either fixed or grew at an exogenously given rate, a central feature of classical theory was that population growth was assumed to be an endogenous variable. This followed from the Malthusian theory that population increased when the standard of living of workers, determined by their wages, was above the subsistence level, and declined when the standard of living was below that level.

At any point of time, there is an inelastic supply of labour, L_t, determined by the given population. The given supply of labour is assumed to be fully employed. There is also a given wage fund, C_t, used to pay wages during the growing season. Therefore the wage rate in the short period is given simply by $W_t = C_t / L_t$, that is, the demand curve for labour is a rectangular hyperbola determined by the given wage fund. The equilibrium wage determined in this way has nothing to do with the marginal product of labour. The marginal product of labour depends on the amount of labour applied to the fixed stock of land, and declines with the amount of labour because of diminishing returns. Competition among capitalists allocates labour to different farms so as to make the marginal product of labour the same in all farms. The excess of the marginal product over the wage rate accrues to the capitalists as profit. The margin of cultivation is extended to the farm which is of such low productivity that the average product of labour is equal to its marginal product, and therefore there is nothing left out of total product as payment for land. On the intra-marginal farms, the average product of labour is higher than the marginal product;

therefore there is a surplus of total output over the shares of labour and capital, which accrues to landlords as the rent of land.

This short-term model is then set in historical motion by introducing two dynamic influences. At a given point of time, the wage rate may be above or below the subsistence level. If the market wage rate w_t is above the subsistence level s, population will increase and with it, the labour force will grow, say, from L_t to L_{t+1} in the next period. Conversely, if the wage rate is below the subsistence level, the labour force will decline.

The other dynamic influence is the growth of the wage fund. The classicals assumed that landlords did not save anything out of their incomes, spending it instead on the employment of 'unproductive labour', by which they meant labour that did not create any capital. It was the capitalists who saved a large part of their profit incomes and invested their savings to increase the wage fund, say, from C_t to C_{t+1}, depending on the amount and rate of profits. As population grows, labour is allocated to less and less fertile land, pushing the extensive margin of cultivation outward. At the same time, more and more labour is applied to the intra-marginal farms, pushing the intensive margin further. For both reasons, there is a decline in the marginal product of labour. Hence the rate of profit and eventually the amount of profits decline while rent incomes increase. The wage fund stops growing when the rate of profit falls to zero, that is, when the marginal product of labour equals the subsistence level. The economy will then have reached its stationary state. (For a more detailed mathematical analysis, see Booth and Sundrum 1984: Appendix 3.1.)

The principal conclusion of the theory is that the accumulation of capital does not have any effect on the wages of labour, which are tied to the subsistence level. Instead, it only leads to a continuous growth of population. The growth of population leads to a steady rise in the rent of land and a steady fall in the rate of profit. Therefore the subsistence level governing the growth of population plays a central role in determining the wages of labour. But the concept of the subsistence level itself was left unclear. Thus O'Brien (1975:38) has suggested that

> 'subsistence' itself is sometimes treated as a psychological requirement which is variable but usually Ricardo speaks as if it is a physical concept of what is necessary to sustain life – which was consistent with his general theoretical approach because unless subsistence was a physical concept the death control mechanism would not operate.

However, other writers have argued for a psychological or conventional interpretation of the subsistence concept (see, e.g., Hollander 1979). The difference is of some importance because the physiological interpretation would imply considerable uniformity of wages in different regions and over time, while a psychological interpretation would permit some variations over space and time.

But whatever the interpretation of the subsistence concept, the endogenous theory of population growth based on that concept proved false in the subsequent history of the present-day developed countries. In these countries there was a fall in fertility and the rate of population growth with a rapid rise in the standard of living of the mass of the population. The classical theory of demographic behaviour may have applied in the less developed countries in earlier times. Thus, for example, Ishikawa (1967:78) has argued that the more densely settled LDCs may even be interpreted as having reached the stationary state under the prevailing technology and institutions. However, even in the LDCs, the classical theory does not explain more recent experience in which population growth was so greatly accelerated by improvements in public health and medical science that large sections of the people have fallen below the subsistence level, leading to the emergence of mass poverty in many LDCs.

The classical theory also assumed that the available labour supply would be fully employed at all times, and that the growth of population would be accommodated by increasing labour intensity of cultivation. If agricultural technology remained constant, as the classical theorists generally assumed, the increasing labour intensity of cultivation would be subject to the full force of diminishing returns and reduce the marginal product of labour sharply. In fact, however, as Boserup (1965) has argued, the growth of population has induced a steady improvement of agricultural technology, especially by the invention of more productive labour intensive techniques of cultivation. But eventually there is a limit to the improvement of technology induced by population growth. Then labour can no longer be fully employed in the agricultural sector. In the DCs the problem was solved partly by the shift of labour outside agriculture, and partly by the mechanization of agriculture. But in the LDCs there has been a much smaller shift of labour outside agriculture, and agriculture itself has not been able to accommodate the growth of population. Hence a considerable proportion of the labour force in many LDCs suffers from chronic conditions of unemployment and underemployment.

It is convenient to discuss Marx's contribution to the subject here because, at least in his positive theory, he followed the work of the classical economists with a few modifications. The classical theory had been worked out most fully for an agricultural economy. However, Marx wrote at the height of the Industrial Revolution, when manufacturing industry was becoming a much more dominant sector of the economy. Marx therefore modified classical theory to deal with the industrial sector. Hence he was mainly concerned with the distribution of income between labour and capital, and much less with the distribution between labour and land.

Writing under the shadow of the British classical economists, Marx also adopted a subsistence theory of wages, interpreting the subsistence theory of wages to mean that the value of labour corresponded to its cost of production, just as he explained the value of commodities. In sticking to the subsistence theory of wages, he was mainly concerned to deny that wages were at all influenced by labour productivity, either on the average or at the margin. In fact, the difference between wages at the subsistence level and the productivity of labour was the source of the surplus value in which he was particularly interested.

However, he broadened the concept of subsistence to include some conventional elements of the standard of living:

> In contradistinction, therefore, to the case of other commodities, there enter into the determination of the value of labour power, a historical and moral element. Nevertheless, in a given country, at a given period, the average quantity of means of subsistence for the worker is given. (Marx 1946: vol. 1, p. 171)

He did this to account for variations in wages in different places and at different times. By contrast, the largely biological concept of subsistence in classical theory meant fairly uniform wages in all places. But at the same time it meant that the 'historical and moral element' could no longer be explained by the classical theory of demographic behaviour. Instead, Marx's theory of wages 'essentially starts not from population movements but from the accumulation of capital' (Mandel 1971:143).

Marx described the payment of wages at the subsistence level rather than at the productivity of labour as the exploitation of labour by capitalists. To a large extent, this concept of exploitation is a moral or normative judgment. From an analytical point of view, a group may be said to be exploited if their share of total income under some set of institutions is less than what it might be under others. It is along these lines that Roemer (1982) has distinguished different categories of exploitation. For example, feudal exploitation occurs when there are ties of bondage that force labourers to work on the land of their feudal overlords without payment or only for military protection. But under capitalism the labour contract is voluntary and there is no physical coercion. Capitalist exploitation, however, arises from the fact that labourers have to work with capital, which was produced by labour in the past but which is now owned by capitalists. That is, the concept of capitalist exploitation is based on a comparison of the capitalist system with one in which there is no private ownership of the means of production. Within the capitalist system competitive forces should lead to workers being paid wages equal to their marginal product, according to neoclassical economics. Therefore exploitation occurs in the neoclassical model when labour is paid less than its marginal product, as when there is monopsony in the labour market. Roemer also distinguished a category of socialist exploitation, in which some members of society have a privileged access to certain inalienable assets, including the powers of the state.

However, Marx himself goes further. Capitalists' exploitation of labour occurs not just because they own capital, but also through the forms in which capital is accumulated and the ways it is used. In classical theory an increase in the stock of circulating capital leads to an increase in the demand for labour, but this increase in the demand for labour does not have any long-term effect on wages because it is offset by population growth. In neoclassical theory, on the other hand, the accumulation of fixed capital could raise wages by increasing the marginal product of labour. By contrast, Marx argued that capitalists designed their machines to be predominantly labour-saving so that the accumulation of capital in fact led to a reserve army of unemployed labour. It is through creating such a reserve army of unemployed labour that capitalists drive down wages to the subsistence level, albeit a concept of subsistence conditioned by historical and moral factors. Although trade unions could exert countervailing bargaining power against the employers, this could occur only in the short run. In the less densely populated areas of North America, wages may rise rather than fall in spite of the rapid introduction of mechanized production techniques, so long as workers had the option of extending the land frontier (Mandel 1971:148). But when this option has been fully utilized, wages would again be forced down to the subsistence level.

Marx also recognized that there were substantial economies of scale in industrial production. This meant that large capitalists could produce more cheaply than small capitalists and could therefore drive out smaller competitors from business. Hence the ownership of capital would become increasingly concentrated over time. This was the basis of Marx's Law of Concentration. Such a concentration of capital gave capitalists an additional bargaining power in depressing wages to the subsistence level.

Marx's predictions, like those of the classical economists before him, failed to materialize in the subsequent history of the developed countries. Since he wrote, wages in these countries have risen several-fold in line with the great increase of total production. To a large extent this was due to a significant rise in the political power of labour, partly due to the growth of collective bargaining through trade unions, and partly due to the rise in their productive skills through education and training. But at the same time, many aspects of capitalist development which he observed in his writings are also to be found in modern industrial capitalism (Galbraith 1967).

8.3 The dualistic model of Lewis

The distribution of output between wages and profits plays a key role in Lewis's (1954, 1972, 1979) dualistic model of development based on the historical experience of western Europe. In this model the economy is divided into a modern and a traditional sector. The essential feature of the modern sector is that it is capitalistic, that is, it is run by capitalists who hire wage labour and sell the output at a profit. Thus the modern sector is not necessarily the same as the industrial or the urban sectors, although the capitalist mode of production is more prominent in these sectors. In contrast, Lewis assumed the traditional sector to consist mainly of self-employed people, typically peasants cultivating a family farm with their family labour. In this sector there is a surplus of labour in the sense that withdrawing labour from the traditional sector will not reduce the output of that sector. Although most critics of the model have focused on this assumption, it does not necessarily mean that the marginal product of labour (in the sense of hours or intensity of work) is zero; all that it means is that the marginal product of the number of workers is zero because when some workers leave the sector, total output could be maintained by the remaining workers putting in more work.

Because Lewis conceived of the traditional sector as consisting typically of family agricultural enterprises, the standard of living of the workers in this sector was determined by the average product of labour. This is sometimes described as the subsistence level, but the concept is different from that of the classical economists. Under these conditions workers in the traditional sector would move to the modern sector only if the wage offered there was at least equal to the average product of labour in the traditional sector. At that wage, there would be an 'unlimited supply' of labour, that is, a perfectly elastic supply. Hence the wage in the modern sector was fixed institutionally at the level of the average product of labour in the traditional sector. This assumption corresponds to the classical assumption that there is an elastic supply of labour at the subsistence level.

At the wage corresponding to the average product of labour in the traditional sector, employment in the modern sector would be extended to the point at which the marginal product was equal to the wage. The central problem that Lewis was concerned to explain was the process by which the surplus labour of the traditional sector was gradually absorbed by the expansion of the modern sector. Given the institutionally fixed wage, the capitalists in the modern sector saved a high proportion of their profit incomes in increasing the stock of capital in the modern sector. This raised the marginal product of labour and hence expanded employment in the next period. The process would go on until the labour surplus in the traditional sector is fully absorbed, and the marginal product of labour becomes the same in the two sectors. After that point wages in both sectors would rise as analysed in neoclassical theory. When this process is completed the centre of gravity of the economy would have shifted from the traditional or agricultural to the modern or industrial sector. Lewis also takes account of other factors such as the supply of food from the traditional to the modern sector, and changes in the terms of trade between the two sectors.

The dualistic model has been intensively studied as a model of growth.

But here we are primarily interested in the implications for the distribution of income. These are best studied by comparing this model with the classical model. In the classical model wages remained stable mainly as a result of the assumed demographic behaviour. In the dualistic model the average standard of living in the agricultural sector is assumed to be stable because any reduction in the agricultural workforce was offset by greater intensity of work by the remaining workers, while wages are stable in the modern sector because of the infinitely elastic supply of labour. In the classical model there was a steady increase in the rent of land as population pressed on a limited area. In the dualistic model rent is not distinguished as a separate factor, being combined with labour as a source of income of self-employed peasant families. In the classical model the rate of profit was determined in the agricultural sector as the difference between the marginal product of labour and the wage per worker, and savings out of profits were invested to increase the wage fund steadily. In the dualistic model profits are earned in the industrial sector as the excess of output over the wage cost, and savings out of profits are used to invest in fixed capital, thereby increasing employment in the modern sector. The main feature of the dualistic model is that savings depend not so much on the total income, but rather on its distribution between profits and wages.

The dualistic model was advanced as an explanation of the historical experience of the DCs, especially Britain, but much of the controversy surrounding it has been over its application to the LDCs. Of the two basic assumptions on which it is based, namely the elastic supply of labour and the high propensity to save out of profit incomes, most of the controversy has been around the former. In spite of the many criticisms levelled against that notion, it is quite valid at least for the more densely populated LDCs with a very heavy pressure of population on land. In the course of the debate there has been much less discussion of the other basic assumption of the model, namely the high propensity to save out of profit incomes. It is on this account that Singh (1975:236) concluded that 'When we come to testing we find the dualistic models as a whole falsified. This is so most clearly with respect to saving and investment behaviour, which Lewis justly thought to be the central feature of the phenomenon of development.'

While the classical and the dualistic models throw some light on the factors influencing income distribution in LDCs, they suffer from some weaknesses. The classical theory assumes that population growth is tied to the subsistence level, largely through the effects on mortality. But while recent advances in medical science and improvements in public health have been more important influences on mortality than food supply, rising incomes have had a more important effect on population growth through a decline of fertility after a certain level of income is reached. This relationship, known as the demographic transition theory, has therefore come to replace the Malthusian theory.

The classical theory was mainly concerned with a circulating form of capital. While the dualistic theory takes more account of fixed capital, it does so only in the context of the modern, or industrial, sector. But in fact the role of fixed capital in the agricultural sector has important implications for income distribution.

Finally, the dualistic model treats the typical producer in the traditional sector as a self-employed peasant, but in fact a considerable part of the rural labour force consists of hired labour from landless families. An alternative model, embodying some of these modifications, has been advanced by Butt (1960), and is summarized in the following section.

8.4 The mechanization process of Butt

The main object of this model is to study the dynamics of growth and distribution under the influence of population growth and capital accumulation. In contrast to the Malthusian theory, in which population growth is tied to the subsistence level, this model is based on the demographic transition theory in assuming that the rate of population growth increases with the rise of per capita income up to a point, and declines thereafter. Capital consists of fixed capital, each unit of which is described as a 'machine'.

The most important feature of the model is that unlike most versions of the modern theory of growth, the economy is divided into a number of sectors, each with its own individual characteristics. Many aspects of growth and distribution depend on the way in which capital is allocated to the different sectors over time. Particularly important is the agricultural sector. While the modern theory is based on two factors of production, labour and capital, and the classical theory is based on land, labour, and circulating capital, the Butt model of the agricultural sector takes account of three factors – land, labour, and fixed capital.

In order to highlight the role of fixed capital in the nonagricultural sectors, a sharp distinction is made between two types of techniques, namely 'handicraft' techniques which do not use any capital, and 'mechanized' techniques which use capital in the form of machines. Thus capital is introduced into production by substituting mechanized techniques for handicraft techniques; the process is described as 'mechanization'. In order to concentrate on the dynamic aspects, the model is simplified by assuming fixed coefficients between factors and output in each technique. When a mechanized technique is substituted for the handicraft technique in a sector, capital is used to save labour in producing the output. The physical productivity S of capital in each sector is measured by the amount of labour saved per unit of capital; the productivity of capital varies from sector to sector.

The mechanization of each sector goes through two phases. In the first phase the mechanized technique is used together with the handicraft technique. Then the price of the product equals its wage cost in the handicraft technique, and the rate of profit of capital equals the productivity of capital in that sector. In the second phase the sector is completely mechanized and the price of the product falls below its wage cost in the handicraft technique.

As capital accumulates the rate of profit goes on declining. A sector begins to be mechanized, that is, a mechanized technique is introduced into the sector when the rate of profit declines to the level of the productivity of capital in that sector. This means that the various sectors are mechanized in a particular sequence, the sequence in which they are arranged in descending order of their respective capital productivity. Each sector has to wait its turn for mechanization. The pattern is illustrated in Figure 8.1, where S_i is the productivity of capital in the ith sector, and r_t is the rate of profit at time t.

In this figure the rates of return to the various sectors are shown by the flat lines, reflecting the assumption of fixed coefficients between labour, capital, and output. The horizontal sections of the r_t curve represent the first phase of mechanization of a sector when the mechanized technique is used together with the handicraft technique, and the downward sloping sections the second phase when the mechanized technique has completely replaced the handicraft technique.

There are a number of possible outcomes depending on the rate of capital accumulation and the rate of population growth. So long as the capital stock grows faster than population, the process of mechanization moves forward until the rate of profit declines to zero – the stage of the 'euthanasia of the rentier'. This is the state of exhaustion corresponding to the

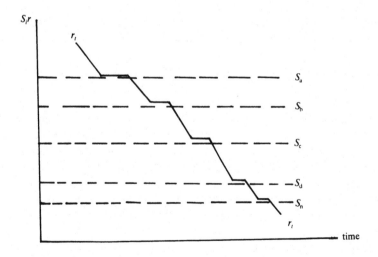

Figure 8.1

classical stationary state, when the 'full possibilities of capitalism are realised'. Accumulation may also cease if the rate of profit is too low to induce saving – the case of exhaustion through improvidence – or if capitalist consumption has reached a satiety point. If wage earners also save and their consumption also reaches satiety, we have the Ramsey case of universal bliss. If at any time the rate of capital accumulation equals the rate of population growth, we have Marshall's (1961) case of the spreading stationary state. If population grows faster than capital, there may be a retrogression of the mechanization process.

So far we have only considered the process of mechanization of the nonagricultural sectors. We now consider its extension to the case of the agricultural sector. This extension is particularly important because the agricultural sector is the major sector of the LDCs. The agricultural sector is important for the study of growth and distribution for two reasons: one is that the product of the agricultural sector, food, is an important item of consumption; the other is that an essential factor of production in this sector is land, whose supply cannot be increased like capital.

In the nonagricultural sectors the productivity of capital was derived by comparing mechanized techniques with handicraft techniques using only labour. In the agricultural sector the techniques which do not use capital are described as 'peasant techniques' using land and labour. Because peasant techniques depend on two factors of production, there is a whole spectrum of peasant techniques differing in the amounts of land and labour required to produce a unit of food output. With peasant techniques only, we have the case analysed by Ricardo. As population pressure increases on a limited area of land, there is a succession of peasant techniques with a steadily increasing labour intensity of cultivation. The price of food, and with it the rent of land, rises; and the real wage of labour falls. The process can be thought of in terms of a peasant calendar, in which the pressure of population on land determines the intensity of cultivation, the rent of land, and the wages of labour.

At any point of time there is a particular peasant technique in vogue. Then the physical productivity of capital in the agricultural sector at that time depends on the comparison between a mechanized farming technique and the peasant technique in use at that time. This depends on the amount of land and/or labour that is saved by the mechanized technique. A mechanized farming technique may be land-saving or land-using, or labour-saving or labour-using. The important point, however, is that the curve showing the rate of return of a mechanized technique in agriculture cannot be drawn as a horizontal line as for other sectors, but as a curve as shown in Figure 8.2. In this diagram, the horizontal axis measures the movement along the peasant calendar, indicated by the rising rent of land, as cultivation by peasant techniques become more and more labour intensive. At each point, the S curve shows the profitability of the mechanized

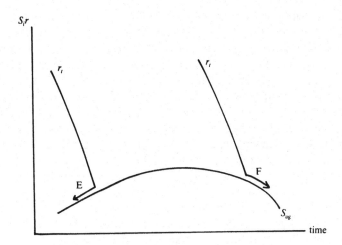

Figure 8.2

technique *vis-à-vis* the peasant technique in vogue at that stage of the peasant calendar. The profitability of the mechanized technique depends on its land-saving characteristic in the rising part of the curve, and on its labour-saving characteristic in the falling part of the curve.

The agricultural sector will be mechanized when the rate of profit falls to the level of the capital productivity of the mechanized farming technique. If this occurs in the early stages of the peasant calendar, the mechanized technique will be land-saving. The mechanization of agriculture will then free the economy from the constraint of the fixed supply of land. The rent of land will decline, thereby relaxing one of the most important conditions for a high inequality of income distribution in LDCs. This is the route followed by the DCs, and is shown by the arrow marked E. But these favourable results may not follow if the mechanization of agriculture is long delayed in the peasant calender. Then agricultural mechanization will be labour-saving and land-using, leading even to a rise in the rent of land, as shown by the arrow marked F. The Butt model is particularly useful in bringing out all the possible outcomes of capital accumulation for growth and distribution. (For a more detailed analysis, see Booth and Sundrum 1984: section 3.4 and Chap. 7.)

8.5 Critique

As noted in section 8.1, the theories summarized in the above sections deal with the functional distribution of income, that is, with the prices of, and the shares of total income accruing to, the various factors of production. These factor prices and factor shares are certainly relevant to explain the personal distribution of income, according to the analytical framework adopted here, but they are only part of the explanation. For a more complete analysis we must also consider the proportions of the population earning their income from each factor of production. One object of the following three chapters is therefore to discuss the ways in which these proportions are determined for the major factors of production.

With regard to factor prices and factor shares, the main thrust of the explanation offered by the theories discussed above is in terms of the factor endowments of countries. Hence changes in these factor prices and shares are explained by population growth and capital accumulation with a given area of land. In the neoclassical theory, the rate of population growth is assumed to be given exogenously, while the rate of capital accumulation is determined by savings behaviour. Then, following the marginal productivity theory, what happens to factor prices and shares depends on the elasticity of substitution between factors and the nature of technological progress. The theory has been developed mainly to explain the stability of factor shares, assumed to have characterized the historical experience of the developed countries. In fact, some of the main features of technological progress are derived from the assumed stability of factor shares.

In the classical theory population growth is assumed to be endogenously determined by the relationship of wages to the subsistence level of income, according to the Malthusian hypothesis. Capital accumulation in the wage fund is also assumed to be endogenously determined by savings out of profits. The interaction between these two relationships then leads to the expansion of the wage fund and a steady growth of population. In this process wages fluctuate around the subsistence level, while the growth of population on limited land leads to a steady fall in the rate of profit and a steady rise in the rent of land.

In the dualistic model of Lewis factor incomes are determined separately in the two sectors of the economy, the traditional sector with a surplus of labour, and the modern sector with a steady accumulation of capital by savings out of profits. Because of the labour surplus in the traditional sector, there is an unlimited supply of labour to the modern sector at a constant wage. The rate at which the surplus labour is absorbed into the modern sector depends on the rate of capital accumulation. Thus while the stock of capital determines wages at any point of time for a given inelastic supply of labour in the neoclassical theory, the stock of capital determines employment in the modern sector for a perfectly elastic supply of labour in the dualistic theory. When all the surplus labour of the traditional sector has been absorbed into the modern sector, the economy enters a neoclassical phase of its growth process.

In the Butt model factor prices are determined by population growth and capital accumulation on a fixed area of land, but this model also takes account of the effect of varying commodity prices. Thus while nominal wages are constant so long as handicraft techniques are used in some sectors, real wages are affected by changes in the price of commodities. The price of nonagricultural goods will fall steadily with their mechanization. The price of food will rise before the agricultural sector is mechanized, with the increasing labour-intensity of peasant techniques. If the agricultural sector is mechanized at an early stage of the peasant calendar, the price of food will fall, but this may not happen if the mechanization of the agricultural sector is delayed. The rate of profit will decline throughout, but the changes in the rent of land will depend on the stage of the peasant calendar in which agriculture in mechanized.

In tracing the influence of factor endowments on factor prices and shares, the above theories have made a number of assumptions about the functioning of factor markets which do not necessarily hold in practice, especially in LDCs. For example, most of these theories assume that available supplies of factors are normally fully utilized, and that factor prices are determined by the equilibrium of supply and demand. But in practice, factor prices are often fixed above their equilibrium levels and factors are not fully employed. This was the basis of the Keynesian theory about the crucial role of aggregate demand in determining incomes and employment. But many economists have argued that this theory is not applicable to explain the widespread unemployment of labour in LDCs (for example, Rao 1952; Dasgupta 1953). Instead, such unemployment is explained by the scarcity of land and capital, and the rigid proportions in which labour is combined with other factors under the prevailing technology (Eckhaus 1955). But factor proportions are not as rigidly fixed as generally assumed; in fact, there is considerable variation of these proportions even in the agricultural sector, both for economic and for institutional reasons (see Booth and Sundrum 1984: Chap. 4). As a result, land and capital are not as fully and productively utilized as they might be. Therefore demand factors play a considerable part even in LDCs in determining the utilization of factors and their prices.

Most theories also assume highly competitive factor markets (Lydall 1979:2–4). Even in DCs, there is only limited competition in many important markets; hence, for example, Kalecki (1942) advanced his theory of the degree of monopoly as a major determinant of income distribution in highly industrialized countries. But competition is also very imperfect in the LDCs. One consequence of imperfect competition is that factor prices will not necessarily be equal to marginal productivity. However, there is also another consequence, namely that persons supplying the same factor of production receive very different prices for it. By concentrating so heavily on the competitive case, these theories fail to take account of the extent to which such price differences contribute to income inequality.

Another limitation of these theories is that they assume all units of each factor of production to be homogeneous. While this is useful to simplify the analysis, it means that these theories do not take account of the inequality of incomes that is due to differences between units of the same factor of production.

Finally, a major weakness of the neoclassical theory is that it has been developed mainly for the case of constant returns to scale, because it is only on this assumption that the marginal productivity theory is consistent with the assumption of perfect competition. But in fact returns are not constant. Just as the classical economists took full account of diminishing returns in agriculture in their analysis of that sector, any theory of factor prices in the industrial sector must take more account of increasing returns, an important characteristic of that sector.

Hence the theories discussed in this chapter suffer from two major weaknesses in their explanation of income distribution in LDCs, namely that their explanation of factor prices rests on highly simplified assumptions about the functioning of factor markets, and they do not take account of the proportions of the population earning their incomes from different factors of production. Therefore some modifications of these theories to remedy these weaknesses are discussed in the following three chapters dealing with the three major factors of production.

Chapter nine

Incomes from land: land distribution and rent

9.1 Agricultural share of the labour force

In the theories discussed in the previous chapter, incomes were distinguished according to the factor of production from which they were derived. This classification of incomes is a useful way of developing an analytical framework for the study of income distribution. Strictly speaking, this approach is fully justified only if each individual or household derives income only from one factor of production. The classical economists, in fact, explicitly assumed this to be the case, but this assumption was criticized by Johnson (1964:177), who argued that 'the time has come to sever the link with the classical attempt to identify categories of income with distinctly different kinds of productive factors, and that a more useful approach would be to lump all factors together as items of capital equipment'. But this criticism was made in his essay on opulence with special reference to the developed countries. These countries had already accumulated a large stock of capital invested, not only in specific capital goods, but also to improve the quality of land and human resources. In the less developed countries, however, there has been much less accumulation of capital and much less investment in land and human resources. Therefore the classical approach is still a useful way of analysing the distribution of income in LDCs. The major exception is the case of farmers cultivating their own farms, in which case their incomes are derived both from the land and from the labour they put into their farms.

But in following this approach the theories discussed in the last chapter had concentrated only on the prices received by the various factors of production and the shares of total output accruing to these factors, mostly for the case of competitive factor and product markets. In most LDCs, however, factor markets do not function in this way. Therefore one task facing us is to modify these theories to take account of other types of market institutions. Further, any explanation of the distribution of income among individuals and households must take account note only of the prices and output shares of the various factors of production, but also of the proportions of the population depending on these factors and the way these proportions change over time. These in turn depend on the distribution of the factors of production among individuals and households. Therefore another task facing us is to explain the distribution of productive assets among the population and the changes in this distribution over time.

The main problem in developing the analytical framework to deal with these problems as they affect income distribution in LDCs is that LDCs vary greatly among themselves. It is clearly not possible to deal with these variations in individual countries. Therefore we shall only consider the typical features affecting incomes from the various factors of production as they apply to LDCs generally, and note only some of the major differences among them.

In this chapter we discuss incomes from land. The topics considered are the agricultural share of the labour force discussed in this section, the size distribution of land discussed in section 9.2, the rent of land discussed in section 9.3, and the extent to which land is leased, discussed in section 9.4.

Even in the LDCs land used as the site of residential and nonresidential buildings is an important source of incomes. But because the supply of such land can be extended by encroaching on the neighbouring rural areas, incomes from land in urban areas can be treated in the same way as incomes from capital. Therefore in the present chapter we shall only consider incomes from land used for agricultural production in rural areas.

An important feature of LDCs is the high proportion of the labour force engaged in agriculture. One of the best established generalizations of development economics is that the agricultural share of the labour force in a country is lower, the higher its per capita income, and declines steadily with the growth of per capita income (Fisher 1935; Clark 1957; Kuznets 1966). This relationship is shown in Table 9.1 by the postwar data from a number of countries, both developed and less developed. The table shows that the agricultural share of the labour force varies inversely with per capita income in each decade, and also declines over time for each group of countries. An interesting feature is that the decline of this share over time has followed a logistic pattern, being slow in countries at a low level of development, then becoming faster at the middle stages of development, and again becoming slow in the most developed countries.

This statistical regularity can be explained in terms of supply and demand factors as follows. The supply factors are the productivity of labour, q_a and q_b in the agricultural and nonagricultural sectors respectively. The demand factors are the proportions k_a and k_b of income spent on the products of the two sectors. It is generally the case that k_a is a decreasing function of per capita income and k_b an increasing function. To simplify the analysis, it is assumed that the supply of output from each sector equals the demand for it; this assumption can be easily modified to take account of foreign trade. Then the following three equations deter-

Table 9.1 Decline in the agricultural share of the labour force

Group of countries	Agricultural share (%) of labour force			Decline of agricultural share of labour force (percentage points)		
	1950	1960	1970	1950–60	1960–70	1950–70
1	92.9	90.1	86.8	2.8	3.3	6.1
2	84.3	80.5	76.7	3.8	3.8	7.6
3	76.3	71.3	65.3	5.0	6.0	11.0
4	66.8	61.7	54.7	5.1	7.0	12.1
5	55.4	48.9	40.3	6.5	8.6	15.1
6	46.1	37.3	28.0	8.8	9.3	18.1
7	33.2	27.4	20.4	5.8	7.0	12.8
8	23.2	17.6	12.0	5.6	5.6	11.2
9	16.7	12.0	8.0	4.7	3.0	8.7

Source: Kuznets 1982: Table 4.1, p. 44.

mine the three variables: per capita income y, and the shares λ_a and λ_b of the labour force engaged in the two sectors.

$$y = \lambda_a q_a + \lambda_b q_b \tag{9.1}$$

$$\lambda_a = y k_a / q_a \tag{9.2}$$

$$\lambda_b = y k_b / q_b \tag{9.3}$$

The characteristic feature of LDCs is that their labour productivity in the two sectors is very low, lower than in the DCs. This is the main reason for their low per capita incomes. At this low level of income, they spend a high proportion on food. Therefore they have a high proportion of their labour force engaged in agriculture.

Next we consider how changes in these supply and demand factors influence the allocation of labour over time. As we shall only be concerned with the *proportions* of the labour force engaged in the two sectors, we may simplify the analysis by assuming that the labour force is constant, without any loss of generality. The supply factors are the rates of growth of labour productivity, $\dot{q}_a$ and $\dot{q}_b$ respectively, where a dot over a variable indicates its rate of change over a given period. At the end of the period, the labour productivities become q_a' and q_b' repectively, using a prime to distinguish final from initial values. The demand factors are the income elasticities of demand ε_a and ε_b.

From these definitions, it follows that

$$q = \Sigma \, q_i \lambda_i \tag{9.4}$$

179

and

$$\dot{q} = (k_a \dot{q}_a + k_b \dot{q}_b) + (\lambda'_a - \lambda_a) \frac{q'_b - q'_a}{q} \tag{9.5}$$

The first term on the righthand side of (9.5) represents the component of overall growth of GDP due to the growth of labour productivity in each sector. The second term refers to the component of growth due to the re-allocation of labour from the sector with lower labour productivity, which may be taken as the agricultural sector, to the sector with higher labour productivity.

Also from the above definitions we have

$$\lambda'_i - \lambda_i = \frac{\lambda_i(\dot{q}\varepsilon_i - \dot{q}_i)}{1 + \dot{q}_i} \tag{9.6}$$

Hence we have two equations for the two variables $\dot{q}$ and $\lambda'_i - \lambda_i$ in terms of the parameters $\dot{q}_i$ and ε_i referring to the rates of growth of labour productivity and income elasticities of demand of the two sectors.

The simplest way to solve these simultaneous equations is as follows. Because of the growth of labour productivity in sector A, the quantity of labour required to produce the initial quantities of output in that sector will decline by

$$\lambda_a - \frac{\lambda_a q_a}{q'_a} = \frac{\lambda_a \dot{q}_a}{1 + \dot{q}_a}$$

and similarly for sector B. Therefore the total labour required to produce the initial outputs of both sectors will decline by

$$\frac{\lambda_a \dot{q}_a}{1 + \dot{q}_a} + \frac{\lambda_b \dot{q}_b}{1 + \dot{q}_b} \tag{9.7}$$

But due to the growth of demand, the output of sector i will increase by $\lambda_i q_i \dot{q}\varepsilon_i$. Then the labour required to produce the extra output of both sectors will be

$$\dot{q} \left(\frac{\lambda_a \varepsilon_a}{1 + \dot{q}_a} + \frac{\lambda_b \varepsilon_b}{1 + \dot{q}_b} \right) \tag{9.8}$$

As the labour force is constant by assumption, the reduction in the labour required to produce the initial outputs, given by (9.7), must equal the addition required to produce the extra outputs, given by (9.8). Equating these two quantities, we get

$$\dot{q} = \left(\frac{\lambda_a \dot{q}_a}{1 + \dot{q}_a} + \frac{\lambda_b \dot{q}_b}{1 + \dot{q}_b} \right) \left(\frac{\lambda_a \varepsilon_a}{1 + \dot{q}_a} + \frac{\lambda_b \varepsilon_b}{1 + \dot{q}_b} \right)^{-1} \tag{9.9}$$

Substituting this expression into (9.6), we also have

$$\lambda_a' - \lambda_a = \frac{\lambda_a \lambda_b (\dot{q}_b \varepsilon_a - \dot{q}_a \varepsilon_b)}{\lambda_a \varepsilon_a (1 + \dot{q}_b) + \lambda_b \varepsilon_b (1 + \dot{q}_a)} \tag{9.10}$$

that is,

$$\lambda_a' \gtrless \lambda_a \quad \text{according as} \quad \frac{\varepsilon_a}{\varepsilon_b} \gtrless \frac{\dot{q}_a}{\dot{q}_b} \tag{9.11}$$

This is a neat formula showing the role of demand and supply factors. According to this result, the agricultural share of the labour force will decline if the ratio of income elasticities of demand, representing the demand factors, is less than the ratio of the growth rates of labour productivity, representing the supply factors. It is because this condition was fulfilled in the DCs that their agricultural share of the labour force declined rapidly for over a century in the past. However, the condition was satisfied to a smaller extent in LDCs in the postwar period so that the agricultural share of the labour force in these countries has declined more slowly in these countries, and a large proportion of the labour force is still engaged in agriculture in these countries. This was partly because the growth of labour productivity in agriculture was smaller relative to other sectors, and also because the income elasticity of demand for food has remained at a high level. It is generally found that the income elasticity of demand for food of households varies with their income. But the national income elasticity of demand involved in the above formulae is an average of the elasticity for different income groups and therefore depends on the distribution of income among these groups. The national income elasticity of demand for food in individual countries therefore depends not only on the growth of per capita income but also on the changes in the inequality of income distribution.

The above analysis was based on some simple assumptions, especially that labour is fully employed and that there is equilibrium of supply and demand at stable prices. These assumptions must be relaxed for a more complete analysis. Further, we must also take account of the role of foreign trade. (For further discussion, see Booth and Sundrum 1984: Chap. 2.)

9.2 Size distribution of land

Given the agricultural population, we next consider their incomes. These incomes depend on the area of land they have for cultivation and the state of agricultural technology. One factor influencing the land available for cultivation is the density of population. The density of population is usually calculated as the number of persons per unit of the geographical area of countries. But the geographical area of countries consists of land of very different qualities, some of which, like mountains, deserts, and forested areas, are unsuitable for cultivation. Therefore a better measure of the land available for cultivation is given by adjusting the geographical area in terms of arable land, by giving a weight of 1 to arable land, 0.5 to permanent pasture land, 0.2 to forest and woodland, and 0.1 to all other types of land, as classified in the FAO *Production Yearbooks*. The per capita adjusted area in different Asian countries is shown in Table 9.2.

These adjusted figures show that there are some remarkable differences between countries. The proportion of the adjusted area which is actually cultivated is high in some long-settled countries, such as those in South Asia, but quite low in other equally long-settled countries such as China, Japan, and Indonesia. These differences are the result of the different strategies of land use that the countries have followed to cope with the growth of population pressure. The countries of South Asia have generally followed the route of extending the land frontier continuously, while the

Table 9.2 Adjusted and arable land areas: selected Asian countries, around 1980

Country	Per capita geographical area (ha)	Per capita adjusted area (ha)	Arable land as percentage of adjusted area
Bangladesh	0.16	0.11	91
China	0.96	0.31	32
India	0.48	0.28	87
Indonesia	1.28	0.36	37
S. Korea	0.26	0.09	6
Malaysia	2.33	0.67	46
Pakistan	0.93	0.33	72
Philippines	0.61	0.31	77
Sri Lanka	0.44	0.18	72
Taiwan	0.20	—	—
Thailand	1.09	0.50	78
LDCs (average)	2.38	0.75	32
Japan	0.32	0.09	45
DMEs (average)	4.17	1.41	36

Source: Food and Agriculture Organization (1985) *Production Yearbook*.

North Asian countries have followed the route of a more intensive culti-vation of a smaller and more fertile proportion of their geographical area. The difference may be due to differences in biophysical conditions of soil conditions, rainfall, and situation of river valleys, as Vaidyanathan (1978) has suggested. But it may also be due to the fact that what Ishikawa (1978) has described as the 'community principle' has been followed to a greater extent in the North Asian countries. Under this principle, surplus labour was used to improve the land for the common benefit of all farmers in a given area, so that more labour-intensive methods of cultivation could be used to raise the yield of land.

Although the geographical area of countries is constant over time, except when it is changed by war and conquest, the arable part of this area varies in the course of population growth. Therefore we must also consider the growth of cultivated land area relative to the growth of population. The changes between 1960 and 1980 are summarized in Table 9.3 for various groups of countries. The land–inhabitant ratio, indicating the abundance of land relative to the agricultural population, varies greatly between coun-tries, both within developed and within less developed countries, with some

Table 9.3 Land–inhabitant ratios, yields, and production per worker, 1960–82

Country groups	Land (ha) per male agric. worker		Yield tons (wheat equiv. per hectare)		Output (by wheat equiv. per worker)	
	1960	1980	1960	1980	1960	1980
DCs						
(a) Land abundant	171.9	265.8	0.43	0.62	83.1	197.3
(b) Medium	14.9	27.9	2.33	3.68	34.1	102.4
(c) Land scarce	6.4	12.4	2.27	3.61	22.6	69.6
(d) Extremely scarce (Japan)	1.2	2.3	8.64	12.23	10.3	27.8
LDCs						
(a) Land abundant	60.0	62.1	0.28	0.42	11.3	20.8
(b) Medium	15.2	15.5	0.48	0.76	7.2	12.7
(c) Land scarce	1.9	1.7	1.26	1.91	5.5	10.5

Note: Country classification:
    DCs (a) Land abundant: Australia, Canada, New Zealand, S. Africa, USA.
          (b) Medium: Austria, Denmark, Finland, France, Ireland, Israel, Norway, Sweden, UK.
          (c) Land scarce: Belgium, W. Germany, Greece, Italy, Netherlands, Portugal, Spain, Switzerland, Yugoslavia
          (d) Extremely scarce: Japan.
    LDCs (a) Land abundant: Argentina, Chile, Libya, Paraguay, Peru, Syria, Venezuela.
          (b) Medium: Brazil, Colombia, Mexico, Turkey.
          (c) Land scarce: Bangladesh, Egypt, India, Mauritius, Pakistan, Philippines, Sri Lanka, Surinam, Taiwan.
Source: Hayami and Ruttan (1985), Table 5.1, p. 120.

LDCs having a greater abundance of land than some DCs. But there is one difference between the two groups of countries. In the DCs the rapid growth of the nonagricultural sectors has reduced the absolute size of the agricultural population, so much so that the average land per agricultural worker in all these countries increased between 1960 and 1980. By contrast, the absolute size of the agricultural population has continued to increase in the LDCs because of the rapid growth of population and the slow decline of the agricultural share of the labour force. In some of these countries, especially the more land-abundant countries, the area under cultivation increased more rapidly so that there was a slight rise in the land–inhabitant ratio. In other countries, especially the land-scarce countries, the scope for land extension was more limited so that there was a decline in the land–inhabitant ratio.

The effect of declining land–inhabitant ratios on the output and incomes of agricultural workers, however, was offset by a tendency for the yield of land to rise. This tendency was greatly accelerated by systematic agricultural research, especially the invention in the international agricultural research centres of new varieties of seed which were very responsive to the use of modern inputs such as fertilizers. The growth of yields was generally faster in countries where land was more scarce. This tendency operated systematically both in DCs and LDCs, offsetting the effect of the declining land–inhabitant ratios.

So far we have only been considering differences in the average land area per agricultural worker between countries and changes over time. But to explain the distribution of income among the agricultural population, we must also consider how the total area of land is distributed among farmers. The situation in a number of countries is summarized in Table 9.4 in terms of the Gini index of land distribution. A serious weakness of these data is that they do not take sufficient account of differences in the quality of land between regions within countries. In the absence of more detailed data, the above measures have to be used as rough measures of the inequality of land distribution.

Taking the typical Latin American countries first, we find that in spite of their relative land abundance, the ownership of land is highly concentrated; there is both a high degree of agricultural proletarianization with large estates cultivated with hired labour, and extensive leasing out of land in small units to tenant farmers. Then there is a second group, typified by conditions in Africa; here there is less concentration of land, but agricultural technology is generally low so that even those with a large area to cultivate earn only a low income. However, many of these countries are rich in natural resources, whose ownership is highly concentrated, so that these countries illustrate dualistic development in an extreme form. There are a few Asian countries with a relatively light pressure of population on land such as Burma, Malaysia, Thailand, and the outer islands of

Table 9.4 Average holding size (ha) and inequality of land distribution

Country (Year)	Average holding size (ha)	Gini index of land distribution
Peru (1961)	20.37	0.947
Venezuela (1961)	81.24	0.936
Argentina (1970)	270.10	0.873
Colombia (1960)	22.60	0.865
Brazil (1960)	79.25	0.845
Uruguay (1966)	208.80	0.833
Iran (1960)	6.05	0.624
Turkey (1960)	5.03	0.611
India (1953–54)	2.20	0.694
(1961–62)	1.84	0.584
(1971–72)	1.60	0.586
Indonesia (1973)	1.01	0.556
Java	0.64	0.486
Outer islands	1.51	0.570
Pakistan (1972)	5.28	0.520
Philippines (1971)	3.61	0.520
Taiwan (1960–61)	1.27	0.474
Japan (1960)	1.18	0.473
Thailand (1978)	3.72	0.460
Bangladesh (1977)	1.42	0.450

Source: World Bank (1975), *Land Reform Sector Policy Paper*; Booth and Sundrum (1984), p. 139.

Indonesia; in these regions, there is less concentration of land ownership and a high degree of tenancy offsets the tendency to proletarianization.

Then we consider various categories among the long-settled Asian countries. At one extreme are Taiwan and South Korea, with a relatively more equal distribution of land and most farms cultivated with family labour. The surplus labour of rural areas has been absorbed by the rapid growth of the nonagricultural sectors. The second important category is illustrated by the historical experience of Japan and China. Although there was considerable inequality in land ownership, there was also extensive tenancy so that operational holdings were more equally distributed and proletarianization was limited. The third category consists of India, Bangladesh, and Java, with intense population pressure on the land; there is a moderate degree of inequality of land ownership but only a limited extent of tenancy so that there is a high and growing degree of proletarianization. Finally, at the other extreme are Pakistan and the Philippines with a high degree of concentration combined with both extensive tenancy and a high degree of proletarianization.

Thus we see that the conditions of land distribution vary greatly among

LDCs. In order to explain this variation, we consider some of the theories that have been advanced in the literature. One of the dominant theories on the subject is the Marxian theory of increasing concentration. This law was first advanced for the industrial sector because of the strong force of increasing returns in that sector, or what Mitrany (1951:27) has described as 'an elemental belief in the superiority and hence the necessity of large-scale production'. Writing in England in the middle decades of the nineteenth century, Marx assumed that the same tendency would also apply in the agricultural sector, leading to a concentration of farms in the large sizes.

However, this theory was criticized by Chayanov and other writers belonging to the 'agrarian school' in Russia and the countries of eastern Europe. These countries were at an earlier stage of economic development and resembled today's LDCs more closely with respect to the proportion of the labour force engaged in peasant agriculture. According to these writers, the force of increasing returns was much weaker in agriculture than in industry so that there was less of a tendency towards increasing concentration. For example, a small farm engaged in livestock and dairy industry may be just as profitable as a large farm engaged in producing grain. In fact, Lenin himself (quoted by Patnaik 1979:408) pointed out that 'agriculture did not develop according to the same pattern as industry; it is subject to special laws'.

The debate hinged on how far small farms were able to survive in the face of competition from large farms. Chayanov argued that peasant families cultivating small farms with family labour behaved very differently from capitalist farmers operating large farms with hired labour. The difference lay primarily in the fact that while capitalist farmers employed labour up to the point at which its marginal product was equal to the wages they had to pay, peasant farmers used their family labour up to the point at which its marginal product just equalled the irksomeness of the extra work (Thorner 1966:xvi). This argument is indeed very close to the 'cheap family labour argument' used by Sen (1964:323), who explained the position in LDCs as follows:

> In a situation of widespread unemployment, the opportunity cost of labour to a family-based farm is very low, but for various reasons (mainly perhaps sociological), the wage rate does not go down below a certain level, considerably higher than the opportunity cost. As a consequence, the family-based farmer applies labour more liberally with less restraint than the wage-based farmer, and this naturally leads to a higher productivity per acre of the *small* farms, because these are mostly family-based farms rather than wage-based farms.

Although capitalist farmers and peasant farmers employ labour in different ways, both approaches are consistent with maximizing behaviour. To the large farmer, hired labour is a variable factor, and profits are maximized when such labour is hired up to the point at which marginal product is equal to the wage rate. But to the peasant household, family labour is a fixed factor of production which does not have alternative uses because of the imperfection of the labour market discussed in the next chapter. Therefore family labour is used intensively up to the point at which its marginal product is close to zero, because that is the point at which the output of the farm is a maximum. This theory is important for our present discussion because it provides a reason why small peasant farms may be able to compete effectively with larger farms, and why there may be no tendency towards concentration of ownership.

In practice, the two tendencies described in these theories have operated in different degrees in various countries. For example, high inequality of land distribution in countries like Pakistan and the Philippines may have been due to a process of concentration as envisaged by Marx. But in the typical Latin American case, the very unequal distribution of land may have been due to the fact that when Europeans settled down in large numbers, they took over large blocks of land for their own use, unlike the Asian colonies which already had relatively high population pressure on the land at the time of the European conquest. The dominance of peasant farming in most other Asian countries is probably the result of the process envisaged by the agrarian economists. But the highly egalitarian distribution of land in countries like Taiwan and South Korea was the result of extensive land reform, especially those undertaken in the postwar period (see Booth and Sundrum 1984: Chap. 6 for a more detailed discussion of Asian countries).

9.3 Rent of land

Given a distribution of land among the agricultural population, we next consider the incomes derived from land ownership. The classical economists based their theory of rent on the assumption that there was a fixed stock of land that was a free gift of nature for society as a whole, so that land did not have any cost of production associated with it. But the existing stock of land was owned by a class of landlords whose income was derived from the rent of land. The land was rented out to capitalists who cultivated it with hired labour. On these assumptions, they concluded that the rent of land was a residual after capital was paid at its prevailing rate of interest, and labour was paid wages at a subsistence level. When the rent of land is determined in this way as a residual, it varied between different farms according to their fertility and rose steadily over time with the growth of population pressure on the fixed area of land.

There are, however, a number of modifications that have to be made to these propositions before they can be applied to LDCs. It is generally true that the rent of land is higher in countries with a greater population pressure on land. But, as argued in the Butt model, the scarcity of land can be relieved to some extent by the investment of fixed capital. According to that theory, if agriculture is mechanized by the use of fixed capital in the early stages of the peasant calendar, the investment will tend to be of the land-saving form, such as the construction of irrigation works and the use of fertilizers. Then such investment will put a brake on the rise of rent in the course of population growth. This explains the relatively low rent of agricultural land in the developed countries. On the other hand, if agriculture is mechanized only in the later stages of the peasant calendar, investment will tend to be of the labour-saving type, such as the use of tractors. Then such investment may even exacerbate the rise of rent. In practice, both forms of investment are being made in LDCs at present, and the effect on rent is the net result of the two forces.

Another modification that has to be made relates to the classical assumption that agricultural production was carried on by capitalists who rented land from landlords and hired workers to cultivate it. By contrast, in the dualistic theory of Lewis it was assumed that agricultural production was carried on by peasant families who owned their farms and cultivated them with family labour. In this case the income of the peasant families consisted of a mixture of rent and wage incomes.

In practice, the typical situation in most LDCs is a combination of the two patterns. Hence we must distinguish at least three cases: (i) the case in which owners of large estates cultivated their land by hiring landless labourers; (ii) the case in which owners of large estates leased out their land in smaller parcels to tenants; and (iii) the case in which owners of small farms cultivated their land using their family labour.

Owners of large estates therefore have two options. One is to cultivate their land with hired labour. Then, if wages paid per hectare are W_a, and the output is Y_a, the net income they derive from their land will be $R_a = Y_a - W_a$. The other option is to rent out their land at a rental of R_b. Then, if the output per hectare is Y_b, the income that tenants derive from their labour and the opportunity to lease in land will be $W_b = Y_b - R_b$.

Landlords cultivating their land with hired labour will employ labour only to the point at which the marginal product of labour equals the prevailing wage rate. On the other hand, tenant farmers will cultivate their land more intensively to maximize output, that is, to the point at which the marginal product falls to zero. Therefore, in general, $Y_b > Y_a$, that is, $(W_b - W_a) + (R_b - R_a)$ will be positive. However, each of these two components will also be positive. As far as the landlords are concerned, the rent they charge their tenants must be at least as great as the income they can derive by cultivating their land with hired labour; therefore $R_b > R_a$. As far as the tenants are concerned, the income they derive as tenants must be at least as great as the income they can derive by hiring out their labour; therefore $W_b > W_a$.

Finally, we consider the case of owner cultivators. It is likely that these farmers will cultivate their land as intensively as tenant farmers. Therefore, as a first approximation, we may take $Y_c = Y_b$. For notional purposes, the rent component of Y_c may be taken as equal to the rent that tenant farmers pay for leasing their land, and the wage component as equal to the income of tenant farmers. Therefore the income of owner cultivators will be greater than that of tenant farmers, and more so than the income of landless labourers.

Given the incomes of the various categories of the agricultural population, determined by these relationships, the distribution of income will depend on the proportions in these categories. The proportion of owner cultivators in the agricultural population will be determined by the forces influencing the distribution of land ownership discussed above. The same forces will also determine the proportion of the agricultural population who do not own their own land. Of these, the division between landless labourers hiring out their labour and tenant farmers will be influenced by the rent charged by landlords. The higher the rent, the smaller will be the proportion of landless persons wishing to lease in land, and conversely. But the market for land leases varies considerably between countries, as discussed in the following section.

9.4 The leasing of land

One of the possible modes of cultivation distinguished in the last section was cultivation through tenant farmers. This is the typical case considered in the classical model. In this section, we consider the extent of tenancy and the factors influencing the rent of leased land, distinguishing between a number of different cases.

If land is abundant relative to the agricultural population, then any household wishing to engage in agriculture can acquire land as a free good, and there will be no need to lease it from others. This situation is unlikely to arise in any long-settled LDC as far as total arable land is concerned, but land is of variable quality and it is possible that there is relative abundance of the less fertile land. Hence we would not expect much tenancy in the case of such land. On the other hand, as Bardhan (1984: Chap. 10) has pointed out, villages with more productive land tend to show a greater incidence of tenancy.

If land is scarce but its ownership is equally distributed among the agricultural population, and if all agricultural households share the same conditions of production, then again there will be no incentive for any individual household either to buy or sell land, or to lease in or lease out land. But if some households are more efficient than others, then it is possible that there is a price at which it will be mutually advantageous for the less efficient household to sell its land to the more efficient one, or alternatively that there is a level of rent at which it will be mutually advantageous for the more efficient household to lease in land from the less efficient one.

It is unlikely, however, that the first option will materalize to any great extent in the typical LDCs. This is partly because, as Lewis (1955:91) remarked, 'there is probably no country in the world where land is bought and sold solely for its value as a factor of production, and no country where non-economic factors do not frustrate schemes which would otherwise increase output'. It is also because the land market is usually very imperfect; the numbers of buyers and sellers are too small, and the competition too limited, for a standard method of valuation to emerge. This is most clearly seen in the failure of farmers to consolidate the many parcels into which their land is often fragmented. These problems are compounded by the weakness of the capital market. Even an inefficient farmer is likely to earn a larger income from his land, to which he can apply his own family labour, than by investing the sale proceeds in any alternative way and seeking wage employment for his labour. On the other hand, it is usually difficult for even an efficient farmer to finance the purchase of land out of his own capital or by borrowing. Therefore only those in desperate need for cash sell their land, and only relatively rich people with their own capital or with easy access to long-term credit can buy land. The latter are not necessarily the more efficient farmers, but may be capitalists in rural or even urban areas acquiring the land as an investment to be leased out to tenants. Under some conditions, funds may be diverted from productive investments in other forms of capital merely to push up the value of land, as Keynes (1936:241–2) argued, but it is also likely that the rent that such investors can earn from the land makes these investments in acquiring land more profitable than other types of investments.

It is therefore more likely that, as between farmers owning equal areas of land, the more efficient farmers will lease in land from the less efficient, than that they will buy the land. The evidence from India that there is little difference between the inequality of owned and operated holdings suggests that the leasing of land mostly occurs between farmers operating similar farm sizes (Raj 1970); such transactions are therefore most likely to be due to differences in efficiency among these farmers. It has also been found that farm households with more adult members tend to lease in more land than those with fewer adult members (Bardhan 1984: Chap. 10). Also, as the better-off farmers owning larger farms are able to exploit the new agricultural technology based on substantial modern inputs more profitably, they tend to evict their former tenants and take back the leased land for their own cultivation.

The next case is one in which the ownership of land is very unequally distributed. If farms of different sizes are cultivated only with family labour and with the same technology, then the yield per hectare in the large farm will be lower than in the small farm. This raises two possibilities: one is for the large farmer to lease some of his land to the small farmer; the other is for the large farmer to cultivate his land more intensively hiring labour either from the small farmer's household or from landless households. Similarly, the landless household has two options, either to lease in land from the large farmer or to work as hired labour. We must note, however, that these sets of options are not as clear-cut in practice as they are in theory because there is a wide range of forms of tenancy, some of which come close to treating the tenant as a hired labourer.

Countries differ widely in the extent to which the tenancy option is exercised. As mentioned in section 9.2, tenancy was widespread in the historical experience of countries like Japan and China. By contrast, in south and southeast Asian countries such as India and Indonesia, larger owners tend either to cultivate their land with labour hired both on a regular and a casual basis, or to rent their land to tenants in small parcels.

The position regarding the extent of tenancy may therefore be summed up as follows. The extent of tenancy is greater on the more productive land because it is more scarce relative to the number of households wishing to cultivate compared with the less productive land. Tenancy may also occur because of differences in efficiency as more efficient farmers lease land from less efficient owners. Compared with this reason for tenancy, the renting of land by large to small owners as a way of adjusting an unequal distribution of ownership holdings to a more equal distribution of operational holdings varies greatly between countries, being very limited in densely populated LDCs nowadays compared with the historical experience of countries like Japan and China.

Finally, we have to consider the terms on which land is leased. In the classical model, the rent of land is determined by the competition between landlords and capitalists. Because the capitalists also have considerable financial power, they are able to maintain their share of output at the marginal product of labour times the number of workers, and hence to limit rent to the difference between the average and the marginal product of labour. In the LDCs, however, there is no distinct class of capitalists who act as entrepreneurs leasing land from the landlords and cultivating it with hired labour. Instead, rent is determined by the competition between landlords and workers who have to provide both labour and management. Because of the weak bargaining position of workers under conditions of extensive unemployment, the rent tends to a level which only leaves a subsistence level of income to the tenants. In fact, it has been found in India that tenancy is more widespread in regions with more unemployment (Bardhan 1984:135), suggesting that landless people become tenants when they are unable to get secure employment as wage labourers, and that the position of the small tenant is not necessarily superior to that of the regular labourer.

There are many forms of tenancy, which may be broadly classified according to the way rent is paid. The two major types are those in which the rent charged is a fixed amount in cash or in kind, or it is charged as a given share of the crop. The share-cropping form of tenancy is very prevalent in many LDCs and was very common in the earlier history of DCs as well. The explanation for the prevalence of this form of tenancy has provoked a large literature on the subject (see, e.g., Basu 1984: Chap. 10). The reason for this extensive discussion is that it has seemed to economists that this form of tenancy would lead to an inefficient cultivation of land. If land is leased on a fixed rent, the tenant will apply labour on the land up to the point at which the marginal product of labour will equal the wages that the tenant can earn by hiring out his labour to other employers. But if land is leased out on a share-cropping basis, the tenant will only apply labour on the land up to the point at which the alternative wage he can earn will equal the marginal product of labour multipled by the rent share he has to pay.

Various attempts have been made to solve this puzzling feature. One approach has been to explain share tenancy as a way in which the uncertainty afflicting agricultural production is shared between the landlord and the tenant. Another approach, following Cheung (1968), emphasizes that landlords not only fix the share of the crop that has to be paid as rent, but also the amount of labour that tenants have to put in. Thus, by controlling the labour input, landlords can ensure that land is cultivated as intensively as in the fixed rent case. If landlords can specify the labour input by farmers, they can choose this amount so as to maximize their rents, and the rent share they charge will vary according to the conditions of farming such as the productivity of land. But in practice, the share of the crop that is usually charged is remarkably constant, at around half, under widely differing conditions. Another method that landlords can follow is that while charging rent at the customary share of output, they can ration the amount of land leased to individual tenants so as to maximize output and their share of it. The intensity with which land is cultivated under share-cropping will also be influenced by whether the landlord shares in the costs of production to the same extent as in the harvest.

The discussion in the above sections of this chapter may be summarized as follows. According to the analytical framework adopted here, the distribution of income in a country is explained both by the prices of the various factors of production and by the proportions of the population earning their incomes from each factor of production. This chapter dealt with incomes derived from land. It has been concerned both with the rent of land and with the proportions of the agricultural population with varying access to land. The distribution of the population according to their access to land is determined by institutional factors which vary widely among countries. Therefore we can only consider some of the general principles determining such distribution.

The access to land depends partly on the distribution of land ownership. The distribution of land ownership is very unequal in some countries, especially in Latin America, mainly for historical reasons such as the colonization by Europeans. In other countries the growth of population pressure has led to a more equal distribution of land, while the average size of holdings declined. The access to land depends also on the extent to which the leasing of land to tenants is prevalent. The incidence of land leasing also varies considerably between countries, being significant in the north Asian countries and quite limited in the south Asian countries. Both the distribution of land and the incidence of tenancy are influenced by institutional conditions which vary greatly between countries.

Where land is leased out to tenants, there is a wide variation in the nature of rent contracts, ranging from cases in which the rent is fixed either in cash or in kind to those in which it is a fixed share of output. The main influence on the level of rents is the pressure of population on scarce land, depending partly on the extent to which labour is absorbed into the non-agricultural sectors, and partly on the extent to which the scarcity of land is relieved by the investment of fixed capital and land-saving techniques. Finally people without any access to land earn their incomes as agricultural labourers. The wages of such labourers are discussed in more detail in the next chapter.

Chapter ten

Incomes from labour: wages and employment

10.1 Categories of labour

The present chapter deals with incomes mainly derived from labour. Workers earning such incomes are generally classified as 'employees' in population censuses and labour force surveys. The proportion of such workers in the labour force is generally lower in the LDCs (about 40 per cent around 1970) than in the DCs (around 80 per cent). The main reason is that the agricultural sector is a large part of the economy of LDCs, and a high proportion of the labour force in this sector consists of farmers working on their own account and of unpaid family workers.

Most of the theories discussed in Chapter eight treat labour as a homogeneous factor of production, and explain the income of labour in terms of a single rate of wages. But for a more detailed study we must distinguish different categories of labour with very different levels of income, both because of different rates of wages and different levels of employment.

One distinction among categories of labour is according to the sector of their employment. If labour was fully mobile between sectors, and if there was perfect competition between all sectors of labour employment, then all workers of the same qualifications would earn the same wages. But labour is not fully mobile and competition is not perfect. As a result there are significant difference in wage rates between sectors. In particular, wage rates of labour in the agricultural sector are typically lower than in other sectors. This is true even in the DCs (Cornwall 1977:51), and more so in the LDCs. Therefore we must distinguish categories of labour according to the sector of their employment.

With few exceptions, the theories discussed in the last chapter assumed that labour was fully employed. But a high proportion of the labour force in LDCs is severely underemployed or unemployed, with significant effects on their incomes. Therefore we must also distinguish between categories of labour according to the level of their employment.

Third we must distinguish categories of labour according to their skills and qualifications. The most important reason for differences in labour skills and qualifications is the level and type of education of workers. Therefore we must also distinguish labour according to the level of education.

Among wage employees the largest group in most LDCs is that of agricultural labourers; therefore they are considered in more detail. Some of the typical features of their wages and employment are listed in section 10.2, illustrated with data from a few countries. Then in section 10.3 we consider how far existing theories explain these features. Other categories of labour mostly working in urban areas are then discussed in section 10.4.

10.2 Agricultural wages and employment: data

In many LDCs the supply of labour in the agricultural sector comes from landless households, but some labour is also supplied by owners of small farms whose land is so small that it is not sufficient to employ the family labour fully. The demand for agricultural labour comes from the owners of farms so large that they cannot be cultivated with family labour, and from absentee landlords and land owners engaged primarily in other, more profitable, occupations. Further, even small farms hire in labour at times of peak demand for labour.

Therefore both the supply and demand for labour are determined by the size of the agricultural population and the distribution of land among this population. In countries with a very unequal distribution of land, there is a large supply of labour from people without access to their own land. The distribution of land is more equal in some densely populated countries of Asia, but because of the scarcity of land relative to population, landless labourers emerge as a considerable proportion of the agricultural population. This proportion has been estimated at 30 per cent in countries such as India and Indonesia.

These supply and demand conditions then determine the wages and employment of agricultural labour. Some of the typical features of agricultural wages and employment may be listed as follows. The first feature to note is that agricultural wages are very low compared with wages in other sectors and with other types of income. This is due to a number of reasons. One reason is that, owing to intense population pressure, land is cultivated very intensively and therefore the productivity of labour is low due to diminishing returns. Another reason is that the stock of capital in LDCs is low, and most of it is invested in the nonagricultural sectors. Therefore little capital is invested in agriculture. Finally, agricultural labourers are generally unskilled workers with a low level of education and therefore have a low productivity. Because of their low wages, agricultural labourers are among the poorest people in the LDCs.

The second feature of agricultural labour markets in most LDCs is that the wage rate is different for different agricultural operations, but the wages for each operation tend to be quite uniform within villages. The main exception to this pattern is that female workers tend to get lower wages than male workers. Male and female workers are often employed for different operations, but female workers tend to get lower wages than male workers even when they perform the same operation.

Even though wage rates tend to be quite uniform within villages at any time, village labour markets tend to be isolated from each other. Therefore agricultural wages vary considerably in different regions even of the same country. The magnitude of these differences may be illustrated by data on the daily wage rates of male agricultural labourers in the different states of India in 1984–85 (Table 10.1).

These daily wage rates vary from Rs 7.3 in Karnataka and around Rs 8.5 in Madhya Pradesh, Orissa, and Tamil Nadu to more than twice these figures in Haryana and Punjab. The table also gives the net domestic product per worker in the agricultural sector of each state. This shows that the states with high wages are also the agriculturally most advanced states of India. The correlation coefficient between male agricultural wages and the net domestic product of agriculture per worker in that sector is very high (0.88). This suggests that the productivity of labour has a significant influence on wages. In a more detailed study covering 52 agro-climatic regions of India, Bardhan (1984) found that more than half the variation in

Table 10.1 Daily wage rates (in rupees) of male agricultural labourers: India, 1984–85

State	Daily wages (Rs)	NDP per age-worker (Rs)
Andhra Pradesh	10.41	2,642
Assam	12.87	4,768
Bihar	9.88	2,598
Gujarat	12.58	4,843
Haryana	19.35	8,391
Himachal Pradesh	12.55	3,442
Karnataka	7.31	3,553
Kerala	16.86	8,061
Madhya Pradesh	8.53	2,279
Maharashtra	9.46	3,378
Orissa	8.42	3,489
Punjab	18.13	10,709
Rajasthan	12.63	4,640
Tamal Nadu	8.83	1,512
Ultar Pradesh	10.54	3,251
West Bengal	10.59	6,133

Source: Jose (1988), p. A-48.

wages could be explained by a regression of productivity-related variables such as rainfall and the use of fertilizers. He also studied the variation of wages across villages of West Bengal and found highly significant regression coefficients of such productivity parameters, though with lower R^2s.

These regional variations are quite large and persistent in the LDCs because developments in any region that raise labour productivity there do not spread rapidly to other regions. Thus, describing conditions in cocoa-producing countries of Africa, Lewis (1976:27) says

> The differences can be astonishingly wide: the average income in the cocoa region may be five times as high as the average income of surrounding provinces – a degree of difference which could not persist very long in a developed country, where labour would be flowing rapidly to the richer region and capital flowing rapidly to the poorer.

He has therefore argued that it is the failure of growth to spread horizontally rather than the failure of growth to trickle down vertically which leads to growing inequality in the process of development.

The fourth important feature of agricultural labour markets in LDCs is that a high proportion of agricultural labourers is either unemployed or severely underemployed, especially in the slack seasons of the agricultural year. Under traditional systems labour would be employed on a regular basis, and employed for nonagricultural and domestic duties during the slack seasons. Under these systems the payment for labour was not only wages but also various forms of support that employers gave their workers and their families.

With growing commercialization of the labour market, labour has tended to be employed more and more on a casual basis. They are then employed for particular operations of agricultural production as the need arises. Therefore they are unemployed during the slack seasons of the agricultural calendar. Further, some of them may be unemployed even during the peak seasons. But in the absence of social security systems, they cannot afford to stay idle. Instead, they do some work to support themselves and often report themselves as employed. Hence the rates of unemployment reported in population censuses and labour force surveys are usually low, and underestimate the true extent of their unemployment. Some authors therefore suggested that the concept of unemployment should be modified to include not only people who were openly unemployed, but also those earning low incomes from the work they actually do (e.g., Turnham and Jaeger 1971; and Hauser 1974). But this approach has been criticized by Sen (1975:38) who argued that 'to identify unemployment with poverty seems to impoverish both notions since they belong to somewhat different categories of thought'. The difficulty is that some people are fully employed and may even be working very hard, but they are poor because their productivity is low; they were described as the 'working poor' in the ILO employment report (1972) on Kenya. But there are also people who are poor because they cannot find work which they are capable of and willing to do.

Under these conditions a better index of the extent of unemployment is given by the proportion of casual workers in the rural labour force. This relationship is supported by the close correspondence between the careful estimates of rates of unemployment made by Indian statisticians and the proportion of casual workers in the labour force in different states of India (Table 10.2).

Unemployment of labour in the agricultural sector in fact reflects the unemployment of labour in the whole economy. As Dandekar (1962:170) explains it:

> This is because the non-agricultural sector in these economies is usually organized on the capitalist principles, and hence does not permit workers in unless they can contribute to the production of more than the wages they receive in return. Consequently, the entire residual population is thrown on to agriculture which by its nature and tradition employs or accommodates whatever population is thrown on it without reference to the marginal productivity of labour.

Table 10.2 Unemployment and casual labour by states: India

States	Unemployment rate: 1973–74	Proportion of casual workers in labour force	
		1973–74	1982–83
Andhra Pradesh	11.2	32.2	34.6
Assam	1.9	10.2	17.6
Bihar	10.0	26.9	35.2
Geijarat	5.4	23.8	32.9
Haryana	2.9	9.1	15.7
Karnataka	8.6	31.2	36.2
Madhya Pradesh	3.4	19.4	24.3
Maharashtra	9.4	37.6	33.9
Orissa	10.2	30.6	33.6
Punjab	3.9	13.9	20.7
Rajasthan	3.2	5.2	12.9
Tamil Nadu	10.5	37.3	40.7
Uttar Pradesh	3.4	13.2	17.7
West Bengal	10.7	32.6	38.0
India	7.8	26.6	28.8

Sources: For 1973–74, Visaria (1981); for 1982–83, Parthasarathy (1987).

Finally, we consider the variation of agricultural wages over time. Agricultural wages vary between different seasons of the agricultural year, being higher during ploughing and harvesting than at other times mainly because of the variation in the demand for labour. But we are more interested in the variation of wages over longer periods of time, covering a number of years or decades. Some of the most detailed data have again been collected in India; they are summarized in Table 10.3 for the country as a whole.

In this table the index of real wages is derived by taking a simple average of the values for individual states. The table also shows an index of the growth of agricultural production. Up to the mid-1970s, there was little change in real wages, although there was a significant increase in agricultural production. In fact, Bardhan (1984:190) has pointed out that real wages of agricultural labour households declined by 16 per cent between 1964–65 and 1974–75, while net production of food grains went up by 20 per cent and net domestic product of the agricultural sector (in 1960–61 prices) rose by 11 per cent. Since the mid-1970s average agricultural wages for the country as a whole has been growing faster, at about the same rate as agricultural output.

For this period we also have data on the growth of real wages and of agricultural production for individual states of India (Table 10.4). Again we see that there is only a weak relationship between growth of wages and growth of agricultural production. Particularly interesting is the case of Punjab, where there was a rapid growth of agricultural production but little change in agricultural wages during this period.

The data on the growth of agricultural wages in real terms in some other Asian countries are summarized in Table 10.5. Wages grew rapidly in South Korea, where there was a rapid growth of GDP, and to some extent

Table 10.3 Agricultural wages (male labour) and production: India, various years

Period	Index of male real agricultural wage	Index of agricultural production
(a) Average index (1956–57 = 100)		(Index = 100)
I 1958/9–1960/1	104.6	106.5
II 1966/7–1968/9	104.3	121.1
III 1974/5–1976/7	108.7	153.1
IV 1982/3–1984/5	137.1	196.3
(b) Percentage change		
Between periods I and II	−0.3	13.7
Between periods II and III	4.2	26.4
Between periods III and IV	26.1	28.2

Sources: Jose (1988); Unni (1988).

Table 10.4 Growth of agricultural wages (male workers) and agricultural production by state: India, 1974–77 to 1982–85

State	Index of real wages 1982–85 as percentage of 1974–77	Food grain production 1982–85 as percentage of 1974–77
Andhra Pradesh	156	126
Assam	126	120
Bihar	115	103
Gujarat	142	144
Haryana	126	146
Himachal Pradesh	119	97
Karnataka	110	110
Kerala	136	96
Madhya Pradesh	140	132
Maharashtra	158	112
Orissa	126	126
Punjab	103	173
Rajasthan	127	125
Tamil Nadu	123	98
Uttar Pradesh	113	153
West Bengal	105	102
Average	127	123

Sources: For wages, Jose (1988); for food grain production, Government of India (1981)
Economic Survey 1980–81 and Government of India (1987) *Economic Survey 1986–87*.

also in Sri Lanka, but grew very slowly or even declined in other countries such as Bangladesh and Malaysia in spite of the rapid economic growth in the latter economy. Particularly interesting is the case of the Philippines, where wages actually declined in spite of rapid agricultural development based on the new rice fertilizer technology.

10.3 Agricultural wages and employment: theory

From the last section, we see that any theory of the wages of agricultural labourers in LDCs must explain two significant features. One is the fact that agricultural wages vary considerably between different countries and between different regions of the large countries. The other is the fact that, while there is considerable seasonal fluctuation of wages, their average values over the agricultural year tend to be remarkably constant over time in most countries, especially the densely populated countries in which the nonagricultural sectors are not expanding rapidly. The extreme case of these features of agricultural wages may be illustrated diagrammatically as in Figure 10.1.

Table 10.5 Index of real wages of agricultural labour (1965 = 100)

Year	Bangladesh	S. Korea	Malaysia	Philippines	Sri Lanka
1965	100	100	——	100	100
1966	94	108	100	102	99
1967	91	117	95	104	99
1968	104	129	97	102	107
1969	98	141	100	92	100
1970	101	152	98	82	95
1971	97	159	93	81	103
1972	105	165	91	76	103
1973	148	177	89	79	97
1974	130	189	100	85	102
1975	102	189	90	92	117
1976	114	212	112	103	130
1977	110	238	102	106	120
1978	112	300	107	95	154
1979	113	385	119	100	——
1980	112	377	——	54	——
Annual rate of change (%)	1.36	8.72	1.01	−0.29	2.44

Source: Palacpac (1980, 1985) *World Rice Statistics.*

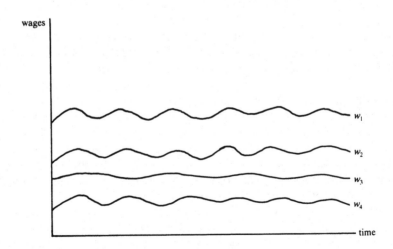

Figure 10.1

In the neoclassical theory the wages of agricultural labourers, like those of all categories of labour, are assumed to be determined by the equilibrium of supply and demand. The demand comes from the larger farmers and is explained by the marginal product of labour, while the supply consists of landless agricultural labourers and is explained by their marginal disutility for labour. Agricultural labourers in LDCs are very poor; therefore their demand for employment is likely to be more intense than their preference for leisure. Hence their supply of labour is unlikely to be very elastic with respect to wages. For example, using Indian data, Bardhan (1984: Chap 1, p. 28) concluded that 'market agricultural labour supply seems to be primarily determined by other economic, social and demographic conditions, not by the wage rate. The labour supply function looks more like a vertical line than the horizontal one commonly assumed in the development literature'. Given a fairly inelastic supply of labour, differences in wages are primarily due to differences in demand as determined by marginal productivity conditions. In fact, differences in wages between regions do correspond to differences in agricultural productivity, as illustrated by the Indian data in Table 10.1. Further, there is also a systematic seasonal fluctuation in wages corresponding to variations in the demand for labour. Hence Bardhan (1984:56) concluded that 'there is substantial evidence that the wage rate is quite sensitive to demand and productivity factors, contrary to the implications of subsistence or other theories of wage invariance to these factors'.

However, there are two problems with this explanation. One problem is that if agricultural wages are fixed by the equilibrium of supply and demand, then labour must be fully employed at that point. But in fact, as argued in the last section, a considerable proportion of landless labourers in LDCs is severely underemployed. The second problem is that if agricultural wages are determined by productivity conditions, as assumed in this theory, they must have risen with the growth of productivity over time. But in fact these wages have not risen significantly even in countries and regions with rapid agricultural development, and in some cases have even declined. Therefore the neoclassical theory does not provide a satisfactory explanation of agricultural wage determination.

By contrast, the classical theory assumed that the supply of labour was highly elastic with respect to wages. This assumption refers to the elasticity of the long-run supply of labour, whereas Bardhan's conclusion about the inelasticity of labour supply refers to the position in the short run. A high elasticity of the long-run supply of labour would then be consistent with the observed stability of agricultural wages over time.

The classical economists explained the high elasticity of the long-run supply of labour by their theory of demographic behaviour. According to this theory, the supply of labour would be highly elastic at the subsistence level of incomes. This theory has come up against considerable criticism, but the reasons for its inapplicability to present-day conditions in LDCs must be considered carefully.

The main criticism has been that the subsistence level is unlikely to vary greatly between regions of the same country and therefore a theory of wages based on this concept cannot explain the regional variation of wages that is observed in practice. But this criticism is only valid against a physiological interpretation of the subsistence concept, and much less so for a psychological or conventional interpretation of the concept. Even on the physiological interpretation, the subsistence level may vary in different regions. As Bardhan (1984:49) points out,

> Apart from the fact that there is no one subsistence level (even assuming the same basal metabolic rate of the body and the same level of external temperature), there is the dismal fact that in poor countries, the majority of agricultural laborers have a level of living or a daily calorie intake significantly below even the barest minimum recommended by most nutritionists, and yet they survive.

A more serious weakness of the classical theory is that under modern conditions, population growth even in LDCs is determined more by advances of medical science and improvements of public health than by the relationship between wages and the subsistence level, however that may be interpreted. Another major weakness of the classical theory is that while it may be consistent with regional variations in wages, it is not consistent with these regional wage differences being correlated with productivity differences as strongly as they seem to be.

The classical theory also assumed that labour was always fully employed. This assumption was used to determine the wages in the short run depending on the wage fund, and to determine population size in the long run depending on the subsistence level.

Thus we see that each of these theories is consistent with some features of the agricultural labour market in LDCs, but inconsistent with others. The neoclassical theory explains the regional variations of wages but does not explain either the unemployment of labour or the slow growth of wages over time. On the other hand, the classical theory explains the stability of wages over time but not the regional variation of wages according to productivity conditions. What is needed therefore is a theory that explains all these features to a sufficient degree of approximation.

One suggestion that has been studied intensively in the recent literature is the efficiency wage hypothesis (Leibenstein 1957; Mirlees 1975; Bliss and Stern 1978; Basu 1984). According to this hypothesis employers take advantage of the fact that the efficiency of workers, as measured by their productivity, depends on the level of their consumption, as determined by their wages. Therefore they choose to pay workers more than the equilibrium level of wages. Hence part of the labour force does not get regular

employment; indeed, the main object of the theory is to explain the existence of unemployment. This theory would also be consistent with the long-
run stability of wages. However, this theory has also been criticized, mainly
because the wage which maximizes efficiency of workers in unlikely to vary
much between regions, and hence the theory cannot explain the regional
variation of actual wages. Another theory with similar implications and
similar drawbacks is the labour turnover theory, based on the assumption
that employers may pay higher than equilibrium wages in order to reduce
the cost of recruiting labour (Stiglitz 1974; see also Basu 1984: Chap. 7).

A theory that attempts to explain both the regional variation of wages
and the existence of unemployment was proposed by Booth and Sundrum
(1984:241–3). In this theory the coexistence of these two features of the
labour market is explained as the result of two relationships between the
wage rate and the level of unemployment. One relationship derived from
the usual supply and demand curves is shown by the curve A in Figure
10.2. According to this relation, the level of unemployment is an increasing
function of the wage rate. The other relationship, illustrated by the curve B,
represents the extent of competition between employed and unemployed
workers. The neoclassical theory assumes that this competition is so intense
that, whenever there is unemployment, the wage rate would fall sufficiently
to eliminate the unemployment. Then the B curve would coincide with the
vertical axis, and the equilibrium would be given by the point P. But this
theory is inconsistent with the observed existence of unemployment. The
various fixed wage theories, on the other hand, assume that the competition between the employed and the unemployed is so weak that the exist-

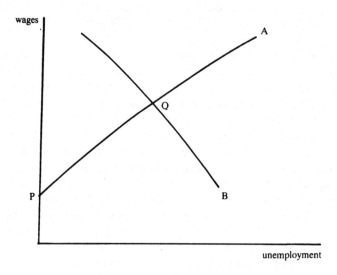

Figure 10.2

ence of unemployment has no effect on the wage rate. Then the B curve would be a horizontal line. On these theories, the actual wage would not be affected by the demand and supply conditions involved in the A curve for different regions. In fact, the degree of competition between the employed and the unemployed is likely to be intermediate between these two extremes. Then the B curve would be a downward-sloping curve in the diagram, showing the wage rate as a decreasing function of the level of unemployment. The intersection of the A and B curves determines the wage rate and the level of unemployment. Thus this theory explains both the existence of unemployment and the variation of wages in accordance with productivity.

The dualistic model of Lewis explained the stability of wages in the modern sector in the historical experience of the present-day DCs by assuming that there was an unlimited supply of labour from the traditional sector at a wage rate corresponding to the average product of labour in that sector. Underlying this argument, the traditional sector was assumed to consist of peasant families who worked harder to maintain the average product of labour, as more and more labour was absorbed in the modern sector. As discussed in Chapter eight, this assumption also is not very realistic of the agricultural sector of most LDCs, mainly because the surplus labour in the agricultural sector consists mainly of the unemployment and under-employment of landless labourers.

The main problem with the Lewis theory is its assumption that the agricultural sector consists entirely of peasant families, deriving their income both from their land and their labour. Instead, we must distinguish at least between landowning households and landless labourers. Landless labourers earn their income only from the wages of their labour. These wages are generally fixed at customary levels above the equilibrium level so that not all landless labourers are employed. So long as there is such unemployment, there is no tendency for agricultural wages to rise, even if there is considerable increase in output and productivity. It is only when all labour has been absorbed into employment that wages begin to be influenced by the level and growth of productivity.

But even this theory does not explain the level at which wages remain stable. A popular view is that these wages are ultimately determined by the bargaining power of employers *vis-à-vis* workers. This approach has been applied to the DCs, where wages are determined by collective bargaining between highly organized groups of workers and employers. In a recent contribution, Datt (1989) has suggested that collective bargaining may also occur in a tacit way without such formal organizations. This view is supported by the fact that there is considerable uniformity of wages within village labour markets. In the Nash (1950) model of such collective bargaining, it was assumed that there is symmetry between the two parties, and the outcome depended only on the inequality in the initial economic position of the two parties, described as their disagreement payoffs. Datt, however, considers an asymmetrical version of the model in which the outcome depends also on the relative bargaining power of the two parties. Estimating the coefficients of the relative bargaining power of the parties involved using some detailed data from some Indian villages, he finds that employers have a much higher bargaining power than workers, and also that, among workers, males have a higher bargaining power than females. In this approach, wages would vary with the conditions of productivity but would not necessarily be at the equilibrium level of full employment. However, the behaviour of wages over time would be influenced by changes in agricultural productivity, even if the relative bargaining power of employers and workers remains constant, but Datt has argued that this influence may be quite small.

The various theories considered above are summarized in Table 10.6 according to the extent to which they explain some of the major features of agricultural wages and employment in LDCs.

10.4 The urban labour market

10.4.1 The urban labour force

We turn now to consider wages and employment in the urban labour markets of LDCs. The first question to consider is the size of the urban labour force. Until comparatively recent times, the urban labour force was quite small, consisting mostly of workers engaged in public administration, foreign trade, and wholesale aspects of domestic trade, and a few centres of secondary and tertiary education; the modern industrial sector, mostly located in urban areas, was quite small and employed only a small fraction of the urban labour force.

Table 10.6 Alternative theories in relation to major features of rural labour markets

Theories	Extent to which theories explain:		
	Variations between regions	Stability over time	Unemployment
Neoclassical theory	+	−	−
Classical theory	−	+	?
Efficiency theory	−	?	+
A–B model	+	+	+
Modified dualistic model	+	+	+
Bargaining model	+	?	+

In more recent times the urban labour force in LDCs has grown very rapidly owing to a high rate of rural–urban migration. This migration is due to a combination of pull and push factors. According to the push factor, people are pushed out of the rural sector because of difficulties in earning an adequate income in rural areas. These difficulties have grown in the postwar period by the acceleration of population growth affecting both rural and urban areas. Because of the growth of population in rural areas, new entrants into the rural labour force were unable to get sufficient land to cultivate or to get other employment opportunities, inducing many of them to migrate to urban areas. Some evidence of this effect is provided by the fact that rates of rural–urban migration in different countries have been positively related to their rates of growth of total population. In fact, it is generally found that the growth of urban population is usually double the growth of total population. However, one problem is that on this argument, the people who migrate must be those who are economically worse off in the rural areas. Instead, many surveys show that it is usually the economically better-off among the rural population who migrate to urban areas.

Then there are the pull factors, one of which is the fact that urban wages are usually higher than rural labour incomes. To some extent, the higher urban wages only reflect the higher cost of living in urban areas and the fact that many goods and services which are available free in rural areas have to be paid for in urban areas. But even after allowing for this factor, urban wages may be higher than the corresponding income levels in rural areas. It will be recalled from section 8.3 that this was a basic assumption of the dualistic model, which Lewis (1954:411) explained in terms of 'the psychological cost of transferring from the easy going way of life of the subsistence sector to the more regimented and urbanized environment of the capitalist sector'. There is also another pull factor, namely the fact that employment opportunities in urban areas have been rising faster because of the rapid expansion of public administration, trade, and education, and also to the growth of the industrial sector.

In fact, it has been observed that the urban population has grown faster than employment opportunities in urban areas. Hence a considerable proportion of the urban labour force is in fact unemployed. Such unemployment is much more visible than its rural counterpart. Further, the amount of rural–urban migration that actually takes place cannot be explained only by the difference between urban and rural wages; if this were the case, the amount of urban unemployment would continue to grow so long as urban wages are greater than rural wages.

The existence of urban unemployment and the fact that the volume of such unemployment does not keep growing indefinitely is explained in the Harris–Todaro model (1970). According to this model, the decision to migrate is based on a comparison of the rural income with the *expected* urban income, that is the actual urban wage multiplied by the probability of getting employment at that wage. This probability itself is equal to the ratio of employment to the total labour force. Therefore rural urban migration reaches an equilibrium level when the rural wage equals the expected urban wage, that is when

$$w_r = \frac{L - U}{L} \, w_u \qquad (10.1)$$

where w_u and w_r are the urban and rural wages respectively, L is the urban labour force, and U the amount of urban unemployment. It then follows that there is an equilibrium rate of urban employment, given by

$$\frac{U}{L} = \frac{w_u - w_r}{w_u} \qquad (10.2)$$

that is, the equilibrium rate of urban unemployment will be equal to the urban–rural wage gap as a ratio of urban wages.

Apart from accounting for the existence of urban unemployment, this theory also explains the fact that migrants are usually not the economically worse off people of rural areas, but rather those who have sufficient skills and training to get urban jobs. In some versions of the theory, it is assumed that while the urban wage is rigidly fixed by various institutional factors, the rural wage is flexible at a market clearing level. Hence there is no unemployment in the rural areas. In fact, however, as discussed in earlier sections, the rural wage may also be quite rigid and there may be considerable unemployment in rural areas also. Then the unemployment in rural areas may be involuntary, while that in urban areas may be much more of a voluntary phenomenon (for a review of the literature on the theory, see Basu 1984: Chap. 6).

10.4.2 Segmentation of the urban labour market

A significant feature of the urban labour market is that it is usually highly fragmented into a number of segments with very different wages and employment conditions. First, there are the workers in the public sector who are mostly located in urban areas. The public sector generally seeks to act as a 'model' employer. It employs a high proportion of the more educated workers. The wages of these workers are usually determined by political decisions rather than by market forces; these wages are usually quite high compared with the per capita income of the countries concerned. The wage disparity in turn leads to a great demand for public sector jobs, but the employment in that sector is limited by the financial resources of the government. Because the public sector is the major employer of educated labour, the wages paid in that sector have a signif-

icant influence on the income differential between educational categories
of labour.

Then there is a segment of the urban labour market consisting of trade
and other service activities. These activities are mostly in the private sector,
and wages and employment conditions generally determined by market
forces. However, there is considerable variation among these enterprises,
ranging from small trading and service activities to large trading firms and
the advanced professional services, with a corresponding variation of wages.

The next segment of the urban labour market consists of the large-scale
modern industrial enterprises, especially state enterprises and foreign firms.
These enterprises generally use highly capital-intensive techniques of
production. Workers in this part of the urban labour market tend to be
highly unionized and consequently get high wages. This is also the part of
the urban labour market in which wages are more systematically regulated
by minimum-wage laws. This sector of industrial employment is therefore
sometimes known as 'high wage islands'.

Fourth, there is also a segment of smaller industrial enterprises using
more labour–intensive techniques of production. The main difference
between these firms and the large-scale enterprises is that workers are
much less unionized and wages are determined by market forces at a lower
level.

Finally, there is an informal sector in which people engage in petty
trading and small-scale industrial activities, usually on their own account
but also employing small numbers of workers. This sector is characterized
by ease of entry. Therefore it is often the first sector of the urban economy
into which migrants from rural areas are absorbed. Hence the wages of
labour are close to the level prevailing in rural areas.

10.4.3 Industrial wages

Next we consider the growth of industrial wages over time. In Lewis's dualistic model, discussed in section 8.3., it was assumed that the modern sector
was able to absorb labour from the traditional sector at a fairly constant
rate of wages. However, this model was based on the historical experience
of the developed countries, especially Britain. It is therefore interesting to
see how far the model has applied to the recent experience of LDCs.

Some data on these trends were compiled by Webb (1977) for a number
of LDCs up to the early 1970s. They are summarized in Table 10.7. In
contrast with the stability of agricultural wages over time (Tables 10.3,
10.4, and 10.5), this table shows that industrial wages in LDCs have generally risen with their per capita income, and sometimes even faster.

The *World Labour Report* (1987, no. 3), published by ILO has
compiled more recent data on the growth of wages from regular urban
employment in LDCs. These are summarized in Table 10.8.

Table 10.7 Trends in GDP per capita and manufacturing wages: LDCs, 1956–72

Country	Average rate of growth of GDP per capita 1959–71	Average rate of growth of manufacturing wages 1956–72
Slow-growth countries (9) (< 2% p.a.)	1.2	2.1
Medium-growth countries (8) (2–3% p.a.)	2.2	2.7
Fast-growth countries (9) (≥ 3% p.a.)	4.3	3.9

Source: Webb (1977), p. 241.

Table 10.8 Growth of GDP per capita and real wages: LDCs, 1971–85

Countries (number of countries)	Average growth of GDP per capita	Average growth of real wages
Slow-growth countries (13)	−1.4	−4.1
Medium-growth countries (11) (< 2% p.a.)	0.8	−1.4
Fast-growth countries (15) (> 2% p.a.)	4.4	1.2

Source: ILO (1987), *World Labour Report*, no. 3, p. 100.

The *World Labour Report* (ILO 1987, no. 3, pp. 97–8) has summarized the main trends as follows:

Since the beginning of the 1970s, real wages have fallen in more countries than they have risen. Of the 41 countries included, 20 show real wage declines of more than 1 per cent per year, while 14 experienced an increase of more than 1 per cent per year. Countries with high rates of growth have generally seen real wage increases and vice versa. In other words, there is a rough positive correlation between the rate of economic growth and real wage improvement. Changes in real wages nevertheless appear to have fallen well behind the rate of economic growth in most LDCs. Real wages rose faster than GDP per capita in only nine of the 41 countries over the period. In some of these countries, the difference in growth rates is quite small and may be spurious or clearly attributable to special circumstances such as the tight labour markets occasioned by exceptionally fast growth in the Republic of Korea or the impact of oil in Venezuela and Ecuador or simply the highly irregular movement of wages. On the other hand, in many countries where the comparisons show real wages lagging behind, the differences have been substantial suggesting that other incomes have been rising much more rapidly than wages.

One of the most interesting cases in the last category is that of Thailand, where per capita GDP is estimated to have grown at 4.3 per cent per annum during the period 1977–84, while real wages declined at 4.5 per cent per annum (see also *World Development Report 1987*, Figure 5.2, p. 97).

Noting the positive correlation between real wages of urban workers and the rate of economic growth, the ILO *Report* (p. 98) goes on to say that 'while this may not seem surprising, it does conflict with the predictions of the labour surplus development models and is not in line with earlier comparisons that have generally found little correlation'. However, this was recognized by Lewis (1972) in his statement that

> When we turn to the less developed countries of our own time and ask what is happening to the industrial wage, the answer, from a very large number, if not from all, is that the wage is rising, even in situations where there is open mass unemployment, not to speak of under-employment.

10.4.4 Wages and employment of educated workers

One of the main sources of income inequality in LDCs is the differences in incomes of individuals according to their educational qualification. The data, presented in section 4.4.3, showed that these differences are quite large in the LDCs.

One explanation is that the salary structure according to educational level is still in the process of adjustment. In earlier times, the wages of more educated workers were very high because educated labour was very scarce and consisted largely of expatriate workers. Since then, however, there has been a steady expansion of the educational system in LDCs. With the increase in supply, the wage differentials between educational categories are being narrowed, but the process is slow (Blaug 1969: Chap. 1).

One reason for the slow adjustment of wage differentials to the growing supply of educated workers is that a large proportion of these workers are employed in the public sector, and the public sector is slow to respond to market forces. Another reason is that the more educated workers have a greater opportunity of migrating to the developed countries, and therefore their wages tend to be linked to the salaries prevailing in those countries. This is supported by the evidence on the substantial 'brain drain' from the LDCs to the DCs.

Economists have tried to explain these differences as the return to the 'human capital' invested in individuals. If the capital market is a perfect one, then the differences in earnings of people with different levels of education would correspond to the cost of the capital invested in their education. In fact, however, the rates of return represented by these income differences are usually higher than any reasonable estimate of the cost of capital. One implication therefore is that the capital market is far from perfect. Another implication is that because of imperfections in the capital market, only persons who are already better-off are able to finance their further education and benefit from that opportunity.

One of the most serious problems in explaining these educational differences in incomes by market forces is the difficulty of measuring the productivity of educated workers. The difficulty is particular serious in the case of workers in the public sector. Especially in that sector, workers are paid according to their educational qualifications rather than according to any measure of their productivity.

The main consequence of the large income differential between educational categories is that there is an almost insatiable private demand for education which has forced governments to expand the educational system rapidly, especially at the higher level. But at the large income differentials, the economy is unable to absorb the growing supply into productive employment. This leads to a growing problem of educated unemployment. The typical situation is illustrated by recent data from the urban areas of Indonesia, summarized in Table 10.9.

Unemployment rates are very high among young people as they seek employment with high expectations of wages, after completing their education. In most cases they are prepared to wait for a chance of a job in the high-wage segments of the urban economy. Hence their unemployment is voluntary to some extent and similar to the Harris–Todaro phenomena discussed above. Eventually, they lower their expectations and most of them get employed by the age of 30. As a result, the wage differentials slowly narrow.

The discussion of this chapter may be summarized as follows. The wages of labour in LDCs are generally low because of the abundance of labour relative to other factors of production. Among labourers, wages also very considerably according to sector of employment; in particular, the wages of agricultural labourers are lower than those in other sectors. Agricultural wages also vary in different regions of the country according to agricultural productivity. But there is considerable unemployment of labour in rural areas. Because of this pool of unemployed labour, agricultural wages have not risen significantly even in countries where there has been a considerable growth of agricultural production. Instead, agricultural wages have remained quite stable at levels determined largely by institutional factors of the rural labour market.

Table 10.9 Unemployment rate by age and education: Urban areas of Indonesia, 1986

Age	Completed education					
	Below primary	Primary	Junior high	Senior high	Tertiary	Total
Males						
10–14	3.6	5.1	—	—	—	4.1
15–19	10.2	16.2	20.4	62.2	—	21.2
20–24	8.1	12.2	20.3	39.5	45.2	26.1
25–29	5.6	3.6	5.2	10.0	18.2	7.1
30 and over	0.9	1.6	1.8	1.1	1.6	1.4
Total	2.5	4.2	6.5	13.7	6.6	6.9
Females						
10–14	10.4	5.0	—	—	—	7.9
15–19	4.9	11.4	21.6	60.7	—	16.6
20–24	4.3	6.1	24.9	40.1	50.0	24.4
25–29	2.1	2.0	11.9	11.2	14.2	7.0
30 and over	0.9	1.8	1.7	1.6	0.7	1.3
Total	1.8	4.5	11.2	21.5	13.4	8.1

Source: Biro Pusat Statistik (1986) *Labour Force Survey* (SAKERNAS).

Urban labour markets are also highly fragmented, with widely differing conditions of wages and employment. A major source of wage differentials are differences in education qualifications. These differentials are quite large because of the scarcity of educated workers, but they decline only slowly in the course of educational expansion. The relatively high wages of labour in urban areas lead to a steady flow of migrants from rural areas, who cannot all be absorbed into employment. Hence there is a pool of urban unemployment, determined by the wage differential between urban and rural areas.

Chapter eleven

Incomes from capital: interest and profits

11.1 Interest and profits

In economics there is a sharp distinction between income in the form of interest and income in the form of profits. The analysis of these two types of income is simplified by associating them with different categories of income receivers, who may be described as rentiers and entrepreneurs respectively. Interest is the price that persons with surplus funds earn for lending these funds to borrowers. Hence it is generally expressed as a percentage of the funds for a given period such as a year or month or even a week. Profit, on the other hand, is the reward of entrepreneurs who organize production by employing various factors of production, including borrowed funds, and taking the risks involved in such production.

It is even possible to make rough estimates of these two categories of income in the developed countries. The estimates for the United States were shown in Table 2.9. From that table, we note that interest and profit incomes are quite small proportions of total income, being about 6 and 9 per cent respectively. By contrast, compensation of employees was over three-fourths of the national income. However, a great deal of capital is invested in the workers of the developed countries, especially in the form of their education and training; therefore their wage incomes include a considerable component of interest on this capital.

The position in the less developed countries is much more complicated. The main reason is that a much larger proportion of the population work on their own account, using their own capital and managing their own businesses. This is particularly the case in the unorganized sector of these economies. As illustrated by the Indian data summarized in Table 2.10, 42 per cent of all incomes are earned in this mixed form, the proportion being 65 per cent in the unorganized sector, especially among the large proportion of owner cultivators. Where interest incomes can be estimated separately, they constitute about 7.6 per cent of all incomes, higher than in the United States. The proportion is even higher at 13.2 per cent in the organized sector, where all incomes are classified into the separate categories.

The standard explanation of these two categories of income is that given in the neoclassical theory. Like any other factor price, the rate of interest is assumed to be determined by competitive market forces, in this case by the supply of and demand for capital. The supply of capital is provided by savings. Savings is explained by the willingness of people to postpone consumption of a part of their income, but because they value future consumption at a lower rate than current consumption, due to what Pigou described as a defect of the telescopic faculty, they are willing to do so only at a price. Therefore the amount that people are willing to save out of their incomes is assumed to be an increasing function of the rate of interest. Countries differ in the amounts they are willing to save even at the same rate of interest. One reason for these differences is that people not only save more as their incomes rise, but they also save a higher proportion of their bigger incomes, Another reason for these differences is explained by their rates of time preference, that is, the rates at which they discount future consumption. It is often argued that persons in the LDCs have a higher rate of time preference and therefore save a smaller proportion of their incomes than people in the DCs.

The demand for savings is typically assumed to come from people, who wish to invest them in durable producers' goods such as machinery and buildings, say for industrial production. These capital goods enable producers to use roundabout methods of production which are more productive. Therefore people are willing to pay interest for borrowing funds to purchase and use such capital goods. In the Austrian theory of capital, the productivity of funds employed in this way is related to the period of production, that is, the length of time after which capital goods produce output. The productivity of capital is known as the marginal efficiency of capital; this is the rate of interest at which it just pays investors to borrow funds for purchasing capital goods. Hence the demand for capital is given by the marginal efficiency of capital. Because of diminishing returns, the marginal efficiency of capital, and hence the demand for capital, is a decreasing function of the rate of interest. The equilibrium between the demand and supply of funds then determines the rate of interest.

When firms invest such funds in their productive activity, their net receipts are usually greater than the interest they have to pay on the borrowed funds, and the difference accrues as profit. One explanation of profits is that they are the reward for organizing the production process, that is, for hiring and paying for the various factors of production, using them to produce output, and selling the output. Two levels of profits are distinguished: normal profits and abnormal profits. Normal profits are the profits earned under equilibrium conditions, when the output is sold at its equilibrium price and the factors of production are paid at their equilibrium prices. Under perfect competition such normal profits are zero, but it takes time for profits to reach this equilibrium level. In the process, firms may earn abnormal profits which may be positive or negative. When abnormal profits are negative, the marginal firms leave the industry; when abnormal profits are positive, new firms enter the industry. It is this process that leads the marginal firm to be of optimal size at which it earns normal profits of zero, and each industry is of equilibrium size. Abnormal profits are therefore a transitional phenomenon which signals producers to adjust their production in accordance with the demand of consumers.

In this explanation, profit is only the reward for performing a managerial function. But the role of producers does not consist only of such a managerial function. To the extent that such a managerial function is needed, it can be performed by professional managers hired at a wage. Another function of producers, which is more important in practice, is the entrepreneurial function, that is, the function of making decisions about the type of goods it would be profitable to produce, the quantities of such goods that can be sold at a profitable price, the technology that would be most profitable to produce these goods, the type and amount of factors of production that should be hired, and so on. Marshall therefore introduced the idea that profits are the reward for such an entrepreneurial function. The level of profits then depends on the success with which producers perform this entrepreneurial function.

Among the many aspects of this entrepreneurial function, Schumpeter stressed a particular aspect, namely the introduction of technical innovations in production and sale of output. The firm which is first to introduce a successful innovation earns a high level of profits. In the course of time other firms imitate the innovation and the level of profits from its use falls. These innovations tend to be bunched together in a number of industries, and there is a general rise in profit levels and a general improvement in economic conditions. Hence there is a fairly regular pattern of cyclical fluctuations in capitalist development, the phenomenon of the trade cycle.

The above arguments explain profit in the competitive case. However, production is not always organized under such competitive conditions. In many cases competition is not perfect. Then firms earn abnormal profits either because they have some monopoly power in the sale of their products, or some monopsony power in the purchase or hiring of the factors of production. An important source of market imperfection occurs in the industrial sector, namely the increasing returns to scale, which is particularly important in this sector. Because of the economies of large-scale production, once a firm achieves a large size, it is able to supply its products at a lower price than other smaller firms and to increase its share of the market; therefore it gains some monopoly power and earns a high level of profits.

In the developed countries the financial transactions of firms are carried out through the capital market. Firms which wish to raise funds issue a variety of financial instruments which are then bought by persons with surplus funds to invest. At one extreme, firms issue bonds, which earn interest at a specified rate. In this case the purchasers get back their capital on maturity. At the other extreme are equity shares, which give purchasers a share in the assets of the firm and hence a share in the profits. In between are a range of other instruments, with the yield on capital varying with the riskiness of the investment. When there is an efficient capital market investors can sell the stocks or shares they have bought in companies, either because they wish to get their money back, or to invest in some other companies. The active trade in these financial assets then plays a significant part in regulating their prices by the competition among investors. Further, firms can raise a large volume of financial resources for their investment activities from a large number of individuals, each investing only a small sum of money. On the one hand, this has led to a rapid accumulation of capital. In particular, it transfers resources from people with savings to others with better and more profitable opportunities to invest. On the other hand, it has led to a wide distribution of the ownership of capital assets among a large number of individuals, each earning a share of the profits from such capital. One further consequence is that there has emerged a sharp distinction between those who finance investments, such as the shareholders of joint-stock companies, and those who control the investments, such as the managers and directors of these companies.

The other important way in which firms finance their investment is by borrowing from the banking system. In this system there is a variety of banks, some specializing in short-term loans mainly for working capital, while others specialize in longer-term loans for fixed capital. The loans that the banks make come partly from the savings of people, which are held in banks as deposits. But banks also have the power of creating credit because people, including the borrowers themselves, hold a fairly stable fraction of their funds in the form of such deposits. Hence banks are able to lend out a multiple of the funds deposited with them. The ability to create credit depends ultimately on people's confidence in banks and the monetary system. Therefore the banking system is constantly under control by monetary authorities of the government regarding the amounts of bank lending, the rates of interest at which banks lend, the purposes of loans, and the amounts that banks have to keep in reserve. An important consideration underlying such control of the banking system is to ensure that bank lending is not so excessive as to lead to inflation.

When the capital market is well developed and there is an extensive banking system, persons with ideas for profitable investment opportunities are able to get the funds for implementing these ideas. The rate of investment is determined by the dynamism of entrepreneurs, their expectations about future profits, and the technology that is available, rather than just the amount of savings and the rate of interest at which it can be borrowed.

The level of investment may even exceed the amount of voluntary savings in the economy. Then if there are idle resources in the economy which can be used for investment, such investment will increase the level of national income sufficiently to bring about the corresponding amount of savings. But if resources in the economy are already fully utilized, such investment will only lead to inflation.

11.2 Capital stock and distribution in LDCs

In this section we consider some of the important differences between DCs and LDCs in the amounts of capital and the incomes people earn in the form of interest and profits. The difference in the stock of capital may be illustrated by some estimates from the United States as an example of a developed country, and from India as an example of a less developed country. In 1971 it was estimated that the total capital stock of the United States was about $2,600 billion. This represents a stock of about $13,000 per member of the population; even if we take only the private stock of capital, it amounts to $7,500 per member of the population. In 1971 the GNP of the United States was estimated at about $1,050 billions. Hence the average capital output ratio taking only the private capital stock was around 1.4.

The distribution of this stock among various categories is shown in Table 11.1. Some interesting features of this distribution may be noted. Over 40 per cent of the stock was owned by the government, especially as infrastructure and defence equipment. Two-thirds of the capital stock consists of structures; in fact, about half consists of residential structures. Only a small proportion of capital is in the farming sector, a quarter is used for the manufacturing industry. The bulk of private capital is used in sectors other than farming and manufacturing. A particularly notable feature is that three-quarters of private capital is owned by the corporate sector, mostly in the nonfinancial corporate sector, and only a quarter in the noncorporate sector.

There is no official estimate of the capital stock in India, but some unofficial estimates have been made by the Central Statistical Organization. According to these estimates, the stock of reproducible tangible assets in the country in 1971 was about Rs 88,000 crores, that is, about $120 billion at the prevailing official exchange rate. Hence the amount of capital per head of the population was only around $200. In that year the net national product was estimated at around Rs 34,500 crores. Hence the average capital output ratio was 2.55 higher than in the United States. Thus it seems that the low per capita income is due both to the slow stock of capital per head of population, and to its lower productivity on the average. In fact, the average capital output ratio has been rising from 1.96 in 1950–51 to 2.14 in 1960–61, 2.55 in 1970–71 (Roychoudhury and Mukherjee 1984:262) and to 2.67 in 1978–79 (Raj 1982:114–15). This is mainly

Table 11.1 Distribution of capital stock: United States, 1971

Category	Amount ($ billion)	Percentages of total
Total	2,574	—
By ownership sector		
Private	1,479	57
Government	1,095	43
By type		
Equipment	927	36
Structures	1,587	64
Private capital by industry		
Farming	99	7
Manufacturing	364	24
Others	1,016	69
Private capital by type of institution		
Corporate	1,084	73
financial	41	3
nonfinancial	1,043	70
Noncorporate	395	27

Source: US Department of Commerce (1981) *Survey of Current Business.*

because of the high proportion of the increase in the capital stock allocated to the more capital-intensive sectors.

The distribution of capital stock in India and its variation from 1971 to 1979 are summarized in Table 11.2. A third of the capital stock, slightly lower than in the United States, is in the public sector, especially for power and transport infrastructure, but this stock has been growing faster. The average capital output ratio in this sector is much higher than in the private sector. A large part of the capital stock in India consists of residential buildings, as in the the United States. However, according to these estimates a large part of the capital stock is employed in the agricultural sector, and a much smaller part in manufacturing. Within the manufacturing sector, most of the capital is employed in the registered firms, that is, larger firms using modern techniques and therefore having a high average capital output ratio.

The capital stock in LDCs is not only limited but also very unequally distributed. For example, Roychoudhury and Mukherjee (1984:246) have estimated that in the rural areas of India, over 80 per cent of all assets were owned by the top 30 per cent of households, the share of the top 10 per cent being over 50 per cent. They also estimated the Gini coefficient of asset ownership to be 0.66 in 1971–72, a slight increase from 1961–62. Such information is not available for asset ownership in urban areas of India, but some idea of the position in these areas is given by the distri-

Table 11.2 Composition and growth of capital stock: India, 1971–79

Sector	Percentage of capital stock		Growth rates and Capital stock	Average capital output ratio	
	1971	1979	1971–79	1971	1979
Directly productive activities					
Agriculture	23.65	23.59	4.41	1.21	1.44
Manufacturing					
registered	11.94	12.22	4.75	3.66	3.28
unregistered	2.94	4.50	10.15	1.49	2.10
Construction	1.33	1.06	1.56	0.63	0.55
Trade	1.48	1.75	6.63	0.29	0.30
Real estate	25.11	21.03	2.16	21.31	19.74
Services	2.15	2.23	4.92	1.15	1.39
Subtotal	68.61	66.38	4.02	1.95	2.03
Infrastructure					
Electricity, etc.	6.18	8.50	8.69	17.14	17.35
Transport	14.88	13.94	3.60	8.33	6.89
Public administration	10.33	11.18	5.48	5.57	5.07
Subtotal	31.39	33.62	5.34	7.85	7.13
Total	100.00	100.00	4.45	2.55	2.67

Source: Raj (1982) Capital Formation and Savings in India, 1950–51 to 1979–80, pp. 114–5.

bution of capital stock in industrial firms according to the size of their employment (Table 11.3). There is a sharp dichotomy between the small and the large firms, with the bulk of industrial capital being located in the large firms. Over 80 per cent of the capital stock is in firms with more than 500 employees which, however, employ only 2.5 per cent of industrial workers in these factories. Thus larger firms are much more capital intensive than small firms. However, the capital–output ratio does not vary much except in the largest firms.

We now consider some theoretical explanations for the differences between DCs and LDCs. One important explanation lies in the fact that the capital market in LDCs is very undeveloped. There are few companies which command sufficient confidence for people to be willing to invest in their shares. Therefore few companies are able to raise large amounts of capital by issuing such shares. Although there are a number of people who have surplus funds from their savings, these savings are not invested in financial instruments. Instead, people with savings either hoard them in unproductive form, or invest them in their own enterprises. This is a major reason for the slow accumulation of capital in LDCs.

There is a banking system in most LDCs but this also is not very developed, partly because the banking habit has not spread widely among the population, most of whom are too poor to have bankable funds. The banking system is highly concentrated in urban areas. Even there, most banks only provide short-term loans for working capital, especially in the trade sector. Access to such loans is also limited because few people can comply with the formal procedures and the credit-worthiness criteria imposed by these institutions. But when banks make loans, they charge a relatively low rate of interest, compared with the cost of capital in the rest of the economy.

Governments of LDCs have taken a number of measures to expand the banking system. They have set up new banks empowered to lend on a long-term basis for fixed capital. They have encouraged banks to expand into rural areas and to provide loans for small-scale borrowers. In some countries the banking system has been nationalized, and is run under direct government control. In most cases the interest rate at which banks lend is also controlled at a low rate by government policy. Therefore persons who have access to bank loans enjoy a special privilege.

In spite of these measures, the extent to which banks supply credit for capital formation in LDCs is quite limited. Further, the opportunity for raising funds in the capital market or for borrowing from the banking system is very unequally distributed among the people. Therefore the stock of capital in LDCs is limited compared with DCs. Further, the ownership of this stock of capital is highly concentrated among a small section of the population.

Much of the capital formation in LDCs is therefore financed by a limited

Table 11.3 Factories by size of employment and capital: India, 1980–81

Number of employees	Share of			Average no. of workers	Capital per worker (Rs 000)	Capital output ratio
	Number	Employment	Capital stocks			
0–50	78.4	13.8	5.4	14.1	21.8	2.30
50–100	10.6	9.0	3.0	67.9	18.9	1.97
100–200	5.3	9.2	3.8	137	23.4	1.96
200–500	3.2	12.1	7.0	299	32.2	1.94
500–1,000	1.1	9.7	11.5	695	66.2	2.99
1,000–2,000	0.8	13.7	13.0	1,406	52.8	2.95
2,000–5,000	0.5	15.9	12.1	2,878	42.5	2.36
5,000 and over	0.1	16.6	44.2	13,526	148.4	9.07
Total	100.0	100.0	100.0	79.9	55.9	3.61

Source: Central Statistical Organization (1982) *Annual Survey of Industry*.

group of individuals who have been able to accumulate their own savings. Because of the limited quantity of such investments, these investors earn a high income and are able to accumulate capital faster. Hence incomes from capital not only contribute to a high inequality of income distribution, but the inequality also increases cumulatively.

Next we turn to the profit incomes earned by entrepreneurs. It is also often alleged that there is a limited supply of entrepreneurship in LDCs. It is even argued that this is due to the concentration of entrepreneurial skills among particular groups, or even races, of people. It is more likely that the latent supply of entrepreneurial skills is just as widely distributed among the people of LDCs, and among all groups and races in those countries, but these skills are not utilized as widely in other countries partly because of the financial constraints imposed by the underdevelopment of the capital market, and partly because of the slow progress of technology. It may also be that persons with capital resources of their own find it more profitable to invest these resources in such assets as land and residential properties, from which they earn high incomes in the form of rent. For whatever reason, the active supply of entrepreneurs in LDCs is limited and as a result, the limited number of entrepreneurs earn a high rate of profit for their skills. Persons earning such profits, like those earning interest income from their capital, are among the richest people in LDCs. This cannot be identified easily in statistical data because in most cases, the profits of entrepreneurship are combined with the income of the labour and the capital which entrepreneurs also contribute to their enterprises.

11.3 The organized and unorganized sectors

Another important feature of the capital market in LDCs is that it is sharply divided into two sectors, usually described as the organized and the unorganized sector. The organized sector is that in which the limited capital market and the banking system are concentrated, and therefore is located mostly in urban areas. Because of its relatively easier access to capital, it also consists of the largest industrial and other business enterprises in the country. These are the enterprises which engage in wholesale and foreign trade. The organized sector also consists of industrial enterprises that use highly capital intensive techniques, but because they also use modern technology to produce goods for richer consumers, they are also highly profitable.

By contrast, the small-scale industrial and trade enterprises, and most enterprises in rural areas, belong to the unorganized sector. These enterprises generally use traditional or intermediate techniques. Their main characteristic, however, is their limited access to institutional sources of capital and credit.

Therefore one major source of capital in the unorganized sector is the savings of the entrepreneurs themselves. But many of them, especially farmers, do not have enough savings to finance their own capital needs. For such people, the major source of credit is the moneylender. These lenders charge a high rate of interest, generally much higher than in the organized money market (for a recent survey, see Tun Wai 1977). Hence the unorganized money market provides a profitable avenue of investment for people with some money capital of their own. But moneylenders charge a high rate of interest even when they are able to borrow funds at a low interest rate from banks for relending in the unorganized money market. At the high interest rate charged in the unorganized market, there is little demand for loans to finance investments, especially for agricultural production, Instead, a high proportion of lending is in the form of consumption loans, especially during the growing season.

A number of reasons have been put forward to explain the high interest rate in the unorganized money market. For example it has been argued that the high interest rates are due to the high cost of lending. Moneylenders in the unorganized sector typically make loans in small amounts to a large number of borrowers so that higher costs are involved in lending a given total amount in the unorganized market than in the organized market. But this factor alone cannot explain the big difference between interest rates in the two sectors because, unlike banks, rural moneylenders carry on their business in a very informal manner, usually within a single village.

Second, it has been argued that moneylenders have to charge a high rate of interest because they face greater risks of default. There are two types of risks. One type, known as borrowers' risks, refers to the chance that borrowers may suffer such serious losses that they cannot repay their loans. This risk is particularly serious in the agricultural sector, which depends heavily on natural conditions in the LDCs, and therefore is subject to greater uncertainty due to natural vicissitudes. The other type of risk, known as lenders' risk, relates to the chance that even if the borrower is able to repay the loan, he may refuse to do so. When loans are given for consumption purposes, there is no increase in income in the future out of which to repay the loans with interest. Hence the chance of default is greater.

However, the risk of default as a reason for the high interest rates is often exaggerated. Moneylenders operating in small local areas usually have enough information to be able to judge the ability and willingness of borrowers to repay loans, and also have many ways of ensuring that they do so.

11.4 Inter-linked markets

An important phenomenon in LDCs, especially in their unorganized sectors, is the inter-linkage between markets. One important form of such market linkage is the case in which employers of labour are also the persons who supply credit to their employees. Another important form is the case in which large landowners are also moneylenders who lend to their tenants.

One consequence of such market linkage is that the income of employers and landlords who are also moneylenders cannot be separated into different categories such as profits, rent, and interest. But another consequence is that moneylenders can adjust the terms at which they supply credit by taking account of the terms at which they rent land or hire labour. Therefore, even if separate negotiations are carried out for different transactions, the terms of these transactions do not necessarily reflect the prices at which they are ostensibly made.

The inter-linkage of markets therefore has significant effects on the terms of credit. For example, when a moneylender deals with his customer in a number of transactions, he faces a smaller risk of default than banks or government agencies that lend money. The moneylender can generally recover the loan by forcing the employee to work for the loan or by confiscating the produce of the land rented out to tenants.

In fact, Basu (1984) has argued that the possibility of reducing the risk of default is an important reason for the inter-linking of rural factor markets. Moneylenders cannot afford to lend to people with whom they have no other dealings because the legal machinery for enforcing repayment is extremely limited in the unorganized sector of LDCs. But when markets are inter-linked, moneylenders are better informed about the borrowers and their ability to repay loans. Further, it is even possible that moneylenders may charge a low rate of interest on loans as an inducement to borrowers also leasing land or providing labour on much more favourable terms to the moneylender. The inter-linkage of markets therefore increases the bargaining power of the better-off people, and hence leads to a cumulative increase in inequality in the absence of more competitive market forces.

Chapter twelve

The structure of production and income distribution

12.1 Growth and structural transformation

One way of studying the distribution of income among individuals and households is in terms of the incomes derived from the various factors of production. This is the model which economists have generally followed since it was first introduced by Ricardo. Most theories, however, have concentrated on the question of the prices of the various factors of production and their shares in the national income. They have also considered these factor prices and income shares mainly for the special case of highly competitive factor markets. In practice, there are many ways in which the functioning of factor markets in LDCs differs from this assumption. Further, these factor prices and shares only relate to the functional distribution of income. In order to explain the personal distribution of income we must also consider the proportions of the population deriving their incomes from the different factors of production. Therefore the preceding three chapters discussed a number of ways in which prevailing theories have to be modified to take account of these limitations.

The incomes of individuals and households depend not only on the various factors of production from which they are derived, but also on the sector in which they are employed. This is partly because the intensity with which the various factors of production are used varies from sector to sector. Thus the main factors involved in the agricultural sector are land and labour; those involved in the industrial sector are labour and capital; and much of the income of the service sector is produced by and accrues to labour. Therefore the incomes generated in the various sectors gives some indication of the incomes accruing to the different factors of production. For example, the considerable share of the service sector even in the poorer LDCs is due to some extent to the role of the traditional part of that sector as the employer of last resort, and to some extent to the high salaries that the more educated workers earn in the modern part of that sector, especially in public administration. Another important reason why the sectoral composition of national income and the sectoral allocation of labour have a significant influence on the distribution of income is that the productivity of labour varies so much from sector to sector.

Because of these influences we consider the statistical evidence on differences in the structure of production in different countries, their changes over time, and the statistical relationship between the structure and the distribution of income in this section. In later sections we consider some theoretical explanations of these relationships.

12.1.1 The structure of production and employment

In section 4.3 we considered the statistical relationship between income level and income distribution and found that the relationship was not very strong. By contrast, development economists have found a much stronger relationship between the structure of production and the level and growth of income levels (see especially Kuznets 1971). Some recent data on this relationship are summarized in this section.

The structure of production is usually studied in terms of the three major sectors of the economy: agriculture, industry, and services. On this basis, data from a large number of countries have been compiled in the annual series of the *World Development Reports*. Although great care has been taken to compile these data, they cannot be taken as completely reliable. In particular, there is the problem that the definition of these sectors in the data on the composition of output does not correspond exactly with the definition in the data on the allocation of the labour force. Therefore too much weight should not be given to differences between individual countries; however, some useful patterns may be derived by comparing broad groups of countries. Some of these broad differences are shown in Table 12.1.

As may be expected, the agricultural sector is larger in the LDCs, both as a share of GDP and of the labour force, than in the DCs. Within the LDCs the agricultural share declines and the industry and service shares rise as per capita income rises. An interesting feature is that the service sector is generally larger than the industry sector, even at the lowest levels of per capita income.

Kuznets (1971) has also summarized time series data for individual developed countries which correspond to the patterns indicated by these cross-section data. The structural transformation of the economy is one the best-documented aspects of economic growth. An explanation for the changes in the agricultural and nonagricultural sectors in terms of supply and demand factors was given in section 9.1. The same model can be extended to explain the varying shares of all three sectors (Sundrum 1990: Chap. 3).

In general, the shares of the various sectors in GDP differ from their shares in the labour force because the productivity of labour is different in

Table 12.1 Sectoral composition of GDP and allocation of labour force, 1980

Countries	(Number)	Percentage share of GDP			Percentage share of labour force		
		A	M	S	A	M	S
LDCs by per capita GDP (1981 in US$)							
<300	(12)	50	16	34	79	8	13
300–600	(20)	31	25	44	69	12	19
600–1,000	(12)	22	31	47	58	17	25
1,000–2,000	(16)	17	33	50	41	20	39
2,000 and over	(9)	6	42	52	18	29	53
Total	(69)	26	29	45	56	16	28
DCs	(21)	6	37	57	11	37	52

Note: A — agriculture; M — industry; S — services.
Source: World Bank (1982) *World Development Report*.

the various sectors. The magnitude of these differences is indicated by the relative labour productivity in each of these sectors (i.e., labour productivity in a sector as a ratio of labour productivity in the economy as a whole). Estimates of the relative labour productivity in a sector may be obtained simply by dividing the sector's share of GDP by its share in the labour force. Some estimates are summarized in Table 12.2. Labour productivity is lowest in the agricultural sector. Labour productivity in the service sector is higher than that in the industrial sector in the poorest LDCs and again in the DCs, but is considerably lower in the middle-income LDCs.

We may also consider the growth rates of GDP and employment in the three sectors over time. The data for the postwar period are summarized in Table 12.3. From such data, we can derive the growth rates of labour productivity in the various sectors. These are summarized in Table 12.4.

The growth rate of labour productivity is usually the lowest in the agricultural sector. It is higher in the DCs and the richest LDCs, but in these countries the share of the agricultural sector is quite small. The growth rate of labour productivity is usually highest in the industrial sector, except in some of the richest LDCs.

These differences play an important role in explaining differences in the overall growth rate. On the average, GDP has grown faster in the LDCs than the DCs, but because population and labour force have also grown faster, per capita income growth has been slower in the LDCs. In fact, these growth rates conform to a logistic pattern, that is, a tendency for growth rates to be low at low levels of income, to be higher at intermediate

Table 12.2 Relative labour productivity by sectors

Countries (number)	Relative productivity of labour in:			
	A	*M*	*S*	*G*ₛ
LDCs by per capita GDP (in US$, 1981)				
<300 (12)	0.63	2.67	2.95	0.309
300–600 (20)	0.48	2.55	3.02	0.313
600–1,000 (12)	0.39	2.00	2.22	0.394
1,000–2,000 (16)	0.42	1.94	1.37	0.286
2,000 and over (9)	0.39	1.49	1.01	0.190
Total (69)	0.47	2.20	2.22	0.331
DCs (21)	0.67	1.00	1.11	0.079

Note: A — agriculture; M — industry; S — services; G_s — inequality of labour productivity by sectors.
Source: As for Table 12.1.

levels of income, and to be low again at the highest levels of income. One part of the explanation of this logistic pattern is the difference in the growth rates of labour productivity in the various sectors and the dominance of different sectors at different levels of income. Thus the agricultural sector usually has the lowest growth rate of labour productivity, while the industrial sector usually has the highest growth rate. As the per capita income of countries rises from a low to an intermediate level, the share of employment in the agricultural sector declines while that in the industrial sector rises. Hence the high growth rate of the industrial sector gets more weight in determining the overall growth rate and there is an acceleration of growth during this phase of the transition. But as income rises from the intermediate to the highest levels, the labour force share of the service sector rises at the expense of the industrial sector. This shift of labour increases the weight of the sector with a low rate of growth and therefore leads to a deceleration of growth in this phase of the logistic pattern.

Another part of the explanation of the logistic pattern lies in the reallocation of labour between sectors of unequal labour productivity. Labour productivity is lowest in the agricultural sector and highest in the industrial sector. Therefore, as labour shifts from the agricultural to the industrial sector, the growth rate accelerates because of this reallocation of labour from the sector with a low labour productivity to the sector with a high labour productivity. This reallocation effect is a powerful one and can produce a logistic pattern in overall growth, even when the growth of labour productivity is the same in all sectors (for a more detailed analysis, see Sundrum 1990: Chap. 3).

Table 12.3 Growth of GDP and employment by sectors: 1965–80

Countries (Number)	GDP		Agriculture		Industry		Services	
	ρ_Y	ρ_L	ρ_Y	ρ_L	ρ_Y	ρ_L	ρ_Y	ρ_L
LDCs by per capita GDP (in US$ in 1980)								
<500 (15)	4.07	2.31	2.61	1.67	5.18	4.04	4.92	4.19
500–1,000 (14)	5.38	2.55	3.72	1.39	7.13	4.54	5.39	4.87
1,000–2,000 (13)	7.18	2.67	3.87	0.51	9.91	4.67	7.56	4.67
2,000 and over (6)	6.35	2.98	2.68	-0.83	6.70	4.36	6.72	3.86
Total (48)	5.58	2.56	3.29	0.96	7.22	4.40	6.00	4.48
DCs (18)	4.15	1.09	1.57	-2.71	4.36	0.51	4.37	2.91

Note: ρ_Y = growth of GDP; ρ_L = growth of employment.
Source: World Bank (1982) World Development Report.

Table 12.4 Growth rate of labour productivity by sector: 1965–80

Countries (Number)		Growth rate of labour productivity of:			
		GDP	Agriculture	Industry	Services
LDCs by per capita GDP (1980 in US$)					
<500	(15)	1.76	0.94	1.14	0.73
500–1,000	(14)	1.83	1.33	2.59	0.52
1,000–2,000	(13)	4.51	3.36	5.24	2.89
2,000 and over	(6)	3.37	4.51	2.34	2.86
Total	(48)	3.02	2.33	2.82	1.52
DCs	(2)	3.06	4.28	3.85	1.46

Source: As for Table 12.3.

12.1.2 Relationship to income distribution

The structure of the economy and its changes over time influence not only the growth path of the economy but also the distribution of income. This is mainly because of the variation of labour productivity between sectors. The productivity of labour, measured simply as the GDP produced in the sector divided by the labour employed in the sector, does not, of course, determine the incomes of all those employed in the sector, but is an important influence on these incomes.

Given the data on the proportions of the labour force engaged in the three sectors and the relative labour productivity in these sectors, the inequality of labour productivities in the economy can be measured by the Gini index just as inequality is measured from data showing the population classified into various income groups, assuming that labour productivity is uniform within sectors. Such an index of sectoral inequality of labour productivity then indicates the distributional effect of the structure of the economy. Average values of such an index are shown in the last column of Table 12.2, under the heading G_S. This index is much higher for LDCs than for DCs; we also find that, among LDCs, G_S rises with per capita income up to a point and declines thereafter.

In Table 12.5 the values of G_S are shown for all LDCs and DCs for which some recent estimates of G, the Gini index of income distribution, are also available. There is very little correlation between the two indices G and G_S. The index G refers to the inequality of income distribution among households classified into income classes, while the index G_S refers to the inequality of labour productivity among sectors of the economy. The income of a person would be influenced by the sector in which she works, but would not be closely or linearly related to the average labour pro-

Table 12.5 Gini index of income inequality and Gini index of inequality of sectoral labour productivity

LDCs	G	G_s	DCs	G	G_s
Mali	0.366	0.350	Portugal	0.414	0.169
Bangladesh	0.369	0.232	Yugoslavia	0.311	0.173
Tanzania	0.416	0.313	Israel	0.326	0.027
India	0.402	0.347	Spain	0.318	0.132
Nepal	0.505	0.342	New Zealand	0.379	0.038
Kenya	0.545	0.482	Italy	0.359	0.099
Sierra Leone	0.439	0.401	UK	0.322	0.092
Sri Lanka	0.411	0.288	Netherlands	0.266	0.142
Sudan	0.433	0.431	Finland	0.311	0.045
El Salvador	0.396	0.303	Japan	0.277	0.084
Indonesia	0.424	0.425	Belgium	0.272	0.053
Zambia	0.531	0.505	Australia	0.398	0.027
Philippines	0.445	0.299	France	0.353	0.092
Egypt	0.396	0.337	Denmark	0.326	0.068
Thailand	0.418	0.521	Norway	0.312	0.050
Mauritania	0.523	0.135	W. Germany	0.304	0.029
Ivory Coast	0.550	0.539	Sweden	0.321	0.068
Peru	0.561	0.383	Canada	0.338	0.036
South Korea	0.371	0.187	USA	0.336	0.033
Turkey	0.495	0.357			
Costa Rica	0.481	0.082			
Malaysia	0.495	0.327			
Chile	0.444	0.227			
Brazil	0.599	0.199			
Mexico	0.516	0.282			
Panama	0.564	0.251			
Argentina	0.435	0.116			
Hong Kong	0.392	0.293			
Trinidad and Tobago	0.435	0.166			
Venezuela	0.487	0.235			

Notes: For LDCs: correlation between G and G_s — 0.106.
For DCs: correlation between G and G_s — −0.054.

Source: World Bank (1989) *World Development Report*

ductivity in that sector. Therefore it cannot be expected that there would be a high correlation between the two indices of individual countries.

Although the relationship between the values of G and G_S for individual countries is practically nonexistent, we get a closer relationship when countries are classified according to income level. Two aspects of this relationship are illustrated in Table 12.6. First, the average value of G_S varies in the same manner as the average value of G, rising with per capita income up to a point and declining thereafter. Second, within groups of countries at the same income level, the more unequal countries with a higher average value of G also have a higher average value of G_S than the less unequal societies. Therefore the distribution of the labour force among the different sectors of the economy and the differences in labour productivity among these sectors are part of the explanation for the variation of the Gini index of income inequality with the income level of countries which has often been noted in the literature. Some theoretical bases for this statistical relationship are discussed in the following sections.

Table 12.6 Average values of G and G_S by income level (number of countries in brackets)

Per capita GDP (US$)	Less unequal	More unequal	Total
<500	$\bar{G} = 0.388$ $\bar{G}_S = 0.311$ (4)	$\bar{G} = 0.525$ $\bar{G}_S = 0.412$ (2)	$\bar{G} = 0.434$ $\bar{G}_S = 0.344$ (6)
500–1,000	$\bar{G} = 0.421$ $\bar{G}_S = 0.370$ (5)	$\bar{G} = 0.531$ $\bar{G}_S = 0.505$ (1)	$\bar{G} = 0.439$ $\bar{G}_S = 0.392$ (6)
1,000–2,000	$\bar{G} = 0.420$ $\bar{G}_S = 0.386$ (3)	$\bar{G} = 0.545$ $\bar{G}_S = 0.352$ (3)	$\bar{G} = 0.482$ $\bar{G}_S = 0.369$ (6)
2,000–3,000	$\bar{G} = 0.457$ $\bar{G}_S = 0.236$ (5)	$\bar{G} = 0.560$ $\bar{G}_S = 0.244$ (3)	$\bar{G} = 0.495$ $\bar{G}_S = 0.239$ (8)
3,000 and over	$\bar{G} = 0.421$ $\bar{G}_S = 0.192$ (3)	$\bar{G} = 0.487$ $\bar{G}_S = 0.235$ (1)	$\bar{G} = 0.437$ $\bar{G}_S = 0.203$ (4)
LDCs	$\bar{G} = 0.423$ $\bar{G}_S = 0.300$ (20)	$\bar{G} = 0.538$ $\bar{G}_S = 0.335$ (10)	$\bar{G} = 0.461$ $\bar{G}_S = 0.312$ (30)
DCs	$\bar{G} = 0.306$ $\bar{G}_S = 0.054$ (12)	$\bar{G} = 0.368$ $\bar{G}_S = 0.098$ (7)	$\bar{G} = 0.329$ $\bar{G}_S = 0.077$ (19)

Source: As for Table 12.5.

12.2 The traditional and modern sectors

One of the most important features of LDCs is that their economies are sharply divided into a traditional sector and a modern sector. The two sectors differ in many respects. In the traditional sector the technology of production is one inherited from the past, having evolved over long centuries by trial and error. However efficient the technology may have been in the past, it is less efficient than the technology of the modern sector, which has been developed, mainly in the DCs, by the deliberate application of modern scientific methods. Therefore, as a general rule the average level of income in the traditional sector is much lower than in the modern sector.

There is also a difference in the forces influencing income distribution in the two sectors. In the modern sector income distribution is more likely to be determined by the working of market forces which are largely unconcerned with the inequality of income distribution. But in the traditional sector there are likely to be quite powerful social forces, based on custom and tradition, which tend to keep income differences within moderate bounds. Therefore the inequality of income distribution is likely to be greater in the modern than in the traditional sector.

The two sectors also differ in the types of commodities they produce. The main reason is that even if the modern sector has an absolute advantage over the traditional sector in producing all commodities, each sector has a comparative advantage over the other in different commodities. For example, the traditional sector has a comparative advantage in agriculture and some traditional manufactures and therefore tends to specialize in these activities. The modern sector then tends to specialize in modern manufacturing and service activities, in which it has a comparative advantage. The commodity specialization of the two sectors also depends on the extent of their contact with the more developed countries with their advanced technology.

The process of development may be broadly considered as one in which modern technology is substituted for the traditional technology of LDCs. We start with a situation in which there is a large traditional sector, with a lower average income and a lower inequality of income distribution than the modern sector. Then the process of development can occur in two ways, which may be described as the modernization of the traditional sector and the extension of the modern sector respectively. In both patterns we assume that the level of inequality in each sector remains constant. The modernization of the traditional sector may be taken as the process in which the proportions of the population in the two sectors remain constant, but there is a steady rise in the average income in the traditional sector as a ratio of that in the modern sector. By contrast, the extension of the modern sector may be taken as the case in which the ratio of incomes in the two sectors remains constant, but the proportion of the population in the modern sector increases steadily.

These two paths of development have very different consequences for the inequality of income distribution. The principal conclusion is that if development proceeds mainly by the modernization of the traditional sector, there will be a continuous decline in income inequality over time. But if development proceeds mainly by the extension of the modern sector, as has tended to occur in most LDCs, there will be a tendency for income inequality to increase up to a point and decline only thereafter.

This conclusion may be derived from the formula for the decomposition of the Gini index for the case in which the population is divided into two non-overlapping groups, described there as the rich and the poor (section 3.3.5). In section 3.5 we then discussed how the Gini index of income inequality was affected by two types of change, namely changes in the proportion of the population in the two groups, representing the process described as the extension of the modern sector, and changes in the income ratio of the two groups, representing the process described as the modernization of the traditional sector. It was shown in Figure 3.5 that the Gini index will decline continuously along the path of the modernization of the traditional sector, while the Gini index will rise up to a point and only decline thereafter along the path of the extension of the modern sector.

The theorem about the rise and fall of overall inequality for the model based on the extension of the modern sector has been proved in different ways by a number of authors (e.g. Kuznets 1955: 269–72; Lydall 1979: Chap. 12). This theoretical result about the variation of overall inequality corresponds to the statistical generalization observed historically and in international cross-section data for inequality to rise with per capita income up to a point and decline thereafter. Therefore some authors have used this theorem to explain the statistical finding. This implies that in the past development has proceeded mainly by the extension of the modern sector rather than by the modernization of the traditional sector. This may, in fact, have been the case historically but it need not necessarily be the case in the future. Even in the case in which development proceeds primarily by the extension of the modern sector, it is not the only explanation of the statistical finding. It is possible that it is also due to an increase of inequality within each sector.

12.3 The influence of demand patterns

In the previous section we considered how the structure of production influenced the distribution of income through the differences in the income levels and income inequality of the various sectors. There is also an influence from the distribution of income on the structure of production through the patterns of demand, that is, because individuals at different income levels have different patterns of demand for the commodities produced in the various sectors. At low levels of income, an individual spends the bulk of his income on food and only a small proportion on manufactures and services. At higher levels of income, the proportion of income spent on food becomes quite small, with larger proportions being spent on manufactures and services. These differences can also be described in terms of income elasticities of demand. The typical situation, shown by household expenditure surveys all over the world, is that the income elasticity of demand for food is less than one, and that for manufactures and services is greater than one.

These income elasticities do not remain constant, but vary with the level of income. As income rises, each commodity goes through different stages. First, it is a 'luxury' with a high income elasticity of demand; then it becomes a 'necessity' with a low income elasticity of demand; finally it reaches a 'satiation point' when income elasticity of demand is zero. Each commodity goes through these stages at different income levels. Therefore commodities may be arranged in a hierarchy according to the income levels at which they pass through these stages (Cornwall 1977:100–2; Pasinetti 1981:71–5). The three types of commodities enter into this hierarchy in the order: food, manufactures, and services. This explains why these commodities have income elasticities of demand in ascending order at the levels of income observed in LDCs.

Strictly speaking, these patterns apply to the relationship between the income of an individual and her income elasticity of demand. In addition to these patterns, the national income elasticity of demand is also influenced by the distribution of income, especially by whether it becomes more or less equal over time. To analyse this effect in the case of, say, food, consider a simple model. Suppose society is divided into two groups 1 and 2, representing the poor and the rich respectively. Let m_i represent the income share, p_i the proportion of income spent on food, and ε_i the income elasticity of demand, of the ith group. The typical situation will be $p_1 > p_2$, and $\varepsilon_1 > \varepsilon_2$. Also let

$$Z = \frac{m_1 p_1 \varepsilon_1 + m_2 p_2 \varepsilon_2}{p}$$

represent the weighted average of the two income elasticities of demand, the weights being the shares of the two groups in the total expenditure on food. Then let r_i be the rate of growth of the income of the ith group over a given period. It follows quite simply from this definition that the national income elasticity of demand for food E is given by

$$E = Z + \frac{m_1 m_2 (r_1 - r_2) [p_1 \varepsilon_1 - p_2 \varepsilon_2]}{p(m_1 r_1 + m_2 r_2)} \qquad (12.1)$$

Hence the national income elasticity of demand for food E will be equal to the weighted average Z of the income elasticities of demand for the two groups only when $r_1 = r_2$, that is, when there is no change in the distribution. To see what happens when there is a change in income distribution, note that the expression in square brackets will be positive in the typical case. Hence we find that $E \gtreqless Z$ according as $r_1 \gtreqless r_2$, that is, the national income elasticity will be greater if the distribution of income becomes more equal, and less if the distribution becomes less equal.

Thus we see that the structure of production and the distribution of income are related with each other in two ways. On the one hand, the structure of production influences the distribution of income because of differences in the income levels of the various sectors. On the other hand, the distribution of income influences the structure of production because of differences in the demand patterns of individuals at different income levels. The result of these two relationships operating at the same time means that the structure of production and the distribution of income are jointly determined by the differences in sectoral incomes on the one hand, and differences in demand patterns of different income groups on the other. This interaction is so important that it may be useful to explain it in terms of a simple model.

Consider an economy divided into three sectors, namely agriculture (A), industry (M), and services (S). Also, let the population be divided into three equal-sized groups, namely the poor, the middle, and the rich. Let X be a (3×1) column vector of the outputs from the three sectors, and let Y be a (3×1) column vector of incomes accruing to the three income groups. The two relationships between X and Y may then be represented as follows. Let A be a (3×3) matrix of element a_{ij}, representing the income accruing to the ith group in the course of producing one unit of output in the jth sector. Then it follows that the distribution of income Y in the economy as a whole is determined by the structure of production X by the equation

$$Y = AX \qquad (12.2)$$

Next, let B be a (3×3) matrix of elements b_{ij}, representing the expenditure on the output of the ith sector out of a unit of income of the jth income group. Then the structure of production X will be determined by the distribution of income Y according to the equation

$$X = BY \qquad (12.3)$$

In practice, the consumption expenditure of the various income groups is not the only source of demand for the output of the various sectors, and the various income groups do not spend all their incomes on the output of the various sectors. But to simplify the analysis, we neglect all interindustry transactions and exogenous sources of demand, and assume instead that the value of the output of each sector is fully distributed as incomes of the various groups, and all incomes are fully spent on the output of the various sectors. Then from (12.2) and (12.3) we get

$$X = BAX \qquad (12.4)$$

a homogeneous set of equations which completely determines the structure of outputs up to a scale factor for given A and B; and

$$Y = ABY \qquad (12.5)$$

another homogeneous set of equations which completely determines the distribution of income, again up to a scale factor.

Example
Let the matrix A be given by

	Agriculture	Industry	Services
Poor	0.12	0.20	0.15
Middle	0.40	0.33	0.25
Rich	0.48	0.47	0.60

This means, for example, that 12 per cent of the output of the agricultural sector accrues as income to the poor, 40 per cent to the middle, and 48 per cent to the rich, and so on for the other sectors. Alternatively, the income of the poor consists of 12 per cent of agricultural output, plus 20 per cent of industrial output, plus 15 per cent of service output, and so on for the other groups. Let the matrix B be given by

	Poor	Middle	Rich
Agriculture	0.80	0.51	0.40
Industry	0.13	0.29	0.36
Services	0.07	0.20	0.24

This means, for example, that the poor spend 80 per cent of their income on agricultural products, 13 per cent on industrial products and 7 per cent on services, and so on for other groups. These numbers reflect an economy in which agricultural is the dominant sector and income distribution within this sector is extremely concentrated, two characteristics that are highly representative of many LDCs. Then equations (12.4) and (12.5) may be solved to give

$$X = \begin{bmatrix} 0.50 \\ 0.30 \\ 0.20 \end{bmatrix} \begin{matrix} \text{(Agriculture)} \\ \text{(Industry)} \\ \text{(Services)} \end{matrix} \qquad Y = \begin{bmatrix} 0.15 \\ 0.35 \\ 0.50 \end{bmatrix} \begin{matrix} \text{(poor)} \\ \text{(Middle)} \\ \text{(Rich)} \end{matrix} \qquad (12.6)$$

Measuring the inequality of overall distribution of income and the inequality of income distribution in individual sectors, by the respective Gini indices, we get

Sector	Inequality
Agriculture	0.24
Industry	0.18
Services	0.30
Total	0.234

It is easy to see that overall inequality is the weighted average of the sectoral inequalities, the weights being the respective shares of total output:

$$G = w_1 G_1 + w_2 G_2 + w_3 G_3 \qquad (12.7)$$

This model is useful to show the interaction between the structure of production and the distribution of income, but it is a very simple one limited to the case in which the distribution of income is the only influence on the structure of production, and the structure of production is the only influence on the distribution of income. It has therefore to be extended to deal with other influences on each of these aspects of the economy. For example, the structure of production may be determined not only by consumer demand within the economy, but also by the nature of the country's foreign trade. Some ways in which foreign trade might influence both the structure of demand and the distribution of income are discussed in the next section. Similarly, the distribution of income may be determined not only by the distribution of incomes arising from productive activity but also by policies of the government. Some ways in which the policies of income redistribution might influence these two aspects of the economy are discussed in Chapter sixteen. (For other extensions, see Booth *et al.* 1981).

12.4 Foreign trade and income distribution

The previous section analysed the relationship between the structure of production and the distribution of income on the assumption that all output was produced in response to domestic demand, and all income was spent on domestic output. But in practice, some output is produced for export to other countries, and some income is spent in imports from other countries. Such foreign trade accounts for a considerable part of economic activity in LDCs, especially the small and medium-sized countries. In these countries the sort of commodities exported are usually very different from those which are imported. Therefore foreign trade has a considerable effect on the structure of production, and hence also on the distribution of income. Some of these effects are discussed in this section.

12.4.1 Neoclassical trade theory

We first consider the neoclassical analysis of the relationship based on the Heckscher–Ohlin model of international trade. In this model a country's comparative advantage depends on the relative endowment of the factors of production. Then, using the standard neoclassical model of the competitive functioning of product and factor markets, the influence of foreign trade on the distribution of income is analysed in terms of the effects on factor prices brought about by the change in the structure of production. The principal results of the theory may be summarized by considering three types of changes in foreign trade.

(i) Free trade in commodities

Consider first the case in which an LDC which had hitherto been largely isolated from other countries is opened up to world trade under conditions of free trade. This is what happened in many LDCs in the eighteenth and nineteenth centuries when they came under the domination of DCs and there was a rapid growth of trade. A large part of this trade was between the LDCs and the DCs, especially the colonial powers.

To analyse this type of trade, consider two countries, A representing the typical situation of LDCs and B representing the typical situation of DCs, such that the stock of capital relative to population and labour is lower in A than in B. Then, if the two countries have the same technology and demand patterns but there is no trade between them, wages will be lower and the rate of profit higher in A than in B. Hence the cost of labour-intensive commodities will be lower in A than in B, while the cost of capital-intensive commodities will be higher in A than in B.

Suppose the two countries begin to trade with each other. Then country A will export labour-intensive commodities that it can produce more cheaply, in exchange for imports of capital-intensive commodities which can be produced more cheaply in B. Consequently, the demand for labour will increase and the demand for capital will fall in A, while the demand for capital will increase and the demand for labour fall in B. These changes in demand will raise wages and lower the rate of profit in A, and lower wages and raise the rate of profit in B. Hence Ohlin (1933) argued that the trade in commodities will reduce the differences in relative factor prices between the trading countries. Pursuing this line of argument, but applying the neoclassical model of markets rigorously, Samuelson (1948, 1953) then showed that when the free trade in commodities equalizes commodity prices in the trading countries, it will also completely equalize factor prices, provided only that the number of freely traded commodities produced in both countries is greater than the number of immobile factors of production.

The equalization of factor prices, of course, will not equalize per capita incomes, for these incomes depend on the stock of factors. But because the average income derived from wages is lower than the average income derived from profits, the effect of foreign trade will be to reduce income inequality in LDCs and increase it in DCs. The magnitude of these effects will depend on the distribution of capital among the people.

(ii) Protection

Next we analyse the effects of protection by considering the difference between the free-trade situation and the case in which a country imposes a protective tariff on some of its imports. In DCs such tariffs have been imposed on labour-intensive commodities imported from LDCs, and in the LDCs such tariffs have been imposed on capital-intensive commodities imported from the DCs.

Such protection will then have two effects acting in opposite directions on the income of the factor of production used intensively in producing the protected commodity. On the one hand, the rise in the price of the commodity will tend to raise the relative price of that factor of production, and hence its share of the national income. On the other hand, the departure from free trade will reduce the national income. It is therefore not obvious which effect will dominate.

However, on the basis of the usual neoclassical model, such as those discussed in the factor price equalization theory discussed above, some definite results have been derived. For example, Jones (1965) showed that the change in the relative price of commodities will have a magnified effect on the relative price of the factor prices. Also, Stolper and Samuelson (1941) showed that there will be an absolute increase in the income of the protected factor of production, that is, that the factor price effect will dominate over the national income effect. Thus the protection of labour-intensive commodities will raise the real wages of labour in DCs, while the protection of capital-intensive commodities will raise the rate of profit in LDCs.

(iii) Promotion of labour-intensive exports

Finally, we consider the effect of policies to promote the exports of labour-intensive commodities. Compared with the free-trade situation, these policies will raise wages but will reduce the national income. The balance between these two opposing effects on the incomes of labour can then be analysed as in the case of protection. But policies to promote labour-intensive exports are followed by LDCs, not so much from an initial situation of free trade according to the neoclassical model, but rather because the conditions assumed in that model do not obtain in practice. Therefore we consider some of the ways in which the actual conditions affecting trade deviate from those assumptions.

12.4.2 Some complications

(i) Pricing of factors

The first complication is that factors of production are not priced in LDCs according to their marginal productivity, as assumed in the neoclassical model. This is because factor markets are not very competitive. They are not always in equilibrium, and they are highly fragmented according to categories within each type of factor and according to sector of employment. Instead, as discussed in Chapters nine to eleven, factor prices are often fixed at levels determined by a variety of institutions affecting factor markets, and remain quite rigid over time independently of supply and demand variations induced by trade.

Therefore factor prices, especially the wages of labour, do not change significantly with changes in the foreign trade situation, such as the opening up of countries to trade, the protection of manufactures, or promotion of labour-intensive exports. Where these changes in the foreign trade regime affect factor prices in the sectors directly involved in trade, these efforts are not communicated to factor prices in other sectors.

(ii) Utilization of factors

Another complication is that because factor markets are not in equilibrium, the available factors are not always fully employed. This was particularly the case in many LDCs before they were opened up to trade. Then, the main benefits that countries derived from the trading opportunity was not so much in the prices of factors but rather in the fuller utilization of surplus resources of land and labour, that is, trade provided these countries with a 'vent for surplus'. This was one of the basic arguments underlying Adam Smith's advocacy of free trade, and was advanced by Myint (1958) as the main explanation for the great expansion of exports of LDCs in the colonial pattern of development.

(iii) Differences in technology

In order to concentrate on differences in factor endowments as the principal source of comparative advantage of countries, most applications of the Heckscher–Ohlin model have assumed that the technology of pro-

duction was the same in all trading countries. In fact, the basic characteristic of LDCs is that while much of their trade is with DCs, they have not
been able to absorb the modern technology which is widely prevalent in
DCs. Hence the basic reason for the low wages of labour in LDCs relative
to those in DCs is the lower level of technology.

The factor price equalization tendency of the Heckscher–Ohlin model
may still operate even if the technology of production differs in the trading
countries. For example, if the technology of production in LDCs is
uniformly lower than in the DCs in the sense that the productivity of
factors in LDCs is lower than in the DCs by the same proportion in all
sectors, then the two types of countries may be assumed to have the same
production function when factors are measured in 'efficiency' units rather
than in 'natural' units. The effect of trade will then be to reduce differences
in the prices of the factors in efficiency units. If factor prices are equalized
in efficiency units, then the prices in natural units will be lower in LDCs by
a uniform fraction representing the technical inefficiency of LDCs. But, in
fact, the technical inefficiency of factors in LDCs varies according to the
sector in which they are employed. Therefore the tendency for factor prices
to be equalized will operate to a much smaller extent.

(iv) Primary product specialization of LDCs

An important condition for the factor price equalization tendency is that a
sufficient number of commodities are produced in all trading countries. But
the difference in factor endowments and in technology between LDCs and
DCs is so great that LDCs came to be highly specialized in primary
products and DCs in manufactures. In fact, to the extent that trade
between these countries lowers the returns to capital in LDCs and raises
them in DCs, and to the extent that the supply of capital responds to these
changes, the effect of trade will be to widen the differences in factor
endowments of these countries, and hence the tendency towards specialization (Findlay 1970; Stiglitz 1970). When countries are so highly specialized, trade does not have the postulated effect of equalizing commodity
prices leading to the equalization of factor prices.

The effect of trade was therefore to expand the sectors producing
primary products and to limit the sectors producing manufactures. Hence
the distribution of income within the agricultural sector came to have
greater weight in determining the overall distribution of income, as
discussed in the above section.

(v) Terms of trade effect

When commodity prices are not equalized, an important influence on
factor prices are the terms of trade between countries. Further, there are
significant changes in these terms of trade as a result of technological
progress. Most neoclassical analyses of the effects of technological progress

on the terms of trade assume that the same commodities are produced in all trading countries but in different proportions. But when countries are highly specialized in the commodities they produce, a more relevant model is that of Lewis (1954, 1969, 1978) which assumes that some of the traded commodities are highly specific to particular countries. Lewis has argued that the wages of labour in each country are determined by its productivity in the commodities produced in both countries, typically food. Then, technical progress in food production will raise wages, while technical progress in the specific commodity exported by the country will only reduce its price without affecting wages.

Historically, technical progress has tended to occur faster in the export sectors of LDCs than in the sectors producing non-tradable goods produced in both DCs and LDCs. Hence the gains from technical progress only led to a deterioration in the terms of trade of LDCs rather than improvement of factor prices (for a review of the literature, see Sundrum 1983:11.3(b)).

(vi) International mobility of factors

International trade theory has typically assumed that factors of production are immobile between countries, while being completely mobile within countries. But most factors have had only a limited mobility within LDCs, leading to fragmented factor markets, while some factors have been highly mobile between countries. Thus there was considerable movement of labour from the densely populated to the sparsely populated countries of Asia during the expansion of trade in the colonial period which limited any tendency for wages to rise in the course of the growth of trade. Similarly, there was a considerable flow of capital from the DCs to some of the export sectors of LDCs, but the profits from such investment accrued to the foreign capitalists rather than to the domestic population.

Chapter thirteen

Conclusions of Part II

13.1 Explaining the cross-section patterns

In the preceding chapters of Part II we considered various economic factors influencing the distribution of income in different countries. Some of the principal conclusions of that analysis are brought together in this final chapter of Part II to explain some of the major patterns in income distribution observed in Part I dealing with the statistical approach. The first section is devoted to explaining the cross-sectional differences in income distribution in different countries, and the next section to explaining changes in income distribution over time.

It is not, of course, possible to explain the distribution of income of each country because their individual distributions are affected by too many factors specific to each of them. Instead, we consider only some of the most important factors, as they affect broad groups of countries, about which we can say something in the light of the analysis in the previous chapters. In particular, we compare the low-income LDCs with the middle-income LDCs, and the LDCs with the DCs.

The statistical data considered in Part I of the book show a broad tendency for income distribution to be more unequal in the middle-income LDCs than in the low-income LDCs. This is the pattern that corresponds to the upward phase of Kuznets's law which postulates a tendency for income inequality to rise with income level in the earlier stage of growth. However, we found that not all low-income LDCs have low inequality, and not all middle-income LDCs have high inequality. That is why the statistical relationship between income level and income inequality, often used to support Kuznets's law, is not a very strong one. Hence we cannot explain income inequality only in terms of the level of income. Instead, we have to explain it by a number of other factors, such as those usually considered in conventional economic analysis.

Some of the most important of these proximate factors are those dealing with the structural differences between various groups of countries, especially the differences in the allocation of the labour force to the three

245

main sectors. As pointed out in Chapter twelve, this allocation varies systematically with the income level of countries. At the lowest level of income, most of the labour force is engaged in the agricultural sector. At the highest income level, only a small fraction of the labour force is engaged in this sector, with the bulk of the labour force in the industry and services sectors. The proportions of the GDP originating in the three sectors also vary in the same way, but the differences are smaller. Using these two aspects of economic structure, we find that there are quite large differences in the productivity of labour in the various sectors. In almost all countries, it is lowest in the agricultural sector. The relative position of the industry and the service sectors regarding labour productivity, however, varies with income level, being higher in the service sector at low levels of income and the industrial sector at higher income levels. There is also a tendency for the labour productivities of the various sectors to become less unequal as income level rises.

Although these structural differences are not directly related to income distribution, they have a considerable influence and in particular, explain the variation of income inequality with income level to some extent. To see the connection, for example, suppose all households engaged in any sector earn the same income, equal to the average income of that sector; then we can derive some implications for income distribution. In the poorest countries income inequality is low because most households are engaged in just one sector, namely the agricultural sector. But at higher income levels labour is more widely distributed among sectors with different income levels, and hence income inequality is higher. At the highest income levels, labour is again concentrated in the nonagricultural sectors, and at the same time, labour productivities become more uniform among different sectors. Therefore there is a tendency for income inequality to be lower at this level of income.

But these structural differences are only part of the explanation of the differences in income inequality. There are also other influences to be considered. One of the most important of them is the fact that the combination of factors of production varies from sector to sector. Thus labour and land are the most important factors of production in the agricultural sector, which is the dominant sector at the lowest levels of income. Further, the poorest countries are often those in which the pressure of population on land is particularly acute. Given such an intense pressure of population on land, incomes derived from the rent of land will be high relative to incomes derived from the wages of labour, as explained in the classical theory. But while the classical theory assumed full employment of labour, the intense population pressure on land has led to considerable unemployment and underemployment among agricultural workers in the poorer LDCs. Therefore the effect of intense population pressure has generally been to make income inequalities higher in the low-income LDCs as compared with the middle-income LDCs. However, countries have differed greatly in coping with such population pressure. Some countries, especially those in northeast Asia, have been more successful in developing labour-intensive methods of cultivation than others, for example, the south Asian countries. Hence the effect of population pressure on income inequality varies considerably between these groups of countries.

Income inequality depends not only on the stocks of the various factors of production, but also on how these stocks are distributed among individuals and households. Thus the inequality of income distribution in the agricultural economy depends not only on the ratio of rent incomes to wage incomes, but also on the distribution of land among individuals and households. The classical economists assumed that the ownership of different factors of production was concentrated in different social classes, and in particular that most of the land was owned by a relatively small land-owning class. On this assumption, it follows from equations (7.11) and (7.12) that the Gini index of income inequality would be high, being the difference between a high rent share of income and a small proportion of the population receiving income in the form of rent.

The classical assumption about the distribution of land was derived from the situation prevailing in Britain at the time, largely inherited from the preceding feudal system. But the way land is distributed varies greatly among LDCs at present. It is highly concentrated in some LDCs, such as those in Latin America. Land ownership also seems to have been highly concentrated in many of the northeast Asian countries at the time that they were still quite poor. But at that time there was also a widespread tendency for large owners to lease their land out to small-scale farm operators. Since then these countries have carried out quite extensive programmes of land reform leading to a more equal distribution of land among the tillers, especially former tenants.

By contrast, land is much more equally distributed in some other countries such as Thailand. This may be explained partly by Chayanov's theory that small farmers use their family labour more intensively on their own family farms, and are thus able to withstand the competition from large farmers relying mainly on hired labour. Hence the trend towards increasing concentration has not operated as strongly in the case of land ownership and control as Marx had argued was the case in regard to industrial capital. Another difference between countries is in the operation of the moral economy, in which powerful social forces tend to protect the rights of the less privileged groups in competition with the more affluent. Such differences in the distribution of land and the operation of social forces are an important cause for the variation of income inequality even among the poorest countries.

Together with land, we must also consider the effect of the natural resources endowment of countries. Many countries with a high level of income derive it from an abundant endowment of natural resources. But in countries with such an abundant endowment of natural resources, their ownership tends to be highly concentrated among a few people. Hence abundant natural resources generally tend to be associated with high-income inequality in the middle-income LDCs.

Another characteristic feature of low-income LDCs as compared with the middle-income LDCs is a much greater scarcity of capital. This scarcity by itself would lead to a higher rate of profit on capital in the low-income LDCs, but because of the small quantity of capital accumulated, the profit share of total income may also be quite small and therefore may not have much effect on overall inequality of income distribution. By contrast, not only is the profit share of total income higher in the middle-income countries, but the ownership of capital is also highly concentrated in a small proportion of the population. Therefore the effect of the distribution of capital is to contribute to greater inequality in the middle-income LDCs.

Next we consider the effect of the level of technology. Because of the scarcity of capital, the low-income LDCs have preserved to a greater extent a traditional technology evolved over long periods of time. Hence techniques of production are more labour intensive in low-income LDCs, while they are more capital intensive in middle-income LDCs, especially those which are modernizing their economies rapidly. The more labour-intensive techniques in the low-income LDCs mean greater demand for their abundant labour resources, and hence have an equalizing effect. The state of technology also depends on the skills of the labour force, especially as they are influenced by education. There is generally a higher level of education in the middle-income LDCs; this by itself would have the effect of reducing the effect of income differentials between educational categories on overall income inequality. But even in countries with a higher average level of education, educational opportunities are very unequally distributed among the people so that many middle-income LDCs are in the transitional phase of high inequality arising from the educational system.

Finally, we consider the effect of the ways in which factor markets function. In the low-income LDCs the working of factor markets is much affected by social norms which have survived from traditional practices of earlier times. These forces generally tend to prevent extreme destitution by such means as spreading employment opportunities more widely and by putting lower limits to the wages of labour. Thus, on balance, they tend to reduce income inequality below what it would otherwise have been. In the middle-income LDCs, however, the process of commercialization has gone further and eroded many of these traditional safeguards; but on the other hand, factor markets are not as fully competitive as generally assumed in neoclassical theories. Therefore the functioning of factor markets tends to contribute to more inequality in the middle-income LDCs.

Thus we see that there are a number of influences on income inequality which act in different ways in low-income and middle-income LDCs. A drastic summary of these effects is indicated in Table 13.1. In this table, a plus sign indicates an effect leading to higher inequality, and a minus sign to lower inequality. However, it must be stressed that these signs only give a rough indication of the direction of the various effects and cannot be assumed to operate in a rigid way in all countries. They do give an impression of a preponderance of positive effects over negative effects in the middle-income LDCs, which goes some way towards explaining the observed pattern of greater inequality in these countries as compared with the low-income LDCs.

Next we consider some explanations for the relatively low income inequality in the DCs compared with most LDCs, especially the middle-income LDCs which we noted in Part I. The first point to note is that the lower income inequality in DCs cannot be attributed only to their higher level of income. This is partly because the statistical relationship between income levels and income inequality among DCs is not very strong. It is also because income distribution patterns have not changed very much in recent times in spite of large changes in income levels. In fact, a more significant decline in income inequality occurred in these countries in the first half of this century when they were undergoing significant development in their basic economic institutions. Since the middle of the century the decline in income inequality in these countries seems to have slowed down

Table 13.1 Factors influencing income distribution in low- and middle-income LDCs

Factors	Effect in low-income LDCs	Effect in middle-income LDCs
Structure of economy		
Allocation of labour force	−	+
Sectoral differences in		
labour productivity	+	−
Population pressure	+	+
Asset distribution		
Land	−	+
Natural resources	−	+
Capital	?	+
Technology		
Labour intensity	−	+
Education	−	+
Factor market performance	−	+

considerably as they had already achieved their present levels of development.

Even in the DCs the productivity of workers in the agricultural sector is significantly lower than in the other sectors, but the agricultural share has become much less important, with a labour force share of 11 per cent, compared with 37 per cent in industry and 52 per cent in services. The corresponding GDP shares were 6, 37, and 57 per cent respectively. They show that differences in the productivity of labour between the industrial and service sectors which employ the bulk of the labour force are smaller. This is one reason for the low inequality of income distribution in these countries.

Because of the small size of the agricultural sector, and because a great deal of capital and advanced technology are used to overcome any scarcity of land in the DCs, the distribution of land is not a significant factor affecting income distribution in these countries. At the same time, these countries have a larger stock of capital, which has led to lower rates of profit. Further, the stock of capital is more evenly distributed among the people.

The most important factor leading to the low income inequality of the DCs is the special position of labour. Because of the dominant position of the industrial and services sectors, and because of the relatively more abundant stock of capital, there is a scarcity of labour relative to other factors of production. This by itself is a factor leading to high wages. Further, the labour force is much more skilled as a result of higher levels of education. This is another factor leading to higher wages relative to incomes from other factors. Finally, labour is much more highly organized in trade unions, so that the bulk of the labour force gets high wages by collective bargaining and also have considerable political power to influence government policies in their favour. These influences are not just the result of higher levels of income, but the result of significant differences in the institutions governing the working of their factor markets.

13.2 Explaining the historical trends

After having considered the cross-sectional differences in income distribution in the previous section, we turn now to an explanation of the historical trends in income distribution. It is only by providing such an explanation that we will be able to project future changes in income distribution, and hence design more effective policies to achieve various distributional objectives.

The first point to note is that explanations of historical changes cannot be derived from observed cross-sectional patterns. The cross-sectional patterns showed, for example, that the average income inequality of middle-income LDCs was higher than that of the low-income LDCs. From this, we cannot assume that income inequality in the low-income LDCs would necessarily increase in the early stages of their growth as their incomes rise to the levels obtaining in the middle-income LDCs. Similarly, the cross-sectional patterns show that the average income inequality in the DCs was lower than that in the middle-income LDCs. This again does not guarantee that income inequality of the middle-income LDCs will necessarily decline in the later phases of their growth as their incomes rise to the level of the DCs.

One reason why the cross-section relationship between income inequality and income level cannot be used to explain historical trends is simply that such a statistical relationship explains only a small part of the statistical variation in the cross-sectional data. This is because, as argued in the previous section, differences in income inequality between countries are due not only to differences in income levels, but also to differences in many other aspects.

But a more important reason is that in order to use the cross-section pattern to explain historical trends, we must assume that all countries are following the same dynamic path and that differences between them are only due to differences in the stage they have reached on this path. This is a crucial assumption whose validity is subject to serious doubt because, as argued in the previous section, there are some factors such as population growth and capital accumulation which may affect income distribution in all countries in a fairly uniform manner as considered in the usual economic analysis, but there are also many other factors involving the economic and social institutions of countries which do not vary in any systematic pattern with the economic growth of countries. Then the dynamic changes of inequality in the course of economic growth in individual countries may differ widely among themselves, and also with the pattern shown by the cross-section relationship between inequality and income at any point of time. These differences may be illustrated as in Figure 13.1. In this diagram, the unbroken lines show the changes in inequality in the course of economic growth in particular countries, while the broken line shows the cross-section pattern between income level and income inequality at a point of time.

Therefore any attempt to explain historical trends only on the basis of cross-sectional patterns is fraught with danger. Instead, it must be based on historical data on changes in income distribution over time. As noted in Chapter five, quantitative historical data on income distribution over any long period are available only for a few developed countries. These data show a significant decline in income inequality dating from the early decades of this century. But we also found that this process of declining inequality has slowed down considerably, so that their income distributions have remained remarkably stable since World War II, in spite of a long period of rapid economic growth.

Quantitative data are not available for the earlier period of modern

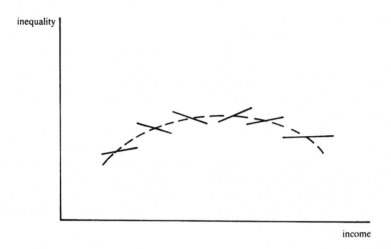

Figure 13.1

economic growth in the DCs in the initial phase of their industrial revolution. On the basis of contemporary evidence of a largely qualitative kind,
Marx advanced his thesis of the increasing misery of the masses during
capitalist development. Kuznets (1955:276) also assumed that inequality
increased during this phase, but in his case, this assumption was a conjecture based on a particular theoretical model of growth and inequality.
He specifically admitted that 'no empirical evidence is available for checking this conjecture of a long secular swing in income inequality', especially
of a rise in the earlier phase. On balance, it is highly probable that there
was in fact a rise in income inequality during this phase.

Accepting the conclusion that income inequality increased in the early
phase of economic growth of the presently developed countries does not,
however, necessarily mean that it would also increase in the early stage of
growth which present-day LDCs are going through. After all, the former
episode occurred in a small sample of countries which had gone through a
particular historical experience and were faced with a situation very different from that confronting the LDCs in more recent times.

Therefore we have to study the historical trends of income distribution
in the LDCs on the basis of their own experience. But in their case, data on
changes in income distribution over time are even more limited and are
available only for a few countries covering much shorter intervals of time in
the post-World War II period. These data do not show any consistent
pattern. In some countries there was an increase in income inequality,
especially in countries which started with a rather unequal distribution of
income. On the other hand, there are more detailed data from Japan and
the newly industrializing countries of Asia, such as Taiwan, South Korea,

Hong Kong, and Singapore, which indicate a decline of income inequality during a period of particularly rapid economic growth. Therefore the problem before us is not one of explaining any single historical trend of income distribution which is uniformly followed by all countries as their economies grow. Instead, we have to explain widely divergent paths followed by different countries.

In fact, there are just too many factors influencing income distribution for us to be able to get a complete theory of the subject. All that we can hope for is to isolate a few dominant conditions which account for the difference between those cases in which income inequality increased in the process of growth, as in Brazil and Mexico, and those which show a declining trend of income inequality, such as Taiwan and South Korea. The most important of these conditions is the initial distribution of assets. In countries where the initial distribution of assets is very unequal, not only is the distribution of income also unequal, but it becomes progressively more so over time. This was particularly the case in the DCs at the onset of their modern economic growth, coming as it did after the feudal phase of their history. But in countries where the initial distribution of assets was more equal, as it was in the Asian NICs at the time they began their rapid growth in the postwar period, the distribution of income becomes progressively more equal over time.

Apart from this condition, there are a number of reasons for a cumulative increase in inequality, as noted by Kuznets (1955:263–5). The most important is that richer people save more, accumulate assets faster, and therefore become even richer. This was also the basis of Marx's Law of Increasing Concentration of property. Another reason, which has been stressed by Kuznets, is that the early stages of growth are characterized by a steady shift of population from the predominantly agricultural rural areas, with a relatively lower average income and a more equal income distribution, to the predominantly industrial urban areas, with a higher average income and a more unequal income distribution. This is the process which we have described in Chapter twelve as the extension of the modern sector, as distinct from the modernization of the traditional sector. Countries with an initially unequal distribution of income are more likely to follow the route of extending the modern sector than that of modernizing the traditional sector.

Another reason for a cumulative increase of inequality is the tendency for the wages of the mass of labourers to remain quite firmly tied to something like a subsistence level, leaving most of the benefits of economic growth to accrue to the owners of capital and land. This is particularly likely to be the case when there is a high degree of unemployment among workers. The more unequal the distribution of income between workers and employers to begin with, the more likely it is that employers will use their superior bargaining power to widen the gap still further.

To the extent that poorer people have access to educational opportunities, this provides an avenue for their individual economic advancement. But at least in the early stages of growth, educational opportunities are extremely limited and such educational opportunities as exist tend to be very unequally distributed. Thus education, which is often looked to as the great leveller, may itself become the means for increasing inequality.

Against these forces leading to a cumulative increase of inequality, especially in the early stages of growth, there are other forces leading to declining inequality, which operated more strongly in the later phases of economic growth of the presently developed countries. In explaining the decline of inequality in these countries, Kuznets laid great emphasis on legislative interference and political decisions, reflecting the greater political power of the working classes. He also pointed to the growing importance of technological progress and of the service sector as factors which reduced the role of material assets, and hence their influence on overall income distribution.

But even without these forces, which operated only at a late stage in the economic development of the DCs, income inequality has shown a declining trend in other countries at a much earlier stage of development. We refer particularly to the experience of the newly industrializing countries of Asia. The most significant feature of these countries is that they started their era of rapid growth from a position of a relatively greater equality, especially in the distribution of productive assets. In the case of countries such as Japan, South Korea, and to some extent also of Taiwan, this was the result of extensive war damage to capital, so that the further accumulation of capital proceeded on a broader base. In all these countries there was also a considerable redistribution of land away from landlords to actual cultivators.

Thus in these countries the cumulative forces leading to increasing inequality discussed above were weaker and offset by other forces which moved in an equalizing direction, mainly because they started with a more equal distribution of assets. For example, workers had greater bargaining power *vis-à-vis* their employers. Educational opportunities were more widespread. But perhaps most important was the effect of the more equal initial distribution of income on the pattern of growth, operating through demand factors. In particular, there was greater demand for labour-intensive commodities, leading in turn to greater demand for labour and hence to higher wages than would otherwise have been the case. Either for this reason or as a result of deliberate policy, economic growth followed the route of modernizing the traditional sector to a greater extent than that of extending the modern sector only. In the case of these countries this trend was reinforced by the deliberate policy decision to encourage the growth of exports of labour-intensive manufactures, at least in the initial stage of their export-led growth. All these factors together explain the decline of income inequality in some of the LDCs in the more recent period.

After this analysis of inter-country differences and historical trends in income distribution, we turn to the implications for distributional policies in Part III.

Part III

The policy implications

Chapter fourteen

The policy objectives

14.1 The distributional objective

In Part II we were mainly concerned with the influence of market forces on the distribution of income. However, the distribution of income is also influenced by the policies of governments. In some cases these effects are the inadvertent consequences of policies followed for some other purpose; in others, they are the results of policies deliberately pursued to influence the distribution of income. Therefore we must also consider how the distribution of income has been and might be influenced by government policies; this is the subject of Part III.

Just as the egalitarian distribution of income provided a convenient point of departure for the measurement of inequality in Part I, and the random distribution of income the point of departure for the analytical discussion of Part II, we need a point of departure for the study of policy implications. For this purpose, the most convenient concept is the socially desirable distribution of income. Once such a concept is defined in a satisfactory way, it can be used to evaluate policies according to the extent to which they lead to this goal, and to improve these policies to make them more effective from this point of view.

However, there is much controversy about what is the socially desirable distribution of income. The position has been well described by Pen (1974:7) as follows:

It is difficult to imagine a more controversial subject. The inequality of incomes has been debated for centuries without passions waning or a clear picture emerging. The facts are the subject of differences of opinion, the theories are many and often conflicting, and above all people fail to agree on just what a proper or fair income distribution should be. Everybody knows that incomes are unequally distributed, but everybody has his own ideas about the causes of this and about the steps that would lead to an improvement. Come to that, some think that there has been far too much of a levelling. The differences of opinion are partly the product of opposing interests: many people feel that others receive unjustifiably high incomes, that others cause inflation with their wage demands or their increased profits, or even that other people's incomes are entirely misplaced (interest!). The debate has generated more heat than light. But in addition it cannot be denied that the cooler, theoretical approaches differ greatly.

In fact, Pen (1974: Chap. 7) compiled a list of 21 norms that have been suggested for the socially desirable distribution of income. But on closer scrutiny we find that the basic theme is that of equality. The very word 'equity' is derived from equality. The controversies in the subject relate not so much to whether equality is or is not an appropriate distributional objective, but rather to how it should be balanced against other social objectives and what instruments of policy should be used to promote the distributional objective. These other issues are important and will be discussed later. But as far as the distributional objective itself is concerned, the most widely accepted view is that a more equal distribution is to be preferred to a less equal one.

Economists have tried to justify the egalitarian distribution of income on welfare grounds, that is, taking the ultimate social objective as the maximization of social welfare in some sense. This was the approach used to derive the welfare measures of income inequality discussed in section 3.4. Social welfare may be defined in various ways. For example, it might be defined as the aggregate utility obtained by adding the individual utilities of all members of society, where these individual utilities are assumed to be functions only of individual incomes. Then the socially desirable distribution of income is the distribution which maximizes aggregate utility.

One problem with this approach is the assumption that the utility of individuals depends only on their own incomes or consumptions. In fact, the utility of individuals depends also on the incomes of other individuals in the same society through feelings of envy or sympathy. This interdependence of utility functions is an important source of the social concern with inequality. To neglect this interdependence is to neglect a central issue involved in defining a socially desirable distribution of income. But even leaving this problem aside, this approach does not necessarily lead to an egalitarian distribution of income because the maximization of aggregate utility will only equalize the marginal utilities of individuals. But as individuals have different utility functions, the equalization of marginal utilities will not equalize their total utilities or their incomes. As Friedman (1947:310-1) put it, 'suppose a hundred persons in the United States are enormously more efficient pleasure machines than any others, each of these would have to be given an income ten thousand times as large as the income of the next most efficient pleasure machine in order to maximize aggregate utility'.

As an alternative, it might be argued that where individuals have different utility functions, the goal should be not the maximization of aggregate utility, but rather the equalization of the total utilities of individuals. But even this criterion will not lead to an egalitarian distribution of income. In fact, it would mean that persons who are more efficient in deriving utility from their incomes should be given less income than others, exactly opposite to the criterion of maximizing aggregate utility.

One way of avoiding these problems is to say that although people differ in the utilities they derive from their consumption or income, we have no reliable means of knowing these utility functions beforehand. Therefore Lerner (1944) argued that in this state of ignorance, we should apply the Bayesian principle and assume that the probability that a person has a particular utility function is the same for all persons. Then it follows that the mathematical expectation of social welfare is maximized by an equal distribution of income. Since then, the theorem has been proved on the basis of much more general assumptions regarding social welfare and the utility functions on which it is based (see, e.g., Sen 1973b).

Another way of avoiding the difficulty is to argue that even if individual utility functions are different, society as a whole should treat all individuals as if they had the same utility functions. Further, it may also be assumed that the utility that a poor person derives from an additional unit of consumption should be given more weight than the utility that a rich person derives from the same addition to his or her consumption, in other words, that the utility function which is assumed to apply to all individuals from the social point of view is subject to the law of diminishing marginal utility. Once this assumption is made, it then follows that total social welfare is maximized when all individuals get the same income.

Many of the problems of the welfare approach to defining the desirable distribution of income discussed above arise from a simple concept of the social welfare function. Recently, however, much theoretical work has been done assuming a sophisticated social welfare function using, for example, the concept of the marginal utility of income to different income groups, to derive optimal rules for various types of taxes (see, e.g., Atkinson and Stiglitz 1980: especially Lecture 12; and Newberry and Stern 1987). In these applications, it is assumed that the parameters of the social welfare function are given by the policymaker to the economist. The results for policy recommendations, however, depend crucially on these parameters, and these parameters are usually not available. It is doubtful therefore whether the welfare approach based on all these assumptions has added much to the choice of the distributional objective. On the other hand, this approach only detracts from other considerations which make the egalitarian distribution desirable from a social point of view. Such a distribution is desirable not only because it maximizes social welfare in some sense or other, but because it promotes social harmony and encourages collective action towards common goals. An unequal society is an unhappy society with a constant potential for social conflict. Such a society is also undesirable because richer people may exercise too much control over society as a whole not only in influencing the allocation of resources in the economy, but also because they have greater political power to influence the government of the day. For all these reasons, the ultimate goal of distributional policy may be taken as the egalitarian distribution of income, just as equality before the law and equality of political rights are taken as social objectives in other spheres.

The real problem, however, is how the concept of the egalitarian distribution should be interpreted in practice. One problem is that while it is easy to say that all people in the same position should earn the same income – the case of horizontal equality – it is much more difficult to define what is meant by complete equality for individuals differing widely in their personal circumstances, such as age, sex, health, place of residence, family obligations, or educational qualifications. (For the problems of defining horizontal and vertical equity, see Atkinson and Stiglitz 1980:350-6.) For example, it might be accepted that people at different ages must have different incomes, but this raises the question of how incomes should vary with age. One solution is to apply the concept of equality not to incomes at a point of time, but rather to the incomes that individuals earn over their whole lifetime. One of the important influences on such lifetime incomes is the degree of social mobility. A high degree of social mobility leads to a low inequality of lifetime incomes, even though the static distribution of incomes at a point of time may be unequal.

Then there is the question of whether it is income which should be equalized or consumption. It may be widely agreed that it is consumption levels which should be equalized, but this does not necessarily mean equal incomes because people with high incomes may spend a large proportion of these incomes on investment rather than consumption. In a well-known statement, Keynes (1919:18) in fact argued that this is what happened during the early stages of modern economic growth in Europe:

> Europe was so organized socially and economically as to secure the maximum accumulation of capital. While there was some continuous improvement in the daily condition of the mass of the population, society was so framed as to throw a great part of the increased income into the control of the class least likely to consume it. . . . Herein lay in fact the main justification of the capitalist system. If the rich had spent their new wealth on their own enjoyment, the world would long ago have found such a regime intolerable.

However true this may have been in the historical experience of the European countries, it is certainly not true to the same extent in the LDCs of today. Much of the increased incomes of the rich people in these countries is spent on consumption in highly conspicuous ways, leading to wide disparities in standards of living between the rich and the poor. Therefore, in these countries, attempts to equalize consumption standards must be based on greater equality of incomes as well.

Sometimes the ideal of equality is applied not to the entire consumption of individuals, but to particular types of consumption or particular activities. This is the distinction which Simon (1948; see also Tobin 1970) draws between general egalitarianism and specific egalitarianism. Specific egalitarianism is the case in which certain items of consumption, such as basic food and shelter, education, medical and health services, are to be equally distributed to all members of society irrespective of their incomes, an approach that is sometimes followed during periods of acute scarcity such as wartimes and famines.

Sometimes the distributional objective is seen primarily in terms of the people at the bottom of the income scale. This may be interpreted as the extreme case of assigning distributional weights, for example, as the case in which the improvement in the income of the bottom group is given an infinitely greater weight than that of the higher groups. By this criterion, societies are evaluated according to the income of their poorest members, the principle advocated by Rawls (1971). The distributional objective can then be taken as maximizing the minimum level of consumption. A more practical variant of this approach is the eradication of poverty. Some of the issues involved are discussed in section 16.3.3. While the eradication of poverty is a highly desirable objective, it may be taken as an immediate objective, while the ultimate objective of distributional policy is taken as equality.

Many of these problems in interpreting the egalitarian distribution, however, relate to that concept as the ultimate goal of distributional policies. Whatever solution we arrive at, this goal is not something which can be achieved in the near future. Therefore it is not very profitable to pursue this definition in great detail. The more important question from a practical point of view is the direction in which the prevailing distribution should be currently modified by government policies. For this purpose, it may be sufficient to say that the distributional objective should be to reduce the inequality of income distribution, however imprecise that concept may be, so long as it helps to evaluate the policies that are followed in the near future.

A more serious problem from the practical point of view is that the distributional objective of reducing income inequality is not the only goal of social policy. Social policy must also take account of other goals, such as the rapid growth of total national income. This is a particularly important goal in the LDCs, where average incomes are very low, lower not only in comparison with DCs, but also lower than what can be achieved. It is the balance that has to be struck between this goal and the movement towards the equal distribution of income that raises the most serious questions about the policies that have to be followed. The issues involved are discussed in the following section.

14.2 The choice between growth and equity

Given two objectives such as growth and equity, there would be no problem if they are independent of each other, in particular if policies to promote one objective did not have any adverse effect on the other. But there is a widespread feeling among economists that there is a conflict between these objectives. Given such a conflict, they also feel that LDCs should give greater weight to the growth objective than to the distributional objective.

For example, this was the position taken by J.S. Mill (1923 edn, p. 749) a long time ago, when he argued that 'it is only in the backward countries of the world that increased production is still an important object; in those most advanced, what is economically needed is a better distribution'. It may also be recalled that Marx also took the view that the capitalist system should be allowed to develop the productive forces of society fully before attempts are made to improve the distribution of income. More recently, the same view was expressed by Johnson (1958:153, 159) as follows:

> [T]he remedies for the main fault which can be found with the use of the market mechanism, its undesirable social effects, are luxuries which under-developed countries cannot afford to indulge in if they are really serious about attaining a high rate of development. . . . There is a conflict between economic efficiency and social justice. The extent or importance of this conflict is likely to vary according to the state of economic development. . . . An advanced country can afford to sacrifice some growth for the sake of social justice. But the cost of greater equality may be great to any economy at a low level of development that wishes to grow rapidly; . . . it would therefore seem unwise for a country anxious to enjoy rapid growth to insist too strongly on policies aimed at ensuring economic equality and a just income distribution. I should add that the problem may not in fact be as serious as I have made it out to be, since in the course of time rapid growth tends in various ways to promote a more equal distribution of income.

It is with respect to such arguments that Sen (1973a:70) remarked, 'I have heard it argued that equality is a "luxury" that only a rich economy can "afford", and while I cannot pretend to understand fully this point of view, I am impressed by the number of people who seem prepared to advocate such a position'.

On the other hand, many socialist economists and governments in the recent past have given greater priority to the equality objective. The alternative views may be illustrated diagrammatically as in Figure 14.1. In this

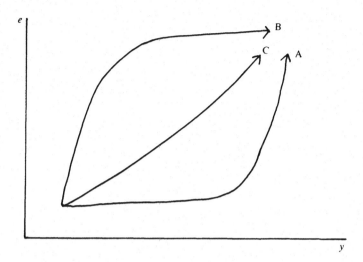

Figure 14.1

diagram average incomes are measured on the horizontal axis, and the degree of equality on the vertical axis. The path marked A represents what may be described as the growth-oriented strategy; according to this strategy, LDCs should concentrate on increasing their average incomes rapidly until they have reached a high level, even if this involves an increase of income inequality in the process, and only then seek to make the distribution of income more equal. By contrast, the path marked B represents what may be described as the equity-oriented strategy; according to this strategy, LDCs should concentrate first on making the distribution of income more equal, and only after a high degree of equality has been achieved should they seek to increase their growth more rapidly. The path marked C then represents a compromise solution in which both growth and equity are pursued together, at least ensuring that there is no increase of inequality in the process of economic growth.

In view of this diversity of opinion, it is worth considering the issue in more detail using the standard model by which economists analyse the optimum choice of policies relating to two objectives. In this method the solution depends on two types of relationships (Figure 14.2). One of the relationships refers to the technical constraints, showing the trade-off between the two objectives. This is expressed as a functional relationship showing how the maximum amount of one objective which can be attained for a given amount of the other objective, that is, by the transformation curve TT in the figure. As drawn, the curve illustrates the case in which there is a conflict between the two objectives; hence the transformation curve is a downward sloping curve which is usually taken as concave to the

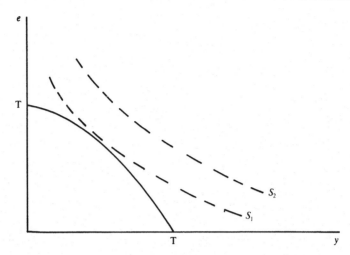

Figure 14.2

origin. Each policy followed by the government will lead to a particular result in terms of growth and equity, and the transformation curve describes the outcomes of all the policies that might be followed. The other relationship refers to the choice between the two objectives based on the social preference system. These preferences may be illustrated by a set of social indifference curves, S_i, which are downward sloping and usually taken as convex to the origin. The optimum policy or set of policies to be followed will then be given by the point at which the transformation curve TT is tangential to the highest social indifference curve between the two objectives. Thus the optimum path to follow is not just a reflection of social preferences as interpreted by different people, but depends also on their views about the transformation possibilities in the economic system.

In recommending the growth-oriented strategy shown by the curve A in Figure 14.1, authors such as Johnson assume that there is an inevitable conflict between the goals of growth and of equity. We consider this assumption in the next section. In the present section we consider some arguments which have been offered about the choice between the two objectives, assuming that there is a conflict between them.

Economists may have a certain competence in describing the technical conditions of the trade-off between these objectives; they are much less competent to identify social preferences as they exist or as they should be. To distil the social preferences from the preferences of individuals is a complex, perhaps a hopeless, task, as indicated by Arrow's (1966) Impossibility Theorem. In a sense, what matters for the choice of policies is the preferences of policymakers. But it is almost as difficult a task to identify a consistent set of preferences underlying their decisions, because they are so often made on an ad hoc basis.

Under certain conditions, an optimal choice of policies may be derived from technical relationships in an economic system. This is the case considered in the 'turnpike' theorem (see, e.g., Dorfman *et al.* 1958: Chap. 12). This theorem shows that the optimum route to a distant objective will lie mostly along a 'maximal' path determined only by the transformation possibilities in the system. But the growth-oriented strategy recommended by the economists cited above has not been based on this argument.

Instead, most economists have relied on the welfare approach to the problem of determining the social preferences between the objectives. The basic difficulty in this approach is that economists have eschewed the possibility of making inter-personal comparisons of utility. Hence the furthest they have been able to go in making welfare judgments is the criterion of Pareto optimality, which is a very limited criterion. By this criterion, a situation in which a few people are rolling in luxury while large numbers are destitute would still be described as Pareto optimal, so long as the position of the poor cannot be improved without some sacrifice on the part of the rich. Further, by this criterion, there may be a number of situations which are all Pareto optimal; then the criterion does not give us any guidance in choosing between these situations. Such a limited criterion does not permit us to make any strong recommendations either for growth or for equity.

Attempts have, however, been made to circumvent the difficulty and make out a case for giving priority to the growth objective. In most cases, government policies will benefit some and hurt others, but it has been argued that if the policy promotes growth of the national income, the sum of the benefits will be greater than the sum of the losses. If we cannot compare these gains and losses, we cannot evaluate the policy. But if these policies are supplemented with measures by which the gainers compensate the losers, then there will be a net gain, even by the limited test of Pareto optimality.

However, some economists have gone further and argued that a policy should be followed if the gainers, however rich, could compensate the losers, however poor, even if compensation is not actually paid. This is the 'compensation principle' originally proposed by Mill and revived by Kaldor (1939) and Hicks (1940). If this argument is valid, then the choice of policies could be made only on the basis of their effects on growth. As Kaldor (1939:144) put it,

> where a certain policy leads to an increase in physical productivity, and thus of aggregate real income, the economist's case for the policy is quite unaffected by the question of the comparability of individual satisfactions; since in all such cases it is *possible* to make some people better off without making anyone worse off.

However, this principle cannot be accepted as it has since been conclusively demonstrated that it leads to inconsistent results in the case where compensation is not paid (Graaff 1957: Chap. 5; Chipman and Moore 1976; see also Meade 1976: Chap. 3 for a lucid exposition). Thus this approach does not lend any support for giving more weight to the growth objective than to the distributional objective in the case in which there is a conflict between the two.

Next we consider whether a method of determining the balance to strike between the two objectives may be derived from the welfare measures of inequality discussed in section 3.4. For example, according to the criterion of the generalized Lorenz curve, any growth of national income is to be preferred which increases the incomes of some individuals without reducing the incomes of any others, whatever be the change in the degree of inequality. But it must be recalled that this criterion is based on the assumption that the utility of an individual depends only on her own income, and therefore does not take much account of the effect of inequality on social welfare.

In some versions of the argument, particular forms have been suggested for social welfare as a function of the two objectives of growth and equity, such as the welfare index $m(1 - G)$ suggested by Sen (1974), where m is the average income and G is a measure of inequality. On this basis the optimum policy can be chosen as that which maximizes this index. However, this particular combination of the two measures is quite arbitrary, and different combinations will lead to different policy choices.

A major distributional problem in LDCs is the extent of absolute poverty. The reduction of poverty depends both on rapid growth of national income and reduction of income inequality. Therefore one approach which may be more relevant to LDCs is to choose the combination of the two objectives that leads to the maximum reduction in the extent of poverty. As pointed out in Chapter four, the results of this approach may be quite different from that based on the generalized Lorenz curve.

Another approach which may be considered is the proposal of Chenery *et al.* (1974) for a measure that takes account of both the growth and the distribution of national income. Suppose the population is divided into k fractile groups according to rising incomes. Then the growth rate of total national income is just the weighted average of the growth rates of the incomes of these groups:

$$R = \Sigma \ w_i R_i \tag{14.1}$$

where w_i is the initial income share of the ith group and R_i the growth rate of their income. Hence this measure gives more weight to the growth of the incomes of the upper-income groups than to the growth of the incomes of the lower-income groups. Therefore these authors have proposed that a better index is the simple average of the growth rates of income of the various groups, giving equal weights to each of them:

$$R_e = \frac{1}{k} \Sigma \, R_i \qquad (14.2)$$

From these formulae, we get

$$R - R_e = \Sigma \left(w_i - \frac{1}{k} \right) (R_i - R) \qquad (14.3)$$

This shows that R_e will be equal to R if the initial distribution of income is completely egalitarian, however unequal may be the final distribution. Also, R_e will be equal to R if all groups experience the same rate of growth of their incomes, however unequal the initial and final income distributions may be. Therefore this measure does not always take account of the extent to which the distribution of income may become more unequal in the process of growth. Using R_e as an index for evaluating alternative outcomes, the optimum choice would be one in which increases in national income are allocated only to the lowest income groups. However, mainly for reasons of political expediency, these authors have in fact recommended a policy in which the incomes of the upper-income groups are stabilized.

Thus we see that there is no commanding hypothesis about the social preferences between the growth and equity objectives that we can rely on. However, this problem arises in an acute form when there is a conflict between the two objectives, as is often assumed. It is therefore more important to consider whether there is in fact such a conflict between the objectives of growth and equity.

14.3 The trade-off between growth and equity

According to one view, there need be no conflict between growth and equity. This is the 'trickle-down theory' which has been explained by Todaro (1977:439) as follows:

> [T]he prevalent view of the 1950s and 1960s in which development was seen as purely an economic phenomenon in which rapid gains from the overall growth of GNP and per capita income would automatically bring benefits (i.e. trickle down) to the masses in the form of jobs and other economic opportunities. The main preoccupation was therefore to get the growth job done while problems of poverty, unemployment and income distribution were of secondary importance.

However, since then the more common view among economists has been that there is a conflict between the two objectives. One possible basis for this opinion may be Kuznets's law, which states that there would be a rise in income inequality in the early stages of growth, and a decline only in the late stages. But as discussed in Chapter thirteen, the statistical basis of this relationship is very weak. Such statistical evidence as has been used to defend the proposition has largely been based on cross-section data from countries at different levels of development. Before we can rely on such a statistical generalization, it must first be explained in terms of the under-lying economic and social forces which lead to rising inequality in the earlier stages of growth, and particularly the way this trend may be modi-fied by the policy instruments within the control of modern governments. It is only then that the cross-section pattern can be applied to project future trends in the LDCs.

Another difficulty with the cross-section patterns is that they are affected by major institutional differences between countries, unconnected with differences in income levels. Therefore a better basis for projecting probable future trends is to use time series data describing historical changes in individual countries. But, as discussed in Chapter thirteen, such time series data as are available do not show any uniform pattern in LDCs. While there has been rising inequality with growth in some countries, there have also been cases of declining inequality in the course of growth in other countries, especially the newly industrializing countries of Asia.

There are also some theoretical reasons why many economists believe in the conflict between the growth and equity objectives. One such reason is based on their views about the role of the market system, as argued by Johnson cited above. Some economists believe that rapid economic growth depends on the freedom of market forces, which will lead to rising inequa-lity of income distribution. Hence they conclude that government policies to interfere with the free working of market forces for distributional reasons would necessarily have adverse effects on economic growth. However, these propositions are not self-evident and need to be verified in individual cases. While market forces may be efficient in allocating given resources most efficiently to meet effective demand on the basis of a given distribution of income, it is not obvious that they will also necessarily lead to the fastest growth of which an economy is capable. Further, even in the case in which market forces do lead to rapid growth, it is not obvious that they will also necessarily lead to greater inequality. Whether they do so or not depends crucially on the initial distribution of incomes and assets.

Another reason why some economists are convinced about the conflict between growth and equity is based on the role of savings. According to this argument, an unequal distribution of income is necessary to generate the savings needed for rapid growth. However, there are many weaknesses in this argument. In the first place, rapid growth does not depend on invest-ment alone; a more important factor is technological progress, which does not necessarily depend on an unequal distribution of income. Second, a high rate of investment does not necessarily depend on a high rate of voluntary savings; instead, it depends on profitable opportunities of investment. When such opportunities exist, they may be financed by borrowing from banks or foreign sources or by inflation. Third, a high rate of investment may be undertaken by the public sector out of its general revenues. Finally, the rate of growth does not depend only on such supply factors as investment, but also on demand factors. Under some conditions, it may be a more equal distribution which generates the demand stimulus for rapid growth (Sundrum 1990).

Whether rapid growth leads to rising inequality or not depends on the policy instruments that governments use for promoting these objectives. Most of the arguments suggesting a conflict between the two objectives is based on a narrow view of the policy instruments that governments can employ. In fact, governments have a wider range of policy instruments at their disposal. We consider these policy instruments and their effects on growth and distribution in the following two chapters.

Chapter fifteen

Regulation of markets

15.1 Incentives and the market system

The policies that governments can follow to influence the distribution of income may be broadly divided into two groups, those relating to the regulation of market forces, and those involving redistribution of incomes and assets independently of the working of markets. The first group of policies is discussed in this chapter, and the second in the next chapter.

Whether markets should be regulated and if so, how they should be regulated, is one of the most serious controversies among economists. Economics as a science began with the discovery of the classical economists of the systematic way in which market prices provide the incentives to harness the self-interested energies of individuals to promote the welfare of society as a whole, as if guided by an invisible hand. But any system of prices plays two roles; one as an allocator of resources, and the other as a distributor of incomes. Even if the prices emerging from the free working of markets are efficient in their role as allocator of resources, the resulting distribution of income is not necessarily the most desirable. In fact, the very unequal distribution of income that was associated with the early stages of modern economic growth in the western countries gave rise to the socialist view that markets should be tightly regulated or even supplanted by a system of central planning in order to achieve a more equal distribution of income. But the market system based on individual incentives is a powerful instrument of social control. Countries in which incentives play a significant role have been among those with a high rate of growth. On the other hand, socialist countries in which incomes of individuals are protected to any extent so that the incentives for effort are muted have generally performed poorly. This is one reason that many of these countries have in recent years been experimenting with ways of restoring the market system based on individual incentives.

In view of this confusion, it is necessary to review the working of markets in more detail. In modern neoclassical economics, the case for free markets is based mainly on their static role in the efficient allocation of resources. But when the classical economists advocated the system of free enterprise, they were mainly concerned with the dynamic role of free markets in promoting the growth of national income (Myint 1948; O'Brien 1975). As J. Robinson (1979:20-1) put it, 'the famous invisible hand is not directing the allocation of scarce resources between alternative uses, but guiding investment into the most advantageous channels and so promoting the growth of means to employ more labour and create more wealth'.

The difference in emphasis is related to two functions that markets perform, which Kaldor (1972) distinguished as the 'creative' and the 'allocative' functions. The creative function of markets is concerned with the accumulation of resources and the efficiency with which these resources are used, both through the advancement of technology and the competitive selection of the most efficient entrepreneurs. By contrast, markets perform their allocative function by allocating given resources to alternative uses in accordance with prevailing consumer tastes and preferences.

In so far as the rapid growth of national income is necessary in LDCs to raise the standard of living of all sections of the population, and particularly of the lower-income groups, markets perform a useful role. Therefore if markets are regulated, it should be done in ways which interfere as little as possible with the creative function of markets. The same cannot, however, be said about the allocative function of markets.

The main reason is that even when markets function efficiently in a competitive and equilibrium manner, they only respond to effective demand based on the prevailing distribution of income and assets. The allocation of resources is then optimal only with reference to that distribution of income. But if that distribution of income is very unequal, the market allocation of resources may not be desirable from a social point of view and may only serve to perpetuate the inequality of income distribution. Therefore it may be necessary to regulate markets to achieve a more desirable allocation of resources from a distributional point of view. If markets are efficient and competitive to begin with, such regulation may be at the expense of long-run growth and efficiency.

But markets, especially in LDCs, do not always work efficiently and competitively. As Lewis (1969b) put it,

> The merits of the market depend on the existence of competition, and perfect competition is rare. It is clear that nothing in the market mechanism either establishes or maintains competition. Only state action can assure competition.

Therefore one form of market regulation is to promote competitive conditions. Another form of government intervention is to regulate the market determination of prices and production. If markets are not efficient and competitive to begin with, the adverse effects of market regulation on long-run growth and efficiency may not be as serious as often assumed, especially if such regulation is confined to a few areas of strategic importance.

Market regulation, however, raises serious problems of implementation in an honest and efficient manner. In fact, it may be recalled that Adam Smith advocated the system of free enterprise not so much because of his belief in the efficiency of that system, but rather because of his profound distrust of the motives of government (Stigler 1975). To some extent this is also true of his modern successors; as Lewis (1971:672) claimed, 'liberal economics is not, as it pretends, a science, but is merely a by-product of individualistic philosophy'. That is why even so great a critic of the system of free enterprise as Joan Robinson (1982) argued that

> if a government is not efficient and honest enough, it is far better to let markets express themselves, otherwise control will lead to more control, corruption, abuses and inefficiency. Therefore, the degree of government action to be taken in an economy should be considered in the light of the efficiency and honesty of a government.

15.2 Varieties of socialism

The main concern of socialism, on the other hand, is with the distribution of income. As Lewis (1969b:iii, see also Lewis 1971) has explained the evolution of socialist thought,

> Early socialist writing says nothing about economic growth; the societies described are most often static; and the problem is only how to divide up the economic pie. Karl Marx recognised the importance of growth, but took it for granted that the problem had been solved; invest more capital, and output would automatically grow. By the time socialist parties began to come into power, between the two world wars, the problem was not how to ensure growth but how to prevent decline, since unemployment was the biggest problem of the times. Securing a per capita increase of 2 to 4 per cent per annum was not elevated into a national objective in the countries of Western Europe until after the second world war.

Marx himself had argued that the productive forces of society should first be developed to the fullest extent under capitalism, and only then replaced by a socialist regime. He therefore reserved his most violent criticisms for 'utopian' socialists who wished to introduce socialist policies prematurely. Marx had coined the slogan 'to each according to his need', but this policy was intended for the time when society had already achieved a high level of productive capacity so that it could fulfil the needs of all. However, in spite of being called neo-Marxists, many modern socialists have been mainly concerned with securing an equitable distribution of income right away rather than with maximizing the rate of growth.

In the socialist analysis, the unfair distribution of income in the capitalist system was mainly due to the unequal distribution of productive assets among the people. The solution was therefore seen in the abolition of private property in the means of production, and the central planning of economic activity by the state. Hence, as Lewis (1969a:55) expressed it:

> the word socialism has been used to cover three distinct sets of ideas. The first relates to the degree of inequality in the distribution of income. The second set of ideas relates to the ownership of property. And the third set relates to the powers of the state.

Each of these socialist ideas has come to be interpreted in different ways, giving rise to innumerable varieties of socialist opinion and practice, such as the Indian concept of the socialist pattern of society, the Burmese way to socialism, the Arab way to socialism, and so on. As Lewis (1969a:59) says, even allowing only three different interpretations for each of these three goals gives rise to 27 varieties of socialism.

But the essence of the socialist goal is the fair distribution of income, and the other two elements of socialist dogma are means to that end, rather than ends in themselves. It is particularly these two elements which have to be reconsidered if socialism is to be reconciled with the objective of economic growth. It is from this point of view that we consider various policies that governments can pursue in the LDCs in order to achieve rapid growth with progressive improvement in the distribution of income.

15.3 Regulation of prices

We now discuss the various policies that governments can follow, with special reference to their effects on each of the two objectives of growth and equity. With regard to their distributional effects, we consider also what the effects will be in the short term and in the long. We begin with policies concerned with the regulation of prices.

15.3.1 Promotion of competitive conditions

One of the factors influencing the distribution of income is the set of prices of commodities and factors that results from market forces. If these forces work in a competitive and efficient manner and lead to an equilibrium between supply and demand, they serve a useful purpose in utilizing resources fully and allocating them efficiently to alternative uses. Further, within the market for individual factors they will also equalize the prices of these factors for different suppliers, and therefore also promote income equality to some extent.

But as we have seen in Part II, markets, especially factor markets, do not function in this manner, only as a result of the maximizing behaviour of individuals. Goods and services are not very mobile between markets and regions. Prices do not adjust speedily to their equilibrium levels, resulting in surpluses and deficits in different parts of the country, and unemployment and shortages in different sections of the market for the same goods or services. Workers earn very different wages in different sectors and occupations. People have to pay very different rates of interest for the loans they borrow for consumption or investment. Because of the shortage of credit, moneylenders in the informal capital markets have considerable monopoly power. Because of the shortage of employment opportunities, employers have considered monopsony power in the labour market. The market for land also works very inefficiently, so that land is often cultivated inefficiently by the owners rather than being leased out to tenants who may be able to cultivate it more efficiently.

Therefore one way in which governments can improve the working of market forces is to promote competitive conditions. This policy has been summarized by Meade (1976:191) as follows:

> A first set of measures to equalise incomes is the removal of restrictive practices and other impediments to competitive conditions which prevent people from moving themselves and their resources from low-paid to high-paid occupations, industries or regions. One great attraction of measures of this kind is that there is no conflict between the objectives of economic equality and of economic efficiency. When a restrictive practice which maintains an unduly high, monopolistic reward in a privileged and protected occupation is removed, the entry of new persons from lower paid, unprivileged, unprotected occupations represents an increase in economic efficiency as well as an increase in economic equality.

The weakness of competition does not depend only on restrictive practices. It may also be due to limitations of market infrastructure, such as transport and communications, and of education and information among workers. Therefore improvements in these aspects of infrastructure are also an essential part of the promotion of competitive conditions.

However, there are some limitations on the extent to which the promotion of competitive conditions alone can solve the problems. One is that in some cases, production has to be carried out on a large scale in order to secure the benefits of economies of scale. Then, especially in low-income countries, the number of such enterprises may be too small to ensure sufficient competition. Second, competitive conditions will only promote equality of incomes among persons with the same endowments, and may even increase the income differentials between persons with unequal endowments. Third, to the extent that the promotion of competitive conditions leads to greater equality, it will do so only in the long run. Therefore this policy must also be supplemented with others in the short run.

15.3.2 Taxes and subsidies

At any given time there will be a certain amount of inequality in the distribution of income determined by market forces alone. People in different income groups have different patterns of expenditure. Therefore their real incomes will depend on the prices of goods. Thus the real income of the poor will be greater, the lower the prices of essential goods on which they spend the bulk of their incomes. Therefore the distribution of income in real terms can be influenced by regulating prices.

One way to do this is by indirect taxes and subsidies. In order to improve the distribution of income, the government might subsidize essential commodities on which the lower-income groups spend a high proportion of their income, and tax luxuries mostly consumed by the rich. But we must also consider the effect of such taxes and subsidies on the allocation of resources. It is from this point of view that Ramsey (1927) first considered the 'optimum' structure of commodity taxes. He defined this concept as the system of commodity taxes which raised a given amount of resources for the government with a minimum distortion of the allocation of resources brought about by free-market forces. He then showed that the tax rate on a commodity should vary inversely with its price elasticity of demand.

But the essential commodities on which the lower-income groups spend a high proportion of their income have a low elasticity of demand, and therefore attract a high rate of tax on this principle. In fact, LDCs rely on such taxes for a large part of their revenues, mainly because of the administrative convenience of collection; therefore the actual structure of such taxes have a significant regressive effect on income distribution. Economic theorists have tried to modify the Ramsey rule to take account of the distributional objective (see, e.g., Atkinson and Stiglitz 1980:386–91), but even the adjustments suggested by the new approaches on the basis of plausible estimates of parameters are not sufficient to overcome the regressive effect of these taxes. (For an analysis of fuel taxes, see Hughes 1987.) The main reason is that while the poor spend a high proportion of their income on essential commodities, these commodities are also consumed by the rich; therefore, even with the adjustment based on distributional weights, these commodities attract a high rate of tax. But commodities which can be classed as luxuries are consumed more exclusively by the rich. Therefore, if indirect taxes are used to collect a large part of government revenues, they should be collected as far as possible by taxes on these luxuries.

15.3.3 Maximum prices of essential goods

Another approach that is often followed to improve income distribution is to fix the maximum prices at which essential commodities can be sold. If the poor can buy at least the same quantities as at the original market prices, they will be better off. But we must also consider the effects on the supply and demand for the commodities. These effects will depend on what initially caused the high prices of these commodities.

Suppose the commodity was produced and sold under competitive conditions. Then its price will be high because the demand is high relative to the supply. In this case, fixing the price at a low level by law will discourage the expansion of its supply. For example, the control of house rents has generally slowed down the construction of new houses and discouraged landlords from maintaining their house properties in good condition. Hence economists generally criticize these policies because they 'raise in an acute form a clash between the objectives of economic equality and of economic efficiency' (Meade 1976:193).

The control of prices may be useful as a way of helping the poor in the short run, but in the long run the best way to lower the prices of essential goods is to expand their supply. Therefore the policy of price control must be combined with measures to expand the supply of these goods. One way is for governments to influence the structure of production, as discussed in the next section. Another way of lowering the price of essential goods without reducing the incentive to expand supply is to subsidize the commodity. When a commodity is subsidized, the price paid by the consumer is lower than the price received by the producer. The subsidy can then be adjusted so that one set of prices can be used for the distributional objective and another set of prices for the efficiency and growth objectives. The costs of the subsidy can then be financed by taxes on luxuries and other less essential goods. If the high price of an essential commodity is due to some degree of monopoly on the part of the producer or seller, then the control of its price will not necessarily reduce its supply. Then the effect of the price control will be to transfer the monopoly profit of the producer or seller to the consumers.

An important problem with a method of price control is that of implementation. If the legal prices are set below the equilibrium level, demand will be greater than supply. Hence this policy must be combined with measures to ration the limited supply. In practice, such schemes often lead to black marketing. Attempts to control such activities are usually not very effective (see, e.g., Mukherji *et al.* 1980) and open up avenues for extensive corruption.

The most widespread application of the price control policy has been to food. In this connection, the Indian experience of agricultural price policy is particularly instructive. The authorities in India have tried to use the instrument of food price policy to attain a number of objectives such as improving the nutrition of the poor, increasing the supply of food, and expanding the employment of labour. But the attainment of several such objectives requires at least as many policy instruments. In the early years after independence, the price of food was kept low in the interests of consumers. This policy has been blamed for the slow growth of agricultural production. Since the mid-1960s, government has fixed the price of food at a higher level to induce faster growth of output, but this has meant that the poor have had to spend an increasing proportion of their incomes on food (Sundrum 1987: Table 6.10, pp. 151–2). There was a rapid growth of food production which was not only due to the improved agricultural terms of trade, but also to the introduction of the new agricultural technology, the substantial investment of resources in irrigation and research, and the subsidy of modern inputs such as fertilizers.

India has also set up an extensive system for the public distribution of food at low prices, especially in urban areas. One problem with this approach is that the price of food is subsidized both for the poor and the rich. In fact, because the public distribution system is more extensive in urban areas, urban consumers are subsidized more heavily than rural consumers. Therefore the policy of subsidizing food must be combined with measures to supply subsidized food mainly to the lower-income groups. If this can be done, one method that is followed in some parts of India is to acquire a part of the harvest at controlled prices, for distribution among the poor at low prices. Farmers are allowed to sell the rest to the non-poor at higher prices in the open market. It is then possible, depending on the respective elasticities of demand, that the average prices received by producers may actually be higher as a result (see Appendix 15.1 for a simple proof).

15.3.4 Minimum wages

On the production side, the main application of price control is in fixing the minimum wages of some categories of labour, especially that supplied by the lower-income groups, above their free market levels. Then workers who continue to be employed will earn higher incomes from their labour. However, we must also consider the effect on employment.

If the labour market was initially a competitive one, with wages at the equilibrium level where supply equals demand, then the price of the product would rise, reducing the demand for the product and hence for labour as well. Even for the same quantity of output, the demand for labour will fall, as the higher wages will be an incentive to employers to substitute capital for labour. At the same time, the higher wages may also increase the supply of labour. Therefore the result will be unemployment of labour. Whatever initial unemployment was there will be exacerbated. Thus, while minimum wages may improve the incomes of those who continue to be employed, the incomes of those who lose their jobs will suffer. Therefore, if the objective is to ensure that all workers enjoy the benefit of higher wages, the policy of minimum wages must be combined with measures to maintain or increase the level of employment, for example, by providing additional employment in the public sector or influencing the structure of production in favour of labour-intensive commodities and the choice of techniques in favour of labour-intensive techniques.

However, labour markets in LDCs are often not competitive; rather, individual employers often have considerable monopsony power to reduce the wages of their employees below the competitive equilibrium level. Then it is possible that fixing minimum wages above the initial level will not only increase the incomes of workers but also expand the amount of employment that maximizes the profits of the employer. Another consideration is that while higher wages may reduce the demand for the products through the cost effect, there may also be demand effects, as the effective demand of workers will rise because of their improved incomes.

Whatever the theoretical arguments, there are minimum wage laws in most DCs. They have also been introduced in many LDCs, but the problem in these countries is that they are enforced only to a limited extent, and even then only in favour of workers who are already in a privileged position, such as the employees of the public sector, and large enterprises, especially those run by foreign companies.

15.3.5 Inflation

In the above two sections we were mainly concerned with particular prices. We must also consider policies relating to the general price level. Many LDCs have used inflationary methods to finance their budget deficits. Apart from their effects on the growth process, such inflationary methods have generally been criticized on the ground that they would have a regressive effect on income distribution, especially because the profit incomes of the upper-income groups tend to rise faster than the wage incomes of the lower-income groups. Whether wages lag behind prices, however, is a matter for empirical investigation. At the lower end of the scale, wages may adjust to price changes fairly speedily. It is for the middle-income groups that wages and salaries are likely to be adjusted less frequently, so that they suffer more from inflationary periods.

Ultimately, whether inflation improves or worsens the distribution of income depends on the way real forces work. Suppose there is a shortfall of food supply, to take a fairly typical source of inflation in LDCs. Its effects on income distribution depend on how the shortfall is distributed among different sections of the people. A fairly common tendency is for food producers to maintain their own consumption, so that the major impact is on the marketable surplus. If labourers engaged in food production are paid the whole or part of their wages in kind, this will also stabilize their real incomes to some extent. Then food prices will rise sharply for other consumers, disproportionately more than the actual shortfall in total supplies. This reflects the extent to which the upper-income groups are able to compete in order to maintain their usual levels of consumption. Some workers, especially those employed in the public sector, may be compensated fairly promptly by salary increases based on the cost of living. Such adjustments throw the burden of adjustment to reduced supplies more heavily on the unprotected group of workers.

15.3.6 Structural adjustment and income distribution

Especially since 1980, a number of LDCs have experienced serious balance-of-payments problems. The World Bank (1988b:1) has argued that 'those problems stemmed from the sharp deterioration in the terms of trade for oil-importing countries and from the legacy of weaknesses in domestic policies and institutions'. In fact, even oil-exporting countries such as Indonesia faced serious balance-of-payments problems because of the sharp fall in oil prices after 1981, and the costs of servicing the foreign debt accumulated during the period of high oil prices. A more serious cause of the balance-of-payments problems of LDCs was the decline in world economic activity, mainly triggered off by the contractionary demand policies followed in major developed countries. These demand policies were pursued in an attempt to control the high rates of inflation, but while they have not reduced inflation to the levels prevailing before the oil shocks, they have reduced world trade and increased unemployment to high levels.

A special feature of the recent period, however, is that many LDCs have followed policies of structural adjustment recommended by the international economic agencies – the World Bank and the International Monetary Fund – as the condition for loans to deal with the balance-of-payments problem. While it is claimed that 'by promoting growth and efficient resource allocation, adjustment programs on the whole play a constructive role in safeguarding the long-term interests of the poor', it is also found that 'some of the macroeconomic policies that aim at restructuring production may aggravate the plight of some vulnerable groups in the short run' (Heller 1988:3). This is because 'many countries have reduced public expenditure on social services and subsidies, cut back on public sector staffing, and experienced higher unemployment and reductions in real wages' (World Bank 1988a:45–6).

Economic and social conditions vary so much in different countries that the effects of structural adjustment policies on income distribution cannot be studied on the basis of any single theoretical model. Therefore a number of studies have appeared which examine the actual experience of selected countries (see, e.g., the UNICEF-sponsored study by Cornia et al. 1988; the World Bank-sponsored study by Demery and Addison 1987; and the IMF-sponsored study by Heller et al. 1988). The general conclusion suggested by these studies is that the adjustment policies by themselves have tended to have adverse effects on the lower-income groups of these countries, but that in some cases these adverse effects were offset or reduced by other measures, such as land reform, educational expansion, or employment programmes, that were followed simultaneously to help the poor.

However, even these compensatory schemes will help the poor only in the long run. Therefore they should be followed as part of a long-run strategy for improving the distribution of income, rather than only as an adjunct to adjustment policies. When they are followed only in the course of implementing the adjustment policies, they tend to be forgotten after the crisis in the balance of payments is over. Because these schemes are not followed as a long-term strategy and therefore do not have a significant effect on the distribution of income, the short-term adverse effects of adjustment policies on the lower-income groups give rise to widespread discontent and hence to serious political instability. Apart from pursuing these positive measures to improve the distribution of income and to relieve poverty, countries facing balance-of-payments problems should also design their adjustment policies so as to minimize the adverse effects on the lower-income groups, for example, by increasing public revenue mainly by taxes falling on the upper-income groups, and by reducing public expenditure on services whose benefits accrue mainly to these groups.

15.4 Regulation of production

Apart from the control of prices, many of the policies followed by LDC governments are directed to the regulation of production. The two major objectives of these policies are to influence the structure of production and the choice of techniques of production. We discuss these policies and their effects in this section.

15.4.1 Structure of production

One of the objectives underlying LDC policies to influence the structure of production has been to accelerate their rates of growth. It is generally assumed that their low levels of income and slow rates of growth are mainly due to the dominance of the agricultural sector. Therefore LDC governments have been specially interested in promoting their industrial development. The experience of the developed countries has shown that the acceleration of their growth has been mainly due to industrial development, but this was true because there had already been a prior development of their agricultural sectors. If the agricultural sector is not developed to its fullest extent, it will be a constraint on industrial development. Therefore, for a successful growth outcome, the agricultural sector of LDCs must be developed until it fulfils its historical mission and is no longer a constraint on industrial development. The development of the agricultural sector requires the active role of government policies because it is subject to powerful institutional factors which impede its development under ordinary market forces. But once agriculture has been developed, the industrial sector may develop rapidly under market forces and may not require an active role of government policies (Sundrum 1990).

LDC policies on the structure of production have also been influenced by distributional considerations. Compared with the structure of production in a society in which income is distributed fairly equally, a society with an unequal distribution of income and subject only to market forces will tend to produce more of the 'luxuries' demanded by the rich, and less of the 'necessities' needed by the poor. Therefore LDC governments have tried to influence the structure of production in favour of the commodities on which the lower-income groups spend a high proportion of their incomes. This has been the main consideration underlying their programmes for agricultural development. Faster agricultural development will not only increase food supplies, but will also lower food prices and hence improve the welfare of the lower-income groups. In addition, as noted above, faster agricultural development will also promote overall growth.

However, as noted in Chapter twelve, the structure of production both influences and is influenced by the distribution of income. One of the main problems is that the distribution of income within the agricultural sector is usually very unequal, mainly due to the scarcity of land under prevailing techniques, so that many rural people do not have their own land to cultivate and become landless labourers suffering from extensive underemployment, and earning low wages when employed. Further, the policies followed in many cases for agricultural development have encouraged the use of capital-intensive methods, which have reduced the absorption of labour in the agricultural sector. Therefore, while agricultural development helps the lower-income groups by expanding food supply and reducing food prices on the one side, it may hurt them by worsening the distribution of income on the other side. Therefore these policies must be combined with other measures to improve the distribution of income within the agricultural sector.

Other policies used to promote agricultural development may also have an adverse effect on the distribution of income. For example, the adoption of the new agricultural technology depends heavily on the availability of credit for the purchase of modern inputs such as fertilizers. However, sufficient credit has generally not been provided. Therefore the main benefits of the new technology have generally accrued only to those who have their own resources for buying these inputs. Even where credit is available, it has sometimes been very unequally distributed to the richer farmers with privileged access to the banking system.

Sometimes the methods used by governments to bring about changes in the structure of production have not been well suited for the purpose. For example, one of the most common policies is to restrict the import of so-called luxury commodities, partly because they are considered non-essential, and partly also to economize the use of limited foreign exchange resources. But given the demand for such commodities, the usual result is that they are then produced domestically. Therefore, if it is really desired to reduce the supply of such commodities, policies to restrict their import must be combined with policies to restrict their domestic production also.

So far we have been considering the required changes in the structure of production only from the consumption point of view. We should also consider the implications for the scale and types of investment. A high level of investment will increase total output in the future but will reduce present consumption. We have to consider how these changes will affect the distribution of income. The effects will depend on two factors, namely the way the investment is financed, and the sectors to which the extra investment is allocated. To the extent that the investment is financed by diverting resources away from the production of goods mainly consumed by the lower-income groups, the consumption of the poor will be reduced. Similarly, to the extent that the investment is allocated to sectors producing goods mainly consumed by the relatively rich, there will be less benefit for the poor. Therefore the ideal solution from the distribution point of view would be to finance the investment by diverting resources away from the production of goods mainly consumed by the rich, and allocating them towards the production of goods mainly consumed by the poor.

15.4.2 Choice of techniques

As argued in Chapter ten, one of the main causes of poverty in LDCs is chronic unemployment, especially of landless labourers in rural areas. Therefore we now consider what can be done to increase the demand for labour and thereby reduce unemployment and the associated poverty.

One possible solution is to adopt policies to expand the production of labour-intensive commodities in place of capital-intensive commodities. In the last chapter it was argued that policies to reduce the inequality of income distribution would result in such changes in the structure of production to some extent. Another approach, widely recommended in the literature, is for LDCs to produce more labour-intensive commodities, especially manufactures, for export. However, the more successful the LDCs are in doing so, the greater will be the protective barriers they will face in the DCs.

Another possible solution is to substitute labour-intensive techniques for capital-intensive techniques; this is the problem of the choice of techniques. In the past it has often been alleged that governments in LDCs have kept interest rates in the organized credit market too low and the exchange rate too high, and thereby subsidized the purchase of capital goods at home and from abroad. This tends to induce an excessive shift to capital-intensive techniques. But in the industrial sector, the most profitable modern techniques are usually embodied in capital goods imported from the DCs with rigid factor proportions, so that relative prices have little effect on the choice of techniques. Further, these techniques may be technically so efficient that they not only save labour, but also capital, per unit of output. Such techniques will promote growth faster and thereby expand future employment opportunities more rapidly. The possibilities of absorbing more labour in agriculture can be increased by more investment, especially in a land-saving form.

Most governments have been mainly concerned to expand employment opportunities in the nonagricultural sectors. But it is in these sectors that the available choice of techniques are sharply divided between highly productive modern techniques which are, however, also highly capital intensive, and traditional techniques which are more labour intensive but also less productive. Therefore the prospect of expanding such non-agricultural employment by policies relating to the choice of techniques alone are rather limited. Instead, these opportunities depend much more on the supply of wage goods. Kaldor (1965:98–9) has put this argument forcefully as follows:

> The amount of employment created outside agriculture looked at *in toto* is not primarily a matter of technology at all. What are the limits of wage employment in any country at any time? As many people as will not create an inflation. As many people as you have wage goods to pay for their work. So the total employment capacity of a country depends simply and solely on the supply of wage goods. . . . [I]t is food that is the primary factor and the size of the agricultural surplus is the vital factor which limits the wage labour force. That decides the wages a country can afford. When you realise this, then you see immediately that all this tremendous discussion about technology is really rather beside the point. (For a more detailed analysis, see also Rakshit 1982.)

Food is an important element of wage goods. As argued above, food supply can be increased by employing additional workers on the land using more labour-intensive techniques. Therefore in this sector it is possible to increase both output of wage goods and employment by the same techniques. However, food is not the only item of wage goods; there are other important items, particularly clothing. A rapid expansion in the supply of clothing is also necessary to expand employment but in the textile industry, there is a choice between efficient capital-intensive modern techniques and less productive traditional labour-intensive techniques. Some countries, notably India, have limited the use of factory techniques in the textile industry in favour of handicraft techniques. The result has been that per capita availability of clothing has remained practically constant over nearly three decades of planned development, and has been one factor in the slow growth of nonagricultural employment. While the benefits of the policy went to a relatively small section of the population, its adverse effect has fallen on a larger group. In such cases a better policy would be to increase production as rapidly as possible by as efficient a technique as possible (Chelliah 1983). This not only improves the standard of living of the poor but, by reducing the cost of an important wage good, also enables more labour to be employed in other sectors.

An alternative approach would be to increase employment opportunities in the public sector in constructing public works. This is the principle of the Employment Guarantee Schemes undertaken in many countries, especially in some states of India. In such activities it may be possible to use labour-intensive methods as efficiently as other methods. The great advantage of this approach is that it also leads to faster capital accumulation and hence to the long-term growth potential of the economy. It therefore represents a method by which LDCs can convert labour, of which they have an abundant supply, to capital, which is scarce, the central theme of Nurkse's (1953) analysis of the problems of development of LDCs. For maximum benefit to the poor, these programmes should be primarily directed to public works which increase the productive capacity of the poor and those which expand the supply of the goods needed by them. Such programmes are usually objected to by employers in the private sector on the ground that they will raise the wages of labour. To overcome this type of criticism, the employment in the public works schemes should be directed primarily at workers currently suffering from severe unemployment or underemployment. To the extent that this can be done, the employment offered under such schemes need not be limited to public works, and may be extended to capital works in the private sector also, with some subsidy of the wage cost from the government.

Appendix 15.1 Effects of a compulsory levy on food production

Let the equilibrium situation before the levy be as illustrated in Figure 15A.1. S is the supply curve. D_1 and D_2 are the demand curves of the poor and rich consumers; by adding them horizontally we get the aggregate demand curve D. The equilibrium price is p. At this price, the quantity supplied is Q, of which q_1 is bought by the poor and q_2 by the rich. Let η_1 and η_2 be the elasticities of demand of the poor and the rich respectively, and let ε be the elasticity of supply. Also let λ be the initial proportion of total supply going to the poor, that is,

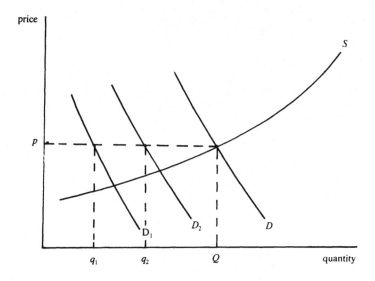

Figure 15A.1

$$\lambda = \frac{q_1}{Q} \qquad (15\text{A}.1)$$

The government now imposes a levy of $\lambda' > \lambda$ on total production, and sells the quantity so obtained exclusively to the poor. The effects are shown in Figures 15A.2a and 15A.2b.

Because $\lambda' > \lambda$, the supply to the poor is increased and the supply to the rich decreased. Hence the price paid by the poor is reduced from p to p_1 and that paid by the rich is raised from p to p_2. The quantity bought by the poor is increased from q_1 to q_1', while the quantity bought by the rich is reduced from q_2 to q_2'. Let $Q' = q_1' + q_2'$ be the total quantity supplied after the levy. The average price received by the producers after the levy is

$$p' = \lambda'p_1 + (1 - \lambda')p_2 \qquad (15\text{A}.2)$$

The problem is to find the conditions under which p' is higher than the original price p.

From the definition of the elasticities of demand and supply, we have

$$q_1' = q_1 \left(1 + \eta_1 \frac{p - p_1}{p}\right) \qquad (15\text{A}.3)$$

$$q_2' = q_2 \left(1 - \eta_2 \frac{p_2 - p}{p}\right) \qquad (15\text{A}.4)$$

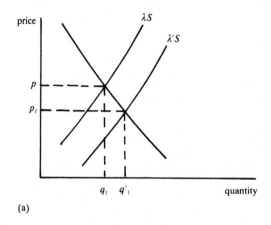

(a)

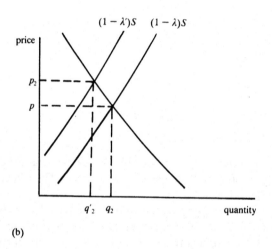

(b)

Figure 15A.2

$$Q' = Q \left(1 + \varepsilon \frac{p' - p}{p} \right) \tag{15A.5}$$

From these definitions, we have

$$\lambda[\eta_1(p - p_1) - \varepsilon(p' - p)] = (1 - \lambda)[\varepsilon(p' - p) + \eta_2(p_2 - p)] \tag{15A.6}$$

Hence

$$\frac{p_2 - p}{p - p_1} = \frac{\lambda \eta_1 + \lambda' \varepsilon}{(1 - \lambda)\eta_2 + (1 - \lambda')\varepsilon} \tag{15A.7}$$

For $p' > p$, we must have

$$\lambda' p_1 + (1 - \lambda') p_2 > p$$

that is,

$$\frac{p_2 - p}{p - p_1} > \frac{\lambda'}{1 - \lambda'}$$

Thus, using (15A.7),

$$\frac{\lambda \eta_1 + \lambda' \varepsilon}{(1 - \lambda) \eta_2 + (1 - \lambda') \varepsilon} > \frac{\lambda'}{1 - \lambda'}$$

which on simplification gives

$$\frac{\eta_1}{\eta_2} > 1 + \frac{\lambda' - \lambda}{\lambda(1 - \lambda')} \tag{15A.8}$$

that is, the demand curve of the poor must be more elastic than that of the rich by a sufficient margin to satisfy (15A.8). Alternatively, the condition may also be written

$$\lambda' - \lambda < \lambda(1 - \lambda)(\eta_1 - \eta_2) \tag{15A.9}$$

that is, the levy must not exceed the initial proportion bought by the poor beyond the limit shown in (15A.9). For a more detailed discussion of the Indian system, see Hayami *et al.* (1982).

Chapter sixteen

Redistributive policies

16.1 Equality of opportunity

As discussed in the previous chapter, competitive markets are a powerful force to elicit the maximum effort from individuals and harness their self-interested action to promote the growth of the national income of society as a whole. But from a distributional point of view, competition must not only be free; it must also be fair. With free competition alone, the incomes of individuals depend not only on their efforts but also on the resources they own and the opportunities they have for participating in the market economy. When these resources and opportunities are unequally distributed, it is as if a race was being run with different starting points for the participants. The distribution of income resulting from the operation of market forces alone may be modified to some extent in the short term by the policies discussed in the previous chapter for the regulation of the resulting prices and structure of production. But to make competition also fair, individuals must be enabled to start on a more equal footing.

One of the circumstances which determines an individual's starting point in the race for economic advancement is the amount of resources with which he is endowed. Some policies for making the distribution of these resources more equal are discussed in the next section. In the present section we consider the inequality of opportunities and how it can be reduced.

16.1.1 Positive discrimination

Traditional societies have generally been characterized by a static technology. Their main concern was therefore to maintain stable conditions to preserve that technology from deteriorating. For this purpose, they evolved a rigid system of social stratification in which individuals had to live out their lives in the class into which they were born, and pursue the occupations assigned to that class. As new technologies became available the traditional stratification of society gave way, but only slowly. Thus these stratified systems survived in the developed countries until quite recently in historical time, and are still powerful influences in many less developed countries even today, such as the caste system of Hindu society in India and tribal distinctions in Africa.

Because the system of stratification declines only slowly as new technologies appear, the gains from the technological progress are very unequally distributed among different sections of society in the early stages. This was one of the main reasons for the rise of inequality in the early stages of growth of the western countries. Less developed countries can avoid this experience to some extent in modern times by policies to equalize opportunities for gaining from new technologies. Many countries have in fact done so by legislation to prevent discrimination according to any of the bases of social stratification. The problem, however, is that of implementing these laws in practice.

Some countries have gone further to legislate for positive discrimination in favour of groups which had traditionally been underprivileged. The best example is the reservation policies of India, which have reserved places in schools and jobs in the public sector for the people of the lower castes. However, this has given rise to some problems, for under the changing conditions of modern times, the congruence between social status and economic conditions is no longer a complete one. Thus some poor people have been disadvantaged because they belong to higher castes, while some people of the lower castes have benefited unfairly even though they enjoy a higher economic condition. Thus, speaking of the Indian situation, Beteille (1983: 121) has commented:

> This society made a terrible mistake in the past in believing that merit was an attribute not of individuals but of groups, that being born a Brahmin was in itself a mark of merit. We shall make the same kind of mistake if we act on the belief that need too is always, and not just in special cases, an attribute of groups rather than of individuals.

16.1.2 Education

One important way which helps individuals improve their market opportunities for benefiting from technological progress is education. Hence an alternative approach for promoting equality of opportunity is through the educational system. The case for equalizing opportunities through this system has been expressed by Lewis (1969a:56) thus:

> If one is concerned with incentives for effort, as any serious thinker must be, the emphasis rests naturally on equality of opportunity rather than on equality of reward. The latter survives only in the form of a concern to eliminate extremes from both ends of the income scale. Equality of

opportunity centres these days on trying to ensure that every young person shall have equal access to the fullest education from which he can benefit and thereafter equal access to every job irrespective of tribe, class, race or religion. If incomes were based only on opportunity, the result would be poverty for the handicapped and the unlucky, and riches for the talented or the lucky. Here the sentiment for equality of incomes comes in to cut off both ends.

The educational route to equalization of opportunity is particularly valuable because it is much more under the control of governments, which provide a large part of educational facilities in LDCs. For the educational system to play this role, three conditions must be satisfied. First, there must be a rapid expansion of the educational system. This will not only improve the distribution of income but will also promote a more rapid growth of the national income by enabling a more skilled labour force to absorb new technologies. When the educational system is very limited to begin with, there is bound to be an increase of educational inequality for a time. The more rapid the expansion of education, the shorter will be the duration of such a transitional rise in educational inequality.

The second condition is that in the process of educational expansion when educational facilities are still inadequate to serve the entire population, the limited educational opportunities must themselves be equally distributed among the people. In fact, in many LDCs these opportunities themselves are very unequally distributed. One reason is that governments tend to give a higher priority to the higher levels of the educational system in their bid to hasten the modernization of the economy. Hence a large proportion of the educational budget is earmarked for subsidies to students at the higher educational levels, who generally come from better-off families. Another reason is that upper-income groups, because of their better economic position, are able to gain higher levels of educational qualification. Thus while past generations of the relatively rich have relied on greater physical assets for their higher incomes, they are followed by a new generation of rich people whose higher incomes are based on their superior educational qualifications. By contrast, poorer people are often not even able to benefit from the educational facilities offered by the government. Therefore, apart from just providing the educational facilities, poorer families must be assisted to get a better education for their children.

A given inequality of educational qualifications will give rise to a greater inequality of incomes if the income differentials between educational categories are large than if they are small. Therefore the third condition for the educational system to play a role in improving the distribution of income is that these income differentials must be narrowed down as rapidly as possible. These differentials may narrow down as a result of market forces, but the process is usually very slow. In fact, the process is often delayed by the public sector itself maintaining large differentials, especially by the practice of determining salaries on the basis of educational qualifications rather than the responsibilities of the job concerned. Thus the educational system, which is often looked upon as a great levelling force, may actually become a major source of rising inequality in the process of growth.

16.2 Redistribution of assets

One of the most important causes of income inequality in LDCs is the unequal distribution of productive resources, such as land and capital, which are scarce and therefore earn high incomes, in contrast to the relative abundance of labour which earns low wages. The unequal distribution of productive assets that prevails in most LDCs is largely an historical accident, because a large fraction of the assets owned by the present generation is inherited from the past generation. In countries that have been settled for a long time and where there has been little extension of cultivable area, most of the land has been inherited in this way. In the case of capital, the fraction accumulated by the present generation will be higher depending on the rate of capital accumulation. Thus if capital accumulates at 5 per cent per annum, about half the present stock may have been accumulated within the past 15 years, taken as the average adult life of the present generation; at 3 per cent, this fraction will be only one-third.

Even more important is the fact that if the historical distribution of assets is unequal to begin with, it tends to become cumulatively more unequal in the course of time. People who are well endowed with assets are able to save more out of their larger incomes and increase their asset holdings faster than those who start off with little or no assets.

Because the distribution of assets, which is a major cause of poverty and inequality of incomes, depends so much on historical factors, policies to improve the distribution of income by redistributing assets are less likely to have adverse effects on the activities of the present generation in promoting growth. Such policies are therefore a particularly important instrument of distributional policies. We consider the methods and effects of such policies in some detail in this section.

16.2.1 Land reform

One way of improving the distribution of assets is to redistribute assets from the rich to the poor, that is, from those who now own large amounts of any asset to those who own little or nothing. This is most obvious in the case of land, whose total stock is limited and cannot be expanded. The redistribution of land by some type of land reform is likely to be particularly effective in improving the distribution of income in LDCs because land is the most important factor of production in agriculture, and agriculture is the major sector in LDCs both in terms of its contribution to the national income and in terms of its share of total employment. In the case of land, there will also be less adverse effects on productivity, because small farmers and landless labourers to whom land may be redistributed are already engaged in agriculture. On the contrary, the effect may be favourable because small farmers usually cultivate their land more efficiently than large farmers.

Because of the great advantages both for distribution and for growth, and because the case for a more equal distribution of assets is so much stronger in the case of a natural resource like land than in the case of produced means of production like capital, most LDC governments have accepted the need for land reform and even passed legislation for the purpose. However, these laws have rarely been implemented effectively or rapidly, mainly for lack of political will, as those who would be adversely affected have a disproportionate influence on government policies, while potential beneficiaries have not been sufficiently organized to press their interests. We shall therefore be primarily concerned with some of the tactical issues involved in implementing land reform programmes.

If a land reform programme is to be implemented successfully, the first essential is speed. The need for speedy implementation of any such redistributive action has been explained in the context of a socialist programme as follows:

> A socialist government has to decide to carry out its socialization programme at one stroke, or to give it up altogether. The very coming into power of such a government must cause a financial panic and economic collapse. Therefore, the socialist government must either guarantee the immunity of private property and private enterprise in order to enable the capitalist economy to function normally, in doing which it gives up its socialist aims, or it must go through resolutely with its socialization programme at maximum speed. Any hesitation, any vacillation and indecision would provoke the inevitable economic catastrophe. (Lange and Taylor 1938:124–5)

However, the redistribution of land need not necessarily entail other elements of the socialist programme, such as the abolition of private enterprise and the centralization of all economic decisions in the hands of the government. The redistribution of land is quite consistent with leaving subsequent decisions of production and consumption in the private sector, subject to some, but not complete, regulation by the state. Then we can combine the advantages of a more equal distribution of assets with such virtues as the market system may have in promoting economic growth and efficiency. But even in this case, it is important that the act of redistribution must be done speedily and once-for-all, so that the confidence that individuals will get the reward for their effort in maintaining and investing in their property will provide the incentives for maximum effort and efficient use of assets, and this confidence will not be seriously affected by a constant threat of expropriation after the initial step.

This approach has a corollary which must be noted, relating to the rights to be vested in recipients of property under any redistribution scheme. One view is that once any asset has been given to an individual, the recipient should not be allowed to transfer his property by sale or hypothecation. The argument is that if the recipient was given such a right, the distribution of assets would again become unequal. This is likely to happen if the distribution of income itself is very unequal, but one of the main reasons for income inequality will be removed by the act of asset redistribution. Therefore it may not be necessary to impose severe restrictions on the transferability of the redistributed property, so long as the conditions of such transfer are fair to the parties concerned. Such freedom of disposal is particularly desirable in the case of land reform, if the land can only be redistributed in small plots. In the course of time, the expansion of non-agricultural employment opportunities will reduce the population dependent on agriculture, and room must be left for the gradual accumulation of land into larger farms capable of yielding higher incomes to those who remain in agriculture. Therefore there is a case for a once-for-all redistribution of land to be carried out without placing any such restrictions on the transferability of the assets.

Then there are a number of other issues which have not been fully resolved in the policy discussions on land reform. These are the questions of from whom, and to whom, land should be redistributed. One important question is whether land should be redistributed only to small farmers who are already cultivating either as owners or tenants, or whether it should also be distributed to landless labourers working in agriculture. Landless labourers are among the poorest people in most LDCs and therefore have strong claims to land on distributional grounds. But they face quite serious problems in setting up as farmers in their own right, especially for lack of cattle and equipment. Therefore any attempt to include them as beneficiaries must be combined with measures to assist them specially with cattle, equipment, and technical aid.

Land reform policies are usually formulated in terms of a ceiling, such that land above this ceiling is taken up for redistribution, and a floor as a minimum area to which all farmers will be raised. However, these parameters of land reform cannot be specified independently. For any specified group of beneficiaries, there is a tight relationship between the ceiling and the floor. For example, given the 1960–61 distribution of operational holdings in India (as given in Minhas 1974), Table 16.1 shows the relationship between the ceiling and floor for three different groups of beneficiaries. Thus, of the three variables – the beneficiary group, the floor, and the ceiling – any two will determine the third.

Table 16.1 Relationship between ceiling and floor in land redistribution: 1960–61

Ceiling (acres)	Percentage of total land redistributed	Floor level for:		
		Small farmers	Landless	Both
50.00	3.7	1.51	1.53	0.51
30.00	8.8	2.34	2.00	1.11
25.00	11.5	2.74	2.67	1.42
20.00	15.4	3.31	3.73	1.79
15.00	21.5	4.01	4.48	2.28
12.50	25.9	4.44	5.23	2.61
10.00	30.2	4.82	6.65	2.98
7.50	38.4	5.59	—	3.59
6.00	45.8	6.12	—	4.04
5.00	50.3	—	—	4.36
4.50	86.1	—	—	4.51

Source: Minhas (1974), Table 5.

Of these, most of the policy discussion has centred around the ceiling, which tends to be fixed on the basis of what the traffic will bear rather than on what is needed to make a significant impact on the distribution of income. On the basis of the ceilings that are considered practicable, many economists have expressed doubts about whether the resulting floor levels of farm area are economically viable. For example, Minhas (1974:401) concluded that 'by itself, a radical land redistribution policy . . . would not be able to solve the problem of abject poverty. The size of the cake is small and the claimants far too many'. But so long as the recipients of land can actually cultivate the land distributed to them, the poor are better off with some land than with none at all. This is because even if the land so distributed is small, it gives the recipients a better bargaining position with regard to other activities, such as wage employment. Therefore Raj (1975:11) argued that

> The case for setting such floors to the size of holdings along with the imposition of ceilings is, of course, self evident. Indeed there would be nothing to be said against it if it were possible *without* leaving a high proportion of the rural population totally landless, acutely under-employed, and living at semi-starvation levels. But, since it *has* the latter implications in the Indian context, and even a toe-hold on land means a great deal to those who are seriously handicapped because they have none, it seems that one needs to be more circumspect about taking a rigid position on this question.

In fact, the ability to earn a given income is not determined only by the area of land cultivated. It depends also on the intensity with which it is cultivated and the inputs applied. Thus farmers in many countries of east and southeast Asia have been able to earn an adequate income from very small farms. Sometimes it is proposed that the area to be given to an individual recipient should be such that it can be cultivated by his household using only family labour. But as Lewis (1954a:306) has argued in connection with land settlement programmes, this 'is no principle at all. The amount of land a family can cultivate depends on the equipment it has; perhaps three arable acres, if it has only a hoe; 10 to 15 acres with a plough and draught animals; 50 acres and upwards with a tractor' (see also Dandekar 1962:174, for a similar argument).

There is therefore a strong case for land reform as a means of improving the distribution of income as well as increasing the productivity of land and employing labour more fully. But in spite of these advantages, land reform programmes have been slow to be implemented in many LDCs. In some cases, where it was felt that land reform involving extensive redistribution was not politically feasible, countries have opted for the alternative of tenancy reform, giving tenants greater security of tenure than they enjoyed previously and limiting the rents charged to some extent. Attempts have also been made to abolish tenancy in the so-called 'land to the tiller' programmes which have been implemented in some parts of south and southeast Asia. But as Herring (1983: Chap. 7) has pointed out in his discussion of such a programme in the Indian state of Kerala, the main beneficiaries were not the poorer cultivators or agricultural labourers, but rather the middle stratum of agriculturists who already owned some land and who were 'not unambiguously tillers or even primarily engaged in agriculture' (Herring 1983:212).

The main reason for the failure to redistribute land to the poorest members of agricultural society is the political opposition from those who would be affected by such redistribution. The problem would not be so serious if the numbers affected in this way were small. This would be the case if land ownership was highly concentrated in a few hands, as predicted by Marx, or as occurs in many Latin American countries. But in some of the densely populated Asian countries, land tends to be more widely distributed, as suggested by economists of the so-called 'agrarian' school (see Booth and Sundrum 1984: Chap. 5 for a discussion of their views). Therefore governments in these countries have to deal with opposition from a larger number of people who may be adversely affected. But in spite of the wider distribution of land, there is still considerable inequality of land ownership and there are still so many poor people who would benefit from some form of land reform that there is a strong case for implementing such programmes to promote both equity and efficiency (see Hayami and Kikuchi 1981, for a further discussion of these issues in an Asian context).

16.2.2 Redistribution of other assets

Land is a special case of productive assets in two respects. First, the total stock of land is likely to be quite rigidly limited, especially in long-settled countries, and second, a large section of the labour force works on land though they own little or no land of their own, so that they could continue to work efficiently on the land if it were redistributed to them. Therefore the redistribution of assets is particularly suitable to the case of land.

We now consider other types of assets, such as industrial or financial capital. Such assets are also very unequally distributed in LDCs and contribute significantly to inequality of income distribution. Therefore in this case also, a more equal distribution of assets will be useful in bringing about a more equal distribution of income. But the method of redistributing assets which is most appropriate in the case of land is less desirable in the case of capital assets. One reason is that the efficient management of such assets requires certain types of expertise which potential beneficiaries are unlikely to have.

Therefore in the case of capital assets, we have to consider other approaches to reduce the inequality of asset distribution. One possibility is for certain types of assets, or assets owned by individuals beyond a certain size, to be nationalized and taken over by the government without being redistributed to others. A justification for this procedure is to prevent the concentration of economic power in the hands of individuals or small groups. Another justification is that it will reduce the inequality of asset distribution by cutting off its upper extreme. But this effect depends on whether previous owners are compensated in full or not. Even if full compensation is paid, there may still be some benefit if the nationalized property is used more efficiently than it was previously.

The main point, however, is that the ownership is transferred to the government. This does not necessarily mean that it has also to be managed by the government. The various options available have been explained by Lewis (1969a:64) as follows:

> The separation between management and ownership is one of the striking features of the large modern corporation. One does not any longer have to choose between private management of private property and public management of public property. One can also have public management of private property. This, in one sense, is what nationalisation comes to; the assets belong to the public in the legal sense, but they are matched by an equal amount of private wealth, since the original assets are acquired by paying compensation, and new assets are financed by borrowing from the private sector. The fourth alternative, private management of public property, meets the socialist requirement that it brakes the growth of private wealth, and ensures at the same time such virtues as private management may have.

We must now note the second characteristic of capital assets, namely the fact that their stock can be increased by investment. In fact, the rapid accumulation of capital is needed in LDCs not only for accelerating their development but also for improving the distribution of income by reducing the reward of capital relative to the wages of labour.

This has two implications for distributional policy. One implication is that policies towards the ownership of capital must not reduce the incentive for investment. This will be the result if investors are constantly under the threat of expropriation. Therefore the instrument of expropriation should be confined only to cases of excessive concentration of assets or to cases where such assets are managed inefficiently or against the social interest. Rather than apply redistributive policies extensively to such assets, a better approach would be to reduce very high incomes that current owners may derive. This is the case for taxing incomes from property at a higher rate than incomes from work, and for taxes on wealth, gifts, and inheritance.

The other implication of the fact that the stock of capital can be increased over time is that the asset base of the poor can be increased by giving them a greater share of newly created assets, rather than by transferring existing assets from the rich. An example is the Indian experiment with the Integrated Rural Development Programme, in which poor households in rural areas have been helped to get assets such as livestock either free or through subsidized credit arrangements. There are a number of problems, such as identifying the appropriate beneficiaries and giving them sufficient technical assistance to benefit from the new assets, which have reduced the effectiveness of the programme in the past (Rath 1985). However, this does not mean that the programme should be abandoned; rather, greater attempts should be made to solve these problems as they arise.

One type of asset calls for special mention, namely housing. The housing of most poor people in LDCs is very inadequate from a hygienic or social point of view. Therefore improvement in their housing conditions will be an important way of raising their standard of living. Improved housing is justified not only for its own sake, but because it is also likely to increase inhabitants' productive capacities by improving their health and changing their attitudes. Improving the asset base of the lower-income groups in this way is therefore an important contribution to a better distribution of income. This is an area in which governments can play a significant role, either by undertaking the construction of new houses or by subsidizing such construction by private enterprise. To the extent that an extensive housing programme increases the demand for labour, it will also have a beneficial effect on employment opportunities (for an account of an experiment carried out in the Indian state of Kerala, see the United Nations 1975).

16.3 Redistribution of incomes

Apart from the redistribution of assets discussed in the last section, governments can also follow policies for the redistribution of incomes; these policies are discussed in the present section. The redistribution of incomes will have some effects on incentives for effort, because if poor people are assured of some income through transfers, they may not have the same incentive to earn income from their own efforts. However, the effect on the working of market forces will be smaller than when governments regulate prices or outputs. Therefore economists generally prefer the method of redistribution of incomes to the regulation of markets. But one problem with the method of income redistribution is that so long as the primary distribution of income is unequal, there must be a repeated redistribution of incomes to make the secondary distribution more equal. Therefore the ultimate objective should be to make the primary distribution itself more equal by such measures as the equalization of opportunities and the redistribution of assets. But these policies may take a long time to have their desired effect on the primary distribution of income. Therefore policies for the redistribution of income may be followed to some extent for a limited period in order to improve the distribution of income in the short term. Some of the issues involved are discussed below.

16.3.1 Extent of redistribution

We first consider the question of how much income should be redistributed. This, of course, depends on the target level of inequality that governments wish to attain. If the goal is complete equality, then governments should tax the excess of all incomes over the average and use the proceeds to bring all lower incomes to the average level. The proportion of the national income that would be involved in such a redistribution is given by Kuznets's K measure of income inequality. From the data summarized in Chapter four, this comes to about a quarter of the national income in the developed market economies and about a third in the LDCs.

Governments do engage in a certain amount of such redistribution but well below that needed for complete equalization of incomes. Data are not available on the amounts actually involved, but some indication is given by the data on the category of central government expenditures described as 'subsidies and transfers' in the World Bank (1988), *World Development Report, 1988*. According to this source, subsidies and transfers in the industrial countries amounted to 60 per cent of central government spending in 1980, while central government expenditures were 28.6 per cent of GDP in 1986; therefore this item of expenditure amounted to 17 per cent of GDP. In LDCs, subsidies and transfers were about 35 per cent of central government expenditures, which was about 24 per cent of GDP, so that subsidies and transfers were about 8 per cent of GDP.

Instead of complete equality, governments have only tried to reduce the degree of income inequality by these redistributive measures. One way they have done this is by a progressive system of direct taxes based on the principles of ability to pay. In this system, larger incomes are taxed at a higher rate than smaller incomes. However, the extent to which income inequality is reduced depends not only on the degree of progressivity of taxes but also on the average rate of tax. The order of magnitude of the effects may be seen from a simple example. Consider the case in which the top 20 per cent of the population earns 50 per cent of the total income before tax. Suppose the tax rate on this group is k times the tax rate on the rest of the population, so that k is a simple index of the progressivity of the tax system. Then the proportion of income p' received by the top 20 per cent after tax is given by

$$p' = \frac{k + 1 - 2kT}{2(k + 1)(1 - T)} \tag{16.1}$$

where T is the average rate of tax. Some illustrative values are shown in Table 16.2.

For any given average rate of tax, the share of the rich declines faster, the more progressive is the tax system. Similarly, for any given progressivity of the tax system, the share of the rich declines faster, the higher the average rate of taxation. The second effect is often stronger than the first. However, LDCs have such undeveloped fiscal systems that the average rate of direct taxation is quite low. Hence they are much less able to use the direct tax system to achieve significant effects on income distribution. For such low rates of direct taxation, any significant effect on income inequality will require very high rates of progression of the tax system. At such high rates, the tax system will begin to have significant effects on incentives for effort.

Table 16.2 Effect of average rate and progressivity of tax on share of top 20 per cent

Progressivity k	Average rate of tax			
	0	0.10	0.20	0.30
1.0	0.50	0.50	0.50	0.50
1.5	0.50	0.49	0.48	0.46
2.0	0.50	0.48	0.46	0.43
2.5	0.50	0.48	0.45	0.41
3.0	0.50	0.47	0.44	0.39
4.0	0.50	0.47	0.43	0.37

In an influential study, Chenery *et al.* (1974) proposed that resources for redistribution should be raised by taxing away all increases of income above a certain level. This proposal has been described as 'redistribution with growth'. It amounts to a marginal tax rate of 100 per cent on those incomes. In the words of the ILO Employment Report on Kenya (1972:112; see also Jolly 1976), 'the stabilisation of the incomes of the top 10 per cent or less of incomes (affecting under 1 per cent of all income receivers) is the minimum result we would expect'. The approach was later justified by the argument that

> In espousing the general principle of redistributing the benefits of growth, an essentially political judgement was made which is thematic to the volume as a whole. This is that intervention which alters the distribution of the *increment* to the overall capital stock and income will arouse less hostility from the rich than transfers which bite into their existing assets and incomes. (Chenery *et al.* 1974:56)

The effect of fiscal policy on income distribution depends not only on the way taxes are levied but also on the way government expenditure benefits different income groups. It is usually more difficult to estimate the distribution of benefits than the distribution of the tax burden. Such estimates have been made only for a few countries. They show that the distribution of benefits through public expenditure has a greater effect in reducing income inequality than the distribution of taxes. One such set of estimates was made for the United States for 1968 by Musgrave *et al.* (1974). According to these estimates, while the distribution of the tax burden reduced the Gini index from 0.365 before taxes to only 0.359 after taxes, the distribution of the benefits of public expenditure reduced it further to 0.283. Meerman (1979) made some estimates of the benefits of public expenditure in Malaysia accruing to different income groups; these estimates appear to have reduced the Gini index of the quintile distribution of income from an initial value of 0.436 to 0.390. Selowsky (1979) made similar estimates for Colombia which show that the distribution of benefits from public expenditure on education and health care reduced the Gini index from 0.426 to 0.400. Thus the expenditure side of public finance appears to have had a considerable influence on income inequality.

However, these estimates of the effect of public expenditure on income distribution depend heavily on the assumptions made to estimate the allocation of benefits to different income classes (for a discussion of these problems, see Atkinson and Stiglitz 1980:286–8). In some cases they are based on fairly reliable data on the extent to which different income groups participate in the various levels of education and benefit from various types of health and medical facilities provided by the government. In other cases data are not sufficient to quantify the benefits accruing to different sections of the population. Then it is generally assumed that all persons receive the same amount of benefit per capita and that these benefits form a higher proportion of the incomes received by the poor than the rich. This is part of the explanation why such estimates of the benefits of public expenditure appear to have such a large effect on the inequality of income distribution.

When the distribution of income is very unequal, a high rate of tax on the top deciles will yield substantial revenues for the government. However, there has been some concern that such a high rate of tax on the top deciles might reduce the savings of the economy and hence affect its rate of growth. Whether this happens or not depends on how far the growth of the economy is constrained by lack of savings, and also on the extent to which the government uses its revenues for investment. Hence Cline (1972, 1975) found that results varied considerably in simulation studies of different countries (see also Newberry 1987:186-7).

In general, it is likely that the expenditure of government funds are more likely to improve income distribution by helping the lower-income groups than the ways in which these funds are raised by taxation. If such redistributive expenditure can be undertaken on a sufficiently large scale, then tax revenues can be raised in ways which have the least adverse effect on efficiency and growth. But in practice, the extent to which government expenditure can play such a redistributive role is quite limited. Therefore the tax system must also be used to have a redistributive effect.

16.3.2 Form of redistribution

Governments usually raise the resources they need for various purposes, including redistribution, in the form of taxes paid in monetary form. But in using their resources to benefit various groups in the population, they have a choice of different forms. So far we have been considering the case of cash benefits. In this form the redistributive policy only affects the secondary distribution of income. As mentioned above, if the change in the secondary distribution has no effect on the primary distribution, then the income redistribution must be repeated year after year to maintain the improvement in income distribution.

In fact, however, the change in the secondary distribution of income will have some effects on the primary distribution. This is because the change in the secondary distribution of income will alter the structure of production through the differences in the pattern of demand at different income levels and because such changes in the structure of production will affect the primary distribution of income through differences in the pattern of income generation in different sectors. Hence there will be a two-way interaction between the structure of production and the distribution of income, as discussed in section 12.3.

If an improvement in the secondary distribution of income leads also to an improvement in the primary distribution through this interaction, then the redistribution of income carried out over a number of years will have a cumulative effect so that a desired improvement in the primary distribution can be achieved over a finite number of years, and further redistributions will not be necessary. But it cannot be assumed that an improvement of the secondary distribution of income will necessarily also improve the primary distribution. Whether it does so or not depends on the differences in the pattern of demand at different income levels and the differences in the pattern of income generation in different sectors. Some empirical studies carried out in a number of LDCs suggest that the effect may not in fact be favourable.

To explain this possibility, we note that a redistribution of income from the rich to the poor will increase the demand for commodities like food, for which the poor have a large unsatisfied demand. This increase of demand for food might lead to an expansion of the agricultural sector. If the pattern of income generation in the agricultural sector is more favourable to labour and hence to the poor, then there will be an improvement in the overall distribution of income. But in many LDCs the distribution of incomes within the agricultural sector is very unequal because of the dominance of rent and profit incomes accruing to the relatively better-off people. This is one way in which a redistribution of income may worsen the primary distribution of income.

On the other hand, a reduction of the disposable income of the rich will reduce their demand for services, on which they spend a high proportion of their incomes. Some of these services are provided by the relatively poor sections of the population. To this extent, the reduced demand for services will worsen the primary distribution of income. Because of these effects, some simulations of the effects of income redistribution indicate that such policies may make the primary distribution of income more unequal than in the initial situation (see Sinha *et al.* 1979 for India; see also Ballentine and Soligo 1978; and Cline 1972). In such cases the redistribution of income must not only be continued indefinitely but must also be steadily expanded in order to maintain a given improvement in the actual distribution of income.

These are the effects which occur when the benefits to the poor are in the form of cash supplements to their incomes. An alternative form of redistribution is to give the benefits to the poor in kind. The principal example is the provision of public services such as education, health, infrastructure, and other social services. These services alter what we have called the tertiary distribution of income. As noted above, the allocation of these services usually has a greater effect in reducing the inequality of income distribution than the pattern of tax collection. But the net effect is likely to be small because the usual types of social services provided by the government are only a small part of total consumption. In order to have a greater effect, the range of such services may have to be extended in LDCs to include such other services as public housing.

The effects through the secondary and tertiary distributions of income are therefore likely to be small, and sometimes even counter-productive. Therefore a more effective form of redistribution is that which affects the primary distribution itself. This is best done by the expenditure of public funds in ways which improve the productive capacity of the poor.

16.3.3 The eradication of absolute poverty

The most serious problem facing LDCs from the distribution point of view is the widespread extent of absolute poverty on any reasonable definition of the poverty line. Therefore LDCs must give high priority to the eradication of absolute poverty as soon as possible. The extent of such poverty will decline, as it has declined in many countries, with growth of the average income. But in many countries, the rate at which absolute poverty has been declining as a result of overall growth has been too slow. Therefore LDCs may also use the method of income redistribution to speed up the eradication of poverty.

The first step in establishing a systematic programme for poverty eradication is to lay down a poverty line to identify the poor who are to be helped to overcome their poverty. The usual approach to defining the line of absolute poverty has been in terms of a minimum standard of living just sufficient to maintain life. However, this has given rise to much controversy over what is the minimum standard of living needed for survival. In fact, it can be very low. As Anstey (1952:3) put it, perhaps with unconscious irony, 'in many parts of India, it is fatally easy just to maintain life. A handful of rice, a cotton rag, a mud hut and dung-cakes (for fuel) constitute the only necessities'. What is required is not just to maintain life at a miserable level, but rather to provide individuals so that they can at least realize their human personality with some dignity. But it is not possible to lay down physiological limits on such a standard.

A more serious problem is that we do not need a definition of poverty for intellectual curiosity. The definition is needed as an aid to policy. The concept of poverty eradication means a particular approach to the distribution of income. It implies that a higher priority will be given to raise the bottom income groups to a given level than to improve the conditions of those above that level. Therefore the best solution is to define the poverty line as a policy parameter, as part of the government commitment to eradicate poverty. One consequence is that the definition must be based on what the government intends to do to overcome poverty. If the solution is sought in terms of food distribution, then the definition must be based on a norm of food consumption. Similarly, if the solution is sought through educational policy, it should be based on a minimum standard of education and so on.

Most often, however, the poverty line is defined in terms of income. It has been argued that the definition in terms of income can be adjusted to norms in terms of specific needs. For example, in explaining the 'basic needs' approach, Streeton and Burki (1978:413) say:

> One way out of this conceptual impasse is to identify a core of basic needs. The emphasis on a few needs does not mean that others are neglected. It does mean that at the level of income required to meet the core needs, the household would also satisfy other needs. A definition of core basic needs in very poor societies proves to be surprisingly robust, so that counting deficiencies for very different items of the basket yields approximately the same number of people.

Assuming a poverty line in terms of income level, the extent of poverty can be measured in various ways, as indicated in section 3.6. One is the number of persons below that poverty line, the headcount measure. Another is the poverty gap, that is, the proportion of the national income that must be transferred to the poor to eradicate poverty. A third measure is the weighted poverty gap, which assigns greater weight to incomes that are further below the poverty line.

There has been some discussion of the optimum way in which a given amount of funds should be allocated to different sections of the poor in order to achieve the maximum reduction of poverty (e.g., Kanbur 1986). The solution varies with the measure of poverty used. Thus if the headcount measure is used, the funds should be allocated to those who are closest to the poverty line. If the poverty gap measure is used, then any method of allocation will reduce poverty to the same extent. If the weighted poverty gap measure is used, the funds should be allocated to the poorest of the poor.

This problem arises only when limited resources are allocated which are insufficient to eradicate poverty within a reasonable time. A better approach would be to increase the allocation of funds for the purpose. A more serious problem is to identify the poor and to find the best means of alleviating their poverty. Data are usually given only about the numbers of the 'faceless poor', without much indication of their characteristics and the causes of their poverty. Therefore better statistical information about the poor is a matter of high priority.

If the solution is sought primarily through the redistribution of income, the magnitude of the problem is indicated by the poverty gap. According to the data assembled by Kakwani (1980:392–5), using a poverty line defined as per capita income of US$150 at 1970 prices, the average poverty gap for a sample of 31 LDCs was 3.71 per cent of the national income (5.95 per cent in Asia, 6.73 per cent in Africa, and 0.73 per cent in Latin America). The poverty gap is particularly large in the poorer LDCs; thus the poverty gap was 8.6 per cent in India and 6.7 per cent in Indonesia at the time the data were collected.

The extent of redistribution required to eradicate poverty is therefore not beyond the capacity of governments. But solving the problem by just redistributing incomes means that the process has to be repeated year after year. This may be necessary in the case of people who are unable to participate in the normal functioning of the economy. In other cases a better approach is to use the funds to improve the productive capacity of the poor. A useful approach is to lay down a planning target in terms of the proportion of the national income such as, say 5 per cent, that will be transferred through the government budget for poverty relief. With such a target, poverty can be eradicated in most countries within a decade.

Once such a financial target is laid down, then concrete programmes can be set up to identify the poor and the best ways of helping them overcome their poverty. In fact, when such programmes are in place, it may be easier to mobilize aid from developed countries specifically for poverty relief.

16.4 The scope for equitable growth

To conclude the study, we may summarize the conclusions of Part III as follows. In Chapter 14, it was argued that LDCs must orient their policies to promote both a rapid growth of their national incomes and a more equal distribution of incomes, in particular that rapid growth should be pursued in such a way that its benefits are widely shared among all sections of the society.

The historical experience of countries, however, shows that these two objectives have not always been attained to an equal degree in the past. On the one hand, the growth of national income by itself will not trickle down to all sections of the population. This is partly because, under ordinary market auspices, people who are already better off have a greater chance of contributing to growth and benefiting from it. It is also partly because, as Lewis (1976:26, 28) says, 'development must be inegalitarian because it does not start in every part of the economy at the same time . . . [I]n practice, the inegalitarianism of the development process derives not so much from failure to trickle down vertically as from the failure of horizontal spread from the enclaves to the traditional sectors'. This was the experience of the present-day developed countries in the early stages of their growth. The benefits of their rapid growth accrued to the lower-income groups only to a limited extent. Income inequality declined in these countries in the first half of this century, but it was not due to their growth. Instead, it was due to significant changes in the education, organization, and political power of workers.

On the other hand, the pursuit of an equitable distribution of income by itself will not lead to rapid growth. This has been the experience of many of the countries which adopted a socialist approach. Therefore these countries are currently reconsidering their policies to give greater weight to the growth objective.

These conclusions, however, do not mean that there is an inescapable conflict between the objectives of growth and equity. On the contrary, there is considerable scope for equitable growth. The main theme of this and the previous chapter has been that modern governments in LDCs have such a wide range of policy instruments at their command that they can deploy them to achieve the objectives of growth and equity at the same time. The ways in which these policies can be orchestrated are briefly summarized below.

Rapid growth of LDCs depends essentially on their adoption of technology based on modern science, just as they contributed to the modern economic growth of DCs in the past two centuries. For this to be achieved, there must be a rapid expansion of education and modern infrastructure, and improvement of economic institutions. These are essentially the 'duties of the sovereign', the special responsibility of the state (Sundrum 1983; Chap. 5).

The effect of these developments on the distribution of income, however, depends on how the new opportunities are distributed among the people. In many LDCs these opportunities have been distributed very unequally. For example, educational expansion, which was confidently looked upon as a great levelling force, turned out to be a major source of rising inequality. Similarly, infrastructural development to promote the adoption of modern technology has largely been concentrated in areas serving the upper-income groups, becoming another source of rising inequality. To avoid these adverse effects on distribution, governments should distribute the facilities largely provided by the state itself more equally, and even to favour the lower-income groups, who suffer from a greater handicap to begin with. Another way is to expand these facilities as rapidly as possible so that the duration of any transitional rise of inequality can be reduced.

With the growth of national income resulting from these developments, there will be a slowing down of population growth and hence a faster growth of per capita income. In practice, population growth has been faster among the lower-income groups because, while mortality levels were reduced sharply by the official actions of public authorities, fertility levels depend more on the personal circumstances of individual families and were slower to decline. This is another reason why development measures such as the expansion of education and infrastructure must be concentrated more heavily on the lower-income groups.

The growth of the national income depends also on a high rate of investment. In the past, some economists have argued that an unequal distribution of income was necessary to achieve high rates of savings and investment. This may be true if upper-income groups save and invest a high proportion of their larger incomes, as Keynes argued had been the case in the western countries in the early stages of their growth. But this has not been the case in LDCs. Therefore LDC governments must consider some alternative means, such as a higher rate of investment by the state itself. This will also help to allocate investment to the needs of the lower-income groups to a greater extent.

An important question is the role to be assigned to market forces in the mobilization and allocation of resources. Liberal economists have argued in favour of market forces playing this role in order to maximize the rate of growth. In fact, even for this purpose, market forces need to be modified by the state in some ways (Sundrum 1990). Another consideration is that market forces may unleash powerful disequalizing effects on the distribution of income. This will particularly be the case if market prices are ridden with monopoly elements and do not function in a competitive way. Therefore one policy that governments must follow is to promote competitive conditions. On the other hand, one of the principal elements of the socialist approach is that market forces must be severely controlled in the interests of a more equal distribution of income, and hence that economic activity must be planned centrally by the state. However, actual experience has generally shown that countries following this approach have had only a limited growth performance. These experiences suggest the importance of a mixed economy, with market forces playing a significant role but subject to regulation by the state, as a more promising way of achieving both growth and equity at the same time.

The policies discussed so far are long-term policies in the sense that they have to be pursued steadily over a long period of time. We turn now to policies which have to be considered over a shorter period. We start with the policy towards the distribution of assets. An unequal distribution of assets is not only a source of an unequal distribution of income at a point of time; it is also the main reason why income inequality may rise in the process of economic growth, as happened in the early stages of the growth of western countries. By contrast, when there is a more equal distribution of income to begin with, income inequality may actually decline in the course of economic growth as happened in the Asian NICs.

Socialist thinkers were so impressed with the effects of an unequal distribution of assets that they have argued for the abolition of private property in the means of production. But the nationalization of the means of production is often accompanied by their management in state enterprises, which have rarely been very efficient. One alternative is the private management of public assets. Another alternative is that these assets be redistributed more equally among the population. Such a policy need not then have adverse effects on growth.

This was in fact what was done with respect to land in the land reform programmes of countries such as Japan, South Korea, Taiwan, and many socialist countries. For example, as a result of the highly effective land reform in Taiwan, the Gini index of land ownership declined from 0.62 in 1950 to 0.46 in 1960, and the proportion of farm families who owned their land rose from 36 per cent in 1950 to 80 per cent in 1974 (Ranis 1983:88). In these countries the land reform programme and the more equal distribution of other assets was the result of the aftermath of wars and violent revolutions, but these measures can be carried out in a less violent way by other LDCs. These measures must, however, be implemented promptly to avoid loss of confidence and to ensure efficient utilization of resources.

The measures discussed so far will serve both the growth and distributional objectives, but the effects on the distribution of income may take a long time to materialize. If the distribution of income in LDCs is very unequal to begin with, and if it is desired to improve the distribution of income in the near future, these countries must consider other policies as well. One policy to consider is the redistribution of incomes through the fiscal system. In the past, LDCs have relied heavily on indirect taxes because of their greater convenience of collection. Further, these taxes have also been levied at high rates on the necessities consumed mainly by lower-income groups because of their inelastic demand. Hence there have been considerable regressive elements in the tax systems actually followed in LDCs. These systems must therefore be modified to be more equitable. One modification is to levy indirect taxes more heavily on the luxuries consumed mainly by the upper-income groups. The best way, however, is through a progressive system of direct taxes, with the revenues used to assist lower-income groups to improve their productive capacity.

A second policy that LDCs can follow to improve the distribution of income in the short run is to influence the structure of production in favour of commodities mainly consumed by the lower-income groups. A particularly important application of this policy is to expand agricultural production. The faster the food supply is expanded, the sooner will the agricultural sector fulfil its historical mission so that overall growth will no longer be constrained by the agricultural sector (Sundrum 1990: Chap. 5). In this way the policy will promote both growth and equity at the same time.

Finally, the distribution of income can be improved in the short run by a policy of regulating prices. Price control measures have generally been criticized by economists because of their adverse effects on the working of market forces in promoting growth. However, this policy will not necessarily have such an adverse effect if market prices are unduly influenced by monopoly elements. Therefore the price control policy must be applied only in special cases in which they do not have such adverse effects, and also as a short-term solution, until longer-term policies for expanding supplies become effective. A more serious problem is to implement the price control measures in an efficient and honest manner.

One of the most serious problems of income distribution in LDCs is the widespread extent of absolute poverty. The longer-term policies for promoting growth and equity described above will eventually eradicate such poverty in LDCs, as it has been eradicated in the DCs, but absolute poverty is such a terrible blot on the human conscience that it should not be tolerated for a long time. Therefore LDCs must also use the short-term policies discussed above to eradicate poverty as soon as possible. The DCs can also help by directing more of their aid specifically for this purpose. This can be done more effectively through programmes that the LDCs themselves set up for the speedy eradication of poverty.

Bibliography and author index

Numbers in square brackets refer to pages on which works are cited in the text.

Adelman, I. and Morris, C.T. (1973) *Economic Growth and Social Equity in Developing Countries*, Stanford, CA: Stanford University Press. [83]

Adelman, I. and Robinson, S. (1978) *Income Distribution in Developing Countries*, Oxford: Oxford University Press. [154]

Adelman, I. and Whittle, P. (1979) *Static and Dynamic Indices of Income Inequality*, Geneva: World Employment Programme WEP 2-23/WP 74. [138]

Ahluwalia, M.S. (1974) 'Income inequality: some dimensions of the problem', in Chenery, H. *et al.* (eds), *Redistribution with Growth*, Oxford: Oxford University Press.[78, 90–2]

—— (1976) 'Inequality, poverty and development', *Journal of Development Economics* 3:3–37. [79, 81, 86, 89–92]

Ahluwalia, M.S., Carter, N.G., and Chenery, H.B. (1979) 'Growth and poverty in developing countries', *Journal of Development Economics* 6:299–341. [64, 84–5, 101, 113]

Anand, S. (1983) *Inequality and Poverty in Malaysia*, Oxford: Oxford University Press. [18, 20, 77, 117, 119–20]

Anstey, V. (1952) *The Economic Development of India*, London: Longman, Green and Co. [305]

Arndt, H.W. and Sundrum, R.M. (1975) 'Regional price disparities', *Bulletin of Indonesian Economic Studies* 11:30–68. [24]

Arrow, K.J. (1966) *Social Choice and Individual Values*, New York: John Wiley and Sons. [266]

Atkinson, A.B. (1970) 'On the measurement of inequality', *Journal of Economic Theory* 2:244–63. [55–6]

—— (1975) *The Economics of Inequality*, Oxford: Clarendon Press. [37–8]

—— (1981) 'The measurement of economic mobility', in Eijgelshoven, P.J. and van Gemerden, L.J. (eds), *Inkomensverdeling en openbare financien: Opstellen voor Jan Pen*, Utrecht: Uitgeverij Het Spectrum, pp. 9–24. [129]

Atkinson, A.B. and Stiglitz, J.E. (1980) *Public Economics*, London: McGraw-Hill. [261–2, 277, 302]

Bacha, E. (1977) *The Kuznets Curve and Beyond: Wealth and Changes in Inequality*, Washington, DC: World Bank Discussion Paper.[113]

Ballentine, J.G. and Soligo, R. (1978) 'Consumption and earnings patterns and income distribution', *Economic Development and Cultural Change* 26:696–708. [304]

Bangladesh Bureau of Statistics (1984) *Statistical Yearbook of Bangladesh 1983–84*, Dhaka. [119, 123]

Bardhan, P. (1984) *Land, Labour and Rural Poverty*, New Delhi: Oxford University Press. [189, 199, 202–3]

Bartholomew, D.J. (1982) *Stochastic Models for Social Processes*, Chichester: John Wiley and Sons. [130]

Basu, K. (1984) *The Less Developed Economy*, New Delhi: Oxford University Press. [192, 203–4, 208, 225]

Bergsman, J. (1980) 'Income distribution and poverty in Mexico', *World Bank Staff Working Paper no. 395*, Washington, DC: World Bank. [119]

Berry, A. (1978) 'Income and consumption trends in the Philippines, 1959–70', *Review of Income and Wealth* 24(3):313–31. [119]

Beteille, A. (1983) *The Idea of Natural Inequality*, Delhi: Oxford University Press. [291]

Bhattacharya, N. and Mahalanobis, B. (1967) 'Regional disparities in household consumption in India', *Journal of the American Statistical Association* 62:143–61. [50]

Biro Pusat Statistik (1968, 1969) *Cost of Living Surveys*, Jakarta. [25, 27]

—— (1980, 1981) SUSENAS. Jakarta. [22–3, 30, 77, 98, 119, 126]

—— (1982) *Social Accounting Matrix, Indonesia 1975*, Jakarta. [156]

—— (1986) *Labour Force Survey (SAKERNAS)*, Jakarta. [213]

Blaug, M. (1969) *The Causes of Graduate Unemployment in India*, London: Allen Lane Penguin Press. [211]

—— (1974) *Education and the Employment Problem in Developing Countries*, Geneva: ILO. [97]

—— (1978) *Economic Theory in Retrospect*, Cambridge: Cambridge University Press. [8]

Bliss, C. and Stern, N. (1978) 'Productivity, wages and nutrition', *Journal of Development Economics* 5:363–98. [203]

Boersma (1978) 'Opening address', in Krelle, W. and Shorrocks, A. (eds), *Personal Income Distribution*, Amsterdam: North-Holland, pp. xiii–xix. [32]

Booth, A.E. and Sundrum, R.M. (1984) *Labour Absorption in Agriculture*, New Delhi and Oxford: Oxford University Press. [164, 173, 175, 181, 185, 187, 204, 297]

Booth, A.E., Chaudhri, D.P. and Sundrum, R.M. (1981) *Income Distribution and the Structure of Production*, Canberra: Australian National University, Economics Department Seminar Paper. [239]

Boserup, E. (1965) *The Conditions of Agricultural Growth*, London: Allen and Unwin. [165]

Bourguignon, F. (1979) 'Decomposable income inequality measures', *Econometrica* 47:901–20. [48–9]

Brown, J.A.C. (1976) 'The mathematical and statistical theory of income distribution', in Atkinson, A.B., (ed), *The Personal Distribution of Incomes*, London: Allen and Unwin, Chap. 3, pp. 72–88. [39]

Bureau of Census (various issues) *Current Population Report Series 60*, Washington DC. [18, 20, 30, 77, 98, 115]

Bureau of Census and Statistics (1973) *Family Income and Expenditure, 1971*, Manila. [18, 20, 22–3, 27, 30, 35, 77, 98, 123]

Butt, D.M.B. (1960) *On Economic Growth*, Oxford: Clarendon Press. [170–3]

Central Bank of Ceylon (1984) *Report on Consumer Finances and Socio-Economic Survey 1981/82*, Colombo. [18, 25, 27, 30, 96, 98, 119, 123]

Central Statistical Organization (1980) *National Accounts Statistics, 1980*, New Delhi. [33]

—— (1984) *Annual Survey of Industries*, New Delhi. [222]

Chanthawon, P. (1987) 'The decomposition analysis of the sources of income inequality in Thailand, 1962/3 and 1968/9', cited in Mehdi Kronkaew *The Current State of Poverty and Income Distribution in Thailand*, Canberra: Australian National University Conference Paper. [119]

Champernowne, D. (1953) 'A model of income distribution', *Economic Journal* 63:318–51, reprinted in Champernowne, D. (1973), Appendix 6. [133]

—— (1973) *The Distribution of Income Between Persons*, Cambridge: Cambridge University Press. [135]

—— (1974) 'A comparison of measures of inequality of income distribution', *Economic Journal* 84:787–816. [60]

Chelliah, R.J. (1983) *A Review of Economic Development and Policy in India*, New Delhi: Rajaji International Institute of Public Affairs and Administration. [286]

Chenery, H., Ahluwalia, M.S., Bell, C.L.G., Duloy, J.H., and Jolly, R. (1974) *Redistribution with Growth*, London: Oxford University Press. [83, 268, 302]

Chenery, H.B. and Syrquin, M. (1975) *Patterns of Development 1950–79*, London: Oxford University Press. [81, 89]

Cheung, S.N.S. (1968) 'Private property rights and sharecropping', *Journal of Political Economy* 76:1107–22. [192]

Chipman, J.S. and Moore, J.C. (1976) 'Why an increase in GNP does not imply an improvement in potential welfare', *Kyklos* 29:391–418. [268]

Clark, C. (1957) *The Conditions of Economic Progress*, London: Macmillan. [178]

Cline, W.R. (1972) *Potential Effects of Income Redistribution on Economic Growth*, New York: Praeger. [303–4]

—— (1975) 'Distribution and development', *Journal of Development Economics* 1:359–400. [303]

Cornia, G.A., Jolly, R., and Strewart, F. (1988) *Adjustment with a Human Face*, Oxford: Clarendon Press. [281]

Cornwall, J. (1977) *Modern Capitalism*, London: Martin Robertson. [95, 124, 129, 194, 236]

Cowell, F.A. (1980) 'On the structure of additive inequality measures', *Review of Economic Studies* 37:521–31. [48]

Coxon, A.P.M. and Jones, C.J. (1975) *Social Mobility*, London: Penguin Books. [136]

Dagum, C. (1982) 'Income distribution models', in *Encyclopaedia of Statistical Sciences*, vol. 4, New York: Wiley and Sons, pp. 27–34. [39]

Dalton, H. (1920) 'The measurement of the inequality of incomes', *Economic Journal* 30:38–61. [55]

Dandekar, V.M. (1962) 'Economic theory and agrarian reform', *Oxford Economic Papers* 14:69–79. [198, 297]

Dandekar, V.M. and Rath, N.S. (1971) *Poverty in India*, Poona: Indian School of Political Economy. [17]

Dasgupta, A.K. (1953) 'Keynesian economics and under-developed countries', *Economic Weekly* 6:101–5. [175]

Datt, G. (1989) *Wage and Employment Determination in Agricultural Labour Markets in India*, Canberra: Australian National University, Ph.D. thesis. [205]

de Janvry, A. and Subbarao, K. (1986) *Agricultural Price Policy and Income Distribution in India*, Delhi: Oxford University Press. [154]

Demery, L. and Addison, T. (1987) *The Alleviation of Poverty under Structural Adjustment*, Washington, DC: World Bank. [281]

314

Dorfman, R., Samuelson, P.A., and Solow, R.M. (1958) *Linear Programming and Economic Analysis*, New York: McGraw-Hill. [267]

Dornbusch, R. and Fischer, S. (1978) *Macro-economics*, New York: McGraw-Hill. [32]

Eckhaus, R.S. (1955) 'The factor proportions in underdeveloped countries', reprinted in Agarwala, A.N. and Singh, S.P. (eds), *The Economics of Under-development*, London: Oxford University Press, pp. 348–80. [175]

Feller, W. (1966) *An Introduction to Probability Theory and Its Applications*, vol. 2, New York: John Wiley. [144]

—— (1968) *An Introduction to Probability Theory and Its Applications*, 3rd edn, New York: John Wiley. [132, 134, 144]

Fields, G.S. (1980) *Poverty, Inequality and Development*, Cambridge: Cambridge University Press. [2, 119]

—— (1985) 'Industrialization and Employment in Hong Kong, Korea, Singapore and Taiwan', in Galenson, W. (ed.) *Foreign Trade and Investment*, Madison: University of Wisconsin Press, Chap. 8, pp. 333–75. [122]

Findlay, R.E. (1970) 'Factor proportions and comparative advantage in the long run', *Journal of Political Economy* 78:27–34. [243]

Fisher, A.G.B. (1935) *The Clash of Progress and Security*, London: Macmillan. [178]

Fisk, E.K. (1975) 'The subsistence component in national income accounts', *The Developing Economies* 13:252–79. [24]

Food and Agriculture Organization (various issues) *Production Yearbook*, Rome: Food and Agriculture Organization. [182]

Foster, J., Greer, J. and Thorbecke, E. (1984) 'A class of decomposable poverty measures', *Econometrica* 52:761–6. [65]

Friedman, M. (1947) 'Lerner on the economics of control', *Journal of Political Economy* 55:405–16, reprinted in Friedman, M. (1966) *Essays in Positive Economics*, Chicago: Chicago University Press. [260]

—— (1957) *A Theory of the Consumption Function*, Princeton: Princeton University Press. [29]

Galbraith, J.K. (1967) *The New Industrial State*, Boston: Houghton Mifflin. [167]

Government of India (1981, 1987) *Economic Survey*, New Delhi: Government Publications. [200]

Graaff, J.V. (1957) *Theoretical Welfare Economics*, Cambridge: Cambridge University Press. [268]

Harris, J.R. and Todaro, M.P. (1970) 'Migration, unemployment and development', *American Economic Review* 60:126–42. [207]

Hauser, P.M. (1974) 'The measurement of labour utilisation', *Malayan Economics Review* 19:1–15. [197]

Hayami, Y. and Kikuchi, M. (1981) *Asian Village Economy at the Crossroads*, Tokyo: University of Tokyo Press. [297]

Hayami, Y. and Ruttan, V.W. (1985) *Agricultural Development: An International Perspective* (2nd edn), Baltimore: Johns Hopkins University Press. [163, 183]

Hayami, Y., Subbarao, K., and Otsuka, K. (1982) 'Efficiency and equity in the producer levy of India', *American Journal of Agricultural Economics* 64:655–63. [289]

Heller, P. (1988) 'Fund-supported adjustment programs and the poor', *Finance and Development* 25(4):2–5. [281]

Heller, P., Bovenberg, A.L., Catsambas, T., Chu, K-Y., and Shome, P. (1988) *The Implications of Fund-Supported Programs for Poverty*, Washington, DC: IMF. [281]

Herring, R.J. (1983) *Land to the Tiller*, New Haven: Yale University Press. [297]

Hicks, J.R. (1932) *The Theory of Wages*, London: Macmillan. [161-2]

—— (1940) 'The Valuation of Social Income', *Economica* 7:105-24. [267]

—— (1966) *Value and Capital* (2nd edn), Oxford: Clarendon Press. [21]

Hirsch, F. (1977) *Social Limits to Growth*, London: Routledge & Kegan Paul. [2]

Hirschman, A.O. (1945) *National Power and the Structure of Foreign Trade*, Los Angeles: University of California Press. [44-5]

Hollander, S. (1979) *The Economics of David Ricardo*, Toronto: Toronto University Press. [164]

Hughes, G. (1987) 'The incidence of fuel taxes', in Newberry, D. and Stern, N. (eds) *The Theory of Taxation for Developing Countries*, Oxford: Oxford University Press. [277]

International Labour Organisation. (1972) *Employment, Incomes and Equality*, Geneva: ILO. [198]

—— (1987) *World Labour Report*, no. 3, Geneva, ILO. [209-11]

Ishikawa, S. (1967) *Economic Development in Asian Perspective*, Tokyo: Kinokyniya Bookstore. [165]

—— (1978) *Labour Absorption in Asian Agriculture*, Bangkok: ILO-ARTEP. [183]

Jain, S. (1975) *Size Distribution of Income*, Washington, DC: World Bank. [71, 76, 93, 96, 115, 119]

Jitsochon, S. (1987) 'Sources and trends of income inequality: Thailand, 1975/6 and 1981', cited in Mehdi Kronkaew *The Current State of Poverty and Income Distribution in Thailand*, Canberra: Australian National University Conference Paper. [119]

Johnson, H.G. (1958) 'Planning and the market in economic development', *Pakistan Economics Journal* 8:44-55, reprinted in Johnston, H.G. (1964) *Money, Trade and Economic Growth*, London: George Allen and Unwin, pp. 151-63. [264]

—— (1964) 'The political economy of opulence', *Canadian Journal of Economics and Political Science*, reprinted in Johnson, H.G., *Money, Trade and Economic Growth*, London: George Allen and Unwin. [177]

—— (1973) *The Theory of Income Distribution*, London: Gray-Mills Publishing Ltd. [31, 134]

Jolly, R. (1976) 'Redistribution with growth', in Cairncross, A. and Puri, M. (eds) *Employment, Income Distribution and Development Strategy*, London: Macmillan, Chap. 4, pp. 43-55. [302]

Jones, R.W. (1965) 'The structure of simple general equilibrium models', *Journal of Political Economy* 73:561-2. [241]

Jose, A.V. (1988) 'Agricultural wages in India', *Economic and Political Weekly* 23(2):46-58. [196, 199-200]

Kakwani, N.C. (1980) *Income Inequality and Poverty*, London: Oxford University Press. [41, 48, 52-3, 55, 59, 61, 63-4, 70, 73, 76, 84, 100, 124, 147, 306]

Kaldor, N. (1939) 'Welfare propositions in economics', *Economic Journal* 49:549-52, reprinted in Kaldor, N. (1960) *Essays on Value and Distribution*, London: Gerald Duckworth, pp. 143-46. [267]

—— (1965) 'Remarks', in Robinson, R. (ed), *Developing the Third World*, Cambridge: Cambridge University Press, pp. 171-2. [285]

—— (1972) 'The irrelevance of equilibrium economics', *Economic Journal* 82:1237-55. [273]

Kalecki, M. (1942) 'A theory of profits' *Economic Journal* 52:258-67. [175]

Kanbur, S.M.R. (1986) *Budgetary Rules for Poverty Alleviation*, Princeton University, Woodrow Wilson School, mimeograph. [306]

Kendall, M.G. and Stuart, A. (1963) *The Advanced Theory of Statistics*, London: Charles Griffin. [44, 46, 56, 103]

Keynes, J.M. (1919) *The Economic Consequences of the Peace*, London: Macmillan. [262]

—— (1936) *The General Theory of Employment, Interest and Money*, London: Macmillan. [190]

Kuo, W. (1975) 'Income distribution by size in Taiwan', in Council for Asian Manpower Studies *Income Distribution, Employment and Economic Development in Southeast and East Asia*, Tokyo: Japan Economic Research Centre 1:80–153. [119]

Kuznets, S. (1955) 'Economic growth and income inequality', *American Economic Review* 45:1–28, reprinted in Kuznets, S. (1963) *Economic Growth and Structure*, New Delhi: Oxford and IBH Publishing Company, pp. 257–87. [72, 96, 113, 235, 252–3]

—— (1963) 'Quantitative aspects of the economic growth of nations, III: distribution of income by size', *Economic Development and Cultural Change* II: 1–80. [111, 113]

—— (1966) *Modern Economic Growth*, New Haven: Yale University Press. [78–9, 111–12, 178]

—— (1971) *Economic Growth of Nations*, Cambridge, MA: Belknap Press. [227]

—— (1975) 'Demographic components in size distribution of income', in Council for Asian Manpower Studies, *Income Distribution, Employment and Economic Development in Southeast and East Asia*, Tokyo: Japan Economic Research Center, vol. 2, pp. 389–472. [29–30]

—— (1976) 'Demographic aspects of the size distribution of income: an exploratory essay', *Economic Development and Cultural Change* 25:1–94. [16–17, 29, 34]

—— (1982) 'The pattern of shift of labour force from agriculture, 1950–79', in Gersovitz, M., Diaz-Alejandro, C.F., Ranis, G. and Rosenweig, M.R. (eds) (1982) *The Theory and Experience of Economic Development*, London: Allen and Unwin, pp. 43–59. [179]

Lange, O. and Taylor, F.M. (1938) *On the Economic Theory of Socialism*, Minneapolis: University of Minnesota Press. [294]

Lecaillon, J., Paukert, F., Morrisson, C., and Germidis, D. (1984) *Income Distribution and Economic Development*, Geneva: ILO. [22–3, 61, 72–3, 76–7, 79]

Leibenstein, H. (1957) *Economic Backwardness and Economic Growth*, New York: Wiley. [203]

Lerner, A.P. (1944) *The Economics of Control*, New York: Macmillan. [261]

Lewis, W.A. (1954) 'Economic development with unlimited supplies of labour', *Manchester School* 22:139–91, reprinted in Agarwala, A.N. and Singh, S.P. (eds) (1958) *The Economics of Underdevelopment*, London: Oxford University Press. [167, 207, 244]

—— (1954a) 'Thoughts on land settlement', *Journal of Agricultural Economics* 11:3–11, reprinted in Eicher, C. and Witt, L. (1964) *Agriculture in Economic Development*, New York: McGraw-Hill, Chap. 18, pp. 299–310. [297]

—— (1955) *Theory of Economic Growth*, London: Allen and Unwin. [190]

—— (1969) *Aspects of Tropical Trade 1883–1965*, Stockholm: Almqvist and Wiksell. [244]

—— (1969a) *Some Aspects of Economic Development*, Accra: University of Ghana. [275, 291–2, 298]

—— (1969b) *Principles of Economic Planning*, London: Allen and Unwin. [274]

—— (1971) 'Socialism and economic growth', London School of Economics Annual Oration, reprinted in Gersovitz, M. (ed), *Selected Economic Writings of W. Arthur Lewis*, New York: New York University Press, Chap 31, pp. 669–82. [274]

—— (1972) 'Reflections on unlimited labour', in di Marco, L.E. (ed) *International Economics and Development*, New York: Academic Press. [167, 211]

—— (1976) 'Development and distribution', in Cairncross, A. and Puri, M. (eds) *Employment, Income Distribution and Development Strategy*, New York: Macmillan. [197, 307]

—— (1978) *Growth and Fluctuations*, London: Allen and Unwin. [244]

—— (1979) 'The Dual Economy Revisited', *Manchester School* 47:211–29. [167]

Little, I.M.D. (1976) 'Review of Adelman and Morris' *Economic Growth and Social Equity in Developing Countries*, and Chenery *et al.* 'Redistribution with Growth', *Journal of Development Economics* 3:99–106. [83]

Lydall, H. (1977) *Income Distribution during the Process of Development*, Geneva: I.L.O. WEP 2-23, Working Paper 52. [80]

—— (1979) *A Theory of Income Distribution*, Oxford: Clarendon Press. [175, 235]

Mandel, E. (1971) *The Formation of the Economic Thought of Karl Marx*, London: NLB. [166-7]

Mangahas, M. (1975) 'Income inequality in the Philippines: a decomposition analysis', in Council for Asian Manpower Studies, *Income Distribution, Employment and Economic Development in Southeast and East Asia*, Tokyo: Japan Economic Research Center. [50]

Marshall, A. (1961) *Principles of Economics* 2 vols. Variorum edn, London: Macmillan. [172]

Marx, K. (1946) *Capital*, London: Allen and Unwin, English translation. [166]

Meade, J.E. (1976) *The Just Economy*, London: Allen and Unwin. [55, 268, 276, 278]

Meerman, J. (1979) *Public Expenditure in Malaysia*, Oxford: Oxford University Press. [302]

Mill, J.S. (1862) *Principles of Political Economy*, 5th edn (1923), London: Parker, Son and Bourne. [8, 264]

Manhas, B.S. (1974) 'Rural poverty, land distribution and development strategy', reprinted in Srinivasan, T.N. and Bardhan, P.K. (eds), *Poverty and Income Distribution in India*, Calcutta: Statistical Publishing Society. [295-6]

Mirlees, J. (1975) 'A pure theory of underdeveloped economies', in Reynolds, L.G. (ed.), *Agriculture in Development Theory*, New Haven: Yale University Press. [203]

Mitrany, D. (1951) *Marx Against the Peasant*, London: Weidenfeld and Nicholson. [186]

Muellbauer, J. (1976) 'Discussion', in Atkinson, A.B. *The Personal Distribution of Incomes*, London: Allen and Unwin, pp. 93–5. [41]

Mukherji, B., Pattanaik, P.K., and Sundrum, R.M. (1980) 'Rationing, price control and black marketing', *Indian Economic Review* 15:99–118. [278]

Musgrave, R.A., Case, K.E., and Leonard, H. (1974) 'The distribution of fiscal burdens and benefits', *Public Finance Quarterly* 2:259–311. [302]

Myint, H. (1948) *Theories of Welfare Economics*, London: Longman Green. [273]

—— (1958) 'The classical theory of international trade and the underdeveloped countries', reprinted in Myint, H. (1971) *Economic Theory and the Underdeveloped Countries*, Oxford: Oxford University Press. [242]

Myrdal, G. (1968) *Asian Drama*, Harmondsworth: Penguin Books. [72]

Nash, J.F. (1950) 'The bargaining problem', *Econometrica* 18:155–62. [205]

National Statistical Office (1973) *Socio-Economic Survey BE 2511-2512*, Bangkok. [18]

—— (1985) *Report of the 1981 Socio-Economic Survey*, Bangkok. [25, 157–9]

Newberry, D. (1987) 'Taxation and development', in Newberry, D. and Stern, N., *The Theory of Taxation for Developing Countries*, Oxford: Oxford University Press, Chap. 7, pp. 165–204. [303]

Newberry, D. and Stern, N. (1987) *The Theory of Taxation for Developing Countries*, Oxford: Oxford University Press. [261]

Nurkse, R. (1953) *Problems of Capital Formation in Underdeveloped Countries*, London: Oxford University Press. [286]

Nygard, F. and Sandstrom, A. (1981) *Measuring Income Inequality*, Stockholm: Almqvist and Wiksell International. [41]

O'Brien, P. (1975) *The Classical Economists*, Oxford: Clarendon Press. [164, 273]

Ohlin, B. (1933) *Interregional and International Trade*, Cambridge, MA: Harvard University Press. [240]

Oshima, H. (1970) 'Income inequality and economic growth: the post-war experience of Asian countries', *Malayan Economic Review* 15:7–41. [78]

Paglin, M. (1975) 'The measurement and trend of inequality: a basic revision', *American Economic Review* 65:598–609. [31, 53, 107, 110, 115–17]

Palapac, A.C. (1980, 1985) *World Rice Statistics*, Los Banos: International Rice Research Institute. [201]

Papanek, G. (1978) 'Economic Growth, Income Distribution and the Political Process In Less Developed Countries', in Griliches, Z., Krelle, W., Krupp, H.J., and Kyn, O. (eds), *Income Distribution and Economic Inequality*, New York: John Wiley and Sons. [85]

Parthsarathy, G. (1987) 'Changes in the incidence of rural poverty and recent trends in some aspects of agrarian economy', *Indian Journal of Agricultural Economics* 42(1):1–22. [198]

Passinetti, L.L. (1981) *Structural Change and Economic Growth*, Cambridge: Cambridge University Press. [124, 236]

Patnaik, U. (1979) 'Neo-populism and Marxism: the Chayanovan view of the agrarian question and the fundamental fallacy', *Journal of Peasant Studies* 6:375–420. [186]

Paukert, F. (1973) 'Income distribution at different levels of development: a survey of evidence', *International Labour Review* 108:97–125. [79]

Pen, J. (1974) *Income Distribution* (2nd edn), London: Penguin Books. [259–60]

Prais, S.J. (1955) 'Measuring social mobility', *Journal of the Royal Statistical Society*, series A, 118:56–66. [130]

Pyatt, G. (1976) 'On the interpretation and disaggregation of Gini coefficients', *Economics Journal* 86:243–55. [50]

Raj, K.N. (1970) 'Ownership and operation of land', *Indian Economic Review* 5(1):1–42. [190]

—— (1975) 'Agricultural development and distribution of land holdings', *Indian Journal of Agricultural Economics* 30:1–13. [296]

—— (1982) *Capital Formation and Saving in India: 1950–51 to 1979–80*, Bombay: Reserve Bank of India. [218, 220]

Rakshit, M. (1982) *The Labour Surplus Economy*, New Delhi: Macmillan. [285]

Ramsey, F.P. (1927) 'A contribution to the theory of taxation', *Economic Journal*, 37:47–61. [277]

Ranis, G. (1983) 'Alternative patterns of distribution and growth in the mixed economy: the Philippines and Taiwan', in Stewart, F. (ed.), *Work, Income and*

Inequality, London: Macmillan), Chap. 4, pp. 83–107. [310]

Rao, B. (1984) 'Philippines (1970–71)', in van Ginneken, W. and Park, J., *Generating Internationally Comparable Income Distribution Estimates*, Geneva: ILO, pp. 113–8. [26]

Rao, V.K.R.V. (1952) 'Investment, income and the multiplier in India', reprinted in Agarwala, S.N. and Singh, S.P. (1958) *The Economics of Underdevelopment*, Oxford: Oxford University Press. [175]

Rao, V.M. (1969) 'Two decompositions of concentration ratio', *Journal of the Royal Statistical Society*, series A, 132:418–25. [50]

Rath, N.S. (1985) 'Garibi Hatao: Can IRDP do it?', *Economics and Political Weekly* Feb. 9:238–46. [299]

Rawls, J. (1971) *A Theory of Justice*, Cambridge, MA: Harvard University Press.[263]

Republic of China (1987) *Taiwan Statistical Yearbook*, Taipei: Council for Economic Planning and Development. [119]

Ricardo, D. (1952) *Collected Works*, Sraffa edn, vol. 8, Cambridge: Cambridge University Press. [1]

Robinson, J. (1979) *Aspects of Development and Underdevelopment*, Cambridge: Cambridge University Press. [273]

—— (1982) 'Book review', *Economic Journal* 92:758–9. [274]

Robinson, S. and Dervis, K. (1977) 'Income distribution and socioeconomic mobility', *Journal of Development Studies* 13:347–64. [135, 137]

Roemer, J.E. (1982) *A General Theory of Exploitation and Class*, Cambridge, MA: Harvard University Press. [166]

Roychoudhury, U.D. and Mukherjee, M. (1984) *National Accounts Information System*, Delhi: Macmillan. [218–19]

Salter, W.E.G. (1960) *Productivity and Technical Change*, Cambridge: Cambridge University Press. [163]

Samuelson, P.A. (1948) 'International trade and the equalisation of factor prices', reprinted in Stiglitz, J.E. (ed.) (1966) *Collected Scientific Papers of Paul Samuelson*, Cambridge, MA: MIT Press, vol. 2, Chap. 67. [241]

—— (1953) 'Prices of factors and goods in general equilibrium', reprinted in *Collected Scientific Papers*, vol. 2, Chap. 70. [241]

—— (1964) *Economics*, New York: McGraw-Hill. [6–7]

—— (1965) 'A fallacy in the interpretation of Pareto's law of alleged constancy of income distribution', reprinted in Merton, R.C. (ed.) (1972) *Collected Scientific Papers of Paul Samuelson*, Cambridge, MA: MIT Press, vol. 3, Chap. 165. [41]

Seers, D. (1969) 'The meaning of development', *International Development Review* 11:2–4. [2–3]

Selowsky, M. (1979) *Who Benefits from Government Expenditure?*, Oxford: Oxford University Press. [302]

Sen, A.K. (1964) 'Size of holdings and productivity', *Economic and Political Weekly* (February): 323–6. [186]

—— (1973a) *On Economic Inequality*, Oxford: Clarendon Press. [43, 264]

—— (1973b) 'On ignorance and equal distribution', *American Economic Review* 63:1022–4. [261]

—— (1974) 'Information bases of alternative welfare approaches: aggregation and income distribution', *Journal of Public Economics* 4:387–403. [59, 268]

—— (1975) *Employment, Technology and Development*, Oxford: Clarendon Press. [197]

—— (1976) 'Poverty: an ordinal approach to measurement', *Econometrica* 44:219–31. [65]

Shorrocks, A.F. (1980) 'The class of additively decomposable inequality measures', *Econometrica* 48:613–25. [48]

—— (1983) 'Ranking income distributions', *Economica* 50:3–18. [57]

Simon, H. (1948) *Economic Policy for a Free Society*, Chicago: University of Chicago Press. [263]

Singh, S.K. (1975) *Development Economics*, Lexington: DC Heath & Co. [169]

Sinha, R., Pearson, P., Kadekodi, G., and Gregory, M. (1979) *Income Distribution, Growth and Basic Needs*, London: Croom Helm. [304]

Solow, R.M. (1956) 'A contribution to the theory of economic growth', *Quarterly Journal of Economics* 70:65–94. [162]

Srinivasan, T.N., Radhakrishnan, P.N., and Vaidynathan, A. (1974) 'Data on distribution of consumption expenditure in India: an evaluation', in Srinivasan, T.N. and Bardhan, P.K. (eds), *Poverty and Income Distribution in India*, Calcutta: Statistical Publishing Society, pp. 148–62. [28]

Stigler, G.J. (1975) *The Citizen and the State*, Chicago: Chicago University Press. [274]

Stiglitz, J.E. (1970) 'Factor price equalization in a dynamic economy', *Journal of Political Economy* 78:456–88. [243]

—— (1974) 'Alternative theories of wage determination and unemployment in LDCs', *Quarterly Journal of Economics* 88:194–227. [204]

Stolper, W.F. and Samuelson, P.A. (1941) 'Protection and real wages', *Review of Economic Studies* 9:58–73. [241]

Streeton, P. and Burki, S.J. (1978) 'Basic needs: some issues', *World Development* 6:411–21. [306]

Summers, R. and Heston, A. (1984) 'Improved international comparisons of real product and its composition, 1950–80', *Review of Income and Wealth* 30:207–62. [82, 95, 116]

Sundrum, R.M. (1973) 'Consumer expenditure patterns', *Bulletin of Indonesian Economic Studies* 9(1):86–106. [20]

—— (1983) *Development Economics*, Chichester: John Wiley and Sons. [16, 81, 244, 308]

—— (1987) *Growth and Income Distribution in India*, Delhi: Sage Publications. [125–6, 279]

—— (1990) *Economic Growth in Theory and Practice*, London: Macmillan. [227, 229, 271, 283, 309–10]

Swan, T.W. (1956) 'Economic growth and capital accumulation', *Economic Record* 32:334–1. [162]

Theil, H. (1967) *Economics and Information Theory*, Amsterdam: North-Holland. [49]

Thorner, D. (1966) 'Chayanov's concept of peasant economy', in Chayanov, A., *The Theory of Peasant Economy*, Homewood: Richard D. Irwin. [186]

Tobin, J. (1970) 'On limiting the domain of inequality', *Journal of Law and Economics* 13:263–77. [263]

Todaro, M.P. (1977) *Economic Development in the Third World*, London: Longman. [269]

Tun Wai, U. (1977) 'A revisit to interest rates outside the organized money markets of underdeveloped countries', *Banca Nazionale del Lavoro* 122:291–312. [224]

Turnham, D. and Jaeger, I. (1971) *The Unemployment Problem in Less-Developed Countries*, Paris: OECD. [197]

United Nations (1967) *Incomes in Postwar Europe*, New York: United Nations. [115]

—— (1975) *Poverty, Unemployment and Development Policy*, New York: United Nations. [299]

—— (1979) *World Population Trends and Policies*, New York: United Nations, vol. 1. [64]

Unni, J. (1988) 'Agricultural labourers in rural labour households, 1956–57 to 1977–78', *Economic and Political Weekly* 23(26):A:59–68. [199]

US Department of Commerce (1981) *Survey of Current Business*, Washington, DC: Department of Commerce. [219]

Vaidyanathan, A. (1974) Some aspects of inequalities in living standards in rural India', in Srinivasan, T.N. and Bardian, P.K. (eds) (1974) *Poverty and Income Distribution in India*, Calcutta: Statistical Publishing Society, pp. 215–41. [20]

—— (1978) 'Labour use in Indian agriculture', in Bardhan, P.K. *et al.* (eds), *Labour Absorption in Indian Agriculture* (Bangkok: ILO-ARTEP). [183]

—— (1986) 'On the validity of NSS consumption data', *Economic and Political Weekly* 21(3):129–37. [28]

van Ginneken, W. and Park, J. (1984) *Generating Internationally Comparable Income Distribution Estimates*, Geneva: ILO. [22–3, 72–3, 77]

Visaria, P. (1981) 'Poverty and unemployment in India', *World Development* 9(3):277–300. [198]

Webb, R.C. (1977) 'Wage policy and income distribution in developing countries', in Frank, C.R. and Webb, R.C. (eds), *Income Distribution and Growth in the Less-Developed Countries*, Washington, DC; The Brookings Institution. [209–10]

Wiles, ?. (1974) *The Distribution of Income: East and West*, Amsterdam: North-Holland. [43]

—— (1978), 'Our shaky data base', in Krelle, W. and Shorrocks, A.F. (eds), *Personal Income Distribution*, Amsterdam: North-Holland. [17, 21]

Williamson, J.G. (1965) 'Regional inequality and the process of national development', *Economic Development and Cultural Change* 13:3–45, reprinted in Needleman, L. (1968) *Regional Analysis*, London: Penguin Books. [44]

Wolfson, M. (1986) 'Stasis and change – income inequality in Canada 1965–83', *Review of Income and Wealth* 32:337–70. [115–16]

World Bank (various issues) *World Development Report*, Washington, DC: World Bank. [61, 72, 86–8, 95, 114–15, 119–21, 227–8, 230, 232, 300]

—— (1975) *Land Reform Sector Policy Paper*, Washington, DC: World Bank. [185]

—— (1984) *World Tables*, Washington, DC; World Bank. [87–8, 120–1]]

—— (1988) *Report on Adjustment Lending*, Washington, DC: World Bank. [281]

Subject index